TREATMENT OF SCHIZOPHRENIA

PHILIP R. A. MAY, M.D.

Treatment
of
Schizophrenia

**A COMPARATIVE STUDY
OF FIVE TREATMENT METHODS**

Science House

New York

Library of Congress catalog card number: 68-17264

MANUFACTURED IN THE UNITED STATES OF AMERICA

TO

Our Patients and to Those Who Believed
that this Study Should be Done

~~~~~~

AUTHOR

Philip R. A. May, M.A., M.B., B. Chir. (Cantab.),
M.D. (Stanford, U.S.A.), M.R.C.P., D.P.M.
Clinical Director, The Neuropsychiatric Institute,
California State Department of Mental Hygiene and
University of California at Los Angeles.
Clinical Professor of Psychiatry,
University of California at Los Angeles.
Formerly Research Director, Camarillo State Hospital,
Camarillo, California State Department of Mental Hygiene.

CONTRIBUTORS

Gerald J. Aronson, M.D.

Consulting psychoanalyst, Schizophrenia Research Project
9735 Wilshire Boulevard
Beverly Hills, California.

Jonathan O. Cole, M.D.

Superintendent, Boston State Hospital, Boston, Massachusetts.
Formerly Chief, Psychopharmacology Research Branch, National Institute of Mental Health, Chevy Chase, Maryland.

Luther S. Distler, Ph.D.

Assistant Research Psychologist, Psychology Clinic, University of California at Berkeley, Berkeley, California.
Formerly Research Assistant (Psychology), Camarillo State Hospital, Camarillo, California State Department of Mental Hygiene.

Wilfrid J. Dixon, Ph.D.

Professor of Biomathematics and Director of the Computing Facility, Center for the Health Sciences, School of Medicine, University of California at Los Angeles.

Edward G. Feldman, M.D.

Consulting psychoanalyst, Schizophrenia Research Project
435 North Roxbury Drive
Beverly Hills, California.

Sidney Fine, M.D.

Consulting psychoanalyst, Schizophrenia Research Project
450 North Bedford Drive
Beverly Hills, California.

Maimon Leavitt, M.D.

Consulting psychoanalyst, Schizophrenia Research Project
450 North Bedford Drive
Beverly Hills, California.

Genevieve S. May, M.D.

Consulting psychoanalyst, Schizophrenia Research Project
416 North Bedford Drive
Beverly Hills, California.

A. Hussain Tuma, Ph.D.

Chief, Clinical Projects Section, Clinical Research Branch, National Institute of Mental Health, Chevy Chase, Maryland.
Formerly Research Specialist (Psychology), Camarillo State Hospital, Camarillo, California State Department of Mental Hygiene.

Milton Wexler, Ph.D.

Consulting psychoanalyst, Schizophrenia Research Project
Scientific Advisory Board, Foundation for Research in Psychoanalysis
465 North Roxbury Drive
Beverly Hills, California.

Contents

CHAPTER 3   *Methods of Statistical Analysis—*
              Wilfrid J. Dixon, Ph.D. and Philip
              R. A. May, M.D.

CHAPTER 4   *Description of A Patient Sample: The*
              *Schizophrenia Research Project—*Philip R. A. May, M.D.

TREATMENT OF SCHIZOPHRENIA

List of Tables

TABLE OR FIGURE

Foreword

THE READER WILL immediately sense that this is a most impressive study. It is impressive in the scope of its undertaking, the sophistication of its design, the number of workers who had to be coordinated, the years of its duration, the detail and variety of methods employed in analysis of data, the clarity of its major finding, and its implications for treatment, administrative practice and training. Impressive, too, is the persistence and determination required of Dr. May and his group to bring the study to completion, as well as the careful and discriminating job of collation necessary to bring it to book form. Finally, it is impressive that the author has included critical discussion by a group of peers in the published work.

It is relatively uncommon to find good studies testing efficacy of treatment variations within one modality—for example, pharmacotherapy. It is rare to find good studies comparing efficacy across treatment lines. This research is exceptional in its effort to evaluate five different treatments embracing four modalities—drugs, psychotherapy, electroshock and milieu—and one combination of modalities, namely, drugs plus psychotherapy. The number of cases within each test group is reasonably satisfactory in terms of a search for "definitive" results, rather than mere suggestions for others to replicate. This does not imply that further efforts along these lines are not necessary (and that even a replication of sorts might be considered if cost is not prohibitive), but, after reading the report, one is left with a sense of satisfaction that "this could be it" or at least that a Herculean effort has been put forth to the end that this *should* be it.

The study, boiled down to its essence, states that ataractic drugs and drugs plus psychotherapy are the best treatments for "the average run of schizophrenics admitted to mental hospitals," and that no substantial difference in success of treatment can be found between these two treatment groups. There appears to be no significant interaction effect between drugs and psychotherapy. Psychotherapy alone and milieu therapy alone are *far* less efficacious, and electroshock therapy occupies the middle ground. Psychotherapy may contribute something to release of aggression or, perhaps, improvement of insight, but the gains seem hardly worth the greatly added costs. Costs are escalated first by the expense of psychiatric sessions, and second because patients in psychotherapy tend to stay longer in the hospital, especially those who are eventually classed as failures.

These findings may be startling to some and may even be traumatic to those who have special investments in one or another therapeutic form. These individuals, especially, will ask questions designed to find an error in the research that will leave them in possession of their prejudices. Indeed, the implications are so vast that all thoughtful readers would do well to comb over the methods and procedures to see how well the claims meet their personal standards of validity. Fortunately the whole investigation is spelled out in sufficient detail with charts, graphs, instruments, statistical techniques and appendices to make this possible to a highly satisfactory degree.

Perhaps psychotherapy failed to be of significant value because it was carried out by relatively inexperienced therapists—or, more strictly, although therapists' experience covered a wide range, many were psychiatric residents with relatively little training (they had experienced supervisors, however). Perhaps it failed because it was not sufficiently prolonged—the upper limit of duration was one year. Claims have been made that for chronic schizophrenics, psychotherapy may be necessary for five or more years. Perhaps the frequency of psychotherapeutic sessions was too low; perhaps the style, techniques or aims were short of the mark.

The author's defense is a good one. The therapists, their techniques, frequency, and duration were such that, should their approach prove to be successful in treating the "average run" of schizophrenics, there would be reasonable hope that appropriate services could be provided to the many schizophrenic patients in this class, within a practical, dollar- and manpower-dependent world. Of course, there is the pragmatic limitation that only a few variables can be included in any one study. Evaluation of the efficacy of several styles of psychotherapy was simply beyond the scope of the investigation.

All in all, it is difficult to dismiss the impression that this study has dealt the use of psychotherapy, as an essential modality of treatment for hospitalized schizophrenics, a hard blow. It may even turn out to be a mortal blow, especially if support for this finding is forthcoming from other sources. Readers are aware that Freud saw little use for psychoanalysis in the "narcissistic neuroses." The psychotherapy used in May's study, although not psychoanalysis, was analytically oriented and supervised; to an extent, therefore, it might lend weight to Freud's original claim.

Since Freud's pronouncement, many psychotherapists have reported results, mainly anecdotal, supporting the effectiveness of a psychotherapeutic approach in schizophrenia; but recent comparative studies on aggregate samples seem, on the whole, to back up Freud. For example, in a study made at the Massachusetts Mental Health Center,[1] psychotherapy for a minimum of two years by senior psychiatrists, more advanced than May's therapists and probably at the level of his supervisors, produced little change in chronic schizophrenia (generally of poorer prognosis than May's cases), while ataractic drugs did indeed cause significant behavioral improvement on objective tests. Also, in a recent investigation of drugs and social therapy in chronic schizophrenia,[2] of several methods tried, ataractics alone produced significant improvement in behavior of chronic schizophrenics over the short run (six months); however, the suggestion was advanced that an interaction effect between drugs and social therapy occurred over the longer run (eighteen months to three years). May's report does not consider long-term effects of any type, although he gives long-term studies high priority for his future work.

As though one blow were not enough, May finds that psychotherapy prolongs the patient's stay in the hospital, especially if things are not going well. This is supported by numerous observations that when a psychotherapist invests himself heavily in his patient, he becomes reluctant to "give up"; often he believes his patient is doing well or, at least, that a favorable development is just around the corner—in contrast to more objective observers. Therapeutic zeal is, of course, admirable and the stuff of which great physicians are made, but it should not be permitted to take time and money which, if the present report is correct, could have been better allotted elsewhere—for example, in the outpatient or after-care department.

The apparent lack of efficacy of psychotherapy under the conditions of this experiment in schizophrenia does not by itself permit assumptions about its value in other conditions—the neuroses, for example; but such a resounding negative must surely give us pause to reconsider the evidence pro and con for the other diagnostic illnesses. Certainly this research increases the urgency of our need to know where we stand with the use of psychotherapy in nonschizophrenic conditions. Many attempts have been made to evaluate psychotherapy, and some notable reviews of the literature are available. Evaluation of psychotherapy is a very complicated procedure, and on the basis of the published reports, we are today *not* in a good position to defend scientifically the efficacy of the most used and, in fact, most in demand, therapeutic tool on the

---

[1] "Psychiatric Research Center: Studies in the Psychoses," Jack R. Ewalt, M.D., Principal Investigator, Massachusetts Mental Health Center; National Institute of Mental Health, Grant No. MHO5077.
[2] Milton Greenblatt, M.D., Maida H. Solomon, B.A., B.S., Anne S. Evans, M.S., and George W. Brooks, M.D.: *Drug and Social Therapy in Chronic Schizophrenia.* Charles C Thomas, Publisher, Springfield, Illinois, 1965.

current psychiatric scene. Have we oversold the public? Do we supply solace and comfort—balm to the soul, so to speak, without being able to achieve any deep, thoroughgoing "specific" changes? Is psychotherapy by psychiatrists truly more valuable than that administered by less trained professionals or even untrained nonprofessionals?

These very disturbing questions are raised once again, and forcefully, by the implications of the present investigation. It would be worth millions to get the right answers, and all our thinking and planning ahead into the era of community psychiatry might be quite different if we had such answers. Dr. May's brilliant methodological assay should give heart to new investigators that such a demonstration is possible and eminently worth the effort.

While some may be surprised—even a little shocked—at the poor showing of psychotherapy, probably few will be surprised at the good showing of ataractic drugs. It may be relevant that the principal investigators allowed the treating physicians considerable latitude in their choice of dosage and even combination of ataractics consistent with best clinical practice. Drugs so used could have some relationship to the optimum for each patient. It might be argued that the test of the psychopharmaceuticals was a much fairer one than that for the other modalities—psychotherapy or milieu therapy, for instance.

The results above are supported by considerable controlled research showing that tranquilizing drugs are helpful in the rehabilitation of chronic schizophrenic patients. Studies of frequency of relapse of patients in aftercare have been unusually consistent in demonstrating the superiority of drugs over the placebo condition. A fortunate development for this research is that multihospital studies supported by National Institute of Mental Health have generally failed to show a significant superiority of any one ataractic over others in the treatment of chronic schizophrenia. The pharmacotherapeutic agents selected by May and his collaborators have withstood the test of time and have not as yet been superseded.

Fully as difficult to evaluate and as complicated to employ as psychotherapy is the somewhat vaguely designated milieu therapy. Concepts and definitions of this modality vary greatly. Some think of it as comprising the many ongoing activities on the ward, excluding "specific" drug treatment, shock treatment and psychotherapy, which are collectively assumed to be therapeutic. Some think of milieu therapy as related to a series of efforts to develop a "therapeutic community," usually conceived in such terms as "maximizing the therapeutic potential of everyone in the system." A more sophisticated definition might include efforts to mobilize patients and staff to cooperate in improving the physical and social environment in which they live and the collective establishment of a set of progressive expectations that provide goals and challenges for everyone in the movement toward a better life for all.

I think Dr. May's "milieu therapy" leans toward the former idea of a loose collection of "nonspecific therapies," such as occupational therapy, group meetings, and the like, mostly supervised or dominated by nonmedical personnel. In fact, as utilized in this study, it forms a baseline or backdrop against which the more "specific" therapies could demonstrate their potentialities. But this is only one form of therapeutic organization of the environment. It does not necessarily test the full potential of milieu methods.

To illustrate: On more than one occasion we have seen wards and even entire buildings inhabited by chronic schizophrenics, more severe than those included in Dr. May's population, emptied through discharge of the patients to homes, family care situations, day care centers, and so on, within the time period described in this study. One technique for accomplishing this—perhaps a "shock technique"—is to notify the patients that the building must be emptied by a certain date and thus challenge them to cope with a new reality. True, some patients become agitated and even regress; but if the expectation is held constant and personnel are available to assist the patients to meet it, an impasse is negotiated which formerly seemed to be a "life and death" resistance. To be sure, this process is aided by judicious use of drugs, group psychotherapy, individual consultation, work rehabilitation and the like, but impressive results have been achieved in the past without modern ataractics and with few ancillary aids. Obviously it is not *this* kind of milieu therapy that Dr. May's remarkable study evaluates. It is important for the reader to understand exactly to what situations and therapeutic conditions the findings apply.

The results with electroconvulsive therapy would probably fit the expectations of most knowledgeable readers. It has generally been assumed that ECT can be helpful to schizophrenic patients who feature affective disorders, but that it is relatively ineffective for schizophrenics without a prominent affective component. The assumption, too, would be that schizophrenic patients receiving ECT relatively early in their clinical course benefit most by the treatment.

However, experience shows that results with ECT are often transient. This brings up the problem of aftercare and follow-up. The investigators would accomplish a great public service by reporting comparative results over the long term, for these, in the last analysis, are what count the most. We are pleased, therefore, that Dr. May and his group plan to assume responsibility for long-term follow-up, and eagerly await their next report.

This study is obviously of extraordinary importance to all who are involved in planning therapeutic care in hospitals, particularly under the conditions of scarce resources that usually prevail in our mental institutions. I doubt whether any person responsible for administration of a mental facility, or even part of one, can afford to neglect this book. Aside from considerations of economy and efficiency, it is poor medicine to pursue any treatment beyond the point of its indication, and May has helped us to define and delimit the indications for various treatment approaches.

Finally, the implications for training are considerable. Can we justify costly training of psychiatric residents in psychotherapy of the psychoses if this form of treatment yields little clinical benefit to patients? Can residents learn dynamic psychiatry as well or better by working with other types of illness more responsive to psychotherapy?

And what about training programs in psychopharmacology? Modern training for psychiatry puts heavy emphasis on psychotherapy and interpersonal dynamics, with correspondingly little emphasis on pharmacodynamics. May's results seem to encourage greater concern with matters psychopharmacological, since proper therapeutics here may make a great difference in the lives of many schizophrenic patients. We will need to develop a cadre of teachers of psychopharmacology, teachers who know the intricacies of drug prescription and management and who can integrate this knowledge with pharmacology, biochemistry and the main currents of psychiatric practice. The ultimate beneficiary of such a training program ought to feel closer to the mainstream of medicine than the preceding generation of trainees.

The cost of research can be very great, but, under favorable conditions, its rewards can be enormous. These favorable conditions include scientific leadership of the quality responsible for this extraordinary investigation.

MILTON GREENBLATT, M.D.
Commissioner, Massachusetts
Department of Mental Health,
Professor of Psychiatry,
Tufts University

Preface

THE RESEARCH HEREIN reported is based on the premise that there is a serious need for authoritative experimental study of the results of the different forms of treatment for the schizophrenic process. This subject should be of concern to a varied audience. It will be of most direct interest to clinicians, administrators, research workers and other professional personnel of the various disciplines concerned with the treatment of the schizophrenic patient. It is also relevant for anyone who has anything to do with organizing and furnishing treatment services for the mentally ill.

Reviewers and critics have pointed out a wide range of inadequacies and shortcomings in previous investigations of this area, including poorly selected and heterogeneous patient samples; deficient controls; inadequate, ill-defined or unspecified criteria for evaluating outcome; and absent or inadequate follow-up. Remarkably, there is a notable lack of comparative investigation of the relative efficacy of the various treatment methods in current use. This is all the more surprising because, aside from the theoretical scientific implications of the findings of such studies, it would seem self-evident that information obtained by adequate experimental study under specific conditions is essential to patients and their families; to all of the professional disciplines involved in treatment; to administrators of treatment programs and to those concerned with their financial support.

On the face of it, it is unlikely that any one treatment by itself will be a universal panacea, effective in every way, for all types of patients, in everyone's hands, in every type of setting. Since many patients are treated in public mental hospitals, it seemed to us important to compare the effectiveness of different treatments in this particular type of setting. Accordingly, a multidisciplinary research program of considerable magnitude was designed to study the results of treatment methods in common use for schizophrenic patients under the conditions that might reasonably be expected in a good public hospital, presently or within the foreseeable future. This included both an immediate outcome study of the course of in-hospital treatment and a coordinated follow-up for at least two years.

The general aim was to determine, for a carefully selected and studied group of schizophrenic patients, the results of using five different commonly used treatment modalities: (1) ataraxic drugs alone; (2) indi-

vidual psychotherapy alone; (3) the combination of individual psychotherapy and ataraxic drugs; (4) electroshock; and (5) a good level of
plain, reasonable, conservative care without the addition of any of these
"specific" treatments. Since each of these methods has its dogmatic
protagonists and its ardent detractors, we could not avoid "keeping
score." Indeed, it was our scientific responsibility to do so with scrupu-
lous care. The clinician must of course be given general statistics on outcome and relative effectiveness, and these are the main target in this
volume, which is intended to be the first in a series of reports from the
study.

In our future research we hope to go beyond this, to determine
whether it is possible to predict who will respond to each of these treatment methods. This is a much more difficult question to answer, and it
will be some time before we are in a position to publish any findings
in this respect.

To review briefly the contents of this volume: Chapter 1, by Dr. A.
Hussain Tuma, summarizes the background of the problem and places it
in historical perspective. Chapter 2 describes in considerable detail, but
in fairly simple language, the plan of the in-hospital phase of the study.
Concentrating this basic reference material in readily accessible form
eliminates the need for repeated explication elsewhere in this and in
future publications, and helps us to present the results and their implications crisply and without tedious repetition of technical details. The
reader, whatever his professional discipline and whether or not he
thinks of himself as research-minded, will be able to know exactly what
was done and why it was done and to understand more clearly some
of the pitfalls in interpretation of research reports.

There is, however, another important reason for presenting the research design and procedures in detail—our belief that more and better
clinical research is needed, particularly in relation to the results of treating the various forms of psychosis. A great deal of time and effort was
put into planning and working through this study. It is hoped that a
description of procedures and experience and discussion of limitations
and defects will be of help to other investigators and may even encourage a few to carry on the task of improving methodology and adding to our knowledge of treatment outcome. If used by others, some
of the practical operational definitions may perhaps clarify some areas
of muddled thinking and help the research investigator to speak more
clearly to the clinician.

Chapter 3, by Dr. Wilfrid J. Dixon and myself, presents the methods
of statistical analysis and describes their purpose simply and with a
minimum of jargon. This chapter is intended to give the lay reader some

understanding of the procedures used, but it is also hoped that it will be of assistance to the clinical investigator who is planning an outcome study of his own and who may perhaps be hard pressed to understand the experts who advise him.

Chapter 4 aims to describe the patients, briefly and yet in such a way that the reader can have a reasonable picture of the subjects of our study.

Chapters 5 through 9 compare the results of the five methods of treatment in terms of a spectrum of major criteria chosen to provide a multidisciplinary, multifaceted evaluation. Practical hard-fact administrative criteria are included, as well as purely clinical criteria such as the patients' condition as judged by psychoanalysts, ward nurses and treating physicians.

Chapter 10, by Dr. Luther S. Distler and myself, gives the findings for the psychometric measures.

Chapter 11 compares the five treatments in terms of estimates of the cost of the patients' entire stay in the hospital, and Chapter 12 summarizes all the findings in a more compact manner.

The last two chapters contain our conclusions in the form of a presentation followed by a formal discussion. Chapter 13 is my own conclusions and speculations as to the significance and application of the findings. Chapter 14 is a series of contributions arranged as an "Open Forum," in which a number of investigators associated with the project discuss my conclusions and add any other comments that they might care to make. The contributors to this section are Drs. Gerald J. Aronson, Luther S. Distler, Edward G. Feldman, Sidney Fine, Maimon Leavitt, Genevieve S. May, A. Hussain Tuma, Milton Wexler and myself. It ends with a section by Dr. Jonathan O. Cole, providing a viewpoint from outside the project.

Each chapter is preceded by a brief summary and is organized under subheadings to identify discrete units that may be read separately. Thus the reader is readily given the choice of selective attention to detail on the basis of his particular interests and tastes.

As a matter of style, the first person singular has been used deliberately to confer personal responsibility for thoughts and ideas with which I felt my co-investigators might possibly differ; the first person plural has been used for joint efforts and wherever I felt reasonably certain that they would agree. Every attempt has been made to avoid unnecessary research jargon and to use language that should be readily intelligible to persons working with the schizophrenic patient, whatever their profession. In some situations, however, technical terms and abbreviations have been used as an alternative to tedious repetition. Suit-

able definitions and descriptions for this form of shorthand will be found
in the sections on Design and Statistical Analysis and in the List of
Abbreviations.

It must be emphasized that the opinions expressed in this book are
those of the authors, and should not be taken as the official positions
of the various agencies that supported this research.

Philip R. A. May, M.D.
760 Westwood Plaza
Los Angeles, California

Acknowledgments

MUCH OF THE toil and trouble of this project was done by others, and the author and contributors want them to know how much their partnership and support have meant during this long and often tedious enterprise.

The names of investigators and those who were officially employed by the project will be found in the next section. Unhappily, some of the major co-investigators have not been able to take as active a part in the processing and analysis of results and in the preparation of this report as I would have wished. In particular, special credit must be given to Dr. A. Hussain Tuma and Dr. Luther S. Distler, who joined the project during its pilot and planning stages. Having coordinated the follow-up and in-hospital data collection for a long time, they progressed to greater and more responsible positions elsewhere and did not have time to work further with the Schizophrenia Research Project.

There are many to whom our thanks are due. First, to our patients and their relatives and friends whose participation and cooperation provided the fundamental elements of our work and whose names must remain confidential. We hope that this study may throw some light on problems of importance to them and to others.

Throughout this study we have been fortunate to have the active cooperation and participation of Camarillo State Hospital. The friendly support of Dr. Louis R. Nash, Superintendent and Medical Director, provided not only office space and a generous basic staff, but also a climate that encouraged the development of clinical research and that tolerated in good humor the aggravations that it caused.

In the early stages we received research grants from the State of California Department of Mental Hygiene (Dr. Daniel Blain, Director of Mental Hygiene, continued under Dr. James V. Lowry, the present Director). Later, financial support was maintained for the major part of the project by research grants from the Department of Health, Education and Welfare, United States Public Health Service, National Institute of Mental Health (NIMH-04589 and NIMH-02719); and by contract with the Psychopharmacology Research Branch of the National Institute of Mental Health (PH-43-66-49). The Benjamin Rush Research Foundation and the Albert Epstein Fund came to the rescue in moments of crisis.

The Neuropsychiatric Institute of the California State Department of

Mental Hygiene and the University of California at Los Angeles (Dr. Norman Q. Brill, Medical Director and Chairman of the Department of Psychiatry) contributed space and timely assistance, as well as a group of volunteers who became so involved in the project that they have been listed among the regular project staff in the next section. Of these, special thanks must go to Mrs. Ada E. Hirschman who has persevered with style through some of the darker aspects of data processing, contriving to work for the project even while temporarily residing in England. Mr. Ernest M. Sable, Business Administrator of the Neuropsychiatric Institute, reviewed the sections on cost and made some very helpful suggestions and comments about cost analysis and accounting procedures. I am also indebted to Mrs. Jane A. Kirksey for ten years of consistent devotion to accuracy in data processing and cheerful tolerance of idiosyncracy; and to Mrs. Aldine Newton who faithfully followed the manuscript through innumerable drafts and contributed substantially to its polish and final format.

The Health Sciences Computing Facility of the Center for the Health Sciences, University of California at Los Angeles, provided not only computing assistance (sponsored by NIH Grant FR-3) but also consultation and assistance in data reduction, programming and analysis. During the past four years Mr. Daniel N. Frumkes has coordinated much of the data processing.

Dr. Leon J. Epstein—then Director of Research for the State of California Department of Mental Hygiene and now Associate Superintendent at the Langley Porter Neuropsychiatric Institute, San Francisco, and Associate Professor of Psychiatry, University of California, San Francisco—contributed substantially to sharpening the research design in the early planning stages. Dr. Ruth I. Barnard secured the interest of the Research Sub-Committee of the Los Angeles Psychoanalytic Society, whose members welcomed the opportunity to examine the relationship of psychotherapy to other methods of treatment in a public institution and to explore the research and teaching role of the psychoanalyst in that setting.

Mr. Emanuel H. Newman—then Head of the Los Angeles Office of the Bureau of Extra-Mural Social Work and now Chief, Family and Children Division, California State Department of Social Welfare—provided support for our work with the patients' families and in following up our patients after discharge; in fact, he graciously allowed us to "borrow" some of his best staff. Mr. Robert Middlebrook, who took Mr. Newman's place when he left for Department Headquarters, continued the same helpful and friendly relationship.

Dr. Gerald A. Mendelsohn, Assistant Professor, University of California, Berkeley, gave generous and welcome advice in connection with certain preliminary analyses of psychometric data. With his guidance, some of these were done at the Computer Center at the University of California, Berkeley.

At Camarillo Hospital, Mr. Eugene S. Jones and Dr. Herschel Fogelson joined in the early planning, followed by Dr. Benjamin A. Siegel, the present Chief Psychologist. They were instrumental in obtaining the cooperation and assistance of the Department of Psychology. Dr. Vernon G. Bugh, now Superintendent of Pacific State Hospital, Pomona, California, and Dr. Hugh A. Adams, the former Chief of Professional Education, helped in the pilot stages and supervised the treatment of patients with electroshock. Dr. Walter P. Streitel and Dr. Eugene E. Kelemen handled with dexterity the problems of patients and staff in the Admission and Treatment Services, and Dr. Norman C. Mace, the present Chief of Professional Education, worked through matters that involved the psychiatric residents.

The treatment staff of all disciplines at Camarillo Hospital joined with us wholeheartedly. We must acknowledge not only their cooperation with the demands of research, but also their sincere and steady devotion to the difficult task of treating schizophrenic patients. The same is true of the staff of the Bureau of Extra-Mural Social Work who provided aftercare for the patients, and the private psychiatrists and community agencies who helped us.

Research investigators in other parts of the country have been liberal in their assistance, and much that we have achieved rests upon their efforts. Our thanks are due in particular to Doctors Lester Luborsky, Lewis L. Robbins, Helen D. Sargent and Robert S. Wallerstein of the Menninger Foundation Psychotherapy Research Project, for consultation and for permission to use or to modify their scales, forms and ideas. We are indebted also to Doctors Howard E. Freeman and Ozzie G. Simmons for furnishing their questionnaires as a starting point for the design of our structured family interviews.

Dr. Dean J. Clyde, Director, Biometric Laboratory, University of Miami, gave a helping hand in suggesting design and analyses, as well as providing and scoring the Clyde Mood Scale decks that were used in the project.

Dr. Wilfrid J. Dixon, Professor of Biomathematics, University of California at Los Angeles, has persevered with the study from its early beginnings; his continuing sophisticated interventions permeate its substance and have guided us in design, in execution, and in analysis—and in some of the finer points of writing.

Supplies of trifluoperazine (Stelazine) and chlorpromazine (Thorazine) were donated by Smith Kline & French Laboratories, Philadelphia, and procyclidine (Kemadrin) by Burroughs Wellcome & Company, Inc., Tuckahoe, New York.

Finally, special mention must be made of the personal encouragement suitably mixed with scientific advice that we have been fortunate to find in our relationships with the staff of the Psychopharmacology Research Branch of the National Institute of Mental Health. Dr. Jonathan O. Cole and Dr. Solomon C. Goldberg and their staff have been splendid to work with, and I hope that this book will serve as an expression of their direct and personal support of clinical research.

Schizophrenia Research Project

INVESTIGATORS AND STAFF

ALTHOUGH THE AUTHOR and contributors assume full responsibility for the format and writing of this book and for all errors of omission and commission, the substance would not have been possible without the individual and collective work and thought of all the investigators and staff of the project. The quality and degree of completeness achieved in this study reflect their enthusiasm, cooperation and personal investment. A full and proper share of the credit for the work reported here and for any worthwhile idea or finding should therefore be given to them. The names are listed with major investigators first, then full-time project staff, followed by part-time and other members. Alphabetical order has been used wherever this seemed appropriate.

PRINCIPAL INVESTIGATOR
Philip R. A. May, M.D.

NURSING
Mary A. Wilkinson, M.A., R.N.
Betty J. Woodbury, R.N.
Barbara E. Bailey, R.N.
Muriel G. Barrett, P.T.
Dorothy Hamilton, R.N.
Beverly A. Hughes, P.T.
Diamond Maurer, P.T.

PSYCHOLOGY
A. Hussain Tuma, Ph.D.
Luther S. Distler, Ph.D.
Walter F. McKeever, Ph.D.
Jane F. Cazevelan, Ph.D.
Mortimer M. Meyer, Ph.D.
Michael D. Nesbitt, Ph.D.
J. Gordon Tolmie, Ph.D.
Peter J. Ebersole, B.A.

PSYCHIATRY
Wesley H. Kraude, M.D.
S. Milton Ramer, M.D.
David A. Thiele, M.D.
Stuart S. Turkel, M.D.

PSYCHOANALYSIS
Gerald J. Aronson, M.D.
Bernard S. Brandchaft, M.D.
Edward G. Feldman, M.D.
Sidney Fine, M.D.
Maimon Leavitt, M.D.
Arthur Malin, M.D.
Genevieve S. May, M.D.
James M. Mott, M.D.
Milton Wexler, Ph.D.

RESIDENTS AND OTHER THERAPISTS

Ada M. Anderson, M.D.
Seawright W. Anderson, M.D.
Donald A. Ballard, M.D.
Edward M. Bjerk, M.D.
Jack C. Borel, M.D.
Arthur B. Burris, M.D.
Robert Capper, M.D.
Pei Chu Chao, M.D.
John P. Cleary, M.D.
Edward C. Cummings, M.D.
Grant L. Garlock, M.D.
Bernard Goodman, M.D.
Edwin P. Gramlich, M.D.
Herbert Gray, M.D.
Edward L. Green, M.D.
Lawrence E. Johnson, M.D.
Irma M. Karnopp, M.D.
Sara R. Kebe, M.D.
Clarence Langerak, M.D.
Anthony Lapolla, M.D.
Philip W. Lawler, M.D.
William H. Lorack, M.D.
Jerome J. Lubin, M.D.
Gerald E. Maguire, M.D.
Rachel Pape, M.D.
James D. Reardon, M.D.
R. Perry Reynolds, M.D.
Joan H. Shalack, M.D.
John Sheel, M.D.
William M. Shipman, M.D.
Robert J. Sokol, M.D.
Mack E. Sturgis, M.D.
Steven I. Topel, M.D.
Walter R. Townsend, M.D.
Paul E. Wedel, M.D.
H. Weldon Wilkinson, M.D.
Ruth H. Winzeler, M.D.

BIOLOGICAL SCIENCE

Barbara L. Tuma, B.S.

SOCIAL SCIENCE

Eleanor B. Sheldon, Ph.D.
Leo G. Reeder, Ph.D.
Leta M. Adler, Ph.D.
Sherri Cavan
Amelia Fitts
Hilda Johnston
Dorothy Meier
Elizabeth Raymer
Rita Roffers
Carmela M. Ruby
Frederick Thalheimer

SOCIAL WORK

Donald T. Lee, M.S.W.
Gip P. Rogers, M.S.W.
Wilfred D. Coggins, M.S.W.
Dorothy Perrault, P.S.W.
Harold Austin, M.S.W.
John Mack, M.S.W.
Edward E. Roy, M.S.W.
Bernice J. Goodsitt, P.S.W.

BIOSTATISTICS

Wilfrid J. Dixon, Ph.D.

COMPUTER ANALYSIS

Daniel N. Frumkes, B.A
Jochen Haber, B.A.
Jane A. Kirksey
Lois H. Parmalee, B.A.

VOLUNTEERS

Joan D. Bird
Betty Rae Brown
Elizabeth Gordon
Ada E. Hirschman, B.A.

OFFICE STAFF

Sandra S. Bugaj
Carol Carson
Marilyn V. Crothers
Marilyn Cummings
Pearl R. Davis
Ruth J. Dunkelberger
Edess Fargo
Elizabeth A. Fruits
John D. Griffin
Gladys M. Haight
Anne K. Hall
Jean Hayes
Nancy E. Hughes
Margaret Husky
Sarah Frances Jensen
Penelope L. Kellogg
Sarah Koanjakian

Virginia R. Lawrence
Ida J. Lepp
Mary McFall
Patsy J. Melzian
Kathryn Minikin
Aldine Newton
Sheila A. Olson
Joyce Pinkard
Thelma A. Robinson
Darlene Schanfald
Fern Simons
Mildred E. Tarr
Margaret E. Taylor
Jan P. Vandemeer
Denise E. Vandenberg
Walter J. Wager
Sherrylyn R. Young

CHAPTER I

Treatment of Schizophrenia
An Historical Perspective

A. HUSSAIN TUMA, PH.D.

~~~~~~

THE HISTORY OF the treatment of schizophrenia is marked by a great variety of approaches. The development of descriptive psychiatry in the 19th century, followed by dynamic theories of personality and psychopathology and the widespread use of a large number of somatic and psychological therapies during the past few decades, have led to an increasing demand for specificity and differentiation in choice of treatment for the mentally ill. This, it seems, has in turn led to studies of the interacting relationships between the specific methods of treatment and other components of the total treatment situation such as type of illness, characteristics of the patient's personality and background and of the therapist, and the social context of the illness. Concurrently there has developed a general dissatisfaction with the research methodology of the past and an increasing demand for more stringent scientific standards and methodological sophistication.

The current situation seems to be that some progress has been made in the development of a diversity of treatment methods which, on the whole, seem to achieve the reduction or removal of some symptoms and alleviate suffering. However, there is no firm evidence that these result in a greater number of "cures" or lasting remissions or even a reduced incidence of readmissions. Nor do we find sufficient data on the comparative efficacy of the currently used methods of treatment in terms of reducing specific symptom patterns or improving psychological, social or occupational functioning. It follows, therefore, that our present standards for evaluating treatment outcome in schizophrenia must be comparative in character, more specific in reference to behavior, imbued with social and economic as well as clinical realism, and aware that, in general, none of the present forms of treatment can sustain a claim to have produced results beyond the point of amelioration.

BACKGROUND

The history of psychiatric treatment is marked by a great variety of approaches which have been used to deal with mental and emotional disorders. The change from time to time manifest in the approach to a given disorder may be viewed as an expression of a corresponding change in the conception and etiological formulation of the disorder. It may also reflect the technological achievements and sophistication of the times.

It would appear, for instance, that the concept of "Moral Treatment" which prevailed throughout most of the 19th century was based on a fundamental belief that a benign social and physical environment was crucial to provide a suitable background for the path to recovery. The "lunatic" inhabitants of an asylum were deemed to need the shelter and support—in the broadest terms—that was provided there.[1][*] Ordinary kindly and humane attitudes, gentle outdoor activities, productive work, adequate food, rest and cleanliness were the proper "treatment." Healing and reintegration were left to Nature's own devices with little, if any, active intervention. This general approach made no specific assumptions as to the etiology of the disorder; nor did it need to distinguish particularly between one type of disorder and another. Implicit in the approach was the assumption that the pathogenic elements were rooted in the physical and social environments in which the patient lived before his admission.

[1] See references 25, 66.
[*] References may be found at end of chapter.

By the end of the nineteenth century, progress had been made in the development of a descriptive psychiatric classification that differentiated several types of illnesses. The etiology of some organic mental diseases had been identified, but progress toward an understanding of most disorders had been disappointingly slow. Two major and somewhat opposing themes characterized the 20th century, which has witnessed a gradual shift of emphasis from description and classification toward the active use of specific therapeutic methods. On the one hand, there has been the development and application of psychoanalytic understanding to the treatment of the neuroses and more recently of the psychoses; and on the other, a rapidly expanding use of physical forms of treatment.

In general, the various psychoanalytic and psychotherapeutic approaches, whether directive or nondirective, supportive or analytic and uncovering, have in common a dynamic definition of personality structure and function with attention to social and cultural influences in addition to biological factors. They may be said to be essentially rationalistic, i.e., based on a theoretical formulation of psychic structure and of the mental processes involved in the particular disorder under treatment.

In contrast, the development of somatic therapies such as continuous narcosis, psycho-surgery, insulin, electronarcosis, electroshock and ataraxic drugs has been largely empirical; justified partly, perhaps implicitly, on the basis of organic etiological theory and partly on the basis of a general belief that psychological states may be influenced by nonpsychological means. Although clinicians and research investigators who use these physical methods of treatment seem mostly to have started without elaborate or specific theories, many of them have subsequently postulated processes and mechanisms by which their particular method might produce psychological changes or improvement in personal relationships. In other words, with somatic therapy, theory has tended to follow on the heels of empiricism. Indeed, some writers are hopeful that clarification of the mechanisms involved in physical methods of treatment may unravel the anatomic and physiologic substrates of mental disorder and so pave the way for a more rational form of treatment.

During the past few decades there has been an increasing demand for specificity and differentiation in choice of treatment according to the type of illness or the characteristics of the patient. This subject has become a prominent target for scientific inquiry. At the same time, perhaps as the result of a climate that conceptualized schizophrenia as a group of reactions with multiple constitutional (genetic) and psycho-social (experiential) determinants, there has been an increasing trend toward the combined use of somatic and psycho-social treatment methods. This has led to studies of the interacting relationships between the specific methods of treatment and other components of the total treatment situation, such as characteristics of the patient's personality and background and of the therapist and the social context of the illness. On the whole, a multivariate model of etiology (and treatment) is gradually replacing the univariate model for schizophrenia. There remain, however, many investigators who believe strongly that schizophrenia is fundamentally a unitary disease entity and that its primary treatment rests in a single method yet to be discovered.

Somewhere in the middle ground between the two models is the common belief that several separate reaction patterns or disease entities are at present erroneously subsumed under the rubric of "schizophrenia," each the product of different combinations and interactions of experiential and genetic factors and so requiring an individualized treatment approach for each. With this view it is quite possible that one or more of the "schizophrenias" may turn out to be due to very specific genetic or biochemical factors, while others may be determined through faulty development and pathogenic family and social environments, and still others by both. This style of thinking leads to research directed toward the identification and description of alternative etiological models, in the hope that more specific forms of treatment may be developed.

It is clear, therefore, that research on the outcome of treatment for schizophrenia must contend with a great variety of problems, including fundamental uncertainties concerning the identification and conception of "schizophrenia" as well as its etiology and natural history. There are, in addition, methodological problems in the description and measurement of the different dimensions of this illness, and, last but not least, grave practical difficulties in long-range follow-up, particularly among patients who return to mobile and often transient communities.

PRESENT STATUS

It would be foolhardy to attempt a comprehensive review of the published material on the many aspects of research in the treatment of schizophrenia; even if possible, it would take us too far afield. For the present it will suffice to outline briefly the current state of affairs as we see it.

One of the most obvious features in the plethora of reports is a distinct absence of adequately controlled studies comparing the *relative* efficacy and *specific* indications for the various treatment methods in common use. One also cannot escape the impression that many investigators and clinicians have no real expectation of "cure," at least for those patients who are described under the label "process schizo-phrenia." As a result, treatment has been largely focused on the reduction of symptoms and improvement in family and social adjustment.

Moreover, although an effort is often made to postulate a meaningful relationship between certain aspects of schizophrenic pathology and the particular method selected for its treatment, no one as yet has seriously claimed to have discovered a rational and effective cure for the majority of cases. In a very sober vein, the comment has been made that "at present we can say only that we are treating empirically disorders whose etiology is unknown with methods whose action is also shrouded in mystery."[2]

It is also apparent that in the area of treatment, as in other areas, there is a general dissatisfaction with the research methodology of the past and an increasing demand for more stringent scientific standards and methodological sophistication. Consequently, there has been an impressively developing willingness to subject the outcome of therapy to rather sophisticated evaluation and to conduct investigations of salient aspects of the therapeutic process, including the activities, role and characteristics of the therapist.

Reviewers' criticisms of some common methodological defects and our own efforts to avoid these will be discussed in greater detail in the chapter on research design. To summarize, these concerns are expressed in terms of heterogeneity, small size or inadequate description of the patient group, insufficient details as to the type and amount and duration of treatment, disagreement on acceptable objective criteria of outcome, failure to provide acceptable control or comparison groups, biased assignment of patients to treatment, absent or deficient statistical analysis and the drawing of inappropriate inferences on the basis of insufficient evidence. To this may be added a further long list that includes problems of drop-outs and sample attrition, inattention to non-patient factors such as therapist characteristics, or to situational factors such as institutional policies and practices, and finally the absence of post-treatment follow-up and long-range evaluation of main and side effects.

Our own review of the literature reveals that there has been no adequately controlled comparison of the efficacy of the five treatment methods used in this study, although each of them has been in common use for many years. In addition, there has been little published systematic evaluation of psychotherapy in schizophrenia. This is by no means independent of the relatively meager and rather confused state of psychotherapy research in general. Considering the widespread use

[2] See reference 41.

of psychotherapeutic methods, this should indeed arouse deep concern. Our limited knowledge of what can and cannot be accomplished must severely limit our ability to produce meaningful and testable hypotheses, to modify and improve present methods and to develop the necessary techniques and procedures for research in this area.

Some twenty years ago Whitehorn observed that "the large literature on psychotherapy to which the learner might expect to turn for guidance has not been formulated in the same impersonal scientific style as that on pharmacology. It has been written, for the most part, out of the convictions which arise from personal activity rather than from carefully controlled scientific comparison."[3] Although Whitehorn himself was at that time inclined to favor a clinical rather than an experimental approach, he nevertheless cautioned that "the psychotherapist's emotional reactions tend to establish premature convictions; arouse evangelical rivalries and lead to the development of rival 'schools of psychotherapy.'" In the same vein, Hoch pointed out the need for a comprehensive method for evaluating the effectiveness of psychotherapy.[4] Mensh concluded that ". . . the balance still remains on the side of the anecdotal report, the 'clinical instance,' impressions and observations and not on the side of systematic, controlled investigation. . . ."[5] Snyder observed that too many studies of the outcome of psychotherapy are subjective judgments, sometimes by the therapists themselves. "In general . . . the more rigorous the criteria, the less encouraging are the results."[6]

Regarding outcome, Frank comments, "There is little established knowledge about the relative efficacy of various forms [of psychotherapy] and the therapists' expectations seem to influence the length and amount of treatment required to produce improvement."[7] Referring to outcome, he says, "By and large . . . the effect of successful psychotherapy seems to be to accelerate or facilitate the healing process that would have gone on more slowly in its absence. This is, of course, the function of most medical treatments. If psychotherapists did no more than reduce duration of suffering and disability, this would be well worth their efforts."

Eysenck's provocative current position regarding the effectiveness of psychotherapy is summarized in his statement that "the therapeutic effects of psychotherapy are small or nonexistent and do not in any demonstrable way increase the rate of recovery over that of a com-

[3] See reference 65.
[4] See reference 37.
[5] See reference 47.
[6] See reference 53.
[7] See reference 32.

parable group which receives no treatment at all."[8] Earlier it had appeared to him that there was an inverse correlation between recovery and psychotherapy: ". . . the more psychotherapy, the smaller the recovery rate. . . ."[9] Eysenck's tabulations have been criticized as misleading and inconsistent by Duhrssen and Jorswieck.[10] Rosenzweig also challenged Eysenck's conclusions, believing that the more intensive the treatment, the higher the level of recovery.[11] Yet, as pointed out by Meehl[12] and more recently by Bergin,[13] in spite of various attacks upon Eysenck's original logic and data, no one has been able to meet directly his main challenge by offering concrete, experimental evidence favorable to psychotherapy.

Alexander concluded that "the outcome of psychotherapy in schizophrenics in terms of cure or improvement does not appear to differ greatly from the other methods of treatment."[14] And yet Walker and Kelly found psychotherapy to be negatively related to the rate of hospital discharge of schizophrenic veterans.[15] It is evident, however, that an increasing number of workers in this area are finding evidence that psychotherapy leads to greater variability among its recipients by causing some to improve and others to become worse than control subjects.[16] Implications of these observations obviously bear on many aspects of psychotherapeutic transactions, including patient and therapist characteristics.

Strupp, reviewing the conceptual and technical problems of research in psychotherapy, summarized his discontent, shared by the majority of researchers in this area, in the following words: "It is disquieting to contemplate the large discrepancy between clinical and philosophical insights on the one hand, and research accomplishments on the other. As researchers we seem to lack methods for making greater inroads on the phenomena with which psychotherapy deals—the broad spectrum of human experience."[17]

Why this lack of method (and fruitful ideas) after half a century of individual and occasionally group efforts in this direction? Many researchers have attempted to provide an answer to this question.[18] Meehl thought that, given the state of our knowledge, ". . . we do not seem

[8] See reference 30.
[9] See reference 27.
[10] See reference 26.
[11] See reference 50.
[12] See reference 46.
[13] See reference 9.
[14] See reference 2.
[15] See reference 62.
[16] See references 5, 9, 13, 31, 49, 61.
[17] See reference 56.
[18] See references 19, 42, 46.

sufficiently daring and experimental about therapeutic tactics. Even when practical exigencies force a certain amount of trial and error, doctrinaire views about therapeutic theory are likely to be left unquestioned."[19] Colby attributed the chaos in theory and methodology in this domain to the absence of a shared paradigm which commands consensus regarding a set of conceptual, theoretical, instrumental and methodological commitments.[20] For a new paradigm to emerge and to be given a hearing, Colby feels we should ". . . halt and question every assumption in every paradigm in use today." Moreover, as a method of treating the mentally ill, psychotherapy suffers an enormous lack of specificity in definition and purpose. Compared to other scientifically based methods of treatment, it has been thought useful and applied to a fantastic range of human problems and situations by a wide variety of artisans. Therefore, to be more useful and effective than it has been, psychotherapy must become better differentiated: more explicit in characteristic properties and functions, broader in scope to include a multitude of other behaviors besides the verbal, and yet more specific in purpose.

In addition, the emergence of an acceptable paradigm must come from systematic research of a broad base. Perhaps one promising road to this end entails what Meehl suggested some twelve years ago: ". . . a coordinated large-scale research program in which the range of theory and tactics should be widely sampled; designed so as to yield information about the higher-order interactions and the (no doubt tremendous) individual differences among therapists 'officially' homogeneous in views. Multiple criteria of outcome should be used, at least until we know a great deal about the criterion intercorrelations and their post-therapy course."[21] In such a design, we should add, patient groups must be widely represented and identified, therapists' characteristics well described, and treatment schedules clearly specified.

There are more published studies of outcome for the somatic therapies, but the end result still leaves much to be desired. Freyhan, for example, observes that although the introduction of somatic therapies facilitated a steady increase of separations from hospitals, the proportion of permanent separations after single admissions has remained virtually unchanged through the past fifty years.[22] He concluded that there is no indication that somatic therapy or psychotherapy have contributed any measurable increase in the proportion of permanent separations. In a similar vein Kalinowsky and Hoch noted that "empirically, the organic

[19] See reference 46.
[20] See reference 19.
[21] See reference 46.
[22] See reference 33.

treatments produced results. The evidence of those results is naturally open to discussion, and no final determination of their value has as yet been made."[23]

Some fourteen years after the introduction of convulsive therapy by Von Meduna in 1934, Palmer, perhaps one of the greatest enthusiasts about somatic therapy, wrote, "In any syndrome whatsoever in which affective disorder is either dominating or determining the clinical pattern, convulsion therapy offers an almost specific field of therapy."[24] He went on to state, ". . . it is probably true to say that convulsive therapy now holds the field as the most effective single remedy in the whole range of psychiatry in relation to the number of patients deriving benefit from the treatment. Its use should not be restricted to the mental hospital, and any general hospital which is not offering the public this form of treatment is not discharging its responsibility to the sick public."

Now, two decades later, there is still no conclusive evidence regarding the indications for ECT in schizophrenia. Nor do we have an adequate theory as to its mode of action.

The introduction in 1952 of the first major ataraxic drug, chlorpromazine (Thorazine) aroused a great deal of interest, and, in general, pharmacotherapy may be considered to be the most intensively and soberly studied method of treatment for schizophrenia at the present time.

Early clinical investigations were directed toward determining whether chlorpromazine produced any effects in schizophrenia beyond mere sedation or increased enthusiasm and more hopeful expectations in the treatment staff and the patient.[25]

While it is generally well acknowledged that so far pharmacotherapy seems to ameliorate rather than cure, chlorpromazine and several other phenothiazines have been established as useful agents—at least to the satisfaction of the somatic therapists—in producing improvement in psychomotor performance, cognitive functions and clinical status,[26] both in acute and chronic severely ill hospital patients.[27] Other phenothiazines have gradually receded into lesser significance.[28]

Thus, the current situation seems to be that some progress has been made in the development of a diversity of treatment methods which, on the whole, seem to achieve the reduction or removal of some symptoms and alleviate suffering. However, there is no firm evidence that

[23] See reference 41.
[24] See reference 48.
[25] See references 15, 22, 23, 35, 52.
[26] See reference 36.
[27] See references 10, 11, 16, 18, 39, 51, 54, 60, 63.
[28] See references 43, 44.

these indeed result in a greater number of "cures" or lasting remissions or even a reduced incidence of readmissions. Nor do we find sufficient data on the *comparative* efficacy of the currently used methods of treatment in terms of reducing specific symptom patterns or improving psychological (cognitive and affective), social or occupational functioning. It follows, therefore, that our present standards for evaluating treatment outcome in schizophrenia must be comparative in character, imbued with realism and adjusted to the fact that, in general, none of the present forms of treatment can sustain a claim to have produced results beyond the point of amelioration. The sobering facts make it plain that we should utilize realistic criteria of outcome which seem appropriate to the needs of the individual patient and his family, to the goals of the therapist and the hospital administrator and to the expectations of the community.

Although we are aware that the information gathered in this study may throw light on some of the theoretical questions referred to above, our immediate aim is to evaluate empirically in practical terms the effectiveness of the five different methods of treatment. Presently we are not considering the potential contribution of these methods to provide basic scientific knowledge or their ultimate validity or usefulness in explaining the nature of what we now know as "schizophrenia." It is entirely possible that a particular method of treatment may prove to be an extremely valuable research instrument in answering questions regarding the nature, etiology, sociology, physiology, biochemistry or psychology of schizophrenia, even though this same method may not be of great practical value, judged by the number of people it helps, its cost or its side effects. It seems likely, however, that a treatment method that proves to be clinically effective will also point the way to the solution of fundamental theoretical issues.

REFERENCES

(1) Adelson, D. & Epstein, L. J.: A study of phenothiazines with male and female chronically ill schizophrenic patients. *J. Nervous and Mental Disease,* 134:543–554, 1962.
(2) Alexander, L.: *Treatment of Mental Disorders.* W. B. Saunders, Philadelphia, 1953: 200–206.
(3) Arieti, S.: Psychotherapy of schizophrenia. *Archives of General Psychiatry,* 6:112–122, 1962.
(4) Bandura, A.: Psychotherapy as a learning process. *Psychological Bulletin,* 58:143–159, 1961.
(5) Barron, F.: Some test correlates of response to psychotherapy. *J. Consulting Psychology,* 17:235–241, 1953.

(6) Barron F. & Leary, T.: Changes in psychoneurotic patients with and without psychotherapy. *J. Consulting Psychology*, 19:239–245, 1955.

(7) Bateson, G., Jackson, D. D., Haley, J. & Weakland, J.: Toward a theory of schizophrenia. *Behavioral Science*, 1:251–264, 1956.

(8) Bellak, L.: Methodology and research in the psychotherapy of psychoses. *Psychiatric Research Reports*, 17, American Psychiatric Association, 1963.

(9) Bergin, A. E.: Some implications of psychotherapy research for therapeutic practice. *J. Abnormal Psychology*, 71:235–246, 1966.

(10) Bigelow, N., Ozerengin, F., Schneider, J. & Sainz, A.: Carphenazine in the treatment of chronic schizophrenia. In *Third World Congress of Psychiatry*, Vol. II, McGill University Press, Montreal, 1961.

(11) Cacioppo, J. et al: A comparison between trifluoperazine and carphenazine in chronically ill schizophrenic in-patients. *Diseases of the Nervous System* (supp), 22:46–50, 1961.

(12) Cartwright, D. S.: Success in psychotherapy as a function of certain actuarial variables. *J. Consulting Psychology*, 19:357–363, 1955.

(13) Cartwright, D. S.: Effectiveness of psychotherapy: A critique of the spontaneous remission argument. *J. Counseling Psychology*, 2:290–296, 1955.

(14) Cartwright, R. D. & Vogel, J. L.: A comparison of changes in psychoneurotic patients during matched periods of therapy and no-therapy. *J. of Consulting Psychology*, 24:121–127, 1960.

(15) Casey, J. F., Bennett, I. F., Lindley, C. J., Hollister, L. E., Gordon, M. H. & Springer, N. N.: Drug therapy in schizophrenia: a controlled study of the relative effectiveness of chlorpromazine, promazine, phenobarbital and placebo. *Archives of General Psychiatry*, 2:210–220, 1960.

(16) Casey, J. F. & Hollister, L. E.: Combined drug therapy of chronic schizophrenics: controlled evaluation of placebo, dextroamphetamine, imipramine, iso-carboxazid and trifluoperazine added to maintenance doses of chlorpromazine. *American J. of Psychiatry*, 117:997–1003, 1961.

(17) Casey, J. F., Lasky, J. J., Klett, C. J. & Hollister, L. E.: Treatment of schizophrenic reactions with phenothiazine derivates. *American J. of Psychiatry*, 117:97–105, 1960.

(18) Clark, M., Roy, R. S. & Parades, A.: Chlorpromazine in chronic schizophrenic females: a note on predicting response. In *Transcript of 6th Research Conference on Cooperative Chemotherapy Studies in Psychiatry, and Broad Research Approaches to Mental Illness, March 27–29, 1961*, Washington Department of Med. & Surg., VA, 1961.

(19) Colby, K. M.: Psychotherapeutic processes. *Annual Review of Psychology*, 15:347–370, 1964.

(20) Cole, J. O., ed.: Evaluation of drug treatment in psychiatry. *Psychopharmacology Service Center Bulletin*, 2, 3:28–38, 1962.

(21) Cole, J. O. et al: Phenothiazine treatment in acute schizophrenia-effectiveness. *Archives of General Psychiatry*, 10:246–261, 1964.

(22) Cole, J. O., Klerman, G. L. & Jones, R. T.: Drug therapy—1959. In *Progress in Neurology and Psychiatry*, Spiegel, E. J., ed., Grune and Stratton, New York, 1960: 540–576.

(23) Coons, W. H., Boyd, B. A. & White, J. G.: Chlorpromazine, trifluoperazine and placebo with long-term mental hospital patients. *Canadian Psychiatric Association J.*, 7:159–163, 1962.

(24) Davis, J. & Cole, J. O.: Psychotropic drugs. In *The Schizophrenic Syndrome*, Bellak, L. and Loeb, L., eds. (In press).

(25) Deutsch, A.: *The Mentally Ill in America: A History of Their Care and Treatment from Colonial Times*. Columbia University Press, New York, 1960: 88–113.

(26) Duhrssen, A. & Jorswieck, E.: Zur korrektur von Eysenck's berichterstattung uber psychoanalytische behandlungsergebnisse. *Acta Psychotherapeutica et Psychosomatica*, 10:329–342, 1962.

(27) Eysenck, H. J.: The effects of psychotherapy: an evaluation. *J. Counseling Psychology*, 16:319–324, 1952.

(28) Eysenck, H. J.: A reply to Luborsky's note. *British J. of Psychology*, 45:132–133, 1954.

(29) Eysenck, H. J.: The outcome problem in psychotherapy: a reply. *Psychotherapy: Theory, Research and Practice*, 1:97–100, 1964.

(30) Eysenck, H. J.: The effects of psychotherapy. *International J. of Psychiatry*, 1:97–178, 1965.

(31) Fairweather, G. W., Simon, R., Gebhard, M. E., Weingarten, E., Holland, J. L., Sanders, R., Stone G. B. & Reahl J. E.: Relative effectiveness of psychotherapeutic programs: a multicriteria comparison of four programs for three different patient groups. *Psychological Monographs*, 492:1–25, 1960.

(32) Frank, J. D.: *Persuasion and Healing—A Comparative Study of Psychotherapy*. John Hopkins Press, Baltimore, 1961: 208–225.

(33) Freyhan, F. A.: Eugen Bleuler's concept of the group of schizophrenias at mid-century. *American J. of Psychiatry*, 114:769–779, 1958.

(34) Fulkerson, S. D. & Barry, J. R.: Methodology and research on the prognostic use of psychological tests. *Psychological Bulletin*, 58:177–204, 1961.

(35) Gibbs, J. J., Wilkins, B. & Lauterbach, C. G.: A controlled clinical psychiatric study of chlorpromazine. *J. of Clinical & Experimental Psychopathology*, 18:269–283, 1957.

(36) Heilizer, F.: The effects of chlorpromazine upon psychomotor and psychiatric behavior of chronic schizophrenic patients. *J. Nervous and Mental Disease*, 128:358–364, 1959.

(37) Hoch, P. H.: Aims and limitations of psychotherapy. *American J. of Psychiatry*, 112:321–327, 1955.

(38) Hollister, L. E.: Evaluation of psychotherapeutic drugs in patients. Paper read at the University of California Medical Center, January 27, 1962.

(39) Hollister, L. E. et al: Trifluoperazine in chronic schizophrenic patients. *J. of Clinical & Experimental Psychopathology*, 21:15–24, 1960.

(40) Jackson, D. D., ed.: *The Etiology of Schizophrenia*. Basic Books, New York, 1960: 456.

(41) Kalinowsky, L. B. & Hoch, P. H.: *Somatic Treatments in Psychiatry*. Grune and Stratton, New York and London, 1961: 336, 346.

(42) Kiesler, D. J.: Some myths of psychotherapy research and the search for a paradigm. *Psychological Bulletin*, 65:110–136, 1966.

(43) Kurland, A. A., Hanlon, T. E., Tatom, M. H., Ota, K. Y. & Simopoulos, A. M.: The comparative effectiveness of six phenothiazine compounds, phenobarbital and inert placebo in the treatment of acutely ill patients: global measures of severity of illness, *J. of Nervous and Mental Disease*, 133:1–18, 1961.

(44) Lasky, J. J., Klett, C. J., Caffey, E. M., Jr., Bennett, J. L., Rosenblum, M. P. & Hollister, L. E.: Drug treatment of schizophrenic patients—a comparative evaluation of chlorpromazine, chlorprothixine, fluophenazine, reserpine, thioridazine, and trifluopromazine. *Diseases of the Nervous System*, 23:698–706, 1962.

(45) Matarazzo, J. D.: Psychotherapeutic processes. *Annual Review of Psychology*, 16:181–224, 1965.

(46) Meehl, P. E.: Psychotherapy. *Annual Review of Psychology*, 6:357–378, 1955.

(47) Mensh, I. N.: Research in counselling and psychotherapeutic process. In *Progress in Clinical Psychology*, Vol. 2, Brower, D. and Abt, L. E., eds. Grune and Stratton, New York, 1956: 340–360.

(48) Palmer, H.: Recent techniques of physical treatment and its results. In *Modern Trends in Psychological Medicine*. Harris, N. G., ed., Harper Brothers, New York, 1948: 251–255.

(49) Rogers, C. R. & Dymond, R. F.: *Psychotherapy and Personality Change*. University of Chicago Press, Chicago, Illinois, 1954: 416–424.

(50) Rosenzweig, S.: A transvaluation of psychotherapy: A reply to Hans Eysenck. *J. Abnormal and Social Psychology*, 49:298–304, 1954.

(51) Schiele, B. C. et al: A comparison of thioridazine, trifluoperazine, chlorpromazine and placebo—a double blind, controlled study on the treatment of chronic hospitalized schizophrenic patients. *J. of Clinical and Experimental Psychopathology,* 22:151–162, 1961.

(52) Schiele, B. C. et al: Treatment of hospitalized schizophrenics with trifluoperazine plus tranylcypromine: a double blind controlled study. *Comprehensive Psychiatry,* 4:66–79, 1963.

(53) Snyder, W. U.: Psychotherapy. *Annual Review of Psychology,* 9:353–374, 1958.

(54) Solynom, L.: High dosage chlorpromazine treatment in chronic schizophrenic patients. *Canadian Psychiatric Association J.,* 5:230–234, 1960.

(55) Stone, L.: Psychoanalysis and brief psychotherapy. *Psychoanalytic Quarterly,* 20:215–236, 1951.

(56) Strupp, H. H.: Some comments on the future of research in psychotherapy. *Behavioral Science,* 5:60–71, 1960.

(57) Strupp, H. H.: Psychotherapy. *Annual Review of Psychology,* 13:445–478, 1962.

(58) Strupp, H. H.: The outcome problem in psychotherapy revisited. *Psychotherapy: Theory, Research and Practice,* 1:1–13, 1963.

(59) Strupp, H. H.: The outcome problem in psychotherapy: a rejoinder. *Psychotherapy: Theory, Research and Practice,* 1:101, 1964.

(60) Terrell, M. S.: Response to trifluoperazine and chlorpromazine, singly and in combination, in chronic "backward" patients. *Diseases of the Nervous System,* 23:41–48, 1962.

(61) Truax, C. B. & Carkhuff, R. R.: For better or for worse: The process of psychotherapeutic change. In *Recent Advances in the Study of Behavioral Change.* McGill University Press, Montreal, 1963: 118–163.

(62) Walker, R. & Kelly, F. E.: Predicting the outcome of a schizophrenic episode. *Archives of General Psychiatry,* 2:492–503, 1960.

(63) Weston, F. K. & Loftus, A. P.: A terminal double blind trial of trifluoperazine in chronic schizophrenia. *Medical J. of Australia,* 1:776–780, 1961.

(64) Wexler, M.: The structural problem in schizophrenia: the role of internal objects. In *Psychotherapy with Schizophrenics.* Brody, E. B. and Redlich, F. C., eds. International Universities Press, New York, 1954: 179–201.

(65) Whitehorn, J. C.: Psychotherapy. In *Modern Trends in Psychological Medicine,* Harris, N. G., ed. Harper Brothers, New York, 1948: 219–236.

(66) Zilboorg, G.: *A History of Medical Psychology.* W. W. Norton & Co., Inc., New York, 1941: 317–329.

(67) Zubin, J.: Evaluation of therapeutic outcome in mental disorders. *J. of Nervous and Mental Disease,* 117:95–111, 1953.

CHAPTER II

Design and Procedures of the Schizophrenia Research Project

PHILIP R. A. MAY, M.D.

THIS SECTION AND its related appendices are intended to help the reader understand our study and compare it with others. It includes definitions, procedural details and discussion of practical and theoretical points that should be of real assistance to the clinical research investigator who is thinking of doing an outcome study in a hospital setting.

The purpose of this research was to examine the results of the different commonly used methods of treatment for schizophrenic patients under the conditions that might be found in a good public hospital now or in the forseeable future. Since many patients are treated in other settings under conditions that are comparable or equivalent in many respects, the results of this study may have a reasonably wide application.

For this study, 228 schizophrenic patients who had not had significant prior hospital treatment were carefully chosen from male and female first admissions to Camarillo State Hospital. They were chosen on the basis of a clinical estimate by a team of two experienced psychoanalysts that the patient's prognosis was in approximately the middle third of the prognastic range. This "triage" attempted to exclude, on the one hand, patients who were already on their way to rapid "spontaneous" remission and, on the other hand, those who were likely to require more than two years of continuous hospital care. These selected patients with an "average" prognosis were assigned to five treatment methods commonly used or commonly advocated for the treatment of this kind of patient: (1) INDIVIDUAL PSYCHOTHERAPY ALONE, (2) ATARAXIC DRUGS ALONE, (3) INDIVIDUAL PSYCHOTHERAPY PLUS ATARAXIC DRUGS, (4) ELECTROSHOCK and (5) MILIEU, a control group which received none of these specific treatments. A method of randomization was used to try to equate the treatment groups in an unbiased manner in as many respects as possible, including their assignments to treating physicians.

The treating physicians were either in psychiatric residency training or had completed their training with up to three years of subsequent experience. However, a resident was not permitted to carry a patient in psychotherapy until he had completed six months residency training. Each patient's treatment was supervised by a treatment supervisor experienced in the particular treatment that was being given and who believed in its efficacy. Care was taken to see that each form of treatment was given a fair trial under good realistic conditions in suitable dosage for an adequate length of time—until the patient was either successfully released or treatment had been given for six to twelve months and both the treatment supervisor and the therapist agreed that it had been a failure.

Those who were declared treatment failures, having failed to respond on one of the five experimental treatments, were subsequently treated with GROUP PSYCHOTHERAPY PLUS ATARAXIC DRUGS. This was selected as a combination commonly used and advocated in public hospitals for the treatment of schizophrenic patients.

Before and after treatment the patients were given a comprehensive, multidisciplinary evaluation that included both narrative material and quantified ratings and test items provided by nursing staff, psychologist, social worker, social science interviewer, psychoanalyst and treating physician. Less detailed evaluations were done every two weeks and three months. Other recorded data included movement statistics; photographs before and after treatment; treatment dosage (including hydrotherapy, sedation and seclusion as well as the specific experimental treatments); ward staffing and milieu; visitors; and information on therapists such as experience, ratings of effectiveness and some limited test material. The information was sufficiently comprehensive to permit an estimate of the cost of treating each individual patient.

Much effort was put into achieving a low drop-out rate and into tracing and correcting errors and inaccuracies before the data were analyzed. All patients were followed up for at least two years after completion of the experimental treatment.

OVERVIEW

The purpose of this research was to investigate the effectiveness of treatment methods in common use for schizophrenic patients under the sort of conditions that might reasonably be expected in a good public hospital, presently or within the forseeable future—and to carry out the study in a way that would bear the maximum possible relationship to the realities of clinical practice.

This latter aspect needs to be stressed, for the reader will find that controlled research studies of treatment outcome in schizophrenia have commonly used a closed-end design with a fixed treatment period— usually two, four, six, eight or occasionally twelve weeks—and that the results have been analyzed for only those patients who stay in treatment for this fixed period. This kind of approach may indeed be appropriate for laboratory studies of the isolated properties of certain drugs and procedures, but for real-life treatment of an illness with a natural history such as schizophrenia it is an absolute misfit. A clinician seldom treats all his patients for the same arbitrary length of time, and he follows them all, however long their treatment takes. He is well aware that there are substantial differences in speed of response to therapy and that many, if not most, schizophrenic patients remain in the hospital for more than twelve weeks—especially in public hospitals.

It would therefore seem more realistic and meaningful to use an open-ended approach that follows all the patients whether they respond quickly or slowly, and that allows patients who respond slowly to be treated for at least six months, preferably a year. This study attempts to meet these requirements, using a basic design that is essentially a straightforward comparison between five randomized treatment groups.

Selected first admission schizophrenic patients with no significant prior treatment were thoroughly evaluated and then assigned by a random method to one of five treatment groups: (1) INDIVIDUAL PSYCHOTHERAPY ALONE, (2) ATARAXIC DRUGS ALONE, (3) INDIVIDUAL PSYCHOTHERAPY PLUS ATARAXIC DRUGS; (4) ELECTROSHOCK, and (5)MILIEU or CONTROL who received none of these special treatments. Re-examination was carried out at intermediate intervals and at the end of treatment. After this there was a follow-up period of at least two years.

SELECTION OF PATIENTS

MIDDLE PROGNOSTIC RANGE. Zubin, Burdock, Sutton and Cheek have emphasized that outcome studies should deal with samples that are relatively homogeneous with regard to prognosis, and that some idea of each individual's prognosis is important in order to assure that the experimental and control groups are equivalent in expected final outcome. "Only with such equivalent groups can a reliable decision be reached as to the efficacy of a particular therapy."[1] Our study not only deals with a patient group that is relatively homogeneous in prognosis, but also includes actual quantitative pretreatment estimates of prognosis for each individual.

Schizophrenic patients were selected from the admissions to Camarillo Hospital by triage, a clinical judgment that the patient's prognosis was in approximately the middle third of the prognostic range. Patients were excluded if they were considered to have little chance of leaving the hospital in less than two years, or if they were already showing signs of rapid recovery during the initial evaluation period (average sixteen days). The main reasons for selecting "patients with an average prognosis" were: (1) this kind of patient is often treated with one or another of the five methods under study, (2) these are the cases where treatment might make the greatest difference between success and failure and (3) this would enable a study from admission to release to be completed in a reasonable time period. In addition, (4) the inclusion of "good prognosis" patients who appear to have a high likelihood of "spontaneous" remission without specific treatment would be likely to obscure evaluation of treatment effectiveness and (5) their assignment to an unnecessary major form of therapy would violate good clinical practice. Finally, granted that it is necessary to use some kind of selec-

---

[1] See reference 39.

tion method to achieve a degree of homogeneity, triage to "average prognosis" should lead to a fairly reasonable estimate of the "usual" or "average" outcome, even though it limits the range by trimming off the "extremely good" and the "extremely bad" ends.

In practice the clinicians seem to have been remarkably successful in selecting a group of medium-stay patients—the length of hospital stay for this study group ranged between 29 and 840 days, with an average of 197. Those who wish to compare our results with other studies are warned (assuming that there is some degree of validity in our clinicians' judgments of prognosis) that such comparisons should be cautious unless the other study provides an estimate of the prognostic range of its patient group.

PRELIMINARY SCREENING. In the selection procedure, preliminary screening to effect homogeneity for a few specific gross prognostic factors was followed by a more detailed evaluation by a team of two psychoanalysts.

A research psychiatrist reviewed the admission service work-up for all patients diagnosed as schizophrenic and examined the patient to apply the following screening criteria:

(a) Diagnosis "schizophrenia," established at the regular hospital diagnostic conference and confirmed by the research psychiatrist.
(b) "First significant admission" (as defined in Appendix IV). We aimed to exclude patients who had had previous major somatic therapy or substantial prior hospital treatment, without making the acceptance criteria so unrealistic as to make it impossible to execute the study.
(c) Age 16 to 45 inclusive.
(d) No evidence of organic brain damage or epilepsy.
(e) No major physical illness or complicating factor that might question the diagnosis of schizophrenia or complicate or contraindicate the administration of any of the five treatment methods under study.
(f) No history of addiction to alcohol or to any drug. Patients who drank heavily at times could be included if they were not considered to be basically "alcoholic."

PROVISIONAL ACCEPTANCE. Patients who met these rough, essentially nonjudgmental, preliminary criteria were then seen by a selection committee composed of two psychoanalysts with a research psychiatrist as a resource person and nonvoting chairman. Their task was to verify the preliminary screening and to apply additional criteria for provisional acceptance into the study as follows:

(1) Patients were excluded who, during the evaluation period, had already almost recovered from the acute phase of their illness or who were showing signs of improvement such that there was a good prospect of early remission without any specific treatment. This elimin-

ated from the study a group of patients in approximately the upper third of the prognostic range.

(2) Patients were included only if the committee felt that there was a reasonable prospect of their improving sufficiently to leave the hospital within two years after admission.

(3) Special emphasis was placed on excluding from the study those where there was any substantial disagreement or question of the diagnosis of schizophrenia.

The committee first reviewed the record and decided whether to exclude a patient on this basis. The remaining patients were then interviewed, and each member recorded his decision separately and again after a group discussion. If consensus could not be reached, the patient was not accepted.

FINAL ACCEPTANCE. The initial acceptance decision was only provisional. If the more detailed research evaluation led to any question, or if the patient improved rapidly before assignment to treatment, the case was reviewed again by the selection committee. The reader may be confident that there is little doubt that the patients who were finally included in the study were truly "schizophrenic": The diagnosis was established only after meticulous consideration, including interviews by six physicians—the admitting physician, research psychiatrist, physician in charge of the case, assistant superintendent and two psychoanalysts.

Table 2.1. SELECTION OF PATIENT SAMPLE

Total admissions diagnosed schizophrenia 6/18/59 to 12/19/62		6900
Officially designated first admissions		4816
Rough screened as possibly meeting acceptance criteria		640
Selection committee action		
Rejected		372
Provisionally accepted for study		268
Excluded during work-up period, before assignment to treatment		21
Did not meet criteria for acceptance	12	
Released AMA,* AWOL, etc.	7	
Other reasons	2	
Accepted for study and assigned to treatment		247
Removed after being assigned to treatment		19
Did not meet criteria for acceptance (prior treatment)	10	
Released early AMA, Rx incomplete	4	
Released Jury Trial, Rx incomplete	2	
Complications, Rx incomplete	3	
Accepted for final analysis of in-hospital phase		228

* Against Medical Advice.

Table 2.1 shows the final patient sample relative to the total admissions for the period of selection, June 18, 1959, through December 9, 1962. Some 13 percent of the total first admissions diagnosed as schizophrenic were rough-screened as possibly meeting the acceptance criteria. Of these, the selection committee accepted 42 percent (or 6 percent of the total first-admission schizophrenics). Of the 268 provisionally accepted by the selection committee, 21 were eliminated before assignment to treatment. (See Tables 2.1 and 2.2.)

Table 2.2.   REASONS FOR EXCLUDING PATIENTS AFTER PROVISIONAL ACCEPTANCE BUT BEFORE ASSIGNMENT TO TREATMENT

	SEX		
	M	F	T
Did not meet criteria for acceptance			
Remitting too rapidly	4	5	9
Prior admission	1	2	3
Other reasons			
Administrative	1	0	1
OD gave patient ECT	1	0	1
Discharged AMA, Jury Trial, AWOL	3	4	7
TOTAL	10	11	21

STAGGER SYSTEM. A stagger system was used to introduce patients into the study, admitting approximately equal numbers to each treatment group until the psychotherapy groups reached the saturation point, i.e., when all the psychotherapy supervisors' time was booked. Selection was then suspended for all groups until supervisory time became available again, at which time additional patients were admitted to the study.

PATIENTS EXCLUDED AFTER ASSIGNMENT TO TREATMENT

GENERAL POLICY. Sample exclusions are seldom discussed in detail in published studies. However, it is important that the reader be able to judge for himself our position that the exclusions were justified to improve the quality of the analysis. A thorough discussion may also assist other research investigators who face similar problems.

A number of patients were excluded from the final analysis after they had been assigned to one of the five treatment methods. Table 2.1 shows that of the 247 patients assigned to treatment, 19 were subse-

Table 2.3. PATIENTS EXCLUDED AFTER ASSIGNMENT TO TREATMENT
DISTRIBUTION BY TREATMENT GROUP

Reason	M	E	D	P	P+D	T	χ^{2}*	P >	P <
1. Rejects (prior hospital treatment)	2	1	2	1	4	10	3.096	.50	.60
Given full Rx	1	0	1	0	3	5	6.063	.10	.20
Discovered early	0	0	0	0	1	1	4.107	.30	.40
Discovered late, any reason	1	0	1	0	2	4	3.609	.40	.50
Discovered late, overlooked	(0)	(0)	(1)	(0)	(1)	(2)	2.928	.50	.60
Not given full Rx (all discovered early)	1	1	1	1	1	5	No differences		
Alternative classification									
Concealed	1	0	0	0	1	2	3.197	.50	.60
Not concealed	1	1	2	1	3	8	1.989	.70	.80
2. Discharged by Jury or early AMA	2	0	1	2	1	6	2.442	.60	.70
Jury, Rx incomplete and inadequate	1	0	0	1	0	2	3.088	.50	.60
Early AMA, Rx none or minimal	1	0	1	1	1	4	1.043	.90	.95
3. Other (all early)	0	3	0	0	0	3	11.012	.025	.05
4. Drop-outs (total (2+3))	2	3	1	2	1	9	1.453	.80	.90
5. Total all exclusions after assignment	4	4	3	3	5	19	0.831	.95	.98

* Four degrees of freedom: comparing numbers excluded and not excluded, using method described in Cochran (see reference 1), binomial test of the variance, n varying, p estimated.

quently dropped from the final analysis; 10 because it was discovered that they did not actually meet the criteria for acceptance and 9 for other reasons.

Table 2.3 gives further details of the reasons for these exclusions and their distribution by treatment group, with overall χ^2 tests for the differences between treatment groups. Examination of the total numbers excluded shows no evidence of bias for or against any particular treatment group: the probability that the distributions are compatible with chance is 95-98 percent. However, when the reasons are examined in more detail some interesting points emerge.

PATIENTS EXCLUDED AS NOT MEETING THE CRITERIA FOR ACCEPTANCE. Ten patients were excluded because it was subsequently discovered that they had been admitted to a hospital before and did not meet the criteria for "first significant admission." Table 2.4 gives some details for each case.* This represents a procedural failure: Our operations were not sufficiently effective to detect early enough all the cases that should have been excluded according to the specifications of the research protocol.

In two instances concealment of hospitalization was deliberate:

Patient #1: This lady appeared to the nursing staff to be unduly familiar with hospital routines. It also seemed strange that such an attractive and sociable young person should have no friends or relatives. It was therefore suspected that she was not from the Los Angeles community and that she might have been in a hospital before. She denied this vigorously, and although a friend quoted the patient as saying she had once been in Camarillo, no record could be found of any previous admission, nor could any member of the hospital staff recognize her. Many months later she admitted that she had been in several hospitals before—mainly in other states, but including one admission to Camarillo under another name! Fear of being deported from California was her main conscious motive for concealing her true identity.

Patient #2: This lady made fragmentary and disconnected allusions to prior treatment, but as she was quite out of contact and continually making extravagant claims, and as the history from the family referred only to brief outpatient treatment some years before, these were discounted. Six months after admission she told her doctor that she had had insulin treatment at another hospital. This was denied by the family, but she continued to refer to insulin treatment in an evasive, contradictory, inconsistent and fragmented way. Her family was interviewed again, and they insisted that she had never been in hospital before. However, suspicion persisted and later she was cajoled into giving

---

* To preserve anonymity the patient and therapist numbers and initials used in case extracts and tables are fictitious and deliberately misleading.

Table 2.4. PATIENTS EXCLUDED AFTER ASSIGNMENT TO TREATMENT
(PRIOR SIGNIFICANT ADMISSION)

Patient #	Sex	Age	Treatment Group	Doctor	Comment
1	F	31	M	A	Prior admission suspected four days before assignment, but denied. Given full course of treatment. Failure (not released). Patient later found to have concealed prior hospital admission.
2	F	23	P+D	G	Suspicion aroused on 168th day. Given full course of treatment. Partial success (released). Patient confused and family concealed prior hospital admission.
3	F	22	P+D	I	Given full treatment. Success (released). Information received on third day but incomplete. Decided to continue patient on treatment while additional information obtained and to make decision at time of final routine review.
4	F	38	P+D	H	Given full course of treatment. Success (released). Information obtained six days before assignment; not received until later and then overlooked by research staff. Discovered in final routine record review.
5	M	17	D	E	Given full course of treatment. Success (released). Information obtained fifteen days before assignment; not received until later and then overlooked by research staff. Discovered in final routine record review.
6	F	35	D	D	Information obtained on thirtieth day. Excluded after 32 days treatment.
7	M	38	E	C	Information obtained on seventh day. Excluded after 20 days treatment.
8	M	19	P	F	Information obtained one day before assignment, but not received in time. Excluded after nine days treatment.
9	F	21	M	B	Information obtained six days before assignment, but not received in time. Excluded after seven days treatment.
10	F	29	P+D	J	Information obtained four days before assignment but not received until later. Excluded after six days treatment.

the name of a hospital. The hospital in question was unable to find any record, but it was then realized that there were gross discrepancies in the information provided by her—including a claimed military service and birth date that would have made her an army sergeant at the age of three! Pressed for further details, the patient changed her story and the hospital was then able to verify that she had in fact been a patient there and had indeed received insulin coma therapy.

In the other eight cases the physician did not obtain a history of prior hospital treatment, but information from other sources—usually the patient's family—disclosed one or more significant admissions. In two of these eight the social worker was not able to arrange an interview with the family until after the patient had been assigned to treatment. In one case information was received three days after the treatment assignment that there might have been a prior admission. Because no details were available, it was decided to wait for additional history and to review the matter for final decision at the end of data collection. It took two months to establish that the patient had been treated elsewhere with electroshock and tranquilizers. In three cases relevant information had actually been obtained one to fifteen days before the patient was assigned to treatment, but was not transmitted to the research staff until afterward. In two cases the information had been filed and overlooked and was not discovered until the routine double-check of the record by the principal investigator at the end of data collection.

The question may be raised as to whether our search for prior admissions and treatment was more—or less—zealous than that usually exerted in clinical practice. In general, our effort corresponds to that of the conscientious clinician, although admittedly there was an element of special search. We think it proper in research to make some special effort to be accurate.

In every case information was obtained from the patient and from family or friends, and the case record was carefully reviewed by the principal investigator at the end of the study. The degree of special search was not prodigious for the eight patients who did not conceal information, nor was it prolonged beyond the period that a clinician would consider reasonable. For example, the longest delay in obtaining information from the family was thirty days after admission—a case where the family changed appointments frequently and insisted that all information had to be cleared through their attorney. By comparison, the three patients in the study who were released the fastest were in the hospital for 29, 31 and 35 days respectively. Thus there was adequate time to obtain information in all cases, even when the patient was released relatively quickly.

It is possible that other patients may have successfully concealed prior admissions, but the number is likely to be small. In the course of a two year follow-up, only one additional prior hospitalization has been discovered, and correspondence with the hospital established that it was not "significant."

Strict adherence to selection criteria poses practical problems. It may take some weeks to interview a family, and it is hardly feasible to delay assignment to treatment in all cases until the family has been interviewed. Moreover, if cases are excluded merely because there is delay in getting information, there is a risk of excluding a particular type of patient who has special family relationships that may influence outcome. This will skew the sample in a definite direction and so lessen its representativeness and reduce the value of the study. There is also the matter of human error. In this study two cases were overlooked at first even though the information was available in the record. Although this amounts to less than one percent of the total intake, and although it was ultimately detected, it does suggest that investigators would be wise to include in their research procedures an early and thorough double-check of their selection criteria. In retrospect also, things could have been speeded up by insisting that it was essential to *telephone* if it were discovered that the patient had had a prior admission instead of waiting for the history to be typed and transmitted to the research staff.

Some might question the exclusion of any cases, and particularly those cases receiving a full course of treatment, on the technical grounds that once a patient is assigned to treatment any exclusion may result in bias if there has been more diligent search in one treatment group than another. However, if the initial examination and routine final review are carried out carefully in the same manner for all patients, as in this study, the chances of systematic bias are minimized, particularly if hospitalization is not concealed.

In point of fact, it is unlikely that the "prior treatment" exclusions introduced any material bias, as the differences in numbers excluded from the five treatment groups are clearly not significant. One case in each group was discovered and excluded *early* (within 6–32 days). Five patients were excluded *later,* but in all five suspicion had been aroused or definite information obtained early and there was no special search in any particular treatment group. The small number and the nature of the *late* exclusions—a failure from MILIEU; two successes and one partial success from the PSYCHOTHERAPY PLUS DRUG group; and one success from the DRUG ALONE group—should assure the conservative research investigator that the bias, if any, is minimal and in favor of the MILIEU (control) group.

Quite apart from bias, there is another side to this matter. The in-

Table 2.5. PATIENTS DISCHARGED BY JURY TRIAL OR
AMA AFTER ASSIGNMENT TO TREATMENT

Patient #	Sex	Age	Treatment Group	Doctor	Comment
11	M	31	P	K	AMA requested on day 1. Discharged on day 6. Therapist in favor of treatment method.
12	M	24	M	A	AMA requested on day 8. Discharged on day 10. Therapist's attitude not known.
13	F	27	D	C	AMA requested on day 12. Discharge on day 17. Therapist much in favor of treatment method.
14	F	29	P+D	L	Therapist in favor of treatment method. After 18 days treatment, family requested AMA. Patient was taken to another hospital on 23rd day, was released from there after a few months and made subsequent marginal adjustment. History of prior admission was being investigated when family requested AMA.
15	F	32	P	M	Released by Jury after 50 days. Marginal adjustment over next three years. Therapist in favor of treatment method.
16	M	36	M	E	Released by Jury after 90 days. Re-hospitalized elsewhere in a few days. Re-released. Subsequent marginal adjustment over next three years. Therapist considered treatment method of questionable value.

clusion of all or any of the ten "prior significant hospitalization" cases would introduce a serious inaccuracy, and we are not able to accept the thesis that it is helpful or advisable to be knowingly inaccurate in the reporting of research results. The purpose of our study is to tell the clinician what happens to first admission schizophrenic patients who have no significant prior treatment. Accordingly, we have confined our analysis to known first admissions. The clinician appreciates very well that patients and their families may give conflicting or misleading information: we think it safe to assume that when a clinician discovers that a patient has had previous hospital admissions, he will revise his frame of reference (and his prognosis) in line with this added information.

PATIENTS DISCHARGED BY JURY OR AGAINST MEDICAL ADVICE. Table 2.5 shows some details for six patients who were excluded because they were discharged by Jury Trial or Against Medical Advice (AMA). Two of these were released by Jury after substantial but incomplete treatment, and four were early AMA's after no or minimal treatment. There is no statistically significant difference between the treatment groups.

PATIENTS EXCLUDED FOR OTHER REASONS. Three patients assigned to ECT were dropped from the study under circumstances that indicate a specific problem with *electroconvulsive therapy.* This is the only treatment group in which patients were dropped after assignment to treatment for reasons other than not meeting selection criteria or release by Jury or AMA.

> *Patient #17:* A 26-year-old male worked up by therapist *M.* When the assignment to *ECT* was made. *M* said he was strongly opposed to its use for this patient and refused to give the treatment or to allow the patient to be transferred to another physician. The patient was dropped from the study after seven days of negotiation, having received no treatment. He was eventually released from the hospital after 114 days of treatment with individual and group psychotherapy.

> *Patient #18:* A 38-year-old female worked up by therapist *N.* After the treatment assignment was made, *N* expressed mixed feelings about *ECT.* Treatment was started, but *N* soon insisted that the patient was recovering and not suitable for any more *electroconvulsive therapy.* The rating team and supervisor reviewed the case and did not agree: To them and to the research staff it seemed that the patient was still clearly psychotic and in need of further treatment. *N* opposed transferring the patient to another physician, and accordingly the patient was dropped from the study after receiving five treatments in fourteen days. She was discharged nine days later.

Patient #19: A 35-year-old female was assigned to therapist *O* who was very much in favor of treating her with *electroconvulsive therapy.* She was disturbed and extremely obese, so that it was physically impossible to administer intravenous succinyl-choline, and *ECT* had to be given without this muscular relaxant. After five treatments she fractured an ankle by kicking against a door. The fracture was considered to be an absolute contraindication to the administration of further *ECT* without a muscular relaxant, and accordingly the patient was dropped from the study on the 21st day. She was eventually released from the hospital 736 days later, having been treated with various ataraxic drugs.

The dropping of these three cases poses some interesting problems in research design, and other investigators may wish to profit from our experience. It is clearly unethical to continue treatment if a complication occurs that makes it physically impossible to continue without serious hazard to the patient. Similarly, once a patient has been assigned to a physician, if he is opposed to giving the patient a particular treatment, there is no ethical way of getting him to give it. In this situation, an agreed transfer to another physician who feels differently is the only alternative to dropping the case. However, transfer introduces bias due to the change in physicians. It would, moreover, be most unwise if the original physician is opposed (as in our two cases).

If patients are assigned only to physicians who are certain to be cooperative in all instances, the study is restricted to a certain type of therapist and loses a lot of its power. Moreover, it is not easy to predict whether a physician will cooperate in any particular case. Those assigned to patients #17 and #18 had agreed beforehand to accept random assignment and were thoroughly cooperative with other patients assigned to *ECT* and to other treatments. Discussion of each patient beforehand with the prospective therapist might be suggested, but this seems hardly realistic.

On the whole, we had a remarkable degree of success in eliciting the cooperation of physicians in random assignment to treatment—245 successes out of 247 cases (99 percent), or 39 successes out of 41 physicians (95 percent).

DROP-OUTS (ATTRITION). The drop-out rate is a simple objective measure of the vigor and efficiency with which an investigator has carried out his research design, and therefore, by implication, of the confidence that may be placed in the results. Keeping patients in a study takes a lot of effort and a certain acquaintance with the workings of the therapeutic situation. The examples given in previous sections will suffice to show that the realities of the clinical situation impose severe stress on a research design and that some attrition is to be expected. Nevertheless, the reader of a research report is entitled to infer that there may well be something wrong with a particular research study if there is a high drop-out rate or if the rate is not given. He should not allow himself to be deceived by a frosting of research jargon, computer talk and intricate statistical manipulation. He should examine critically the reasons for the drop-outs and their distribution, looking especially for the kind of selective drop-out that leads to bias in the composition of the treatment groups.

There is good reason, for instance, to consider that a drop-out rate that is highest for the "placebo" group in a study that is allegedly "double-blind"* is prima facie evidence that the study was not in fact blind and that the drop-outs were biased. In this situation it is likely that the treating physician could distinguish placebo from drug and that he was acting in accordance with his prejudices against placebo when he eliminated patients from the study, whatever the ostensible reason that he gave the research investigator. It may readily be observed that if a physician does not wish his patient to get a particular treatment he will find it easier to transfer him elsewhere or to give some excuse such as "he no longer needs treatment" or "he is too sick to get it," rather than disclose to the investigator that the "blinding" was ineffective.

One should distinguish sharply between the following categories of attrition:

(1) *Screen-Outs:* Patients excluded *before* assignment to treatment because they do not meet the selection criteria for acceptance into the study.

(2) *Rejects:* Patients excluded *after* assignment to treatment because they do not meet the selection criteria. The reject rate is an index of quality control but is hard to interpret. A low rate may either indicate that the early screening was very effective or the final quality control was lax. Conversely, a high rate would indicate poor early screening but better final control.

(3) *True Drop-Outs:* Patients excluded *after* assignment to treatment, but *before* completion of the experimental treatment period, because of some complication or difficulty with the treating physician or the patient, or because the patient insists that he be released AMA.

(4) *Early Remissions:* Patients discharged from the hospital as treatment successes before the completion of a fixed, arbitrary, minimum experimental treatment period. The Early Remission rate is not an index of the efficiency of a research project. A high rate may indicate either a rapid therapeutic effect or the inclusion of patients who are already on the way to "spontaneous recovery." It is particularly important to distinguish clearly between *early remissions* (who

---

* I.e., neither the patient nor the staff know whether an active drug is being given.

represent "success") and *true drop-outs* (who represent "failure" of either treatment or of implementation of research design).

(5) *Limited Responder:* A patient who has completed a defined adequate period of experimental treatment without "satisfactory benefit." The criteria for "satisfactory benefit" will necessarily vary from study to study. For the purposes of this section, it is sufficient to note that a patient could not be designated as a "limited responder" in our study until after the completion of a minimum period of six months in the hospital. It is obvious that these are not *true drop-outs* as strictly defined above, but rather *treatment failures*. (A more detailed discussion and definition of the criteria will be found in the section on Treatment Duration in this chapter.)

(6) *Missing Data:* In this category the patient meets the selection criteria and completes the experimental treatment period, but some of the data are not obtained, either as the result of a failure by the research staff (*missed data*) or because the patient cannot or will not cooperate in providing the data, e.g., by refusing to answer certain questions or by rejecting the test situation in its entirety (*data unobtainable*). If the distinction between *missed* and *unobtainable* data is made accurately, the *unobtainable data* rate is a measure of the patients' cooperation, assuming that the skill and persistence of the research staff remains the same throughout the study. The *missed data* rate is an unequivocal indication of the efficiency of the research staff.

Corotto has illustrated the biasing impact of missing data, pointing out that it becomes greater as the number of excluded subjects increases.[2] He comments that it is not enough to follow the common practice of omitting untestable subjects from further consideration. Although one can only guess what their test results might have been, it is at least possible to look for bias by comparing them with the remainder of the experimental sample on other available types of information. It would seem questionable to generalize the findings of an investigation to the excluded population, particularly if this is at all sizeable.

In this study a record was kept of the reason for any missing data and we were most rigorous in categorizing data as *missed*. For example, the sixth-months tests for patient #211 (see Appendix IV) were not obtained because at the time they were due she was AWOL. They were classified as *missed* (not as *unobtainable*) because no attempt had been made to test her at home.

TRUE DROP-OUT RATE IN THIS STUDY. The true drop-outs in this study comprise the six patients released by Jury or AMA and the three who were dropped from the ECT group because of complications with the physician or the patient. Expressed as a proportion of those who met the criteria for acceptance into the study, the drop-out rate is 4 percent (9/237).

COMPARISON WITH OTHER STUDIES. The distinctions outlined above have not been made in other studies, and the term "drop-out"

[2] See reference 6.

has been used to cover a multitude of sins—and a few non-sins. It would help a great deal to distinguish clearly between the different reasons for removing a patient from a research study, or for excluding his data from the analysis of results. Our definitions are offered in the hope that their use by other investigators will clarify the situation and enable the reader to compare one study with another in this respect.

Reference to the more recent literature indicates that drop-outs have been a serious problem even in high-quality studies, with high and biased rates the rule rather than the exception. What happens in less meticulous studies can only be imagined. By comparison, our 4 percent drop-out rate is extremely low, especially for a minimum treatment period of six months, and the bias, if any, is minimal.

Drop-outs are obviously more difficult to control in an outpatient study than in a hospital, and they may even have a different significance in the two settings. However, the problem is also prominent with inpatient studies, even in those of superior design and execution. For example, in the Psychopharmacology Service Center nine-hospital study of six weeks of drug treatment in acute schizophrenia, the reasons for "early termination" are given as follows:[3]

Drop-outs for administrative reasons
(1) Incorrect diagnosis	9
(2) Intercurrent medical illness	2
(3) Other, court cases, transfer, elopement, etc.	45

Treatment related removals
(4) Marked early remission	10
(5) Serious complication of treatment	11
(6) Treatment failure	43
Number completing study	344

Applying our criteria, the nine in category (1) are *rejects,* and the ten in category (4) are *early remissions.* The 43 so-called "treatment failures" are not *limited responders* as defined above: They did not complete the minimum period of treatment and should properly be counted as drop-outs. Hence, the *true drop-outs* are those in categories (2), (3), (5) and (6), or a drop-out rate of 101 out of the 455 who met the selection criteria (23 percent). The authors note the existence of bias, pointing out that 36 of the 43 patients who were dropped because of early "treatment failure" were on placebo.

In the Spring Grove Hospital study only 187 of the 277 patients remained in the project for ten days or more, and only 108 completed four weeks of treatment.[4] This would mean a *true drop-out* rate at ten days as high as 90/277 or 32 percent, and at four weeks as high as

[3] See reference 32.
[4] See references 21, 22.

169/277 or 61 percent. Seventy-nine percent did not complete the six-week experimental treatment period, for reasons as follows:

(1) No response or worse according to ward psychiatrist	81
(2) Transfers to other services	44
(3) Transfers out, paroled or discharged	35
(4) Drug reactions	27
(5) Organic conditions not induced by drugs	23
(6) Medication no longer needed	8
Total number terminated	218

Applying our criteria, their *true drop-out* rate for the six-week period lies somewhere between 63 percent and 79 percent, depending on how many of the patients in categories (3) and (6) were actually early remissions. In this study also, the drop-out rate was biased and highest for placebo-treated patients—the rank order correlation between the number of patients removed from the study and the potency of the drug they were receiving was −.96. Because of the bias introduced by drop-outs, the investigators could use only the two-week data.

Lasky defined a drop-out as a subject terminated before the full course of planned treatment is complete, stating "It is virtually impossible to prevent sample attrition during the course of a controlled treatment evaluation study conducted in a hospital."[5] He distinguished between the following categories:

A. Treatment-related drop-outs
  (1) Patient becomes better
  (2) Patient becomes worse
    (a) Treatment failure
    (b) Side effects
B. Not related to treatment
  (3) Incomplete or unscorable data
  (4) Failure to obtain evaluation
  (5) Unwitting change of treatment
  (6) Unanticipated transfer
  (7) Later realization that selection criteria not met

Lasky's category (1) corresponds to our *early remission* category, (3) to *data unobtainable,* category (4) to *missed data,* and category (7) to *rejects.* Categories (2), (5) and (6) would be the *true drop-outs.*

The drop-out rate for treatment-related reasons in Lasky's thoughtfully conceived and carefully conducted twelve-week drug study of depressed patients is given as 102/210 (49 percent). However, his tables distinguish the *early remissions* establishing 30/210 (14 percent) as the minimum *true drop-out* rate according to our criteria. (The actual rate is probably larger, as it would include patients in categories (5) and (6) above, the figures for which are not given in his paper.)

[5] See reference 23.

PREVENTION OF DROP-OUTS. The drop-out rate can be reduced by careful planning, with preliminary pilot runs to test procedures for admission, transfer, discharge and removal from the study. However, more than this is needed to achieve a really low rate. Given the present-day realities of psychiatric institutions, successful control of attrition requires a good deal of hard work to integrate research with the other functions of the institution. It is essential that the research investigator should understand how physicians operate in a hospital treatment situation; that he should have some skill in eliciting their cooperation; and that he be able to empathize with their difficulties in the patient-physician relationship without giving way on fundamental matters of research design.

In this study, by deliberate planning, instead of separating research into an ivory tower apart from the normal hospital functions of treatment and education, every effort was made to integrate the three into close cooperation. The principal investigator arranged to be officially in charge of the Admission Service for the entire hospital, and admitting procedures were revised in such a way that research needs were easily incorporated into normal treatment operation. Admissions could not by-pass the Research Staff. Patients could not be discharged without the knowledge of the research psychiatrist, as well as the approval of the assistant superintendent in charge of the unit; they could not be transferred to another unit without the joint approval of the assistant superintendent and the principal investigator or the research psychiatrist. Only the principal investigator was allowed to "drop" a patient from the study—and he went to considerable pains to make it known that this would be regarded as a major and critical decision.

The research staff relied heavily on informal but deliberate personal contact and rapport with the treatment staff to keep the project running smoothly. There were also weekly meetings of the research staff with the head nurses and separate weekly progress reviews of the physicians' cases.

We found little difficulty in obtaining cooperation from our physicians, provided they were approached in a reasonable way by appealing to their wish to improve patient care, while at the same time being considerate of their professional and personal needs. Actions speak louder than words, and we would think it a waste of time or even harmful to harangue physicians about scientific principles or to make speeches about objectivity and bias. To give a specific example, and to illustrate the blending of research and training, the supervised experience in the treatment of schizophrenic patients provided by the research project was highly regarded by the residents—perhaps not only for its educational value, but also because of the implication that the research investigators were interested in their training and in improving the quality of patient care, and were not just exploiting residents to obtain data.

MATCHING AND ASSIGNMENT OF PATIENTS TO TREATMENT AND TO THERAPISTS

Since the patient group as a whole was selected to be homogeneous for "Schizophrenia—average prognosis," there was no attempt to match the specific treatment groups in terms of further parameters such as type of onset, duration and severity of illness. Patients were assigned to the five treatments by a random method, stratifying by sex and by treating doctor as described in Appendix I.

For residents with less than six months training, if the treatment came up PSYCHOTHERAPY ALONE or PSYCHOTHERAPY PLUS DRUG, the patient was reassigned to another physician for treatment (the next in sequence who could take PSYCHOTHERAPY cases). Thus, assignment of treatment to a physician was random for all treatments except for these two. Seventeen percent of the cases in these two groups were reassigned in this way. This will produce a degree of confounding of the results of treatment with the therapist's experience for these cases only. The remaining 83 percent of the PSYCHOTHERAPY ALONE and the PSCHOTHERAPY PLUS DRUG cases, and all the cases in the other three groups, stayed with the therapist to whom they had been randomly assigned.

Accordingly, the comparison of the five treatment methods is strictly applicable only where a minimum of six months residency training is required before taking a case in PSYCHOTHERAPY.

Some clinically-minded readers may wonder why an elaborate random assignment ritual was preferred over simply assigning patients to whatever treatment method was thought best, or trying to match the groups according to important aspects of the patients' history and examination.

Without attempting to go into all the technicalities, assigning patients to whatever treatment is thought to be best for them biases the selection. It assures that the patients assigned to any one treatment will be different to start with in some way or ways that are thought to be important— and probably in several other ways whose association may or may not be concealed from view. Such a procedure completely eliminates the possibility of valid comparison between treatments. It also prejudges the central issues of the whole research by assuming that someone already knows all the answers about what kind of patient does best with what treatment.

The random method used in this study is preferable to the other alternative—forced matching—because it is easier, simpler, less cumbersome and does not require the assumption that the person who does the matching already knows what is important to match for and what is not. It also provides the best chance of equalizing the treatment groups in an unbiased manner in as many respects as possible.

THERAPISTS AND SUPERVISORS

GENERAL POLICY. The patients were treated by physicians with six years or less of psychiatric experience who were either in residency training or had completed it. This is within the range of experience and training that may reasonably be expected to be found for physicians who treat schizophrenic patients in a wide variety of county, state, federal, university and private hospitals. To ensure a high standard, each patient's treatment was supervised by a psychiatric consultant who believed in the efficacy of the particular treatment that he supervised and who was responsible for discussing tactics and operational details with the patient's physician. Thus therapists often had a number of different supervisors, one for each of their patients over a period of time.

PSYCHOTHERAPY SUPERVISION. The therapists were supervised by psychoanalysts experienced in the treatment of schizophrenic patients, one hour of supervision for each patient carried in psychotherapy, or one-half hour per patient per week.

IDENTIFICATION OF THERAPIST AND SUPERVISOR. To minimize the possibility of contamination by the effects of competition among therapists and supervisors, as far as possible it was not disclosed which patients were being supervised in therapy and which supervisor was supervising which therapist. Therapists, patients and supervisors were identified in the records only by confidential code numbers.

TREATMENT METHODS

GENERAL POLICY. The aim was to study the five treatment methods under "good battlefield conditions" that might be considered reasonably practicable in a good public hospital in the forseeable future. Treatment was not given "blind" and, believing that blindness was not even realistically possible, we did not engage in charismatic maneuvers to create the illusion that it was. Patient, treating physician, family and nursing staff knew what kind of treatment was being given and how much. Even though the independent rating teams and the psychometrist were under general instructions not to try to find out what treatment the patient had received, it would be wise to assume that this may have been communicated to them in a number of instances, consciously or unconsciously, in some way or another.

It may be possible to devise a realistic, economically feasible and ethically acceptable research design to compare these five treatment methods in such a way as to successfully conceal from patient, family, treatment staff and research investigators whether *milieu therapy, electroconvulsive therapy, psychotherapy* or *ataraxic drug* is being given.* The results of such a tour de force would no doubt be of considerable theoretical interest, but would leave unanswered the clinician's question as to what happens when treatment is given the way it usually is given. Under "battlefield conditions" the reactions of the patient, family and staff to a particular treatment method are an integral part of the total treatment situation. In this respect our research was carried out under conditions that can be applied directly to clinical practice.

Although the reader may be assured that the research staff and investigators made every conscious attempt to be unbiased and objective in their assessments, we cannot be certain that any of the sources of evaluation were entirely unbiased. However, it would be a remarkable coincidence if such a heterogeneous group of people and sources were all biased in the same direction. Even the psychological tests might be suspected of bias; after all, if the patient "knows" he is being given "all" or "none" of what he believes to be the "best" or the "worst" treatment, he may "show" this in his test responses and expectations of recovery. Moreover, although the psychometrists were not told what treatment the patient was getting, they did have access to research records, and some patients might have told them what they were getting. Thus the possibility of examiner bias cannot be ruled out—and it has been reported that examiner attitudes may affect the results even of so-called "objective" tests.

MILIEU. Basic ward care and staffing were set at a level that would be considered to be good to superior for a public psychiatric hospital in the United States at the time of the study, and that might be considered to be a reasonable standard in the forseeable future.

There were up to about twenty patients of each sex in the study group

* The research theoretician who wishes to attempt this intellectual exercise should start by taking into consideration the period of unconsciousness and disorientation that follows *ECT,* the extrapyramidal and other side effects of ataraxic drugs and the fact that patients talk freely and gratuitously about their therapeutic experiences to other patients and to the staff.

at any one time, housed in one male and one female unit in the same building with similar staffing patterns and general milieu. The wards were changed twice during the 4½ years of intake and treatment. For the first year the patients were with other similar nonresearch patients in a seven-year-old building in two reasonably colorful and cheerful 74-bed units, in four- to six-bed dormitories with a separate day room and dining room. For the next three months the units chosen were rather larger and older—approximately 100 beds each in a building 23 years old. For the remainder of the study period the patients lived in reasonably attractive individual rooms in two twenty-bed units in the same building as the first year; there was a patio and a separate dining facility.

Administratively, the units functioned as a part of the admission and intensive treatment service under the assistant superintendent of the service and subject to the usual customs, rules and procedures of the hospital. It was an important part of our research design that the units should be a part of normal hospital operation so that the results could be interpreted directly in terms of ordinary clinical practice. The treatment staff were *not* special research personnel. Weekend passes, release, restrictions, etc., were determined in the manner usual for the hospital and *not* by research staff. The general orientation of the research staff was to facilitate the research aims of the enterprise in a tactful and supportive manner without disrupting basic policies and practices.

The total number of service nursing staff assigned to the twenty-bed units (including their attached hydrotherapy units) to cover the entire 24 hours averaged 20.6 on the female side and 19.43 on the male side. For the larger units, the staff-patient ratio was somewhat lower. (The two research nurses, one for each ward, are not included in these figures as they had no assigned service function.)

The general ward program for all patients included nursing care, hydrotherapy and occupational, recreational and industrial therapy. The nursing staff held community-type ward meetings once a week with all the patients, and a half-time social worker was assigned to provide casework according to the patient's needs (this was a separate function from that of the research social work staff who obtained the special background information and history from the family).

The patient's doctor was allowed to prescribe barbiturates and hydrotherapy as he thought fit. Patients assigned to the MILIEU (CONTROL) group received only this level of care and did not receive any specific additional treatment. The treatment of the MILIEU group was supervised directly by the principal investigator, who had been brought up to believe firmly in the efficacy of a conservative, expectant, humanistic approach to the treatment of the schizophrenic patient.

ELECTROCONVULSIVE THERAPY. The number, timing and frequency of electroshock treatments were decided by the therapist in consultation with the supervisor for *ECT* according to what was felt to be best for each individual patient. The general pattern was to give treatment three times a week at first, then reduce to two and then one time a week if the patient showed severe confusion and memory loss.

To make the procedure as easy for the patient as possible and to avoid the musculo-skeletal complications that frequently occur with "unmodified" *ECT,* light anesthesia was induced by intravenous thiopental after premedication with atropine. Succinyl-choline was then given intravenously in dosage sufficient to completely or almost completely abolish muscular contractions, and a Dale electroshock machine was used to give a gradual "glissando" electrical stimulus. Cyanosis was avoided by maintaining a full supply of oxygen from a resuscitator unit before and after the electrical stimulus.

The average number of treatments was 19 for males and 25 for females, ranging from 7–44 for those patients successfully released from the hospital after completion of treatment. The ten patients who were not released successfully (limited responders) were given a fair trial of treatment—they received 18, 25, 26, 33, 34, 36, 37, 39, 40 and 45 treatments respectively. Although a vehement devotee of *ECT* might perhaps contend that results would have been more favorable if treatment had been pushed further, the reader should remember that treatment was only given up after careful consideration of the individual case by an experienced supervisor who was asked to consider particularly the likelihood of benefit from continued therapy.

Two patients developed physical complications while on *ECT:*

Patient #22: This 21-year-old male had a past history of a bleeding peptic ulcer. He improved with ten treatments, then suddenly developed tarry stools. Treatment was discontinued and he was transferred to the medical ward. After a few days of medical treatment he was discharged from the hospital against the advice of the internist. Although he was apprehensive and reluctantly admitted that he still heard voices occasionally, the psychiatrists felt that he was much improved and could be discharged. Thus the case is counted in the statistics as a successful release. He did extremely well during the follow-up period.

Patient #61: This 33-year-old male developed urticaria that was thought to be due to the intravenous thiopental. An antihistamine drug was given, and treatment was continued without adverse effect. He was successfully released after the course of treatment had been completed.

ATARAXIC DRUGS. In this case the stated aim was to give whatever type or dose the drug supervisor judged most likely to be effective for a particular case—to study treatment under "good battlefield conditions," not to conduct a study of one particular drug or one particular dosage schedule. In practice, all the patients assigned to DRUG THERAPY were given trifluoperazine (Stelazine). In addition, a few were given chlorpromazine (Thorazine) as well as Stelazine; this was usually for the more aggressively troublesome, in relatively low dosage or for a short period of time. For either drug, the actual dosage was decided by the therapist in consultation with the supervisor. Uncooperative patients were given intramuscular medication at first, changing to oral tablets as soon as possible.

Patients receiving 10 mg. or more of Stelazine were given procyclidine (Kemadrin) by mouth to prevent, or at least to mitigate, the rigidity, restless shuffling, drooling, spasms and other extrapyramidal side effects that occur commonly when Stelazine is given, especially in high dosage. The usual dose of Kemadrin was equal to one half of the number of milligrams of Stelazine being given.

An attempt was made to withdraw or to reduce drugs before release from the hospital, but 77 percent of the patients in the two DRUG groups were taking maintenance dosage at the time of release.

Stelazine Dosage (DRUG ALONE *group*): In the DRUG ALONE group the average total dose of Stelazine by mouth was 4.02 gm. for males and 3.19 gm. for females. For patients who were released successfully, the total dose ranged from 0.48 gm. to 13.51 gm., and the maximum daily dose from 10 mg. to 120 mg.

Two patients in the DRUG ALONE group were not released successfully (limited responders):

Patient #7: Received a total of 2.53 gm. Stelazine in two courses. She was first given 1.06 gm. in 57 days (maximum daily dose 20 mg.) and improved. She then relapsed, and 34 days later was started on medication again, receiving 1.47 gm. over 88 days (maximum daily dose 20 mg.) without much effect. Treatment was then abandoned. In follow-up she did poorly. She eventually got out of the hospital about a year later and then had two subsequent readmissions, each for substantial periods.

Patient #13: Was given a total of 1.67 gm. Stelazine. In the first course she was given 1.05 gm. in 101 days (maximum daily dose 15 mg.); improved, then quickly relapsed. Twenty-two days later she was given, without benefit, a second course of 10 mg. a day for 62 days, after which treatment was abandoned as a failure. In follow-up she did poorly, leaving the hospital eventually after some nine months of further treatment to make a marginal adjustment with one readmission that lasted about two months.

In these two cases, although the extent of the therapeutic trial will seem adequate and reasonable to many, the maximum daily dose is certainly below that advocated by the more enthusiastic advocates of

Texas-size dosage. As previously indicated, this is a study of the results of treatment under "good battlefield conditions." Each patient's treatment was supervised by an experienced clinician who was acquainted directly with the facts of the individual case; the likelihood of benefit from continued therapy was the main focus in deciding whether treatment should be given up as a failure. It is of interest that both these patients (and the two patients described below who were failures from PSYCHOTHERAPY PLUS DRUG) were in fact actually re-treated later with higher doses: their poor performance in follow-up tends to confirm the original opinion of the drug supervisor.

Stelazine Dosage (PSYCHOTHERAPY PLUS DRUG *group*): In the PSYCHOTHERAPY PLUS DRUG group the average total dose of Stelazine by mouth was 3.71 gm. for males and 2.2 gm. for females. For those patients who were released successfully, the total dose ranged from 0.24 gm. to 13.40 gm., and the maximum daily dose from 4 mg. to 120 mg.

Two patients in this group were not released successfully (limited responders):

Patient #9: Was given 5.86 gm. Stelazine over 335 days (maximum daily dose 30 mg.) before treatment was abandoned as a failure. She did poorly during the follow-up: Although she was discharged about four months later, there were two further readmissions.

Patient #200: Was given 13.37 gm. Stelazine over 359 days (maximum daily dose 40 mg.) before treatment was terminated. He remained in the hospital for another 1¼ years and was then discharged. There were two subsequent readmissions, and he spent most of the follow-up period in the hospital.

Thorazine Dosage: Seven patients in the DRUG ALONE group were given accessory Thorazine by mouth. One female received Thorazine for one day only. Three other females were given an average of 10.2 gm. over 40 days, and three males were given an average of 39.2 gm. over 61 days.

Seven patients in the PSYCHOTHERAPY PLUS DRUG group were given accessory Thorazine by mouth. Of the males, one received Thorazine for three days only; the other three were given an average of 16.0 gm. over 62 days. The three females received an average of 6.23 gm. over 49 days.

INDIVIDUAL PSYCHOTHERAPY. Psychotherapy was deliberately restricted to the kind that might perhaps be considered reasonable and practical in the forseeable future in a good public hospital setting where a large proportion of schizophrenic patients are treated. To meet this standard, *psychotherapy* was given under the supervision of qualified psychoanalysts, by physicians whose experience ranged from a minimum of six months residency training to a maximum of three years residency and three years of subsequent experience. Since psychiatrists with this kind of training and experience often treat comparable schizophrenic patients with this kind of psychotherapy in other settings, the results of this study should be fairly generally applicable.

The *type* of *psychotherapy* that was given varied according to patient, supervisor, therapist and the timing of the therapeutic process. Pragmatically, it could be defined as the kind of therapy that is given by residents and recently graduated residents who are being supervised by specially selected members of the Los Angeles Psychoanalytic Society. These supervisors were all experienced in the treatment of schizophrenic patients and were at the time working with this type of illness in their private practice and in other settings. They had all worked at the Menninger Clinic in the past or had experience reasonably compatible with those who had. It should not be assumed, however, that their theoretical values or practical approaches were necessarily identical or even similar.

From a more theoretical point of view, the therapy was in general ego-supportive and reality defining. There was a minimum of depth interpretation and use of psychoanalytic terminology; a substantial focus on working through the patient's problems in his current life situation; some confrontation with the reality of the patient's own behavior and of the manner in which he was operating; a considerable amount of clarification of perceptual distortion; and emphasis on the therapist acting as a suitable model for introjection.

The research investigator may find it easier to talk about the need to distinguish between *psychotherapy* and *no therapy* than to make the distinction in practice. In this study three criteria were used as a reasonable pragmatic definition of the dividing point between *psychotherapy* and *no therapy* along what might be perceived as a continuum.

(1) *In terms of intent and official designation.* Although individual contacts of many kinds by many different people may be therapeutic (in the sense of "beneficial"), accidentally or by design, they are not all *psychotherapy*. Generally, *psychotherapy* involves a deliberate attempt to focus in a personal and individual way on the patient's sensitivities to life situations and his personal reactions to his life experiences; on gaining insight into these susceptibilities in an effort to strengthen his ability to deal with himself and his reactions; and on gaining mastery of his life situation. In some instances a major focus may develop around those technical maneuvers that increase contact and tend to facilitate primitive and later more mature identifications.

The patients assigned to PSYCHOTHERAPY and PSYCHOTHERAPY PLUS DRUG received this specific personal individualized form of therapy, over and above the management and administrative therapeutic contact that is necessary for the treatment of all psychiatric patients. They were officially designated by both therapist and psychotherapy supervisor as receiving *psychotherapy*. It was part of the therapeutic contract that there was to be a deliberate attempt to do *psychotherapy* in individual interviews with the patient. By contrast, for the MILIEU, DRUG ALONE and ECT patients the therapists and supervisors were under instructions that there was to be a deliberate attempt *not* to do *psychotherapy*, and to confine individual contact to matters of management and administration. For patients in these groups, discussion of personal and psychological problems in individual interviews was to be avoided, although it would be permissible to talk with the patient about his reactions to the particular treatment given or to discuss briefly practical issues that he might raise himself.

(2) *In terms of supervision*. For each patient assigned to the two PSYCHOTHERAPY groups there was a specific weekly review by the therapist and psychotherapy supervisor of the transactions between therapist and patient, the aim being to maximize their psychotherapeutic effect.

(3) *In terms of time spent in individual contacts with the patient, whether in the corridor, on the ward or in the office*, the instructions to therapists and psychotherapy supervisors were that in general, unless there was some very good reason to do otherwise, patients assigned to PSYCHOTHERAPY ALONE or PSYCHOTHERAPY PLUS DRUG should be given an average of not less than two hours of therapy a week, with a minimum of not less than one hour a week, the latter figure being more likely when approaching termination. For patients assigned to MILIEU, ECT and DRUG ALONE, the maximum amount of time that could be spent in individual contact was defined in terms that were felt to be realistic and compatible with good standard clinical practice in the community—"except in very special circumstances, not more than one hour per week nor more than thirty minutes at any one time."

The distinction between *psychotherapy* and *no therapy* is reasonably clear, and our rapport with the therapists was such that we can safely believe that even the most psychotherapeutically-oriented therapists honored the intent and the spirit of the design.

None of the MILIEU, ECT or DRUG ALONE patients received anything designated as *psychotherapy*. Those assigned to PSYCHOTHERAPY ALONE and PSYCHOTHERAPY PLUS DRUG who were successfully released received from 7 to 87 hours of *psychotherapy* (12–106 interviews).* (If other individual contacts are included, the total number of hours and interviews ranged from 10–97 and 20–198 respectively.) The "failure" cases were given substantially more than this before it was decided to give up.

As might be expected, patients assigned to MILIEU, DRUG ALONE and ECT were seen more often in contacts other than *psychotherapy*. How-

---

* 1 hour = 60 minutes (not 50!). These figures do not include time spent by the (future) therapist with the patient during initial work-up and evaluation (this probably amounted to some 3–10 hours).

ever, the contacts for these three groups were of very brief duration, only a few minutes on the average, and the total amount of time was clearly and substantially well below the two *psychotherapy* groups. (A two-way analysis of variance shows that the differences in total contact time and in number of hours contact per week are statistically extremely significant—$p < .0000$.)

In only two instances were *nonpsychotherapy* patients seen in this other kind of individual contact for an amount of time that might raise question. For these, the duration of each session was only fifteen minutes and the average number of hours per month was comfortably below the level defined for *psychotherapy*.

It is reasonable to conclude that there was no attempt to give systematic *psychotherapy* to any of the MILIEU, DRUG ALONE or ECT patients.

The reader is referred to Appendix II for a more detailed account of the amount of *psychotherapy* and *other individual contact* given to the patients in the different treatment groups.

INDIVIDUAL PSCHOTHERAPY PLUS ATARAXIC DRUG. Patients in this group received *milieu* care and *psychotherapy* (as described previously) plus the *drug* dosage considered necessary to achieve the best results from the combination with *psychotherapy*. No limits were placed on the amount of *drug* that might be given, except to specify that *some* had to be used. The instructions were that *drug therapy* was to be integrated with *psychotherapy* in order to facilitate *psychotherapy*, but not as a substitute for it. The drug orders were reviewed by both the psychotherapy supervisor and the drug supervisor.

TREATMENT DURATION

The assigned treatment was continued until the patient (1) was successfully released with the approval of the therapist, treatment supervisor and assistant superintendent; *or* (2) had been treated for one year and there was no immediate prospect of release; *or* (3) had been in the hospital for a minimum of at least six months, and the treatment supervisor and the therapist agreed that the particular treatment had been given a good trial *and* that further treatment with that method was unlikely to succeed.

A six- to twelve-month treatment period was chosen for three main reasons. First, this study was deliberately restricted to methods that might be practical in a well-supported public hospital. It is of course possible that a certain number of patients might respond to a longer trial, even though they have not shown signs of satisfactory response in six to twelve months. However, it is unlikely that in the forseeable future such a hospital would have sufficient staff to permit more than a six-month trial of *individual psychotherapy* without response—or at least some promise of response. Second, six to twelve months is clinically more realistic and more congruent with the natural history of schizophrenia than the shorter periods reported in most studies. Third, it is long enough for realistic examination of two important objective criteria of outcome—length of hospital stay and release rate.

In our actual procedure the case was reviewed by the therapist and his supervisor six months after admission. If at that time things were going so poorly that there was thought to be less than one chance in ten that further treatment would lead to release within one year from admission, the patient was declared a "Limited Responder" and treatment was terminated as a failure. However, if they decided that there was better than one chance in ten, treatment was continued until the patient was *either* successfully released from the hospital *or* declared a "Limited Responder" at a later date *or* had been treated for one year. If at one year treatment was considered to be a success and active discharge plans were in process, the period could be extended for a short while longer; if there was no immediate prospect of release, it was discontinued as a failure.

The reader may perhaps wonder why the euphemism "Limited Responder" is used instead of "Treatment Failure." We found that therapists and supervisors are reluctant to admit that treatment has been a failure—it is more acceptable to ask if the patient has failed to respond satisfactorily.

The shortest length of treatment for any patient successfully released was 21 days (a DRUG ALONE patient); the longest was 406 days (a patient assigned to MILIEU). At the end of one year, this latter patient (#40) was clearly not psychotic and was judged to be well enough to leave. However, she had no funds, her family lived a long distance away and a suitable family-care (foster) home could not be found. She was finally released on her own six weeks after the one-year point.

For the "Limited Responders" the length of treatment averaged 238 days with a maximum of 385 days. In only one case was it necessary to discontinue treatment as a failure before the six-month point—patient #80 whose illness seemed to be following a steady downhill course and who had reached a point at which it seemed unwise to continue. The data for this patient were included in the final analysis: it was agreed by all that he had been given a fair trial, and he had completed 97 percent of the defined minimum period in the hospital, far more than any of the *true drop-outs*. (An abstract of relevant points in this case is given in Appendix II.)

Ten other patients were declared "Limited Responders," having been in the hospital six months or more, but with slightly less than six months specific treatment (168–182 days; see Table 2.6). In retrospect, it might have been preferable to use 183 days of *treatment* rather than *hospitalization* as the minimum point, but the difference is small and it is clear that in terms of treatment duration all the "Limited Responder" patients had a good trial.

Table 2.6.   LIMITED RESPONDERS WITH LESS THAN
SIX MONTHS TREATMENT

Treatment Group*	Patient #	Days in Hospital	Days in Treatment
M	128	194	182
(18)	125	205	178
	17	207	174
	84	194	168
E	29	183	176
(10)	18	184	173
	176	182	170
	20	185	169
P	72	197	182
(16)	144	193	179
	80	154	141
D and P+D	None Less Than Six Months		
(2) (2)			

* Number of limited responders in each treatment group is shown in parentheses.

The figures given in the previous section indicate that the "Limited Responders" were also given a reasonable and substantial trial in terms of amount as well as duration. Treatment was never abandoned as a failure until the treating physician and a consultant experienced in that particular method—both intimately acquainted with the facts of the individual case—had judged that there was little or nothing to be gained from continuing. It must, however, be admitted that although large doses were often given, we did not carry through indiscriminately to Texas-size doses of any of the treatments for every patient.

On the whole we consider that all five treatments were given a fair and even break.

SOURCES OF PATIENT DATA

Evaluation of the patient included a wide range of criteria provided before and after treatment by nurses, psychiatrists, psychoanalysts, psychologists, social science interviewers and social workers, using clinical treatment. The patient data may be grouped according to the following In addition, a more limited evaluation was obtained at intervals during description, rating scales, standardized tests and structured interviews. sources.

INDEPENDENT RATING TEAM. Before assignment to treatment, and also at termination, a rating team of two psychoanalysts who had no connection with the patient's treatment interviewed him and reviewed the descriptive narrative material provided by physicians, nurses and social workers.* (They did not have access to the various psychological tests or rating scales.) They recorded their individual ratings independently, then discussed and recorded consensus ratings. The project psychologist or the research psychiatrist was present to handle procedural matters, but did not participate in the interview or in the discussion. The initial and terminal ratings were done by the same two raters. The following information was obtained from the rating team:

> Menninger Health-Sickness Rating Scale (MHS): This scale was developed by the Adult Psychotherapy Research Committee of the Menninger Clinic ". . . to provide a simple survey instrument for recording shortened judgments of patient status, applicable in a variety of therapies." In general, the level of health is defined by comparing the patient under consideration with a standard series of patients graded in degree of health. The development, rationale and reliability of the scale are described by Luborsky.[6]
> The scale was used to provide initial and terminal global ratings of clinical status. Each time, a prognostic rating was also made to predict what the patient's level would be two years later. At the end of treatment an additional rating was obtained of the estimated amount of change during the treatment period.
> Camarillo Dynamic Assessment Scales (CDAS): Most outcome studies fail to include assessment of psychodynamic factors that, in the opinion of many working in the field of psychotherapy and psychoanalysis, are particularly likely to be of importance. With assistance from members of the Psychotherapy Research Project of the Menninger

* In one exceptional case, vacations and the need to have the same rater do both initial and terminal ratings made it necessary for one of the two raters to supervise the treatment of the case for a short period.
Patient #50: A 22-year-old female assigned to PSYCHOTHERAPY ALONE was eventually declared a "Limited Responder" after a year of treatment during which she had two therapists and two supervisors. She had improved only slightly in certain aspects, not at all in others. The first supervisor had nothing to do with the ratings, but for the last 2½ months there was no one else available and it was necessary to assign one of the two original raters as a supervisor. We doubt that there can be any serious suggestion that bias resulted in favor of the treatment as the initial ratings were quite independent and the separate post-treatment ratings of the supervisor were virtually identical with those of the uninvolved rater—eight of the items were rated identically and two were one point different.
[6] See reference 24.

Clinic, the investigators devised nine assessment scales for this purpose. The items chosen for the study were: Affective Contact; Anxiety Level; Ego Strength; Extent to Which the Environment Suffers; Insight; Motivation; Object Relations; Sense of Personal Identity; and Sexual Adjustment. Initial ratings were made of the patient's current status for each item and of his "best ever" and "worst ever" levels. Ratings were also made to describe status at termination of treatment and the estimated amount of change during the treatment period. The item scores were also summed to give a total score, including and excluding sexual adjustment (which proved in practice to be a difficult and unsatisfactory item).

Precipitating Stress: A description of the precipitating stresses, if any, related to hospitalization and to the onset of the present psychiatric episode, with ratings of the severity and duration of these stresses, separately and for the overall stress situation. For discontinuous events such as deaths, births, divorces, etc., the duration of stress was recorded as the number of weeks from the time of the event. For the overall stress situation, the team was asked to consider all stresses and to rate how stressful the situation would be for the (theoretical) average American male or female.

Personality Pattern and Current Symptom Complex: A descriptive statement.

Duration of Illness: An estimate of the lapsed time from the onset of the psychosis to the present admission.

NURSING STAFF. Obtaining a rating that adequately expresses the ward staff's opinion of a patient's behavior is a problem that has ramifications far beyond the scope of the usual research discussions of reliability and validity. By comparison with physicians' or psychologists' ratings which are customarily obtained by interview, there is considerable room for variation, depending upon fluctuations in the patient's condition during the 24-hour daily observation period; differences in personnel attitude from shift to shift; and the response of the patient to these differences. Schizophrenic patients are notorious for their unpredictable and fickle interpersonal relationships: Their object-splitting is so intense and effective that it would be remarkable indeed if all the nursing staff saw the same thing all the time.

The research investigator must understand that this is not just a matter of the *observer's* unreliability; it involves an unreliability in behavioral and other responses that is a manifestation of the *patient's* illness. Clearly, this is a matter that needs special handling. Obtaining the cooperation of the treatment staff becomes a crucial issue, inasmuch as their investment in the research project may be largely secondary and subject to pressure from other work. After considerable correspondence, discussion and experimentation, we decided that for our purposes the following procedure would combine the maximum of accuracy and validity with the minimum of bias and wasted effort.

To rate a patient, the research nurse met as senior rater with those members of the ward staff who had had the most contact with and were likely to have the best knowledge of the patient. At these meetings, under the guidance of the senior rater, the group reviewed and discussed the rating of each item, and then the senior rater recorded the group consensus—i.e., the final rating was based on the group opinion after a discussion guided by the senior rater's knowledge of the amount of each individual's familiarity and contact with the patient and her insight into their particular tendencies to biased presentation. We deliberately chose this method in preference to merely recording the average of a number of individual independent ratings because it seemed much more important to obtain an accurate measure of the best informed opinion (even though it may contain some bias due to the senior rater) than to average a mixture of ignorance and knowledge.

The following were recorded by nursing personnel:

Narrative Material: Progress notes, summarized every month.

Patient Participation: Before, after and every two weeks during treatment, ratings of the patient's participation in group social activities, occupational therapy and recreational therapy, work therapy, and ward meetings on five-point scales ranging from (0) None to (4) Considerable.

Idiosyncratic Symptoms (ISR): At the same time intervals, ratings on four-point scales of the severity of what seemed to the nursing staff to be the patient's most prominent and troublesome symptoms. (For the instructions given see Appendix III.) The ratings were scored separately and as totals in three ways: directly without transformation (IDIORAT); weighted in terms of nurses' judgments of the seriousness of the symptom per se (WEIGHTED-RAT); and weighted in terms of the amount of trouble or concern that the particular patient caused the staff of the unit (TROUBLERAT).

MACC Scale (MACC):[7] Completed at the same time intervals. This is an economical and reliable behavioral adjustment scale, developed in the V.A. for use with psychotic patients and suitable for ratings by a nursing staff. It consists of 19 items rated on five-point scales to measure behavioral and social adjustment in four relatively independent areas: Motility, Affect, Cooperation and Communication. The total adjustment score is the sum of the area scores excepting Motility. (Motility is not included because both high and low Motility scores may indicate malfunctioning, whereas the other scores indicate a "good" adjustment at the high end of the scale and "poor" at the low end.)

Menninger Health-Sickness Scale (MHS):[8] Before, after and every month during treatment to provide a global estimate of the patient's clinical status.

General Improvement Rating: At the end of treatment, a rating of

[7] See references 9, 10.
[8] See reference 24.

overall improvement on a nine-point scale ranging from (0) much worse to (8) much improved.

PATIENT'S PHYSICIAN (THERAPIST). The treating physician provided the following information:

> *Narrative Material—Clinical History, Examination and Progress Notes.*
>
> *Jenkins Symptom Rating Scale (SRS):* [9] Before, after and every three months during treatment. This is a sixteen-item, modified, abbreviated form of the Lorr Scale that concentrates on areas derived from that scale by factor analysis, providing a quantified description of behavior and symptoms.
>
> *Psychotic Confusion Scale (AA):* Before, after, and every three months during treatment. This scale was added in the second year of intake beginning on July 20, 1960, with patient #69. It is a nine-item subscale of the Ann Arbor Mental Status scale developed by Bostian, Smith, Lasky, Hover and Ging.[10] These authors factor-analyzed sixty scaled items of mental status examination and identified nine factors. Factor 1, psychotic confusion, was the only subscale that met conventional standards of reliability: It represents a pattern of sensorial defect, feelings of depersonalization and estrangement, speech incoherencies, disturbances of attention, defective judgment and planning, delusions and hallucinations, tension, panic and blunting of affect.[11]
>
> *Clyde Mood Scale (CMS):* [12] Before, after and every three months during treatment. This scale was designed to measure changes in mood and behavior produced by drugs. It consists of a deck of descriptive terms printed on IBM cards which are sorted into four categories ranging between "extremely" and "not at all." The original 133-item edition was sorted by the physician to describe the patient, yielding scores for six aspects of mood and behavior: Friendly, Energetic, Clear Thinking, Aggressive, Jittery and Depressed.

PHOTOGRAPHS. Black-and-white photographs were taken before and after treatment using standard lighting and print size; full face, profile of head and shoulders, and a full-length picture facing the camera. The intent was to maximize "self-projection"—the patients knew that they would be photographed, they were allowed to wear whatever clothes and makeup they wished and were free to assume any posture or facial expression. Unfortunately, this segment of data collection was beset by critical personnel shortages beyond the control of the investigators, and the data are relatively incomplete.

PSYCHOLOGICAL TESTING. Limitations of time and resources made it necessary to confine psychological evaluation to tests that are

[9] See reference 20.
[10] See reference 3.
[11] See reference 2.
[12] See reference 5.

quantified, simple to administer and easily scored. Projective tests, much in favor in many clinical circles and severely criticized by some research investigators, were regretfully excluded except for the Draw-a-Person test. The following instruments were finally chosen for the study:

Clyde Mood Scale (CMS):[13] Before, after and every three months during treatment. In addition to the therapist's assessment, the patient was asked to sort the Clyde cards to describe himself (Self-sort) and the way he would like ideally to be (Ideal-sort).

Similarities—Proverbs (Wechsler Adult Intelligence Scale):[14] Included, beginning with patient #10, to provide a standardized measure of conceptual disturbance, administered before, after and every three months during treatment, using the standard administration and scoring procedures.

Shipley Scale:[15] Before, after and every three months during treatment, to provide a quantified estimate of intelligence level and capacity to abstract.

Minnesota Multiphasic Personality Inventory (MMPI):[16] Before and after treatment and at the six-month point if the patient was still in the hospital. For the first 26 patients, the short form was used; after that, the long form. The box form (card sort) was used in occasional instances where the tester felt that it was necessary to obtain a suitable degree of cooperation. The answer sheets were hand scored (standard scores) for all the usual validity and clinical scales—?; L; F; K; Hs+.5K; D; Hy; Pd+.4K; Mf; Pa; Pa+1K; Sc+1K; Ma+.2K; Si. Scores on the Pa, Pt+1K and Sc+1K were summed as an index of psychotic functioning, generally referred to as the Psychotic Triad.[17] It was also decided to include the (raw) scores for three special scales that were thought to be relevant to the problems of schizophrenia and its treatment:

(1) Caudra's Control Scale (Cn).[18] This was originally developed to distinguish between psychiatric patients with varying degrees of incapacity and need for hospitalization.

(2) Barron's Ego Strength Scale (Es).[19] This was developed to identify pretreatment attitudes that might be related to improvement with *psychotherapy.*

(3) Taylor's Manifest Anxiety Scale (At).[20] This was included for exploratory purposes only as there is considerable doubt as to its usefulness. It has been judged by critics to have only a moderate relationship to ratings of manifest anxiety and to have little practical use in a psychiatric center.[21]

In addition, whenever the patient cooperated satisfactorily with the

[13] See reference 5.
[14] See reference 33.
[15] See reference 28.
[16] See reference 19.
[17] See reference 14.
[18] See reference 4.
[19] See reference 1.
[20] See reference 31.
[21] See reference 34.

questionnaire form, the individual items were scored for all the scales in Appendix I of the MMPI Handbook[22] in collaboration with Dr. Gerald Mendelsohn of the University of California, Berkeley. In this particular scoring, items that were left blank were scored as if they had been answered in the direction of "sickness," in effect assuming that failure to reply is a tacit admission of illness. (None of these scores were used in the analyses reported in this volume.)

If the patient was able to complete the MMPI, his scores were included in the analyses reported in this volume unless he had obviously invalidated the test by following some set pattern for marking the form, had answered randomly (patients were always observed while they were taking the MMPI), or had failed to answer more than 150 of the items. This liberal criterion of acceptability means that some MMPI's were included that would have been considered (by some) to be unacceptable because of high $?$ (Cannot say); L (Lie) or F (Validity) scores.

For example, it has been proposed that an MMPI should be rejected if the standard score reaches 70 on the $?$ or L scales or 80 on the F scale, "except that if any abnormal score reaches a standard score of 80, an elevated L score may be ignored since defensive lying could hardly be the reason for such a positive elevation."[23]

We have taken the position that such arbitrary rules as these are not appropriate for the patients in this particular study. Our reasons are as follows:

(1) The use of the $?$, L and F scales to reject cases is intended to avoid the possible contaminating effects of intentional malingering, lying, faking and deception. In our study this is not a serious concern.

(2) It has been pointed out that there is considerable overlap between the personality and "validity" scales, and that it would be a mistake to overlook the relevance of the latter to personality structure.[24] It is reasonable to assume that extreme scores on the $?$, L and F scales may indeed reflect the nature and intensity of the emotional disturbance in relatively severely ill schizophrenic patients.

(3) The three "validity" scales (and the F scale in particular) measure attitudes and behavior that are highly characteristic of the pervasive suspiciousness and interpersonal sensitivity found in schizophrenia.

To be more specific, the $?$ scale reflects patterns of confusion, defensive evasion or paranoid suspicion. The F scale is sensitive to misinterpretation of instructions or of the content of the items; to peculiar thoughts and beliefs; and to lack of interest. Its correlation with the Pa (Paranoia) and Sc (Schizophrenia) scales is high.

The L scale consists of items that assess an individual's tendency to present himself in an unusually favorable light by minimizing aggressive feelings and "bad" thoughts; by denying temptation and lack of control; and by presenting himself as unduly "good." When L scores are used to reject a protocol, the underlying assumption is that the patient must be lying because most people would be willing to endorse these particular items even though they are unfavorable. However, the

22 See reference 7.
23 See reference 26.
24 See references 8, 15, 27.

clinician who has had experience with psychotic patients will recognize immediately that this "unduly good" pattern also characterizes a certain type of schizophrenic.

(4) We wish to determine whether the MMPI as a sample of behavior can provide useful information about schizophrenic patients. As Hathaway points out, preoccupation with whether the patient is really telling the truth may be beside the point, as some kind of "lying" or "role playing" is inevitably a part of personality.[25] In fact, a personality test would be a poor instrument if it were not responsive to patients' distortions. Hathaway also points out that, except for patients who try for high scores with an ulterior purpose, patients who obtain a high score on a scale ". . . are *ipso facto* validly like the group from which the scale was derived. This indisputable statistical validity should be more widely recognized and studied by clinicians."[26]

(5) There is good evidence from the data of this study that application of the proposed acceptability criteria[27] would have excluded patients with a high level of pathology, thus attenuating the relevance of the test results to the problem of schizophrenia and reducing the likelihood of demonstrating any treatment effect.

The mean *Final* score on the *Sc* (Schizophrenia) scale for the patients who might have been excluded was 72.1. This is pathologically high; clearly indicative of the disorder under study; and substantially greater than the mean score for the remainder of the patients (65.9). Only one of the patients with an *F* score of 80 or more had an *Sc* score below 70 (and in this case it was 68).

Draw-a-Person:[28] Before, after and every three months during treatment, patients were instructed to draw a person. When the first drawing was completed, they were asked to draw another one opposite in sex to the first. No other instructions or restrictions were made.

Testability: Considerable efforts were made to obtain the patient's cooperation in testing. In difficult cases the project psychologist or the nursing staff member with the closest relationship to the patient would work with the patient individually, even on occasion sitting for hours with him while he painfully and slowly worked his way through the test battery.

A three-point "testability score" was recorded for each patient for each test:

(1) Fully cooperative, test of good quality.

(2) Partially cooperative; test completed but of reduced or doubtful quality.

(3) Patient refused testing or uncooperative to such an extent that test was not of acceptable quality.

These scores were also summed for all tests as a "total testability" score.

SOCIAL WORKER. As soon as possible after the patient had been provisionally accepted into the project, a social worker interviewed one

[25] See reference 17.
[26] See reference 18.
[27] See reference 26.
[28] See references 13, 25.

or more of the persons in the community who might be able to provide reliable background information. This was most often the nearest relative, but in certain instances information was obtained from friends, landladies and other persons. From these relatively unstructured interviews a narrative background and social history was recorded. A structured questionnaire was also completed at the same time, covering selected items of personal and family history and social background, including a description of the socioeconomic characteristics of the patient's family and the patient's past history of psychiatric illness and treatment.

SOCIAL SCIENCE INTERVIEWER. As soon as possible after the social worker's investigation, a staff member trained to give structured interviews interviewed the respondent designated by the social worker as being the best available outside source of information about the patient. The interview schedules were constructed in collaboration with consultant sociologists and used many items that were identical with or modified from questionnaires used in other studies, in particular that of Freeman and Simmons.[29] They were pretested and were designed to obtain data on social background and family composition; to assess the patient's performance levels and functioning within the family, at work and elsewhere; to identify decisions regarding pathways in and out of the hospital; and to examine role expectations and attitudes toward mental illness.

MOVEMENT STATISTICS

To avoid error from routine hospital statistics, we kept our own records of admission, release, leave, readmission and escape. It was necessary to define certain criteria, details being given in Appendix IV, with some discussion of the issues involved.

In interpreting data from studies of "first admission" schizophrenics, the clinician should be careful to inquire whether an attempt has been made to exclude error due to the mistaken inclusion of patients who have had prior admissions at the hospital in question or elsewhere. If the figures relate to "first admissions to Hospital *X*" with no explanation, the clinician should suspect that no attempt was made and that the margin of error is substantial.

Our experience in this respect coincides with that of Friedman, Lundstedt, Von Meering and Hinko who found that at the Cleveland Neuropsychiatric Institute two out of five readmissions were misclassified as first admissions.[30]

[29] See reference 11.
[30] See reference 12.

Even if the label "first admission" is attached only after interviewing the patient and attempting to exclude prior hospitalization elsewhere, there may still be an appreciable margin of error. In our study, 13/268 or 4.8 percent of patients who were believed to be first admissions after the physician's examination were found later to have had significant previous admissions.* Eleven of these were discovered as the result of additional social work interview with family or friends. In the remaining two instances (0.75 percent) previous admission was concealed and only discovered later during the course of treatment.

It is interesting that most of the cases where the history of prior hospital admission was not readily communicated by the patient were women (nine out of thirteen), and that deliberate concealment of prior hospitalization occurred only in women. Statistically speaking, the odds are about one to seven ($p = .13$) that this might be a chance finding, so the clinical investigator might speculate (and allow for the possibility) that either women dissimulate more about prior treatment or else that the clinician tends to be less effective in obtaining their history. (Each of the patients "missed" had a different doctor and there was no evidence that dissimulation bore more severely on male than on female physicians.)

The clinician should also be careful to inquire into the criteria that were used for "release." As other investigators have discovered,[31] it is difficult to decide what constitutes release from a psychiatric hospital, and one cannot safely use the official date of "trial visit" or "discharge" as the date of release to the community. For many psychiatric patients there is no clear-cut break between hospital and return to the community. Some are discharged outright; some are placed on indefinite leave; others go absent without leave and may or may not be transferred later to leave or discharge status. Most patients at some time go on limited leave for weekends or longer, and this may or may not be converted to discharge or leave status, with or without an intervening period of overstaying the leave limits prescribed by the hospital.

Unfortunately, official records do not always keep up with the actual movements of the patient and, to compound the confusion, therapists and patients speedily develop a facility for bypassing official categories and administrative requirements. Accordingly, we kept close track of when the patient actually left the hospital, whatever the ostensible reason for his going and whether or not there was official hospital sanction for his departure.

DURATION AND ONSET OF ILLNESS

Although it is generally agreed that duration of illness is one of the most important factors in prognosis, how "duration" is to be estimated is

---

* Statistically speaking, we can be 95 percent confident (p < .05) that the true rate would lie between 2.6 percent and 8.1 percent.
31 E.g., see reference 11.

seldom defined in even the most rudimentary way. As seen in the literature the definition appears to be pragmatic—whatever was recorded.

As with so many matters that seem simple at first encounter, the more one thinks, the more complicated it becomes. Is it age at onset, lapsed time since onset, or cumulative time at a particular level of severity that is important? Should one estimate the "duration" of schizophrenia from the first behavioral disturbance, or from the first subjective distress? From the first time when personality difficulty became evident? From the point of maximum severity? From clear-cut psychotic symptoms or from occupational incapacity?

To investigate this area, the principal investigator reviewed all the historical material in each patient's record to estimate the age at onset and the duration of illness according to each of these criteria. Details of the various definitions are given in Appendix V, with some discussion of the issues involved.

MILIEU DATA

Records were kept of certain simple milieu variables that might influence outcome or help to describe more precisely the surroundings in which the patients lived.

VISITORS. The research nurses kept a record of who visited the patient and when, making special effort to be as accurate as possible. They kept in close touch with the patients and were on the alert to obtain information about visitors who did not register in the usual way. It was soon found that some visitors avoided the hospital staff. In some cases this seemed to be merely the avoidance of a troublesome and time-consuming registration ritual; in others it seemed to be a symptom of more deep-seated psychological problems of their own or in their relationship to the patient. The practical lesson is that the routine hospital visitors' record is not sufficiently valid for research purposes: The research investigator who wishes to study this area should keep his own records.

WARD STAFF. Number and composition of the ward staff; changes, sick leave and vacation.

WARD POPULATION. Total number of patients on the ward: admitted, released, on leave, working in industrial therapy on and off the ward, and on ground privileges.

WARD ACTIVITIES. Number of staff meetings; of patients participating in small group activities; of patients wearing their own clothes;

of patients considered by nursing staff to be extremely difficult (e.g., physically assaultive, abusive or incontinent); and "special incidents."*

WARD CLIMATE. The research nurses made monthly judgmental ratings on four-point scales to assess ward noise level; demands by patients on personnel; amount of disturbing and destructive behavior; amount of formal and informal constructive activity; interstaff conflict and tension; and the adequacy of the physical surroundings. A seven-point scale was used to give an overall judgment of the adequacy of the general climate of the ward as a whole.

THERAPIST DATA

There is evidence that characteristics of the physician such as social and ethnic background, attitudes, interests and other personality features may have an influence on the selection, course and outcome of treatment. In our study, treatment was not selected on the basis of the physician's or patient's choice, and each physician's deck of random treatment-assignment cards included equal numbers of each treatment method. By this means the investigators aimed to avoid systematic bias in the outcome of any treatment group due to therapist factors. However, it was also thought important to assess some of these factors in order to detect their relative contribution to outcome.

Information was obtained for each physician who had the patient for more than fifteen days. This eliminated some who took over the management of a case for a relatively short time toward the end of the treatment as a holding operation after the final disposition had been determined by the preceding therapist, but included all "first" therapists and all cases where the patient had only one therapist.

BACKGROUND STATISTICS. Age, sex, race, language or communication problems, amount of experience since internship, experience in treating psychiatric disorders, amount of psychiatric residency training.

MOVEMENT DATA. Dates of assignment to the various residency services, change of residency or staff status and of treating each patient.

STRONG VOCATIONAL INTEREST BLANK.[32] Completed once during the time he was treating patients on the project, usually at the

* Events that might have medico-legal or administrative significance and that are required to be reported to supervisory staff, such as elopements, damage to persons or to property, fires and injuries.
[32] See references 29, 30.

beginning. It was scored in the usual manner and, in addition, the scores were used to classify therapists as type A or B according to the methods used by Whitehorn and Betz.[33]

CALIFORNIA PSYCHOLOGICAL INVENTORY.[34] Completed once during the time he was treating patients on the project, usually at the beginning.

CLYDE MOOD SCALE.[35] Every six months the therapist was asked to sort the cards to describe himself.

GENERAL CLINICAL EFFECTIVENESS. Every six months a rating was made of the therapist's general clinical effectiveness in relation to others of a comparable level of training. For residents, this rating was made by the chief of professional education in collaboration with the principal investigator; for nonresidents, by the principal investigator alone. (The principal investigator was Clinical Director of the hospital when the project started and later Research Director, so was reasonably well-informed in this area.)

EFFECTIVENESS IN PSYCHOTHERAPY. Every six months a rating was made of the therapist's effectiveness in *psychotherapy* with each of the patients he was treating in this way. His supervisors rated the manner in which he had handled each case, taking into consideration the difficulties that were unique to that patient. Since the assignment of supervision was not balanced (i.e., not all therapists were supervised by all supervisors) these ratings were subjected to a nonorthogonal analysis of variance, and the ratings were adjusted to allow for supervisor differences in rating. The final scores for the various therapists were obtained by assuming the original ratings to be the sum of a general mean, a constant unique to the particular therapist, and a constant unique to the particular supervisor.

ATTITUDE TO TREATMENT. Immediately after the therapist had been told the treatment to which his patient had been assigned, he was asked to indicate (on four-point scales) how Appropriate he considered the treatment to be for that particular patient; how Comfortable he felt in having to administer that treatment to the patient; and how Effective he thought the treatment would be. These three ratings were summed to give a Total attitude score. He was also asked to select from a list what

33 See references 35, 36, 37, 38.
34 See reference 16.
35 See reference 5.

he thought would be the treatment of choice for the patient. The alternatives were:

(1) Milieu care only
(2) ECT
(3) Ataraxic drugs alone
(4) Individual psychotherapy alone
(5) Ataraxic drugs and individual psychotherapy
(6) Surgical and other physical treatments (specify)
(7) Outpatient care, does not require hospitalization
(8) Group psychotherapy
(9) Permanent hospitalization—patient not treatable
(10) Any other combination of methods and techniques (specify)

TREATMENT DATA

Records were kept of treatment as follows:

ATARAXIC DRUGS. For each course, the daily dose from the physician's order sheet. This was felt to be the most reliable record of what was actually given, although of course there may have been errors in administration.

SEDATIVES. The number of orders was obtained from the physician's order sheet.

ECT. For each course, the date of each treatment from the physician's record sheet.

HYDROTHERAPY. The number of treatments and the number of hours spent in the different forms of hydrotherapy.

PSYCHOTHERAPY AND OTHER INDIVIDUAL CONTACT. Each month the physician completed for each patient (starting about one quarter of the way through the study) a form showing the number of sessions and hours in *individual psychotherapy* and in *individual contact other than psychotherapy.* We kept a sharp eye out for "bootlegging," and are reasonably sure that the physicians did their best to record all their contacts with the patient and that the figures provide a fair estimate of the amount of therapy given. However, there is undoubtedly a degree of inaccuracy in recording this type of information, and in retrospect it would perhaps have been more efficient to record weekly rather than monthly.

PSYCHOTHERAPY SUMMARY. For *psychotherapy* cases, the therapist made a summary at the end of treatment describing under specific headings what the patient's main problems were and the methods the patient used to cope with them; what changes had taken place for better or for worse; and the possible reason for these changes. The supervisor reviewed this summary with the therapist and added his own comments.

COST OF TREATMENT

The cost of treatment does not seem to have been examined in any controlled research study of the outcome of treatment of schizophrenia, and it is easy to see why—its determination is complicated, difficult, easy to criticize and the subject is loaded with explosive potential. It requires little skill in rationalizing to justify the exclusion of Cost from the area of scientific study. One can properly and wisely express considerable skepticism as to the practicability of determining the true cost of many of the component items, and any figures that may be produced can readily be disputed. Nevertheless, where angels have feared to tread, a few faltering steps have been taken: After all, cost *is* important—to administrator, patient, physician, family and taxpayer. I hope that others will be encouraged to improve on our methods and fill in the obvious deficiencies.

The cost of each patient's hospital stay was determined by computing the estimated cost of the following items:

(1) Ataraxic drugs by mouth
(2) Ataraxic drugs by injection
(3) Basic nursing care
(4) Specific nursing duties related to particular treatments
(5) Electroconvulsive therapy
(6) Hydrotherapy
(7) Individual psychotherapy
(8) Individual contacts with the physician other than formal psychotherapy
(9) Meals
(10) Seclusion
(11) Overhead and special services

The cost of the individual items and categories were computed separately and then summed in different ways to provide various indices of the cost of hospital care for each individual patient from admission to release or termination of treatment. No attempt was made to estimate other expenditures that might perhaps be properly included in attempting to gauge the full financial toll on the community, such as allotments to families by welfare agencies; Veterans Administration expenditures for pensions and disability compensation; and indirect charges on the economy such as the value of productive services that are not performed, or taxes and income lost.

It is particularly important to note that the criterion of comparison used in this study was that of *total* cost, which approaches directly the most important aspect of comparative treatment cost—what is the *total* bill for treating each patient?

I would like to think that we are past the era when it was considered appropriate and sufficient to compare different treatments on a cost per diem basis without taking into consideration turnover and how long the patient has to stay in the hospital. However, hospital costs have been expressed per diem for so long that it is perhaps necessary to give an example to demonstrate the fundamental fallacy of comparing different treatment methods on this basis.

Consider two treatment methods with the same per diem cost. On treatment *A* the average patient has "recovered" after 30 days in the hospital. On treatment *B* the same degree of recovery is obtained, but it takes 300 days. In this example it is obvious that as far as the person paying the bill is concerned, the *total* cost for treatment *B* will be ten times more than for treatment *A*. In other words, the administrator or the legislator who considers only per diem cost falls into the same error as the person buying on credit who inquires only about the *size* of the monthly payment without bothering to ask how *long* he will have to keep on paying.

Appendix VI contains definitions of the various cost indices and details of the formulae used in computation, with some discussion of relevant issues. The serious reader is urged to read and re-read this Appendix with a critical eye so that he may be in a position to understand the limitations of our estimates and of the interpretation that may be placed thereon.

The figures were derived for Camarillo Hospital at the time of the study and were based on 1963–1964 salaries and prices. Many of the items were, at best, little more than educated guesses, and for this reason, formulae are given in detail to permit comparison. For certain items a sex-appropriate cost factor has been used where allowance had to be made for the fact that the cost of a particular operation or unit of treatment was estimated to be different on the male and female units (usually higher for females). In some cases, as in basic nursing care, this sex-differentiation is based entirely on objective facts. Elsewhere it depends on an estimate from the treatment staff, and some might suspect a systematic error in perception—do females perhaps exaggerate (or males depreciate) the amount of time it takes to do a particular task? The possibility cannot be denied, but the differences seem to me to coincide with other differences that may be observed between male and female wards. Those familiar with the day-to-day workings of a mental hospital will perhaps recognize a masculine ward attitude of brisk, suppressive, peremptory efficiency that contrasts with female wards that are often relatively expressive, placating, persuasive and exploratory.

FURTHER TREATMENT AND EVALUATION OF "LIMITED RESPONDERS" AFTER TERMINATION OF INITIAL EXPERIMENTAL TREATMENT

After their post-treatment evaluation had been completed, patients who had been declared "Limited Responders" (see previous section) were re-assigned to treatment with *ataraxic drugs plus group psychotherapy. Drugs* were given in a manner similar to that described in the section on ataraxic drugs. *Group psychotherapy* was given twice a week in 1–1½ hour sessions by a member of the hospital psychology staff. The groups were a mixture of "Limited Responders" from the Schizophrenia Research Project with other patients of similar levels of illness. This second treatment combination was continued for one year unless the patient was released before that time.

Before, after, and during this second treatment period, evaluations were continued in the same way as for the original experimental treatment, except that the ratings by the independent rating team were replaced by the ratings of a single independent psychiatrist.

If at the end of one year on the second treatment the patient was still in the hospital, he was declared a "Double treatment failure" and then given whatever treatment seemed most appropriate.

FOLLOW-UP

All patients were followed up for at least two years after their first release from the hospital, in cooperation with the Bureau of Extra-mural Social Work of the California State Department of Mental Hygiene. Since this volume is concerned entirely with the patients' treatment in the hospital, the design and details of the follow-up phase will not be given here.

REFERENCES

(1) Barron, F.: An ego strength scale which predicts response to psychotherapy. *J. Consulting Psychology.* 17:327–333, 1953. (Reprinted as pp. 226–234 in *Basic Readings on the MMPI in Psychology and Medicine.* Welsh, G. S. & Dahlstrom, W. G., eds. University of Minnesota Press, Minneapolis, 1960.)

(2) Bostian, D. W.: Reliability of the Ann Arbor Mental Status Scale. Unpublished reliability evaluation (personal communication).

(3) Bostian, D. W., Smith, P. A., Lasky, J. J., Hover, G. L. & Ging, R. J.: Empirical observations on mental status examination. *Archives of General Psychiatry,* 1:253–262, 1959.

(4) Caudra, C. A.: A psychometric investigation of control factors in psychological adjustment. Ph.D. Dissertation, University of California, 1953. (Reprinted in part as pp. 235–254 in *Basic Readings on the MMPI in Psychology and Medicine.* Welsh, G. S. & Dahlstrom, W. G., eds. University of Minnesota Press, Minneapolis, 1960.)

(5) Clyde, D. J.: *Manual for the Clyde Mood Scale.* Biometric Laboratory, University of Miami, 1963.

(6) Corotto, L. V.: The excluded research subject: An examination of his impact on research results. *J. Nervous and Mental Disease,* 139:581–587, 1964.

(7) Dahlstrom, W. G. & Welsh, G. S.: Scales and scoring procedures. In *An MMPI Handbook,* University of Minnesota Press, Minneapolis, 1960: 443–468.

(8) Dahlstrom, W. G. & Welsh, G. S.: Validity scale patterns. In *An MMPI Handbook,* University of Minnesota Press, Minneapolis, 1960: 117–157.

(9) Ellsworth, R. B.: *The MACC Behavioral Adjustment Scale.* Western Psychological Service, Santa Monica, Calif., 1957.

(10) Ellsworth, R. B. & Clayton, W. H.: Measurement of improvement in mental illness. *J. Consulting Psychology,* 23:15–20, 1959.

(11) Freeman, Howard E. & Simmons, O. G.: *The Mental Patient Comes Home.* John Wiley & Sons, Inc., New York, 1963.

(12) Friedman, I., Lundstedt, S., Von Mering, O. & Hinko, E. N.: Systematic underestimation in reported mental hospital readmission rates. *American J. of Psychiatry,* 121:148–152, 1964.

(13) Goodenough, F.: *The Measurement of Intelligence in Drawings.* World Book Co., Yonkers, N. Y., 1926.

(14) Gough, H. G.: Diagnostic patterns on the MMPI. *J. Clinical Psychology,* 2:23–37, 1946. (Reprinted in *Basic Readings on the MMPI in Psychology and Medicine.* Welsh, G. S. & Dahlstrom, W. G., eds. University of Minnesota Press, Minneapolis, 1960: 340–350.

(15) Gough, H. G.: The *F* minus *K* dissimulation index for the MMPI. In *Basic Readings on the MMPI in Psychology and Medicine.* Welsh, G. S. & Dahlstrom, W. G., eds. University of Minnesota Press, Minneapolis, 1960: 321–327.

(16) Gough, H. G.: *The California Psychological Inventory.* Consulting Psychologists Press, Inc., Palo Alto, Calif., 1956.

(17) Hathaway, S. R.: Foreword. In Dahlstrom, W. G. & Welsh, G. S., *An MMPI Handbook.* University of Minnesota Press, Minneapolis, 1960: pp. vii–xi.

(18) Hathaway, S. R.: Scales 5 (Masculinity-Femininity), 6 (Paranoia) & 8 (Schizophrenia). In *Basic Readings on the MMPI in Psychology and Medicine.* Welsh, G. S. & Dahlstrom, W. G., eds. University of Minnesota Press, Minneapolis, 1960: 104–111.

(19) Hathaway, S. R. & McKinley, J. C.: *The Minnesota Multiphasic Personality Inventory.* University of Minnesota Press, Minneapolis, 1943.

(20) Jenkins, R. L., Stauffacher, J. & Hester, R.: A symptom rating scale for use with psychotic patients. *Archives of General Psychiatry,* 1:197–204, 1959.
(21) Kurland, A. A., Hanlon, T. E., Tatom, M. H., Ota, K. Y. & Simopoulos, A. M.: The comparative effectiveness of six phenothiazine compounds, phenobarbital and inert placebo in the treatment of acutely ill patients: Global measures of severity of illness. *J. Nervous and Mental Disease,* 133:1–18, 1961.
(22) Kurland, A. A., Hanlon, T. E., Tatom, M. H. & Simopoulos, A. M.: Comparative studies of the phenothiazine tranquilizers: methodological and logistical considerations. *J. Nervous and Mental Disease.* 132:61–74, 1961.
(23) Lasky, J. J.: The problem of sample attrition in controlled treatment trials. *J. Nervous and Mental Disease,* 135:332–337, 1962.
(24) Luborsky, L.: Clinician's judgments of mental health: a proposed scale. *Archives of General Psychiatry,* 7:407–417, 1962.
(25) Machover, K.: *Personality Projection in the Drawing of the Human Figure.* Charles C Thomas, Springfield, Ill., 1948.
(26) Meehl, P. E.: Profile analysis of the MMPI in differential diagnosis. In *Basic Readings on the MMPI in Psychology and Medicine.* Welsh, G. S. & Dahlstrom, W. G., eds. University of Minnesota Press, Minneapolis, 1960: 292–297.
(27) Meehl, P. E. & Hathaway, S. R.: The *K* factor as a suppressor variable. In *Basic Readings on the MMPI in Psychology and Medicine.* Welsh, G. S. & Dahlstrom, W. G., eds. University of Minnesota Press, Minneapolis, 1960: 12–40.
(28) Shipley, W. C.: A self administering scale for measuring intellectual impairment and deterioration. *J. Psychology,* 9:371–377, 1940.
(29) Strong, E. K.: *Vocational Interests of Men and Women.* Stanford University Press, Stanford, Calif., 1943.
(30) Strong, E. K.: *The Strong Vocational Interest Blank.* Consulting Psychologists Press, Inc., Palo Alto, Calif., 1946.
(31) Taylor, J. A.: A personality scale of manifest anxiety. *J. Abnormal and Social Psychology,* 48:285–290, 1953.
(32) The National Institute of Mental Health Psychopharmacology Service Center Collaborative Study Group: Phenothiazine treatment in acute schizophrenia. *Archives of General Psychiatry,* 10:246–261, 1964.
(33) Wechsler, D.: *The Wechsler Adult Intelligence Scale.* The Psychological Corporation, New York, 1955.
(34) Welsh, G. S. & Dahlstrom, W. G.: New scales. In *Basic Readings on the MMPI,* Welsh, G. S. & Dahlstrom, W. G., eds. University of Minnesota Press, Minneapolis, 1960: 178–180.
(35) Whitehorn, J. C. & Betz, B. J.: A comparison of psychotherapeutic relationships between physicians and schizophrenic patients when insulin is combined with psychotherapy and when psychotherapy is used alone. *American J. of Psychiatry,* 113:901–910, 1957.
(36) Whitehorn, J. C. & Betz, B. J.: A study of psychotherapeutic relationships between physicians and schizophrenic patients. *American J. of Psychiatry,* 111: 321–331, 1954.
(37) Whitehorn, J. C. & Betz, B. J.: Studies of the doctor as a crucial factor for the prognosis of schizophrenic patients. *International J. of Social Psychiatry,* 6:71–77, 1960.
(38) Whitehorn, J. C. & Betz, B. J.: Further studies of the doctor as a crucial variable in the outcome of treatment with schizophrenic patients. *American J. of Psychiatry.* 117:215–223, 1960.
(39) Zubin, J., Burdock, E. I., Sutton, S. & Cheek, F.: Epidemiological aspects of prognosis in mental illness. In *Epidemiology of Mental Disorder,* American Association for the Advancement of Science, Washington, D.C., 1959: 119–142.

CHAPTER III

Methods of Statistical Analysis

WILFRID J. DIXON, PH.D. AND
PHILIP R. A. MAY, M.D.

THE PURPOSE OF this chapter is to present—without jargon and in simple language—the methods of statistical analysis that were used for this volume, and to describe their purpose so that the ordinary reader may understand without a glossary what has been done and why. The intent is to explain basic principles and procedures, not to offer alternatives to material that may readily be found in any good textbook of statistics. Since this kind of writing is incompatible with precise, hair-splitting technical definition, we trust that the statistical sophisticate will accept simplification and rough approximations with good grace, and that the statistically naive will forgive any deficiencies in clear simple communication.

The chapter ends with a summary list of relevant abbreviations, conventional terms and notations that are used throughout the text to avoid tedious repetition of statistical material elsewhere.

PRELIMINARY CONSIDERATIONS

In the statistical planning of this study there were two particular considerations. First, it seemed timely and worthwhile to attempt to develop methods that could deal with information processing at a level of complexity that would approach the realities of the clinical psychiatric situation. Second, the task of following a considerable number of schizophrenic patients in a controlled study through as much as a year of carefully supervised treatment and for several years of follow-up is so time-consuming and expensive that it is not likely to be attempted very often—and even more rarely completed.

Accordingly, conventional restrictions on data collection were deliberately disregarded in favor of an attempt to extract the maximum of information from our experiment. Instead of conforming to the data-handling customs of the time that declared that only a small amount of data should be collected, the decision was made to accumulate far more information than it seemed (to some) reasonably possible to handle, far exceeding the capacity of any computer then in existence. This would provide the raw material—and the incentive—to experiment with new approaches: We trusted a rapidly advancing technology to develop the necessary capacities.

In this respect it is our position that ignorance is seldom an advantage. Excess information can always be disregarded if it exceeds the handling capacity of the individual investigator; if it seems to have no practical value for the particular analysis to be undertaken; or if it proves to be below acceptable limits of reliability. However, this aspect of information processing is an area with many misconceptions, and it is necessary to review and examine some of the arguments that have been advanced in favor of collecting only a small amount of information, and against the difficult task of multivariate data collection and analysis.

First, it is sometimes suggested that the problem of "How much is enough?" can be handled in advance by selecting for study only a few variables that are (intuitively) declared to be the most important.* Such a proposition would seem to be more akin to armchair philosophy than to science. It implies that the investigator already knows how many variables are sufficient for an adequate description of all necessary aspects of the treatment situation, and further, that it is possible to

---

* The term "variable" is used here in the technical sense of a "bit" of information that can be quantified or categorized and so expressed in numerical form and stored in computer memory.

know what they are before the facts are known. Moreover, as Gerard has pointed out, the finest measurements are nonsense if one is measuring the wrong thing—witness the "science" of phrenology.[1] For our part, we did not feel sufficiently omniscient to be able to limit data collection to the "gun-barrel" vision of a select handful of *certainly important* variables; on the contrary, variables and points of view were selected because they *might* be important or relevant and they *could* be collected. It is perhaps up to the reader to judge from the presentations in this volume whether, for example, it contributes to our understanding of the length of hospital stay of a schizophrenic patient to look at five ways instead of one of expressing Stay, and to know also whether anything further is added to discrimination by taking leave, AWOL, and work-up period into consideration. Or, to take another example, whether a study based only on one or another preselected MMPI scale—or even a few such scales—would have been of much help to the clinician.

Second, and at another level, some might be misled by an often quoted rubric to the effect that valid comparisons cannot be made if there are ". . . more variables than there are patients." Actually, it is inappropriate to associate this rule with data collection; it relates only to the performance of any one single analysis. Moreover, arguments based on this point apply strictly only to "independent" variables (i.e., items that are not interrelated) rather than to "dependent" variables (i.e., items between which there is usually some relationship). In a multivariate study the correct procedure is to narrow down to an appropriate number the variables to be used in any one analysis. In fact, discrimination can often be improved by combining several variables to form a single composite variable.

Third, restriction of data collection is sometimes supported on the grounds that the more variables analyzed, the greater the likelihood that a certain number will be declared to be statistically significant.* Hence the investigator may be misled into accepting as significant a value that is, in fact, the result of some random process. Further, the story goes, the likely number of such "false positives" will depend on the usually unknown degree of intercorrelation between the variables in question. This group of arguments should be rejected as nothing more than a sophisticated "Don't confuse me with all the facts. Just tell me one thing and I'll tell you if he's guilty." The pontifical assumption is made that

---

[1] See reference 7.

* The term "statistically significant" is used here in the technical sense to mean that "if indeed there is no true association, values (or differences) of this order in samples of this size may be expected to occur as the result of random chance process less often than a stated percent or fraction of the time."

neither the investigator nor the reader have the necessary brains or fortitude to study seriously an admittedly difficult problem, and that therefore one should prefer an answer whose simplicity is derived from ignorance.

CODING AND SCREENING

In attempting to extract the maximum of information from our experiment, considerable emphasis was placed on first minimizing the amount of "noise" that might be introduced by errors and by mislaid data. To this end, wherever information could be quantified or categorized it was transposed in numerical coded form into special code schedules, each schedule being set out to correspond to a single IBM card. The coding was checked by a second coder, punched on IBM cards, verified and transferred from cards to magnetic tape.

Further screening for errors and correction, euphemistically referred to in some circles as "cleaning up the data," was accomplished in stages. First, the punches in each column of each card were checked from a print-out that identified the number of punches in each row of each column. Second, each variable was checked from a print-out that identified the case numbers for which the values fell outside specified "legal" limits. Third, each variable was checked by inspection of a series of separate consecutive frequency distribution plots (histograms) for each sex and treatment group. After each step, information that appeared to be missing was traced to see if it was truly missing or merely mislaid; and values that seemed to be deviant or unlikely were back-checked to the source documents. After any corrections had been made, the data were re-checked to see that the corrections had been completed. As an illustration of the time-consuming nature of the checking process, a total of thirteen full sets of consecutive frequency distribution plots (histograms) were examined before the data were finally declared to be ready for analysis.

The handling of a large number of variables and the detection and avoidance of errors in processing is a tricky and lengthy business: it often involves the checking and even re-coding of all or parts of original code schedules for every patient. It is commonly assumed by those investigators who do not screen their data rigorously that the incidence of error is random and therefore "equalizes out" when comparing groups. In our experience this is definitely not the case. On the contrary, errors are almost always repetitive, systematic idiosyncracies, characteristic of a particular error-maker. Everyone who handles the data—transcriber, checker, coder, key punch operator and up the line—introduces his own particular style and location of error. An individual coder may on occasion, perhaps when tired or distracted, transpose "09" to "90," another will tend to confuse "first" and "last," and yet another skips a particular line or page. The whole subject of error and its detection is a fascinating one that perhaps deserves special attention.

EXTREME AND UNUSUAL CASES

In every sample there are likely to be a number of extreme or unusual cases—so-called "outliers." Rigorous data screening such as that described above reduces the likelihood that an "outlier" is an error due to some gross blunder that should not have been included in the first place. It is then more likely that the explanation for any extreme deviation is one of the following:

(1) Either the individual is radically different from the others in the group, or

(2) The particular rating scale or test used gives irregular or erratic values beyond a certain limit, or

(3) The population genuinely includes a certain proportion of extreme cases and, by chance, the sample happens to include one or more of these.

In any of these situations, one may wish to eliminate extreme values from the sample before making statistical inferences about the population as a whole, or perhaps even better, to both assess the influence of tail-end* values that are not representative and also to arrive at some estimate of the parameters of the basic distribution that is reasonably free from their contaminating effect. In this way it is possible to approach questions such as whether a particular treatment works the same for everybody, or whether there is a difference between treatment methods apart from a few extreme individuals.

There is also a second and compelling reason for adopting a statistical approach that pays attention to this problem. As discussed comprehensively by Tukey and McLaughlin,[2] many of the statistical tests in common use are best known and best understood when the variable under study follows a symmetrical Gaussian or "normal" distribution. For long-tailed or asymmetrical distributions, their validity (i.e., the extent to which any statements of probability are correct or at least conservative) and their efficiency (in the sense of obtaining the maximum amount of information from the sample) are open to serious question. If commonly used statistical procedures such as t and F tests are used against long-tailed distributions, they tend to behave poorly, both rela-

* In statistical circles a population has two tails rather than a head and a tail.
[2] See reference 11.

tively and absolutely. For example, a single wild-appearing observation can seriously affect estimates of both the mean* and the amount of variation. On the other hand, for short-tailed distributions the performance of these same procedures will be even better than for the Gaussian ones.

Unfortunately, the "normal" is frequently not the "usual" distribution. Our experience in this respect coincided with that of Tukey and McLaughlin: The typical distribution of errors and fluctuations has a slope whose tails are longer than Gaussian or are asymmetrical. Since it is precisely this type of distribution that poses the greatest danger, it seems appropriate to give special attention to procedures that attach less weight to extreme-appearing cases.

Various methods have been suggested for this purpose. Rank-ordering has the serious disadvantage that it gives the reader little idea of the amount or degree of any differences that might be observed. Another method is to estimate the probability that an individual observation is not from the same population and then "trim off" and discard these tagged individuals—but this throws away data.

A third approach, the one adopted for this study, is Winsorizing, named in honor of Charles F. Winsor, who actively advocated its use in data analysis.[3] In this procedure a given number (g) of the extreme lowest values are replaced by the value of the next lowest, and a similar number of the highest are replaced by the next highest. For example, in a sample Winsorized once the value for the highest individual is changed to that of the next highest and, at the same time, the value for the lowest individual is changed to that of the second lowest. To use a psychological metaphor, trimming denies or censors completely the extreme values, while Winsorizing merely pays less attention to them. Or from another point of view, trimming rejects the "outlier" as if it were a gross and total blunder with no clue as to its true, real value; Winsorizing treats it as a case that belongs but whose magnitude may have been somewhat exaggerated. From either point of view, Winsorizing seems to be more desirable for rigorously screened data than trimming.

In terms of its effect on precision, Winsorizing removes the major distorting effect of "outliers" when they are present, but will of course make the estimate of mean and standard deviation somewhat less precise if the samples do not contain true "outliers." The loss of precision in the latter case is very small compared with the reduction in precision in the estimates if even occasional extreme values are taken at face

---

* Vulgarly, the average. This latter term is used as a synonym for mean in places elsewhere in this book.
3 See reference 2.

value. Dixon has shown that if the distribution is actually symmetrical and normal to begin with, Winsorizing leads to estimations of the mean and standard deviation which are almost as efficient as the best possible, while improved estimates result even if only mildly extreme values are present.*

For this study all the variables were analyzed non-Winsorized (W_0), Winsorized once (W_1) and Winsorized twice (W_2). The patients were first divided into ten groups—separated by two sexes and five treatments. For (W_1), the first stage of Winsorizing, one individual at each extreme in each of the ten groups was Winsorized, i.e., moved into the next nearest value. This represents a little less than 10 percent of the sample since each group contained 20–25 cases. For (W_2), the second stage of Winsorizing, two individuals (20 percent) in each of the ten groups were moved in.

ESTIMATE OF MEAN, STANDARD DEVIATION AND CONFIDENCE LIMITS

For all variables, the mean, standard deviation** and range were computed for each sex and for each treatment separately; for each treatment with both sexes combined; and as totals. This was done in three stages—non-Winsorized (W_0), Winsorized once (W_1) and Winsorized twice (W_2); 95 percent confidence limits† were also computed for each stage of Winsorizing. Confidence limits are obtained on the assumption that the observations are from "normal" distributions with no aberrant values. The article by Dixon and Tukey[4] shows the methods to be used for various amounts of Winsorizing. In our analyses the confidence intervals for (W_1) and (W_2) were expressed as the ratios of the lengths of confidence limits for (W_0).

The location and effect of extreme individuals was observed by inspection of the effect of successive stages of Winsorization on these statistics. For example, a radical reduction in variance or a sharp decrease in the length of the confidence interval is an indication that the Winsorized individuals were outside a normal distribution, and that the Winsorized data may be more generally representative of the true underlying situation apart from these extremes.

---

* See reference 2.
** A measure of the dispersion of variance in a sample. If the sample has a "normal" distribution, roughly 30 percent will lie outside the range of one standard deviation on each side of the center; roughly 5 percent will lie outside the range of two standard deviations.
† A statement of the precision of the estimate of the mean. "95 percent" of the time, the limits of (   ) and (   ) will contain the "true" value.
4 See reference 4.

As an arbitrary intuitive rule, it was decided that (W_0) would be accepted as most representative if the confidence limit ratio $(W_1)/(W_0)$ did not fall below 0.80. (W_1) would be accepted as the most representative if the confidence limit ratio $(W_1)/(W_0)$ fell below 0.80, unless there was a further substantial decrease (20 percent or more) with (W_2). In the last case (W_2) was accepted as the most representative. Hopefully, sharpened rules will be provided by statisticians in the near future.

CHI-SQUARE

In some instances the chi-square (χ^2) statistic was used to compare the treatment groups for some particular categorical variable such as the number discharged against medical advice or the number of dropouts. This provides a statement of the probability that the true proportions in the groups are equal, and that the observed differences in frequencies are the result of random sampling error.

ANALYSIS OF VARIANCE

Analysis of variance is a statistical technique to decide which of several different kinds of variables operating simultaneously are important and to estimate their effects. The variation of all the observations is separated into parts. Each part measures variation attributable to some specific source, e.g., to sex, treatment, etc. The intensity of the effect from any particular source is expressed as an F-ratio, comparing the variation due to that particular source with the variation within the patient groups.

Variance analyses were performed as follows:

(1) A one-way analysis of variance to determine whether there was any significant difference between the mean values considering each sex and treatment as a separate group (i.e., ten groups— five treatments, two sexes). Wherever the term "one-way analysis of variance" is used in the text, it refers to this specific analysis unless otherwise stated.

(2) A two-way analysis of variance for these same ten groups to determine whether there was any significant effect from any of the five treatments apart from sex; from sex alone; or from any peculiarity of interaction between sex and any of the treatment methods. Wherever the term "two-way analysis of variance" is used in the text, it refers to this specific analysis unless otherwise stated.

(3) A three-way analysis of variance for the MILIEU, DRUG ALONE, PSYCHOTHERAPY ALONE and PSYCHOTHERAPY PLUS DRUG groups

(omitting ECT) provides a separation of the variance into three main parts—variance due to *sex, drug* and *psychotherapy*. It also provides an estimate of the effects of the various interactions between these three. (Technically speaking, this is a 2 × 2 × 2 factorial design with the main factors *sex, drug* and *psychotherapy*.) Wherever the term "three-way analysis of variance" is used in the text, it refers to this specific analysis unless otherwise stated.

All analyses of variance were done three times—(W_0), (W_1) and (W_2). The rule previously outlined in "Estimate of Mean, Standard Deviation and Confidence Limits" was used to designate which of the levels of Winsorizing would be accepted as the most representative.

The "model" used here is the usual "additive effects" model, so-called because the separation of variation is made on the basis of an assumption that any resulting observation is the sum of a quantity unique to each group and an "error" of measurement. For the two-way analysis, a quantity for each sex is added. The three-way analysis has three additive components—*sex, psychotherapy* and *drug.*

The two- and three-way analyses provide an opportunity to look for "interaction" effects which are not the simple sum of two or more additive components. For example, in the two-way analysis of variance model, "interaction" occurs when the two sexes respond differently to one or more of the different treatment methods. Similarly, in the three-way analysis, interactions between *sex, psychotherapy* and *drug* can be detected. For example, an interaction effect will be detected if *drugs* have a different effect depending on whether or not *psychotherapy* is given, *or* if the sexes respond differently to *psychotherapy* or to *drug therapy, or* if the effect of *psychotherapy* is different depending on whether or not *drugs* are given as well.

The only deviation in the computations which is not the same as that which appears in elementary textbooks is that the method described by Scheffé for preliminary calculations in the case of unequal cell* numbers or for quick preliminary analysis was used to compute an approximate F-value for the analysis of variance.[5]

Scheffé points out that this analysis corresponds to the more tedious exact analysis assuming that all population variances are equal, but is, in general, somewhat less efficient. In the case of the one-way layout with two groups, it is identical with the exact analysis; in any case it utilizes the sufficient statistics of sample mean and sample variance. Thus, where there is only one degree of freedom (i.e., only one truly independent comparison to be made), as in determining differences be-

---

* Cell: When a patient group is divided up for the purpose of analysis by subclassification or cross-classification (e.g., by sex, by treatment method or by sex within treatments), the subcategories are known as cells.

[5] See reference 10.

tween the two sexes or in a one-way analysis of variance for treatment effect, the value obtained is exact. In other situations the error in estimation is small and, for the screening purpose of this study, not important enough to be troublesome.

As a check of the use of this method for this particular study, a comparison was made between the exact and approximate F-value for twenty variables when the error was likely to be maximal—where the variance differed greatly from one cell to another or where there was a marked difference in cell numbers. For main effect (comparison between treatments) the difference in computation did not appear to produce a bias in assessment of the level of significance; this was in general somewhat understated in the lower levels of significance. The maximum deviation observed would designate as significant at the .02 level a value that was truly at the .01 level, while for F-values greater than five the deviations from exact values were inconsequential. For interaction effects between sex and treatment, there was a slight bias in the direction of overestimating the significance level in the lower levels of significance. The maximum deviation observed would attribute a significance level of .03 to an exact level of .05, while at higher F-levels the differences were trivial. We believe the differences sufficiently small to allow the use of the approximate F-values throughout.

In assigning a significance level to the F-value computed in this approximate analysis of variance, a method was used that gave the exact percentile for one-way analyses and a good approximation for two- and three-way analyses.

ANALYSIS OF CO-VARIANCE

In evaluating outcome, various measures of the patient's final status at the end of treatment were chosen as the prime *clinical* criteria, as contrasted to *administrative* criteria such as cost and stay.

Where the treatment groups have been in general adequately balanced by random assignment, as was the case in this study, *final status* measures may be accepted as the optimum criteria of treatment effect—provided that the groups were, in fact, satisfactorily equal in respect to their initial level on the particular measures chosen for analysis. If this latter condition is met, the amount of change induced by any of the treatments will be suitably reflected in the measurements of final status. If, on the other hand, random assignment has not worked in such a way as to equalize the groups for this specific variable, some sort of adjustment is in order.

Direct measurement of the difference between pre- and post-treatment scores is an obvious step, and such "pre-post" *change* scores were used, as well as simply measuring *final status*. However, as Wittenborn has pointed out, simple difference scores are relatively fallible as measurements of change because they incorporate not only the errors that enter into the post-treatment assessment, but also the errors that enter into the pre-treatment assessment.[6] A more precise approach to adjusting for initial level involves the technique of co-variance. In this, the differences in the effectiveness of the five treatments were studied with the use of final status outcome variables "controlled" or "adjusted" for initial level—the "co-variate." (Another way of looking at analysis of co-variance is to consider that it is a mathematical way of comparing groups "as if" they were equal at the start.) Like analysis of variance, this procedure leads to a test for differences in group means by a separation of the variation into several parts.

An analysis of co-variance was performed for each of the final status criteria of clinical outcome, using as co-variates sex and initial level on the particular variable chosen for analysis. For administrative criteria such as cost and stay, where "initial level" is obviously inapplicable, sex and initial level on the Menninger Health-Sickness rating scale (a global evaluation) were used as co-variates. All co-variance analyses reported in this volume were performed on non-Winsorized (W_0) data and in the manner described above, unless otherwise specified in the text.

Analysis of co-variance is applicable only to the extent that there is a direct linear relationship between *initial* and *final* level, and then only if the relationship is similar in degree (technically, that the regression lines are parallel in slope for the various treatments).

It is therefore necessary to arrive at some guide for determining in any particular instance whether this latter condition is fulfilled sufficiently to justify an assumption that there will be a gain in precision by using adjusted (co-varied) scores.

This is somewhat similar to the problem of deciding in analysis of variance whether one can average (or pool) "interaction" and "within" sum of squares to obtain a "residual" mean square to use as a denominator in testing for main effects. Accordingly, we adopted intuitively a suggested procedure which has some theoretical justification for the analysis of variance situation—accept *co-varied* scores as the most suitable indicator if the *F*-ratio for homogeneity of regression is less than twice the 50th percentile of the *F*-distribution.[7] In particular this rule was used to assist in the resolution of situations where there was some apparent contradiction between the results for *change* and *final*

[6] See reference 13.
[7] See reference 9.

status, and where it was necessary to decide whether *co-varied* scores should be accepted as the most suitable indicator.

To simplify presentation, the text will focus on outcome in terms of *final status,* although statistics for *change* have been included in the tables. It may be assumed (unless stated otherwise) that the statistics for change and co-variance confirm the final status findings with no material discrepancy. Wherever there seemed to be a possible disparity between change and final status, statistics for *final status adjusted by co-variance* for sex and initial level are reported if co-variance was determined to be applicable under the rule given above. It may also be assumed (unless stated otherwise) that the statistics in the text are at the appropriate level of Winsorizing selected by the rules given previously in the section on "Estimate of Mean, Standard Deviation and Confidence Limits"; that Winsorization (paying less attention to extreme cases) did not alter the rank order of the treatment groups, except perhaps trivially in instances where two groups had almost identical values to start with; that the differences and effects observed were not confined to a few unusual cases; and that the significance level for any difference or effect described as approaching significance or better was unchanged or even increased by Winsorization.

MULTIPLE RANGE TEST

If an analysis of variance shows that there is an overall significant difference among a number of treatment group means, the question arises as to which of the pairs of means may be considered significantly different and which may not. For instance, assume that we are comparing five treatments. If an analysis of variance shows that the overall variation among the five means is large enough to be significant, should we then conclude that there is only a significant difference between the highest and the lowest? Or can we test each treatment against every other treatment to see if any of the other differences are significant?

This is not a simple matter—the more groups there are, the more likely it is that any one of them (and we know not which) may be a rather unusual sample that has misleadingly high (or misleadingly low) values. If ten comparisons are made, comparing each of the five means with each other, the probability that at least one of them will appear to be significant is clearly greater than if only one comparison is made. For example, if we use a 5 percent significance level to test the differences among five means, the probability (p) that one or more of the ten comparisons will exceed the 5 percent value is .40.

This raises the question whether we ought to try to control the frequency with which *any* statement of significance is made wrongly (i.e., an *experiment-wise* significance level) rather than just the frequency with which a wrong statement is made for any one comparison (a *comparison-wise* significance level). Various methods of analysis of this situation have been proposed. Duncan's New Multiple Range Test, which was developed for inter-comparing a number of means or other estimates in all possible ways, was used in this study.[8] In Duncan's method an adjustment is made to the difference between the means to provide more protection against the increased possibility of making an erroneous declaration of significance. Two means are declared to be significantly different only if their adjusted difference exceeds the critical value (protection level) for the particular number of groups in the experiment.*

This test was performed twice on non-Winsorized data, first for the five treatment groups with both sexes combined and second for each sex and treatment group separately (i.e., ten groups). Wherever the term "Multiple Range Test" is used in the text it refers to one of these two analyses unless otherwise stated.

DISCRIMINANT ANALYSIS

This type of analysis was used in certain situations to select from a number of variables the one that (after allowing for any differences that might have been due to differences in sex composition) discriminates best between the five treatment groups, i.e., that puts the maximum distance between them. It also identifies the most discriminating linear combinations of two or more variables. For example, analyses were

---

[8] See references 5, 6.

* By this method the true (experimentwise) significance level for a difference is relaxed as the number of comparisons is increased. The significance level used is based on tabular values for a test at the protection levels listed below:

# groups compared*	(p) for .95% protection levels**	(p) for .99% protection levels***
10	.37	.09
9	.34	.08
8	.30	.07
7	.26	.06
6	.23	.05
5	.19	.04
4	.14	.03
3	.10	.02
2	.05	.01

$$* \quad \text{\# groups} = k$$
$$** \quad (p) = 1 - (.95)^{k-1}$$
$$*** \quad (p) = 1 - (.99)^{k-1}$$

done to determine the most sensitive discriminator from among the various stay and nursing evaluation variables. Non-Winsorized data were used for these analyses, which employed the method described by Dixon.[9]

CORRELATION

Correlational analysis was used wherever it was necessary to express the degree of correspondence between the values of two variables. The value of the resulting Pearsonian correlation coefficient (r) may lie between $+1$ and -1. The coefficient is positive if one of the variables tends to increase with increasing values of the other; negative if the variable tends to decrease with increasing values of the other. To put it another way, if the coefficient is either $+1$ or -1, the two variables are mathematically totally linearly dependent upon one another (but not necessarily causally related). If its value is zero, they are mathematically independent.

MISSING VALUES

For the variables reported in this volume, the data were complete or reasonably so and the analyses are based only on cases for which data were obtained, with no attempt to replace missing values. An exception was made in the case of certain information necessary for the computations of cost, where it was felt to be particularly desirable to report statistics that would be truly representative and where all other data necessary for the computations were available.

The proper determination of missing values is not a simple problem, and it is not completely clear what should be an optimum solution. The discussion of this subject by Afifi and Elashoff suggests that if information is available on items that are known to be closely related, it is best to use this knowledge to estimate what the true value would most likely be.[10] (Technically, when there is a high correlation, estimating missing values by multiple regression equations obtained on the complete data appears to be best for comparison on observations, variances, regression coefficients and mean square error.) To use a relevant example, *if* calculation shows that for a particular group *psychotherapy* was usually given two hours a week, and *if* the patient's length of stay in the hospital is known, *then* one can make a good likely estimate of the amount of *psychotherapy* that the patient actually did receive. This is

9 See reference 3.
10 See reference 1.

preferable to the commonly used method of merely inserting mean values.

Accordingly, for these particular instances the missing values were estimated using a regression equation determined on the cases that did not have missing values, and using as predictors items with high face validity that had been shown to be highly correlated with the variable in question. More than one predictor was used if this was necessary to achieve a substantial correlation, or if the second predictor appreciably improved prediction.

In exploratory computations to select the best predictors, eight items that had a high face validity as potential predictors were used directly as well as in logarithmic and square-root transformations in a multiple regression program:

(1) Sex
(2) Age
(3) Education
(4) Treatment Group
(5) Total sedative orders all types
(6) Selection Stay (adjusted for AWOL and leave)
(7) Menninger Health-Sickness scale (initial consensus rating)
(8) MACC scale (initial Total score)

The final choice of the best predictors was to predict the square root of the missing value for hours of seclusion by regression equation from the number of sedative orders. The square root of the number of times in seclusion was calculated by a different regression equation from the same predictor. The missing values for hours of *physician contact other than psychotherapy* were computed using a separate regression equation for each treatment group, with *adjusted selection stay* as the predictor. The regressions were required to pass through the origin, i.e., computed on the presumption that a patient who was treated for zero days would have no contact with the physician. The missing values for the number of hours of *psychotherapy* were obtained using a regression equation (also through the origin) for cases assigned to the two PSYCHOTHERAPY groups, with *adjusted selection stay* used as a predictor.

SIGNIFICANCE LEVELS

In interpreting the results of comparing one treatment with another, it is important to have some indication of the likelihood that any observed differences might be a "fluke" due to so-called "chance." This involves determination of the level of statistical significance, a term used here in the technical sense to mean "If indeed there is no true association, values (or differences) of this order in samples of this size might be expected to occur as the result of random chance processes less often than some stated percent or fraction of the time."

The level .05 (1 in 20) has customarily been accepted as a reasonable dividing point between "significant" and "not significant" for experiments in general, but it is obvious that significance is a continuum, a matter of degree. The .05 level has been used extensively in agricultural and biometric work and is incorporated in this study, but there is no reason why it should be considered holy for medical investigation. One might well use a higher probability level as the dividing line. The actual level to be chosen as "significant" should depend on the importance of the decision and a consideration of how much wrong is risked either way—by the erroneous rejection of a treatment or by its unjustified acceptance.

In clinical research the use of a high percentage level of significance seems quite appropriate, and levels of statistical significance up to $p = .20$ and even higher are reported in this volume. It may be of little concern to the clinician or to the patient if either of two equally safe treatments is mistaken to be the preferred one, but it is important to be sure of recognizing a difference if it really does exist. A .20 level of significance gives odds of 1 to 4 that differences will be accepted as true when they really do not exist, but it increases the chance that true differences will be recognized; the physician may willingly take the risk that there is 1 chance out of 5 that he is administering a treatment that has really no advantage.

It is important to recognize that the designation of a difference as "statistically significant" does not necessarily mean that it is of practical importance. No matter how certain a difference may be, it is its size that determines whether the difference is important or trivial. Equally so, on the other hand, it is important to recognize that the designation of a difference as "not statistically significant" means nothing more than "on the basis of the present sample, a difference cannot, with the significance probability used, be statistically asserted."

This is not the same as saying that there is *no* difference. Statistical tests of significance are subject to two types of error:

> *Type I* in which the null hypothesis (that the findings arise by chance alone and that the treatments really have no effect) may be rejected when it is in fact true (in racing parlance, the chance that one has picked a treatment as a winner when it is in fact a loser).
> *Type II* in which the null hypothesis may be accepted as true when it is in fact false (the chance that one has failed to spot a winner).

The smaller the number of patients studied, the higher the base rate in the control group; and the higher the arbitrary dividing point for "significance," the greater the chances that a true difference may be overlooked. To take an example relevant to this study, let us imagine that we have compared the effect of treatment A with a control, 50 patients in each group. *If* the true discharge rate in the control group is 60 percent and *if* we set .05 as the arbitrary level that will decide if the rate for treatment A is to be declared significantly higher, *then* there is a 1 in 10 chance of overlooking a real increase in discharge rate to as much as even 85 percent, and a 1 in 5 chance of overlooking a real increase to 80 percent.[11]

As can be seen, many of the significance levels reported in this volume far exceed the .05 level, making this present discussion somewhat academic. Nevertheless, it is important that the clinician not be bamboozled into uncritical worship of arbitrary significance levels. There are those who hold, perhaps somewhat condescendingly, that the clinician should be protected against misguided optimism by withholding from him any significance level below .05. As stated previously, it is our position that ignorance is not an asset; accordingly, as far as possible we have adopted the practice of reporting the significance level directly and with as much precision as was reasonably possible. In addition to this more precise reporting, in order to speak distinctly to the clinician, certain terms have been used in the text as conventional designations for specified ranges of significance. To keep peace among the inferencers, we have branched our decisions into categories much as olives in the following manner:

Not significant	$p > .20$
Approaching significance	$p = .20–.0501$
Significant	$p = .05–.0101$
Highly significant	$p = .0100–.0011$
Very highly significant	$p = .0010–.0002$
Extremely significant	$p < .0001$

ROUNDING OFF

Values in the text and in figures and diagrams have been rounded off as the last step in computation, in accordance with the believed accuracy of the estimate. Rounding off in the intermediate stages was avoided. It is readily shown that rounding off introduces an error of standard deviation equal to $1/\sqrt{12}$ of the rounding-off interval. As Villars comments, "Data are imprecise enough as it is without deliberately adding computational errors to them."[12]

[11] See reference 8.
[12] See reference 12.

LIST OF CONVENTIONAL TERMS, ABBREVIATIONS AND NOTATIONS

To avoid long-winded repetition of statistical phraseology in the text, the aforelisted phrases have been used for significance levels, and the following phrases, terms, notations and abbreviations have also been used:

SIGNIFICANCE LEVELS: NOTATION.

(1) Where the actual level was determined, the significance level (p) is given in parentheses to four significant figures (e.g., .0050). A two-tailed test was used, expressing the significance of values observed for all the patients, not just those at one end of the distribution.

(2) If the p value was determined to lie between certain limits, these limits are given in parentheses (e.g., .0005–.0001).

(3) If only the larger limit was determined, that value is given (e.g., < .05).

(4) If a significance level is given without any notation, it indicates that the data were not Winsorized. (In some situations where it is necessary to distinguish non-Winsorized from Winsorized, the notation (W_0) may be used for non-Winsorized data.) If the data were Winsorized once, the notation (W_1) follows the significance level (e.g., < .05, W_1). If the data were Winsorized twice, the notation (W_2) is used.

(5) If a significance level is derived from analysis of co-variance, the notation Co-V follows it (e.g., < .001, Co-V).

(6) If a significance level is derived from a Duncan New Multiple Range test, it is preceded by the notation "D" (e.g., D < .05). (In this case, however, this is a "protection level," not a significance level.)

TERMS DESIGNATING SPECIFIC ANALYSES.

One-way Analysis of Variance	Analysis for overall differences, ten groups (two sexes and five treatments separately) as previously described.
Two-way Analysis of Variance	Analysis for differences between the two sexes and among the five treatments as previously described.
Three-way Analysis of Variance	Analysis with the ECT group omitted, for the effects of *sex, psychotherapy* and *drug,* as previously described.
Analysis of Co-Variance	Analysis of Co-Variance as previously described.

Multiple Range Test   Duncan's New Multiple Range test
                                       as previously described.

STATISTICAL ABBREVIATIONS.

(W_0)	Non-Winsorized data
(W_1)	Data Winsorized once as previously described
(W_2)	Data Winsorized twice as previously described
D	Duncan New Multiple Range Test
Co-V	Analysis of Co-Variance
F	F-statistic or F-ratio
p	Significance level
r	Pearsonian correlation coefficient
SD	Standard deviation
t	t-statistic (ratio)
χ^2	Chi-square statistic

TREATMENTS, TREATMENT EFFECTS AND TREATMENT GROUPS.

(1) The five treatment groups are identified as follows:
   MILIEU *(M):* The patient group treated with milieu care only.
   DRUG ALONE *(D):* The patient group treated with milieu care and ataraxic drug.
   ECT *(E):* The patient group treated with milieu care and electro-convulsive therapy.
   PSYCHOTHERAPY ALONE *(P):* The patient group treated with milieu care and individual psychotherapy.
   PYSCHOTHERAPY PLUS DRUG *(P+D):* The patient group treated with milieu care, individual psychotherapy and ataraxic drug.
(2) Specific treatment effects separated by analysis of variance are identified as follows:
   Drug: The effect of ataraxic drug.
   Psychotherapy: The effect of individual psychotherapy.
(3) The following terms are used to refer to the respective methods of treatment (as distinguished from the patient groups or the specific treatment effects):
   Ataraxic Drugs
   Individual Psychotherapy
   Electroconvulsive Therapy (or *ECT*)
   Milieu Therapy: A general approach to treatment that includes nursing, occupational therapy, industrial therapy, rehabilitation social casework and supportive care.
   The Combination of Individual Psychotherapy and Ataraxic Drugs

OTHER ABBREVIATIONS.

AA   Ann Arbor Mental Status Psychotic Confusion Scale
AMA   Against Medical Advice

AWOL	Absent Without leave
CDAS	Camarillo Dynamic Assessment Scale
CMS	Clyde Mood-Scale
CPI	California Psychological Inventory
F	Female Sex
ISR	Idiosyncratic Symptoms Rating Scale
L.R	Limited Responder (treatment failure; not released)
M	Male Sex
MACC	MACC Scale (Ellsworth)
MHS	Menninger Health-Sickness Rating Scale
MMPI	Minnesota Multiphasic Personality Inventory
N	Number of patients for whom data were obtained
Rx	Treatment
SRS	Symptom Rating Sheet (Jenkins)
SVIB	Strong Vocational Interest Blank
T	Total

REFERENCES

(1) Afifi, A. A. & Elashoff, R. M.: Missing values in multivariate statistics: #1, Review of the Literature. *J. of the American Statistical Association,* 61:595–604, 1966.

(2) Dixon, W. J.: Simplified estimation from censored normal samples. *Annals of Mathematical Statistics,* 31:385–391, 1960.

(3) Dixon, W. J., et al: Program BMD02R, stepwise regression. In *Biomedical Computer Programs.* Health Sciences Computing Facility, Department of Preventive Medicine and Public Health, School of Medicine, University of California, Los Angeles, 1964: 233–257.

(4) Dixon, W. J. & Tukey, J. W.: Approximate behavior of the distribution of Winsorized "t" (Trimming/Winsorization 2). *Technometrics* (In Press).

(5) Duncan, D. B.: Multiple range and multiple *F* tests. *Biometrics,* 11:1–42, 1955.

(6) Duncan, D. B.: Multiple range tests for correlated and heteroscedastic means. *Biometrics,* 13:164–176, 1957.

(7) Gerard, R. W.: The nosology of schizophrenia: A cooperative study. *Behavioral Science,* 9:311–333, 1964.

(8) Kramer, M. & Greenhouse, S. W.: Determination of sample size and selection of cases. In *Psychopharmacology, Problems in Evaluation.* National Research Council, Washington, D. C., 1959; 356–371.

(9) Paull, A. E.: On a preliminary test for pooling mean squares in the analysis of variance. *Annals of Mathematical Statistics,* 21:539–556, 1950.

(10) Scheffé H.: *The Analysis of Variance.* John Wiley & Sons, Inc., New York, 1959: 362–363.

(11) Tukey, J. W. & McLaughlin, D. H.: Less vulnerable confidence and significance procedures for location based on a single sample (Trimming/Winsorization 1). *Sankhya,* 26:331–352, 1965.

(12) Villars, D. S.: *Statistical Design and Analysis of Experiments for Developmental Research.* W. C. Brown Co., Dubuque, Iowa, 1951: 18–19.

(13) Wittenborn, J. R.: The assessment of clinical change. In *Pharmacotherapy of Depression,* Cole, J. O. & Wittenborn, J. R., eds. Charles C Thomas, Springfield, Ill., 1966: 67–90.

CHAPTER IV

Description of a Patient Sample: The Schizophrenia Research Project

PHILIP R. A. MAY, M.D.

IT IS GENERALLY agreed that a research report should contain an adequate description of the subjects of the study. This task in practice proves to be easier said than done, for it requires not one but several descriptions.

This chapter and its related Appendix VII describe the patients in this study in four ways: in terms of the criteria for selection, a sketch of the "average" patient, detailed summary statistics, and a number of case extracts that illustrate more vividly the range of patients studied from "best" to "worst."

SELECTION CRITERIA

Our patient sample was comprised basically of first-admission schizophrenic men and women between the ages of 16 and 45, selected as being in the average range of prognosis for this disorder and so representing its usual or average outcome, with no serious complicating physical illness and no significant prior treatment. However, the reader will probably want to have a better picture of the patients than can be conveyed by the selection criteria. He will probably also wish some assurance that analyses were made to see if the five treatment groups were in fact comparable and reasonably equated.

THE "AVERAGE" PATIENT

A common (but somewhat misleading) approach to description of a patient group is to portray the "average" patient. This would be a 28-year-old man or woman with a high school education and a verbal IQ of 107 (although functioning below this level as a result of his illness); who has had signs of personality disorder for nine years and overt psychotic symptoms for 39 weeks; either a housewife or employed as a skilled manual worker; usually Protestant (60 percent) or Catholic (30 percent), but sometimes Jewish (4 percent) or professing no religion (4 percent) or an Eastern religion (2 percent). He would be more often a committed (81 percent) than a voluntary admission (19 percent); more often Caucasian (68 percent) than Negro (21 percent) or Mexican (9 percent). Sixty percent had been married (at some time or another), while 40 percent were currently married and living with their spouse. On the Menninger Health-Sickness scale (MHS) the average admission rating was 19.4 (undoubtedly in need of hospital care). The clinical prognosis was that in two years the patient's condition would be rated at 36.3 (e.g., in the community, out of the hospital and probably back at work or functioning as a housewife, but with a considerable amount of disability).

SUMMARY STATISTICS

A more comprehensive (but very dull) approach that appeals to the statistically-minded research investigator, but usually conveys little or nothing to the average clinician, is to provide statistical tabulations for base-line variables that might have a bearing on the eventual outcome. To this end Appendix VII covers 22 demographic and clinical history items, 24 items of pretreatment clinical status, and 28 pretreatment psychological test items. The tables give the mean, range and standard deviation of the entire patient group with significance levels from a two-way analysis of variance.

In general, these statistics show that the treatment groups were equated in a thoroughly satisfactory manner. The differences among the five treatments reached statistical significance ($<$ .05) for only 2 out of the 74 items—*Ever married?* (.0288, W_0) and *Motivation* (.0376, W_0). On all other items the differences were nonsignificant, including crucial major variables such as Menninger Health-Sickness scale pretreatment ratings and two-year prognosis; proportion of voluntary admissions; total scores from the analysts', nurses' and therapists' measures; duration of psychosis, and age at onset of illness.

ADDITIONAL TABULATIONS

The tables in Chapter 2 also describe certain aspects of the patient sample. Table 2–1 provides statistics relating the different stages of selection of the patient sample to the population of admissions to Camarillo State Hospital. Tables 2–2 through 2–5 provide information on patients who were excluded from the study.

In addition, Table I.1 (Appendix I) shows the number of patients of each sex assigned to the five treatment groups and the numbers included in the final analysis.

CASE EXAMPLES

To supplement these more formal approaches, a number of case extracts are given below to illustrate more vividly the range of patients studied, from acute to chronic, from best to worst, oldest to youngest.

OLDEST AGE AT ONSET OF PSYCHOSIS AND ADMISSION TO HOSPITAL.

Patient #205: A 43½-year-old white divorced man, living alone, was the oldest of the male patients at the time of admission and also the one whose psychosis had started at the oldest age.

> He was committed involuntarily to hospital because he had not eaten for seven to ten days and had visited the FBI repeatedly with complaints that he was being persecuted by television, telepathy, radio and religious groups. He had always been withdrawn and isolated, avoiding personal contact, but had successfully completed three years of college education and a full period of military service. Psychotic symptoms had started six months previously, but became continuous three months before admission, at which time he walked off his job and started behaving peculiarly, staring into space and searching around the neighborhood. On admission he was quiet, withdrawn, suspicious and hostile, preoccupied with ideas that he was being used

in an electronic experiment to manipulate his sphincters and other muscles. He did not feel that he was ill or in need of treatment, but talked of throwing himself in front of a truck to avoid his tormentors.

Patient #239: A 44½-year-old American-born married woman of Japanese descent was the oldest of the female patients at the time of admission and also the one whose psychosis had started at the oldest age.

She was committed involuntarily to the hospital after she was found standing by a gas stove with the gas on, unlighted. Before her present illness she had been a happy, hardworking, energetic person, employed full time in a semiskilled occupation in addition to looking after her family of three children. Five weeks before admission she began to slow up and to complain of fatigue, exhaustion and headaches; a week later she started to neglect her household duties. Two to three weeks before admission she knelt and prayed in a corner for several hours, saying that someone was testing her brain and wanted to kill her. From then on she became rapidly worse, talked incessantly in a rambling nonsensical fashion and locked the house with the shades drawn, not permitting anyone to enter or to leave. She said she heard voices and complained that she was being gassed. Admitted to the hospital, she denied that she was in any way ill and demanded to be released instantly. She was untidy, depressed, uncommunicative, panicky, negativistic and resistive, stayed in bed and spat out any food that was given to her.

YOUNGEST AGE AT ONSET OF PSYCHOSIS AND ADMISSION TO HOSPITAL.

Patient #106: A 16½-year-old white single student was the youngest male patient and also the male whose psychosis had started at the earliest age.

He was described as an "active, ambitious, industrious youngster who tried to make too many friends with too many people" until 1½ to 2 years before admission. Then there was an abrupt change and he became quiet and seclusive—he sat and stared at the floor for long periods. Three months before admission he became confused, lost many of his belongings at school and started to fail classes. Then he started to feel that he was being followed by a gang that was out to harm him, and on one occasion ran away in panic until he was exhausted. Three weeks before admission he started to copy the license numbers of cars parked outside his house, said he was being spied on and talked about, that he could hear little people talking to him, that someone had tried to poison his cat and his dog. After he ran around the house in the middle of the night with a baseball bat looking for the gang, he was admitted to the hospital "voluntarily" (signed in by his parents) although he did not think there was anything wrong with him. On the ward he was tense, frightened and suspicious, said that he was going to be killed and refused to eat; at other times he expressed grandiose ideas.

Patient #217: A 16½-year-old white single girl was the youngest female patient and also the female whose psychosis had started the earliest.

The first evidence of overt psychosis was one month after her 15th birthday and one year before admission to the hospital. At that time she made the first "B" in her school career, became fearful, could not sleep and cried a lot. She said that others were making derogatory remarks and that she was being accused of being pregnant. She became progressively more nervous and finally, four months later, was referred to a psychiatrist who advised hospitalization. However, she begged not to go and "improved" with four to six weeks of outpatient treatment. There was a marked change in personality and she gained 25 pounds in weight, became unnaturally active and aggressive and lost all her friends. Two weeks before admission she suddenly stopped eating, did not sleep and refused to go to school, talked about God and begged for forgiveness for her sins. She heard voices and said that she had been transformed into the Virgin Mary, that her food was being poisoned and that she was going to die. In the hospital she was quiet and extremely frightened, bewildered and confused, almost mute, moved very slowly and could not dress herself or make her bed.

LONGEST DURATION OF OVERT PSYCHOSIS.

Patient #62: A 32-year-old white single voluntary admission had the longest duration of overt psychosis among the male patients (nine years).

He had always been lonely and isolated, but he first became aware that he was anxious around people fifteen years previously when he was in the army. However, the first sign of overt psychosis was nine years before admission, when he started to think that he was being (unjustly) suspected of being a homosexual and that he was being subtly kidded and humiliated; somewhere around this time he had a vivid hallucination of a fist coming at his face. During the following years wherever he went he felt that humiliating homosexual references were made about him, so that by six years before admission he was restless, unable to concentrate and always on the go. Although he did manage to complete some years of college, he was never able to do more than a little part-time work and was never able to support himself. One month before admission he got the idea that he was being questioned as an informer for the police and thought that people were looking at him, talking about him and making obscene gestures. Voices followed him in the streets, cars with prominent headlights trailed him and he suspected that the FBI was involved. He became frightened and unable to sleep, thought of suicide and then decided to ask for help. On the ward he was quiet, soft-spoken, emotionally unresponsive and seclusive.

Patient #179: A 39-year-old white woman, separated from her husband, had the longest duration of overt psychosis among the female patients (five years).

Her symptoms apparently started when she "went to pieces" after a hysterectomy seven years before admission, complaining of hot and cold flashes, nagging, being suspicious of her husband and unable to continue in her employment. The situation gradually deteriorated and definite psychotic symptoms appeared some five years before admission. By that time she had become withdrawn and suspicious; she thought cars were following her, that people were calling her names and making derogatory statements about her and that her possessions were being stolen. In the intervening years she moved frequently from place to place and from job to job, being asked to move from several apartments because of her bizarre behavior and paranoid complaints against landlords and neighbors. As the illness progressed she suspected that ventriloquism was being used and that microphones had been placed in her room; she complained to the police that someone was rummaging through her belongings. Admitted to the hospital involuntarily, she was seclusive and withdrawn, did not realize that she was ill and demanded to be released.

SHORTEST DURATION OF PSYCHOSIS OR OF ANY KIND OF SYMPTOMS.

Patient #48: A 25-year-old single Negro had the shortest duration of overt *psychotic* symptoms among the male patients (one week). (Four others were also recorded as one week, but the evidence for abrupt onset was less convincing for them than for Patient #48.)

He had been living by himself, so that background information could be obtained only from his employer (who had known him for a year) and his landlady (where he had lived for two years). According to them he had been a quiet, steady, good worker and no trouble at all except for some occasionally heavy drinking and associations (possibly sexual and homosexual) of which his landlady disapproved. He himself said that he was nervous and that for 1½ years he had felt that people were watching him. (In recording duration of illness this was not considered to be definite evidence of *psychotic* symptoms, although obviously it might be taken as such if less strict criteria had been used.) Overt *psychotic* symptoms appeared quite suddenly six days before admission when he accused his landlady of watching him and telling false stories about him. The next day he told his employer that he was not feeling well and went to another hospital where he said that he was looking for his parents (whom he had not seen for four years) because he thought they had been injured and admitted there. He was finally admitted to the hospital involuntarily. On the ward he was suspicious, mistrustful and avoided contact with the staff. He thought he had a fatal disease, that there was some terrible secret, that he was being used as a tool to accomplish harm throughout the world, that people were laughing and doing other things that had special reference to him.

Patient #58: A 25-year-old white male, married and with one child, had by his own account and by that of his wife and family the shortest duration of symptoms *of any kind.*

He had been regularly employed, and although shy, retiring and timid and liable to have temper tantrums, made many friends. There had been no symptoms whatever until a little less than three weeks before admission, when he returned home in an agitated state and told his wife of an attempt to seduce him; he began to think that he might be God. A week later he telephoned his wife to say that God had told him to contact the President, that there was Communist activity at his place of work, it was going to be blown up and he would be killed. Admitted to the hospital, he told the examiner that he was God or the Holy Ghost or the Son of God, that he could kill everybody and also help them. He talked of visions and asked to be allowed to transmit an important message to the President. He did not seem to realize that he was sick. He escaped from the hospital twice during the evaluation period, and on another occasion he refused to return to the ward after visiting with his wife.

Patient #93: Among the female patients, the most recent onset (both of overt *psychotic* symptoms and of symptoms of *any kind*) was in the case of this 23-year-old white married woman who was admitted involuntarily in a catatonic state—mute, negativistic, dishevelled and trembling, covered with cuts and bruises.

Her illness had started seven days before admission when she suddenly threatened to jump out of a window at work. Although she had always been quiet and kept things to herself, she had up to that time seemed entirely well. She had done satisfactorily at school and at work; according to her parents and her husband, the marriage was a success. No one was able to establish contact with her during the evaluation except that she would sometimes repeat automatically whatever the person said (echolalia). Her condition alternated between mutism and periods of excitement in which she would run at the wall and bang her head or attempt to injure herself in some other way. It was impossible to keep her clothing on; she was uncooperative, and had to be spoon fed; attempted to choke several nurses; almost killed the ward cat by choking it into unconsciousness.

LONGEST DURATION OF SYMPTOMS OF ANY KIND OTHER THAN PERSONALITY DISORDER.

Patient #207: A 33-year-old divorced white woman was the female patient who had had symptoms of some kind for longer than any other female patient (twenty years).

It was evident from the age of two or three that this patient had a serious behavior disorder: she was irritable, belligerent, unmanageable, destructive and had severe temper tantrums. Nevertheless, in spite of these difficulties she was a bright child, especially talented in music and dancing; she could read, write and play the harp and piano before entering school. Later on she rebelled against school and completed her graduation requirements only by going to night school. She then moved from place to place in a career of striptease and related activities, holding clerical and other jobs intermittently, having one illegitimate child and several abortions. Although she had shown signs of behavior disorder from early childhood, it could not be said that she had *symptoms* (as strictly defined by the criteria given in Appendix V) until twenty years before admission (age 13) when she was first taken to a psychiatrist. The first definite signs of *psychosis* appeared about four years before admission, when her employer reported that she had been acting in a strange confused manner and had terrible tantrums. She was admitted to the hospital involuntarily because of temper tantrums, suspiciousness and belligerent acting-out behavior that had kept the family household in a constant turmoil. In the hospital she was aloof, suspicious and superior, hostile and evasive, confused, scattered and disorganized. She attempted to deny or conceal her symptoms and claimed that there was nothing wrong with her. However, she was at times rambling and incoherent or noisy and disturbed, admitting she heard voices. She attacked other patients without provocation, ran away on several occasions and was grossly inappropriate and sexually provocative in her dress and behavior.

Patient #151: A 41-year-old married white man with three children was the male patient who had had symptoms of some kind for the longest period (27 years).

As a child he had been lonely and inadequate, hated school and avoided people. In adolescence he was seclusive, artistic, musical, meticulous and orderly. The remainder of his life was turbulent to an extreme. Actual *symptoms* (as strictly defined in Appendix V) dated back to age fourteen or fifteen when he developed a pattern of homosexuality and fetishism. However, he did not see a psychiatrist until ten years before admission. In the last three years he had become preoccupied with strange religious ideas and had alternating sprees of alcoholism and homosexuality, worse in the past six months. He was admitted involuntarily, complaining of increasing depression, insomnia, nervousness and prolonged loss of appetite, drinking and inability to work. He was confused, apprehensive, excited, suspicious, over-talkative, rambling and circumstantial, thought he was both a radio transmitter and a radio receiver, heard voices speaking to him saying that he was put on earth to be a saint and that he should be a recluse and live a life of monastic celibacy.

HIGHEST PRETREATMENT LEVEL OF HEALTH-SICKNESS.

Patient #57: This 21-year-old white single male was given the *highest* pretreatment Menninger Health-Sickness rating (32 points) for any of the patients, male or female.

Although described as shy, frightened and quiet, enjoying music and art, he had been rebellious and in difficulty since age thirteen and had been placed in Juvenile Hall on several occasions. For a month before admission he had been behaving strangely and was finally brought to the hospital after the police found him walking down the white line in the center of a busy street. He informed them that he had received a radio message that Christ was coming and that his name had been called. On admission he was incoherent and in a state of panic: He felt that everyone was against him and trying to kill him, that there was a plot to control his mind and to make him do things by brainwashing. After the first week in the hospital he was able to put on a facade of normality, denying that he was ill and covering up his delusions. In brief contacts he appeared pleasant, talkative, likeable and friendly, well-dressed, coherent and relevant, asserting that all he needed was a short rest. More extended interviewing revealed that he thought that people did not like him, that someone was trying to kill him because he was Christ, that this was not a hospital, that he could trust no one, that people were trying to control him and make him do things. Under pressure he would become angry and talk about visions and doing battle for humanity.

LOWEST PRETREATMENT LEVEL OF HEALTH-SICKNESS.

Patient #145: Of the four patients given the *lowest* pretreatment Menninger Health-Sickness rating (10 points), this 17-year-old single Negro girl would probably have seemed the sickest to the ordinary observer.

She had always been self-conscious and anxious and had been in a special school for a while because she was backward. For some time she had been complaining that her classmates and friends were plotting against her and talking about her. Two weeks before admission she became upset and confused at school. Sent home, she screamed, pleaded for forgiveness and said she wanted to die. In the hospital she was either almost mute or else excited and frightened, glancing wildly around the room and shouting to imaginary people. She took her clothes off; stayed awake all night screaming and yelling despite large amounts of sedatives; heard voices saying she would be killed; and when taken for a walk by several nurses, she attempted to throw herself in front of a car. The most contact that could be established was that she did tell the examiner her age and say that she was in school and that she knew she was in a hospital.

WORST PROGNOSIS.

Patient #115: This 26-year-old white male was given the *lowest* two-year prognosis for any patient on the Menninger Health-Sickness Scale (26 points—i.e., obviously unable to function autonomously and almost, but not quite, in need of hospital protection).

Up to age twelve he was anemic, sickly, sweet and obedient, studied music and had no friends. At that age a physician noted that he was strange and fearful; psychiatric treatment was recommended but not undertaken. In high school he was a lone wolf with only one interest—music. He could never tolerate criticism and finally quit school in anger because he felt that he was being insulted by his teacher. After this he attended college intermittently and part-time for six years, but he never completed the requirements for a degree. Three years before admission he began to hear voices making flippant comments on what he was doing and he started to see visions. He stayed alone in his room playing records, copying musical scores and doing wood carvings in a desultory fashion and making outrageous demands on his family, threatening them with bodily harm. Eight months before admission he broke up the walls and furniture of his room, but talked his way out of hospitalization when the police were called. He was finally admitted involuntarily after he attacked his mother. In the hospital he was circumstantial and evasive, suspicious and irritable, trying hard to put on a friendly healthy front and to explain away his behavior.

BEST PROGNOSIS.

Patient #214: This 29-year-old white married woman with four children admitted under involuntary commitment was given the *highest* two-year prognosis for any patient on the Menninger Health-Sickness rating (53 points—i.e., in the community, functioning quite well, but probably in need of some treatment or support to continue functioning satisfactorily).

As a child she did not form friendships easily. Since age twelve she had felt that people did not like her and said things about her. She was only a fair student and quit school in the twelfth grade to get married. She was not happy in her marriage and would often have temper tantrums when dissatisfied. However, she said that her husband was a good person and a fine father. She had few friends or outside interests, was shy and retiring, but worked successfully in an unskilled job as well as looked after her family. One month before admission she lost her appetite and started to hear voices telling her that her husband and her family physician were going to kill her, that someone was in love with her and that she should leave home. In the hospital she told the examiner that she knew she was ill, that she recognized that many of her thoughts were unrealistic and imaginary and that she needed help. She had a sense of humor and could, to a considerable extent, talk about her problems in a rational manner. She asked for help with future planning and said she was willing to cooperate with any form of treatment that might be necessary. However, at the same time she was impatient to go home and did not recognize that there might be a connection between her personal problems and her illness.

ADDITIONAL CASE EXAMPLES. The case extracts that were used to illustrate specific points in research design may also help to convey to the reader something of the nature of our patients. They will be found in Chapter 2 in the following sections: patients 1, 2 under "Patients Excluded as Not Meeting the Criteria for Acceptance"; patients 17, 18, 19 under "Patients Excluded for Other Reasons"; patients 22, 61 under "Electro-Convulsive Therapy"; patients 7, 9, 13 under "Ataraxic Drugs"; and patients 40, 80, 200 under "Treatment Duration."

CHAPTER V

Release Rate–A Global Criterion of Outcome

PHILIP R. A. MAY, M.D.

~~~~~~~~~~~~~~~~~~~~~~~~~~~~~~~

THE RELEASE RATES for the five treatment groups fell into two clusters. DRUG ALONE* and PSYCHOTHERAPY PLUS DRUG had high release rates (95–96 percent), while MILIEU and PSYCHO-THERAPY ALONE had relatively low ones (58 percent and 65 percent respectively). The ECT group (79 percent) occupied an intermediate position, the result of a high release rate for males (91 percent) and a low one for females (67 percent). The differences between the high and low clusters are highly significant.

Other analyses indicate that *drug* had an extremely significant effect in increasing the release rate, while there was relatively little effect from *psychotherapy.* There was no evidence of significant interaction between the effects of *drug* and *psychotherapy,* nor did the sex of the patient make any significant difference to the results, except for *ECT.* The data suggest that patients who are not given any "specific" treatment such as *ataraxic drugs, electroconvulsive*

* A list of conventional terms, abbreviations and notations will be found at the end of Chapter 3.

therapy or *individual psychotherapy* may be likely to remove themselves from the hospital prematurely and against medical advice.

RELEASE RATE

An obvious measure of the value of a treatment is whether or not it results in discharge from the hospital. Granted that a number of factors may influence the physician's decision to release a patient, the release rate (defined as the percent of patients released from any particular treatment group) nevertheless expresses in simple numerical form the end result of the complicated interactions of the hospital staff, the patient, his immediate family, and the socioeconomic context in which he functions. In this respect it represents a global assessment that combines the many points of view that focus on the patient.

Table 5.1 shows the relevant analysis of variance.

Table 5.1.   RELEASE RATE: ANALYSIS OF VARIANCE

Significance levels for the various effects at three successive stages of Winsorization, computed to four decimal places. The most representative, W_0, also shows the appropriate F-values in parentheses and a directional sign, (+) indicating better values for a particular treatment or for the female sex.

		W_0	W_1	W_2
Five treatments in general		.0001 (9.31)	.0001	.0001
Ataraxic drug	+	.0000 (37.01)	.0000	.0000
Psychotherapy	+	.5533 (0.35)	.2986	.3837
Sex (ECT included)	−	.3624 (0.85)	.3386	.3157
Sex (ECT excluded)	+	.9534 (0.95)	.9667	.8169
Interaction				
Sex × psychotherapy	−	.8041 (0.06)	.8110	.9563
Sex × drug	+	.4632 (0.54)	.4336	.5421
Psychotherapy × drug	+	.4892 (0.48)	.7657	.6220

There was an extremely significant difference in the percentage of patients successfully released from the different treatment groups. Allowing for the effect of differences between the two sexes, the *F*-ratio for overall treatment differences was 9.31 (.0001, W_0). This could not reasonably be attributed to any initial differences between the five groups as they had been satisfactorily equated. If adjustments are made by analysis of co-variance to estimate the release rates that would theoretically occur if the groups had been equated on sex and initial level on the Menninger Health-Sickness scale, we find that the rates

Figure 5-1   RELEASE RATES FOR THE 5 TREATMENTS

Percent released non-Winsorized (W_o), unadjusted and adjusted by co-variance for sex and initial level of health-sickness.

The lines depict Ducan Multiple Range Tests at the 95% and 99% protection levels, non-Winsorized data (W_o). Groups not connected by these lines are significantly different from one another at that level.

██████ = a lack of statistical significance at the 95% level

▪▪▪▪▪▪▪▪▪▪ = a lack of statistical significance at the 99% level

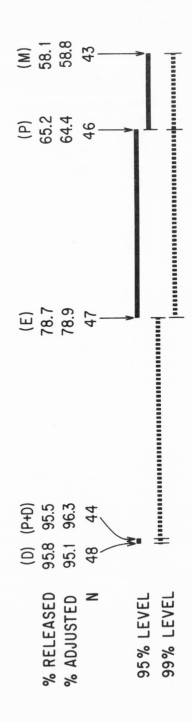

	(D)	(P+D)	(E)	(P)	(M)
% RELEASED	95.8	95.5	78.7	65.2	58.1
% ADJUSTED	95.1	96.3	78.9	64.4	58.8
N	48	44	47	46	43

95% LEVEL

99% LEVEL

and significance level are, for practical purposes, unaltered ($<$ .0005, Co-V).

Figure 5.1 shows the release rates (unadjusted and adjusted by co-variance) for the five treatment groups in rank order with a Multiple Range test.

The highest rates were for DRUG ALONE (95.8 percent unadjusted, 95.1 percent co-varied) and PSYCHOTHERAPY PLUS DRUG (95.5 percent unadjusted, 96.3 percent co-varied); for practical purposes, the release rates for these two could be considered identical. At the lower end, PSYCHOTHERAPY ALONE (65.2 percent unadjusted, 64.4 percent co-varied) had a higher release rate than MILIEU (58.1 percent unadjusted, 58.8 percent co-varied). The difference between these two is relatively small (D $>$ .05), and they are both highly significantly lower (D $<$ .01) than DRUG ALONE and PSYCHOTHERAPY PLUS DRUG. The rate for ECT is intermediate (78.7 percent unadjusted, 78.9 percent co-varied), significantly different (D $<$ .05) from DRUG ALONE, PSYCHOTHERAPY PLUS DRUG and MILIEU but not from PSYCHOTHERAPY ALONE (D $>$ .05).

Figure 5.2 shows the release rates for each treatment and sex separately. It is seen that the intermediate position of ECT is the result of a high rate for males (91.3 percent) and a low one for females (66.7 percent). The appearance of the ten subgroups is that of two clusters: one with high rates (DRUG ALONE and PSYCHOTHERAPY PLUS DRUG, both sexes) and one with low rates (PSYCHOTHERAPY ALONE and MILIEU). The ECT (male) group falls in the upper cluster, ECT (female) in the lower one; the difference between the two sexes being significant (D $<$ .05) for this treatment method only.

Omitting the ECT group from consideration, a three-way analysis of variance (Table 5.1) shows that the main factor in increasing releases was an extremely significant drug effect (F 37.01/.0000, W_0). *Psychotherapy* had no appreciable effect (.5533, W_0); gender was not an important factor for any treatment other than *ECT* (.9534, W_0); and there was no evidence of significant interplay or collision between *psychotherapy* and *drug* (.4892, W_0).

The figures given so far refer to releases in general, and it is of course necessary to consider whether there was any difference in the specific type or manner of discharge. In terms of destination, there was no particular difference between the treatments in the proportion discharged on their own, to relatives, or to a foster home or other sheltered placements. In terms of the hospital's attitude to the release, three patients from the MILIEU group and one from the ECT group left the hospital substantially against the wishes of their physician, although they had completed an adequate trial of treatment and were considered well

Figure 5-2   RELEASE RATES FOR EACH TREATMENT AND SEX SEPARATELY

Percent released non-Winsorized (W_o), unadjusted.

The lines depict Ducan Multiple Range Tests at the 95% and 99% protection levels, non-Winsorized data (W_o).
Groups not connected by these lines are significantly different from one another at that level.

████ = a lack of statistical significance at the 95% level

▪▪▪▪▪▪▪ = a lack of statistical significance at the 99% level enough to be counted as successfully released. In addition (as described in Chapter 2), six patients were discharged by Jury Trial or Against Medical Advice before they could have an adequate trial of treatment.* Taking all ten together, five patients were discharged against advice from MILIEU, two from PSYCHOTHERAPY ALONE and one from each of the three other groups. One hesitates to draw conclusions from such small numbers, but there is a significant difference between MILIEU and the other four treatment groups combined ($\chi^2 = 4.46/.05$—$.025$, W_0), suggesting that patients who are not given a specific treatment such as *ataraxic drugs, electroconvulsive therapy* or *individual psychotherapy* may be more likely to remove themselves prematurely from the hospital. There is no support for the commonly voiced belief that *electroconvulsive therapy* increases and that *individual psychotherapy* decreases the incidence of discharge against advice.

* These six patients were excluded from all analyses except the one described in the remainder of this paragraph, and they are not included in the other computations of release rate referred to in preceding paragraphs of this chapter.

CHAPTER VI

Length of Hospital Stay

PHILIP R. A. MAY, M.D.

CONSIDERING ONLY THOSE who were successfully released, the DRUG ALONE,* ECT and PSYCHOTHERAPY PLUS DRUG patients were released the fastest (130, 135 and 138 days respectively). The PSYCHOTHERAPY ALONE patients stayed the longest (185 days), with MILIEU in the middle (163 days). In the MILIEU group (but not in any of the others) there was a difference between male and female patients, females staying significantly longer. However, this difference would have been reduced if the females had been released when their physician wanted them to be released. *Drug* reduced Admission Stay to a highly significant degree, while *psychotherapy* prolonged it to an extent approaching significance. In fact, if the patients had stayed as long as their therapists had wanted them to, this particular effect of *psychotherapy* would have been highly significant.

There was also indication from the data for Stay to Failure that if a patient is given *individual psychotherapy,* with or without *ataraxic drugs,* the physician is likely to persist much longer before

* A list of conventional terms, abbreviations and notations will be found at the end of Chapter 3.

giving up than if he is using the other forms of treatment; and that he is likely to persist longest if he is using the combination of *individual psychotherapy plus drug.*

If one takes into consideration all patients including the failures as well as the successes, as in Admission Stay (L.R. 432) where the failures are assigned an arbitrary stay of 432 days, and Admission Stay to Failure, the effect of *drug* in shortening the stay becomes extremely significant and there is no substantial difference between the sexes, except in the case of *ECT* where female patients stayed longer than males to an extent approaching significance.

INTRODUCTION

How do the various treatments affect the length of time that the schizophrenic patient will stay in hospital? This is a deceptively simple question, for although hospital stay may appear to be a straightforward, practical, objective, no-nonsense standard for comparison, it is determined to a large extent not by the patient's illness per se, but by its subjective impact on those who treat him and on those to whom he will return. Moreover, the answer must be related to release rate. In fact, release rate may be defined as the proportion of patients discharged during a given period of hospital stay.

ADMISSION STAY

The question may be re-phrased in several ways. First, "Disregarding the failures (who were not released within the first year), if treatment was a success was there any difference between the five methods?" Table 6.1 summarizes the relevant analysis of variance. There was a highly significant difference between the five treatments. After separating out the effect of sex, the F-ratio for overall differences among the treatments was 3.75 (.0060, W_1); adjustment by analysis of co-variance to estimate the Admission Stay that would theoretically occur if the groups had been equated on sex and initial level on the Menninger Health-Sickness scale does not materially change the picture (.025–.01, Co–V). The significance level is increased successively through two stages of Winsorization as we pay less attention to the more extreme cases, signifying that the differences observed are likely to be general throughout the groups and not confined to a few unusual cases. (Extremes were most apparent in the male PSYCHOTHERAPY group, where one patient stayed much longer and one patient got out much faster than the general spread of the remainder.)

Table 6.1.   ADMISSION STAY: ANALYSIS OF VARIANCE

Significance levels for the various effects at three successive stages of Winsorization, computed to four decimal places. The most representative, W_1, also shows the appropriate F-values in parentheses and a directional sign, (+) indicating better values for a particular treatment or for the female sex.

	W_0	W_1	W_2
Five treatments in general	.0191	.0060 (3.75)	.0045
Ataraxic drug	.0074	+ .0039 (8.32)	.0035
Psychotherapy	.1941	− .0987 (2.73)	.0247
Sex (ECT included)	.6887	+ .7945 (0.07)	.7683
Sex (ECT excluded)	.6929	− .7629 (0.09)	.7134
Interaction			
Sex × psychotherapy	.0751	− .0564 (3.61)	.0247
Sex × drug	.0254	− .0219 (6.18)	.0093
Psychotherapy × drug	.5232	− .4685 (0.53)	.4347

Figure 6.1 shows the mean Admission Stay for the five treatments in rank order with a Multiple Range test. The DRUG ALONE, ECT and PSYCHOTHERAPY PLUS DRUG patients were released the fastest (130, 135 and 138 days respectively), significantly more rapidly ($D < .05$) than the PSYCHOTHERAPY ALONE patients who remained in hospital the longest (185 days). The differences between DRUG ALONE, ECT and PSYCHOTHERAPY PLUS DRUG are not significant ($D > .05$). The MILIEU group was in the middle (163 days), not significantly different ($D > .05$) from any of the other groups.

Eliminating the ECT group, a three-way analysis of variance (Table 6.1) shows that the main factor in shortening the stay is a highly significant *drug* effect (F 8.32/.0039, W_1). *Psychotherapy* prolonged the stay to an extent that approached significance (F 2.73/.0987, W_1). There was no significant interaction between the effects of *psychotherapy* and *drug* (.4685, W_1).

Figure 6.2 shows the means for the treatments and sexes separately. Admission Stay for the male and female ECT groups was almost identical; indeed, if one pays less attention to the extreme values (Winsorization) their rank order is reversed. By contrast, there was some evidence that the sexes responded differentially to the other treatments, giving rise to the significant interaction effects shown in Table 6.1. Examination of the means in Figure 6.2 suggests that this could be considered to be mainly a peculiarity of the MILIEU group. For DRUG ALONE, PSYCHO-

Figure 6-1 ADMISSION STAY FOR THE 5 TREATMENTS

Stay is given in days to nearest whole day, non-Winsorized (W_o), unadjusted and adjusted by co-variance for sex and initial level of health-sickness.

The lines depict Ducan Multiple Range Tests at the 95% and 99% protection levels, non-Winsorized data (W_o). Groups not connected by these lines are significantly different from one another at that level.

━━━ = a lack of statistical significance at the 95% level

┄┄┄ = a lack of statistical significance at the 99% level

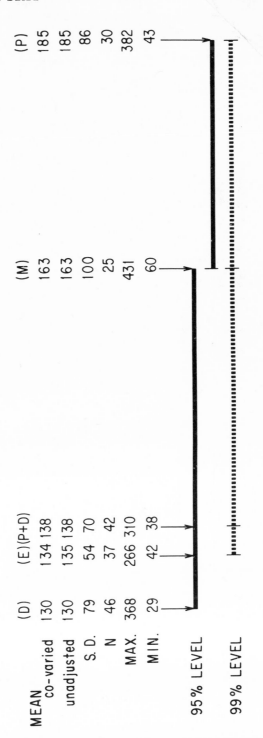

MEAN	(D)	(E)	(P+D)	(M)	(P)
co-varied	130	134	138	163	185
unadjusted	130	135	138	163	185
S.D.	79	54	70	100	86
N	46	37	42	25	30
MAX.	368	266	310	431	382
MIN.	29	42	38	60	43

95% LEVEL

99% LEVEL

Figure 6-2   ADMISSION STAY FOR EACH TREATMENT AND SEX SEPARATELY

Stay is given in days to nearest whole day, non-Winsorized (W_o).

The lines depict Ducan Multiple Range Tests at the 95% and 99% protection levels, non-Winsorized data (W_o).
Groups not connected by these lines are significantly different from one another at that level.

▬▬▬ = a lack of statistical significance at the 95% level

▪▪▪▪▪▪▪▪ = a lack of statistical significance at the 99% level

	$(\frac{M}{M})$	$(\frac{F}{D})$	$(\frac{F}{P+D})$	$(\frac{M}{E})$	$(\frac{F}{E})$	$(\frac{M}{D})$	$(\frac{M}{P+D})$	$(\frac{F}{P})$	$(\frac{M}{P})$	$(\frac{F}{M})$
MEAN	119	121	122	134	135	138	156	183	188	197
S.D.	48	55	54	55	54	98	82	99	72	117
N	11	23	22	21	16	23	20	16	14	14
MAX.	216	286	256	226	266	368	310	382	361	431
MIN.	72	40	38	42	83	29	46	43	52	60

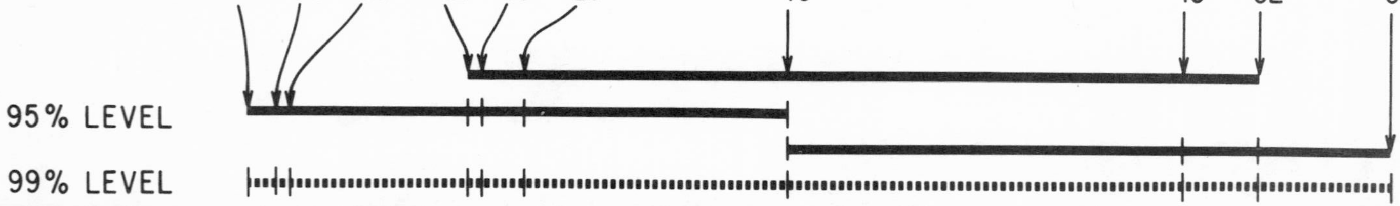

95% LEVEL

99% LEVEL

THERAPY PLUS DRUG and PSYCHOTHERAPY ALONE, males stayed longer than females, but not significantly so. For MILIEU, however, the difference between the sexes is greater and in the opposite direction: Females stayed (197 days) significantly (D < .05) longer than males (119 days). (It should be noted that this is not associated with any particular difference in release rate: The release rate on MILIEU was 55 percent for males, 61 percent for females.)

As a basis for comparison, Admission Stay is somewhat contaminated by the inclusion of the initial evaluation period before treatment was actually started. Subtracting the work-up period heightens the intergroup differences, although only to a small extent. For example, the significance level for differences between the five treatments is raised from .0060 to .0040 (W_1) and for *drug* effect from .0039 to .0028 (W_1). There is little change in the significance levels for *psychotherapy* and other effects.

It is possible to argue both ways on whether periods of leave should or should not be included in computations of stay. In point of fact, however, further adjustment for leave makes little or no difference to the figures given above.

It is perhaps of interest to consider how long the patient's therapist would have liked him to stay in hospital, as well as how long he *actually* stayed. Adjustment from Admission Stay to Ideal Admission Stay raises the average stay for PSYCHOTHERAPY ALONE, PSYCHOTHERAPY PLUS DRUG and ECT by 25, 20 and 14 days respectively. For DRUG ALONE, stay would be reduced by 5 days, for MILIEU by 19 days. The net result would be to promote MILIEU from fourth to second rank in terms of speed of release, second only to DRUG ALONE. The rank order for Ideal Admission Stay would otherwise be the same as for Admisson Stay. There would also be some changes in significance levels. Thus *psychotherapy* would have a very highly significant effect in prolonging Ideal Admission Stay (.0006, W_1), more so than for Admission Stay (.0987, W_1), and the difference between the PSYCHOTHERAPY ALONE and DRUG ALONE groups would be more significant in the Multiple Range test (D < .01). By contrast, the effect of *drug* in reducing stay would be less prominent for Ideal Admission Stay (.0160, W_1) than for Admission Stay (.0039, W_1).

The effect of adjusting for Ideal Stay was much the same in both sexes except in the case of MILIEU, where there was a marked sex difference—the mean stay of male MILIEU patients would have been unchanged if the therapist had had his way, but for MILIEU females it would have been reduced by 25 days. It will be remembered that for Admission Stay there was a significant difference between males (119 days) and females (197 days): Adjustment for Ideal Stay makes this

Figure 6-3   ADMISSION STAY TO FAILURE FOR THE 5 TREATMENTS

Stay is given in days to nearest whole day, non-Winsorized (W_o).

The positions of the DRUG and PSYCHOTHERAPY PLUS DRUG groups have been ghosted in. Multiple Range computations were not done for these two groups because the number of patients was so small.

The lines depict Ducan Multiple Range Tests at the 95% and 99% protection levels, non-Winsorized data (W_o). Groups not connected by these lines are significantly different from one another at that level.

▬▬▬ = a lack of statistical significance at the 95% level

▪▪▪▪▪▪▪ = a lack of statistical significance at the 99% level

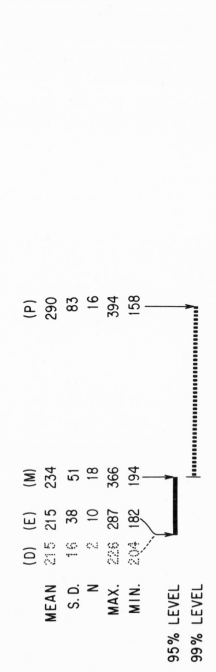

	(D)	(E)	(M)	(P)	(P+D)
MEAN	215	215	234	290	394
S.D.	16	38	51	83	12
N	2	10	18	16	2
MAX.	226	287	366	394	402
MIN.	204	182	194	158	385

95% LEVEL
99% LEVEL

difference less pronounced, although it still approaches the significant level.

ADMISSION STAY TO FAILURE

One might ask, "For the failures, was there any difference between the treatment methods in how long the physician persisted before giving up?" Figure 6.3 shows the treatment group means in rank order for Stay To Failure (i.e., for those patients not released).

For PSYCHOTHERAPY ALONE the average time to giving up (290 days) is highly significantly longer than for DRUG ALONE and ECT (215 days, $D < .01$) and significantly longer than for MILIEU (234 days, $D < .05$). The DRUG ALONE, ECT and MILIEU groups are not significantly different from each other ($D > .05$).

Leaving out the ECT group, a three-way analysis of variance shows that *psychotherapy* had an extremely significant effect in prolonging the time to giving up (F 48.67/.0000, W_0). There is also an extremely significant interaction (F 13.47/.0001, W_0) between the effects of *psychotherapy* and *drug*. When *psychotherapy* was combined with *drug*, the patient was given a *longer* trial than with either of these two treatments alone. However, if *psychotherapy* was not being given, then *drug shortened* the trial period. If treatment was a failure, that conclusion was likely to be reached quicker in the DRUG ALONE group than in MILIEU.

Figure 6.4 shows the means in rank order for each sex and treatment separately. The numbers were not sufficient to examine the influence of sex on Stay to Failure for the ECT, DRUG ALONE or PSYCHOTHERAPY PLUS DRUG groups. For the other two groups there were eight or nine failures of each sex. When treating males, the therapists gave up after about the same length of time ($D > .05$) for MILIEU (247 days) as for PSYCHOTHERAPY ALONE (251 days). However, when treating females, they persisted much longer ($D < .01$) for PSYCHOTHERAPY ALONE (328 days) than for MILIEU (220 days).

With a small number of patients, the possibility of being misled by a few extreme cases is such that one hesitates even to speculate. However, if these figures indicate anything other than the workings of chance, it is that if a female patient is given individual psychotherapy, the therapist is likely to persist longer before giving up than if he is treating the patient with *electroconvulsive therapy, ataraxic drugs* or *milieu therapy*. This is not so for males, and whatever the sex of the patient, the therapist is likely to persist longest if he is using the combination of *individual psychotherapy* and *ataraxic drugs*.

Figure 6-4   ADMISSION STAY TO FAILURE FOR EACH TREATMENT AND SEX SEPARATELY

Stay is given in days to nearest whole day, non-Winsorized (W_o).

The positions of certain groups have been ghosted in where Multiple Range computations were not done because the numbers were so small. Male DRUG is not shown because there were no failures in this group.

The lines depict Ducan Multiple Range Tests at the 95% and 99% protection levels, non-Winsorized data (W_o). Groups not connected by these lines are significantly different from one another at that level.

▬▬▬ = a lack of statistical significance at the 95% level

▪▪▪▪▪▪ = a lack of statistical significance at the 99% level

	$\left(\frac{F}{E}\right)$	$\left(\frac{F}{D}\right)$	$\left(\frac{F}{M}\right)$	$\left(\frac{M}{E}\right)$	$\left(\frac{M}{M}\right)$	$\left(\frac{M}{P}\right)$	$\left(\frac{F}{P}\right)$	$\left(\frac{M}{P+D}\right)$	$\left(\frac{F}{P+D}\right)$
MEAN	211	215	220	230	247	251	328	395	402
S.D.	35	16	46	63	55	80	71	0	0
N	8	2	9	2	9	8	8	1	1
MAX.	287	226	339	274	336	371	394	395	402
	182	204	194	185	206	158	218	395	402

95% } LEVEL
99% }

ADMISSION STAY (L.R. 432)

"Did treatment make any difference to the length of stay, considering not only those patients who were successfully released but also those who were failures and who remained in the hospital?"

Table 6.2 summarizes the relevant analysis of variance. There was an

Table 6.2. ADMISSION STAY (LR 432): ANALYSIS OF VARIANCE

Significance levels for the various effects at three successive stages of Winsorization, computed to four decimal places. The most representative, W_1, also shows the appropriate F-values in parentheses and a directional sign, (+) indicating better values for a particular treatment or for the female sex.

	W_0		W_1	W_2
Five treatments in general	.0001		.0000 (13.35)	.0000
Ataraxic drug	.0000	+	.0000 (54.17)	.0000
Psychotherapy	.8535	−	.9284 (0.01)	.8501
Sex (ECT included)	.4234	−	.4324 (0.63)	.3859
Sex (ECT excluded)	.9185	+	.8782 (0.02)	.8312
Interaction				
Sex × psychotherapy	.2727	−	.2086 (1.58)	.2211
Sex × drug	.5412	−	.5409 (0.37)	.4796
Psychotherapy × drug	.7163	+	.8640 (0.03)	.7972

extremely significant difference between the five treatments. After allowing for the effect of sex differences between the groups, the F-ratio for overall treatment differences was 13.35 (.0000, W_1), and there is no material change in significance level if co-variance adjustments are made for sex and initial level on the Menninger Health-Sickness scale ($< .0005$, Co-V). The F-ratio increases through two successive stages of Winsorization, demonstrating that the differences are likely to be general rather than confined to a few cases. (Outliers were conspicuous in female PSYCHOTHERAPY PLUS DRUG where the longest and shortest stays were distant from the remainder of this particular group.)

Figure 6.5 shows the mean Admission Stay (L.R. 432) for the five treatment groups in rank order with a Multiple Range test. DRUG ALONE and PSYCHOTHERAPY PLUS DRUG are close together at one extreme (142 and 151 days respectively) and not significantly different from each other (D > .05). MILIEU (275 days) and PSYCHOTHERAPY ALONE (271 days) are close together at the other extreme. ECT (198 days) is in the middle, highly significantly shorter than MILIEU and PSYCHOTHERAPY

Figure 6-5   ADMISSION STAY (LR 432) FOR THE 5 TREATMENTS

Stay is given in days to nearest whole day, non-Winsorized (W_o), unadjusted and adjusted by co-variance for sex and initial level of health-sickness.

The lines depict Ducan Multiple Range Tests at the 95% and 99% protection levels, non-Winsorized data (W_o). Groups not connected by these lines are significantly different from one another at that level.

▬▬▬ = a lack of statistical significance at the 95% level

▪▪▪▪▪▪ = a lack of statistical significance at the 99% level

MEAN	(D)	(P+D)	(E)	(P)	(M)
co-varied	144	149	197	273	274
unadjusted	142	151	198	271	275
S. D.	99	92	132	138	154
N	48	44	47	46	43
MAX.	432	432	432	432	432
MIN.	29	38	42	43	60

95% LEVEL

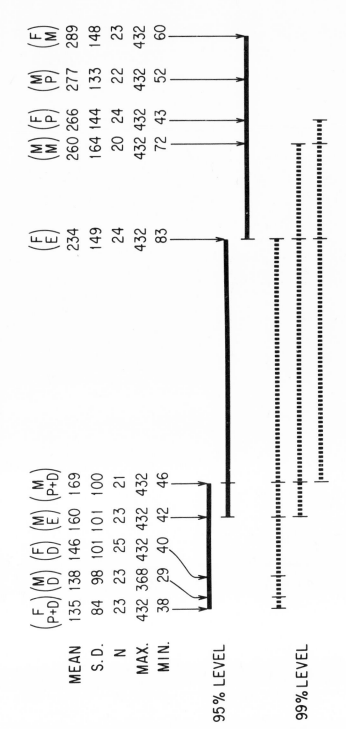

Stay is given in days to the nearest whole day, non-Winsorized (W_0).

The lines depict Ducan Multiple Range Tests at the 95% and 99% protection levels, non-Winsorized data (W_0).
Groups not connected by these lines are significantly different from one another at that level.

━━━ = a lack of statistical significance at the 95% level

▪▪▪▪▪▪▪ = a lack of statistical significance at the 99% level

	$\binom{F}{P+D}$	$\binom{M}{D}$	$\binom{F}{D}$	$\binom{M}{E}$	$\binom{M}{P+D}$	$\binom{F}{E}$	$\binom{M}{M}$	$\binom{F}{P}$	$\binom{M}{P}$	$\binom{F}{M}$
MEAN	135	138	146	160	169	234	260	266	277	289
S.D.	84	98	101	101	100	149	164	144	133	148
N	23	23	25	23	21	24	20	24	22	23
MAX.	432	368	432	432	432	432	432	432	432	432
MIN.	38	29	40	42	46	83	72	43	52	60

95% LEVEL

99% LEVEL

ALONE (D < .01), significantly longer than DRUG ALONE (D < .05) and almost significantly longer (D > .05) than PSYCHOTHERAPY PLUS DRUG. As for release rate, the intermediate position of ECT is the result of a sex difference, although in this case it only approaches significance (D > .05): Female patients given ECT stayed in the hospital longer than male patients (234 days compared with 160). This is shown in Figure 6.6 which presents the means for the sexes and treatments separately.

Table 6.2 shows that, omitting the ECT group from consideration, the main factor in shortening Admission Stay (L.R. 432) is an extremely significant *drug* effect (F 54.17/.0000, W_1). *Psychotherapy* did not significantly prolong Admission Stay (L.R. 432) (.9284, W_1)—in contrast to admission Stay to Failure, which was prolonged to an extremely significant degree. In other words, *drug* shortened hospital stay whatever way you look at the failures. *Psychotherapy,* however, prolonged hospital stay to a significant extent only when stay is measured in such a way as to emphasize (weight) the speed with which a decision as to failure can be reached (as in Admission Stay to Failure). Admission Stay (L.R. 432), gives no credit for speed of decision, as all failures are assigned 432 days no matter how quickly or slowly the decision was reached.*

There was no significant difference between the two sexes for any treatment other than ECT. Interaction between *psychotherapy* and *drug* was not significant (.8640, W_1).

---

* Another way of looking at this statistic is that it represents the situation as it would be if there were no available alternative that could be tried in the event of failure, or as if any alternative was equally ineffective.

CHAPTER VII

Nurses' Assessment of Outcome

PHILIP R. A. MAY, M.D.

~~~~~~

BY THEIR RATINGS for MACC* Affect, Cooperation, Communication and Total Score, the nurses saw an extremely significant difference among the five treatment groups ($.0001$, W_0). PSYCHOTHERAPY PLUS DRUG and DRUG ALONE were the most effective, very close together ($D > .05$) and highly significantly better ($D < .01$) than PSYCHOTHERAPY ALONE or MILIEU, which, as the least effective treatments, were also very close together. ECT was in the middle, distinguishably less effective ($D < .05$ or $.01$) than PSYCHOTHERAPY PLUS DRUG and DRUG ALONE by all four measures, and more effective ($D < .05$) than PSYCHOTHERAPY ALONE and MILIEU by ratings of Cooperation and Total Score. *Drug* had an extremely significant beneficial effect, but the effect of *psychotherapy* was nonsignificant, and there was no indication of interaction between the effects of *psychotherapy* and *drug*.

Essentially the same results were obtained for the ISR except

---

* A list of conventional terms, abbreviations and notations will be found at the end of Chapter 3.

that there was a faint suggestion (clearly not significant) of inter-
action between the effects of *psychotherapy* and *drug*. PSYCHO-
THERAPY ALONE was (nonsignificantly) worse than MILIEU, but
PSYCHOTHERAPY PLUS DRUG was (nonsignificantly) better than
DRUG ALONE.

The findings for the nurses' MHS ratings were similar except
that MILIEU was rated, on the average, somewhat (nonsignificantly) better than ECT and significantly better (D < .05) than
PSYCHOTHERAPY ALONE. There was also a little more (borderline)
evidence of interaction between the effects of *psychotherapy* and
drug.

For MACC (Motility) there was no significant difference among
the five treatment groups and no evidence of significant effect from
either *drug* or *psychotherapy*.

There was some indication of differences in response between
the two sexes. On ECT, males did better than females; significantly
so for MACC (Affect); and nonsignificantly so for MACC (Total,
Cooperation and Communication) and ISR. On PSYCHOTHERAPY
PLUS DRUG, males did significantly better than females as judged
by TROUBLERAT *final* status (but not by TROUBLERAT
change, nor by any of the other nursing measures).

OVERVIEW

The nurses' viewpoint is reflected by their ratings on the MACC (including Total Score as well as the separate factors of Motility, Affect,
Cooperation and Communication); the Menninger Health-Sickness Scale
(MHS) and the Idiosyncratic Symptom Rating Scale (ISR). A preliminary discriminant analysis of the various scores derived from the
ISR showed the simple sum of the ratings for the *most important symptom* and the *second most important symptom* (IDIORAT 1 + 2) was
a good discriminator between the treatment groups. The best discrimination was obtained by weighting this in terms of the amount of trouble
or concern the symptoms caused the staff of the unit (TROUBLERAT
1 + 2). Accordingly, these two scores were chosen to represent the ISR
in this chapter.

MACC (MOTILITY)

The first area of behavior covered by the MACC is Motility, three items
relating to boisterous or agitated overactivity. Although DRUG ALONE

and PSYCHOTHERAPY PLUS DRUG reduced Motility the most, there was no significant difference between the five treatment groups (.5320, W_0); no significant effect from *psychotherapy* (.60–.50, Co-V) or from *drug* (.30–.20, Co-V); and no significant interaction between the effects of *psychotherapy* and *drug* (.9095, W_0).

MACC (AFFECT, COOPERATION, COMMUNICATION, TOTAL SCORE)

Statistics from the analyses of variance for Total Score and the three other MACC subscales (Affect, Cooperation and Communication*) are given in Table 7.1 (A–D). The treatment group means are shown in rank order with Multiple Range tests in Figures 7.1 (E–H). (Higher scores indicate less pathology.) The picture is very similar for all four, with extremely significant differences among the five treatments (.0001, W_0).

The mean scores for PSYCHOTHERAPY PLUS DRUG patients and DRUG ALONE are extremely close together and obviously not distinguishable from each other with confidence (D > .05). Both groups are highly significantly better (D < .01) than PSYCHOTHERAPY ALONE and MILIEU, which are also extremely close together and obviously not clearly separable (D > .05).

ECT is in the middle, significantly or highly significantly less effective than PSYCHOTHERAPY PLUS DRUG and DRUG ALONE in terms of Affect (D < .01), Cooperation (D < .05), Communication (D < .01) and Total Score (D < .01). Although ECT could not be distinguished (D > .05) from either PSYCHOTHERAPY ALONE or MILIEU in terms of Affect and Communication, there was a significant difference (D < .05) in Cooperation and Total Score.

Three-way analysis of variance shows that by all four criteria *drug* had an extremely significant beneficial effect (.0000, W_0), while the effect of *psychotherapy* was not significant (ranging from .9750, W_0 for Affect to .8697, W_0 for Cooperation). There was no evidence of significant interaction between the effects of *drug* and *psychotherapy* (ranging from .9433, W_0 for Cooperation to .5566, W_0 for Affect).

On ECT, males did better than females by all four criteria**, the difference being highly significant for Affect (D < .01) but not significant for the other three measures (D > .05).

---

* The Affect subscale seems to measure a paranoid quality: its three items include the adjectives irritable, grouchy, sullen, bitter. The content of the two other subscales is satisfactorily indicated by their names.
** The *final status* means for the two sexes on *ECT* were as follows: Affect: 9.4 (F), 11.7 (M); Cooperation; 15.3 (F), 16.4 (M); Communication: 15.0 (F), 16.3 (M); Total: 39.7 (F), 44.4 (M).

Table 7.1. MACC: ANALYSIS OF VARIANCE

Significance levels for the various effects at three successive stages of Winsorization, computed to four decimal places. The most representative, W_0, also shows the appropriate F-values in parentheses and a directional sign, (+) indicating better final values (or more change) for a particular treatment or for the female sex.

7.1A. TOTAL	W_0 Change		W_0 Final		W_1 Final	W_2 Final
Five treatments in general		.0001		.0000 (13.32)	.0000	.0000
Ataraxic drug	+	.0000	+	.0000 (49.76)	.0000	.0000
Psychotherapy	+	.6873	+	.9672 (0.00)	.8764	.9676
Sex (ECT included)	−	.6500	+	.9249 (0.01)	.9637	.9837
Sex (ECT excluded)	+	.9468	+	.3369 (0.92)	.3542	.3611
Interaction						
Sex × psychotherapy	+	.3763	+	.3268 (0.96)	.2628	.2776
Sex × drug	−	.1360	−	.8150 (0.05)	.8729	.9629
Psychotherapy × drug	+	.9510	−	.8737 (0.03)	.8452	.8390

7.1B. AFFECT	W_0 Change		W_0 Final		W_1 Final	W_2 Final
Five treatments in general		.0001		.0001 (11.60)	.0001	.0000
Ataraxic drug	+	.0000	+	.0000 (45.12)	.0000	.0000
Psychotherapy	+	.4575	+	.9750 (0.00)	.9576	.9336
Sex (ECT included)	+	.9481	−	.0334 (4.62)	.0288	.0207
Sex (ECT excluded)	+	.4178	−	.3822 (0.76)	.3883	.3513
Interaction						
Sex × psychotherapy	+	.6341	+	.2942 (1.10)	.2807	.2473
Sex × drug	−	.0620	−	.2488 (1.33)	.2116	.2494
Psychotherapy × drug	−	.5629	−	.5566 (0.35)	.5660	.5672

7.1C. COOPERATION	W_0 Change		W_0 Final		W_1 Final	W_2 Final
Five treatments in general		.0001		.0001 (12.20)	.0000	.0000
Ataraxic drug	+	.0000	+	.0000 (45.84)	.0000	.0000
Psychotherapy	+	.8154	+	.8697 (0.03)	.7849	.7633
Sex (ECT included)	−	.6859	+	.2977 (1.10)	.3960	.3585
Sex (ECT excluded)	+	.9986	+	.1022 (2.67)	.1323	.1094
Interaction						
Sex × psychotherapy	+	.3472	+	.5543 (0.35)	.5233	.5787
Sex × drug	−	.1985	−	.9895 (0.00)	.9726	.9777
Psychotherapy × drug	+	.6230	+	.9433 (0.01)	.9966	.9853

7.1D. COMMUNICATION	W_0 Change		W_0 Final		W_1 Final	W_2 Final
Five treatments in general		.0001		.0001 (10.48)	.0001	.0000
Ataraxic drug	+	.0000	+	.0000 (39.31)	.0000	.0000
Psychotherapy	+	.8431	−	.9082 (0.01)	.8922	.8115
Sex (ECT included)	−	.3832	+	.5849 (0.30)	.7195	.7429
Sex (ECT excluded)	−	.7072	+	.2386 (1.39)	.2806	.2789
Interaction						
Sex × psychotherapy	+	.4298	+	.2636 (1.25)	.2481	.2792
Sex × drug	−	.1782	+	.9755 (0.00)	.8616	.7797
Psychotherapy × drug	−	.9442	−	.8705 (0.03)	.8639	.9381

Figure 7-1 E-H NURSES' MACC: FINAL SCORES IN RANK ORDER FOR THE 5 TREATMENTS

Scores are non-Winsorized (W_o), expressed to one place of decimals, unadjusted and adjusted by co-variance for sex and initial level. Higher scores indicate less pathology.

The lines depict Ducan Multiple Range Tests at the 95% and 99% protection levels, non-Winsorized data (W_o). Groups not connected by these lines are significantly different from one another at that level.

▬▬▬▬ = a lack of statistical significance at the 95% level

▪▪▪▪▪▪▪▪ = a lack of statistical significance at the 99% level

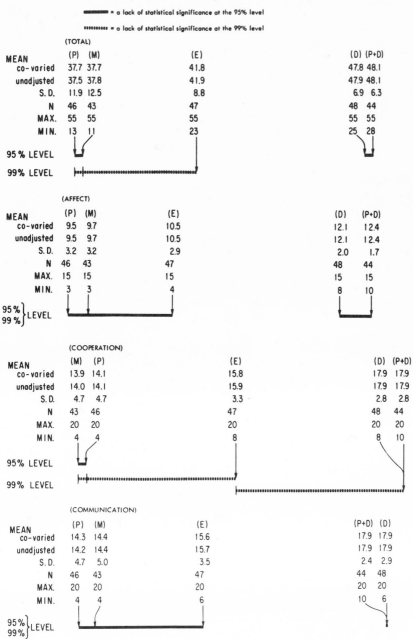

(TOTAL)

MEAN	(P)	(M)	(E)	(D)	(P+D)
co-varied	37.7	37.7	41.8	47.8	48.1
unadjusted	37.5	37.8	41.9	47.9	48.1
S.D.	11.9	12.5	8.8	6.9	6.3
N	46	43	47	48	44
MAX.	55	55	55	55	55
MIN.	13	11	23	25	28

95% LEVEL

99% LEVEL

(AFFECT)

MEAN	(P)	(M)	(E)	(D)	(P+D)
co-varied	9.5	9.7	10.5	12.1	12.4
unadjusted	9.5	9.7	10.5	12.1	12.4
S.D.	3.2	3.2	2.9	2.0	1.7
N	46	43	47	48	44
MAX.	15	15	15	15	15
MIN.	3	3	4	8	10

95% } LEVEL
99% }

(COOPERATION)

MEAN	(M)	(P)	(E)	(D)	(P+D)
co-varied	13.9	14.1	15.8	17.9	17.9
unadjusted	14.0	14.1	15.9	17.9	17.9
S.D.	4.7	4.7	3.3	2.8	2.8
N	43	46	47	48	44
MAX.	20	20	20	20	20
MIN.	4	4	8	8	10

95% LEVEL

99% LEVEL

(COMMUNICATION)

MEAN	(P)	(M)	(E)	(P+D)	(D)
co-varied	14.3	14.4	15.6	17.9	17.9
unadjusted	14.2	14.4	15.7	17.9	17.9
S.D.	4.7	5.0	3.5	2.4	2.9
N	46	43	47	44	48
MAX.	20	20	20	20	20
MIN.	4	4	6	10	6

95% } LEVEL
99% }

On DRUG ALONE, females did better than males in terms of Affect, Cooperation and Total Score† but not significantly so. For the other treatment methods, the differences between the sexes are small and of little significance.

NURSES' MHS

The analysis of variance for the nurses' Menninger Health-Sickness ratings is shown in Table 7.2 and the treatment group means in rank order in Figure 7.2. (Higher scores indicate relative health.)

Table 7.2.   NURSES' MHS: ANALYSIS OF VARIANCE

Significance levels for the various effects at three successive stages of Winsorization, computed to four decimal places. The most representative, W_0 (Change) and W_1 (Final), also show the appropriate F-values in parentheses and a directional sign, (+) indicating better final values (or more change) for a particular treatment or for the female sex.

	W_0 Final		W_0 Change		W_1 Final	W_2 Final
Five treatments in general	.0005		.0151		.0001 (6.27)	.0001
Ataraxic drug	.0002	+	.0017	+	.0000 (16.79)	.0000
Psychotherapy	.1256	−	.7545	−	.0525 (0.76)	.0700
Sex (ECT included)	.7132	+	.3695	+	.9593 (0.00)	.8740
Sex (ECT excluded)	.5764	+	.4790	+	.5962 (0.28)	.5181
Interaction						
Sex × psychotherapy	.7510	−	.4986	+	.7351 (0.11)	.6383
Sex × drug	.5922	−	.4017	+	.6985 (0.15)	.6767
Psychotherapy × drug	.1460	−	.1465	−	.2523 (1.31)	.2545

In the case of *final status* MHS ratings, one stage of Winsorizing was necessary to lessen the effect of unusual extreme cases and so obtain statistics that may be regarded as reasonably representative of the patient groups. In particular, three patients were rated by the nurses as 20–30 points higher than the next lower person in their group (one each in the male and female PSYCHOTHERAPY PLUS DRUG groups and one in the female ECT group). It is also of interest that the non-Winsorized upper range of the *final status* ratings given by the psychoanalysts to the same patients on the same scale corresponds roughly with the twice-Winsorized range for the nurses' ratings—evidently a few patients seem very well to the nurses, but not to the psychoanalysts.

No Winsorizing was necessary to obtain acceptably representative

† The *final status* means the two sexes on DRUG ALONE were as follows: Affect 12.4 (F), 11.8 (M); Cooperation: 18.6 (F), 17.1 (M); Total: 49.6 (F), 46.0 (M).

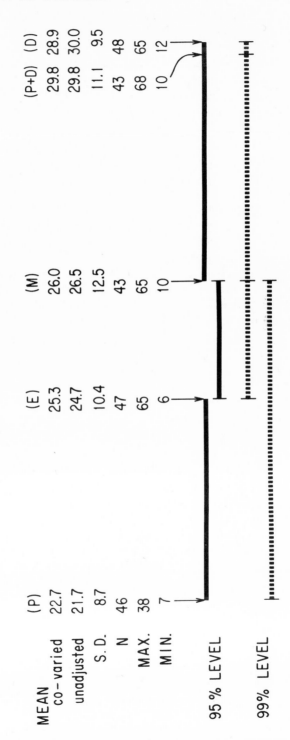

Scores are non-Winsorized (W_o), expressed to one place of decimals, unadjusted and adjusted by co-variance for sex and initial level. Higher scores indicate relative health.

The lines depict Ducan Multiple Range Tests at the 95% and 99% protection levels, non-Winsorized data (W_o). Groups not connected by these lines are significantly different from one another at that level.

▬▬▬ = a lack of statistical significance at the 95% level

▪▪▪▪▪▪▪ = a lack of statistical significance at the 99% level

MEAN	(P)	(E)	(M)	(P+D)	(D)
co-varied	22.7	25.3	26.0	29.8	28.9
unadjusted	21.7	24.7	26.5	29.8	30.0
S.D.	8.7	10.4	12.5	11.1	9.5
N	46	47	43	43	48
MAX.	38	65	65	68	65
MIN.	7	6	10	10	12

95% LEVEL

99% LEVEL

figures for *change* which was not so affected by outliers. However, there was some disparity between the results for *change* and *final status* in that the differences among the five treatment groups and the separate effects of *psychotherapy* and *drug* were assigned somewhat lower levels of significance by the criterion of *change* than *by final status*. In this case, co-variance adjustment (which takes initial level into consideration) is appropriate since a supplemental analysis indicated that outcome depended on sex and initial level to about the same extent for all five treatments. Accordingly, unless specified otherwise, the following discussion will focus on statistics that apply to scores adjusted by co-variance.

In general, there was a very highly significant difference among the five treatments (.001–.0005, Co-V). The PSYCHOTHERAPY PLUS DRUG (29.8) and DRUG ALONE (28.9) groups had the highest (healthiest) mean scores, not significantly different from each other (D > .05) but highly distinguishable (D < .01) from PSYCHOTHERAPY ALONE which had the lowest mean score (22.7). For MILIEU (26.0) and ECT (25.3), which ranked third and fourth respectively, the only intergroup distinctions that can be asserted with confidence (D < .05) are that ECT was less effective than PSYCHOTHERAPY PLUS DRUG and DRUG ALONE, and that MILIEU was more effective than PSYCHOTHERAPY ALONE.

Omitting the ECT group from consideration, three-way analysis of variance indicates that *drug* had a very highly significant beneficial effect (< .001, Co-V), and that *psychotherapy* had a nonsignificant adverse effect (.40–.30, Co-V). There was some (doubtful) evidence of interaction between the effects of *drug* and *psychotherapy* (change .1465, W_0; final .2523, W_1; .10–.20, Co–V). PSYCHOTHERAPY ALONE was worse than MILIEU to an extent approaching significance (.10, Co-V), but PSYCHOTHERAPY PLUS DRUG was (nonsignificantly) better than DRUG ALONE (.70–.60, Co-V). The sex of the patient seemed to make no material difference to outcome for any form of treatment.

IDIOSYNCRATIC SYMPTOMS (ISR)

Table 7.3 gives the analysis of variance for TROUBLERAT 1 + 2, the sum of the trouble-weighted ratings for the severity of each patient's two most important symptoms. Figure 7.3 shows the treatment means in rank order with a Multiple Range test (higher scores indicate more severe symptomatology, more trouble). For change, one stage of Winsorizing was necessary to diminish the effect of extreme cases and obtain suitably representative statistics. However, this did not alter the order of the groups. For final status no Winsorizing was required.

By TROUBLERAT 1 + 2, the differences among the five treatments were very highly (or even extremely) significant (change .0010, W_1; final .0001, W_0; < .0005, Co-V). PSYCHOTHERAPY ALONE, with a mean of 94.6, and MILIEU (90.0) ranked the lowest. These two were very close together (D > .05) and highly significantly worse (D < .01) than PSYCHOTHERAPY PLUS DRUG (50.8), which ranked the highest. DRUG ALONE (60.0) was second ranking, close to PSYCHOTHERAPY PLUS DRUG (D > .05) but significantly better than MILIEU (D < .05) and highly significantly better than PSYCHOTHERAPY ALONE (D < .01). ECT (83.5) was in the middle, distinguishable with confidence only from PSYCHO-THERAPY PLUS DRUG (D < .05).

Table 7.3.   IDIOSYNCRATIC SYMPTOMS (TROUBLERAT 1 + 2):
ANALYSIS OF VARIANCE

Significance levels for the various effects at three successive stages of Winsorization, computed to four decimal places. The most representative, W_1 (Change) and W_0 (Final), also show the appropriate F-values in parentheses and a directional sign, (+) indicating better final values (or more change) for a particular treatment or for the female sex.

		W_1		W_0	W_1	W_2
		Change		Final	Final	Final
Five treatments in general		.0010		.0001 (5.21)	.0001	.0001
Ataraxic drug	+	.0000	+	.0000 (20.24)	.0000	.0000
Psychotherapy	+	.0775	+	.7464 (0.10)	.7594	.7596
Sex (ECT included)	−	.0338	−	.0088 (7.10)	.0069	.0055
Sex (ECT excluded)	−	.0510	−	.0253 (5.01)	.0212	.0171
Interaction						
Sex × psychotherapy	−	.9946	+	.5628 (0.33)	.5717	.5721
Sex × drug	−	.4962	+	.3810 (0.77)	.3471	.3331
Psychotherapy × drug	−	.7714	−	.3564 (0.85)	.3680	.3562

Omitting the ECT group, a three-way analysis of variance showed that *drug* had an extremely significant beneficial effect (*F* 20.24/.0000, W_0). There was some disparity between the findings for *change* and *final status* in relation to the effect of *psychotherapy*. If this is resolved by using *co-varied* scores, it is demonstrated that, on the average, *psychotherapy* had a negligible effect (.99, Co-V). Although PSYCHO-THERAPY ALONE was somewhat worse than MILIEU (.50–.40, Co-V), and PSYCHOTHERAPY PLUS DRUG did better than DRUG ALONE (.50–.40, Co-V), the *F*-ratio for interaction effect is clearly nonsignificant, both for *final status* (.3564, W_1) and for *change* (.7714, W_0).

There were differences between the two sexes for the five treatments in general, significant for both *change* and *final status* (change .0338, W_1; final .0088, W_0). On MILIEU, ECT and PSYCHOTHERAPY PLUS DRUG, females changed less and had more troublesome symptoms at the end

Figure 7-3 NURSES' TROUBLERAT (1 + 2): FINAL SCORES IN RANK ORDER FOR THE 5 TREATMENTS

Scores are non-Winsorized (W_O), expressed to one place of decimals, unadjusted and adjusted by co-variance for sex and initial level. Higher scores indicate more severe symptoms.

The lines depict Ducan Multiple Range Tests at the 95% and 99% protection levels, non-Winsorized data (W_O). Groups not connected by these lines are significantly different from one another at that level.

▬▬▬ = a lack of statistical significance at the 95% level

▪▪▪▪▪▪▪▪ = a lack of statistical significance at the 99% level

MEAN	(P+D)	(D)	(E)	(M)	(P)
co-varied	50.8	59.3	84.7	87.7	96.2
unadjusted	50.8	60.0	83.5	90.0	94.6
S. D.	49.9	52.5	66.5	59.1	61.8
N	43	48	46	43	46
MAX.	142.8	155.8	174.8	174.8	175.5
MIN.	0	0	0	0	0

95% LEVEL

99% LEVEL

of treatment than did males. However, the difference between the two sexes was significant only for PSYCHOTHERAPY PLUS DRUG ($D < .05$) and then only for *final status,* not for *change.* The sex of the patient seemed to make no particular difference in the case of DRUG ALONE and PSYCHOTHERAPY ALONE.

The results for IDIORAT 1 + 2 (where the ratings for the severity of each patient's two most important symptoms were simply summed without being weighted) were essentially the same as for TROUBLERAT 1 + 2, except that the differences between the two sexes were, in general, less prominent (change .1134, W_1; final .0503, W_0) and not significant ($D > .05$) for any of the five treatments.

CHAPTER VIII

The Results of Patients' Treatment as Judged by Their Therapists

PHILIP R. A. MAY, M.D.

IN TERMS OF overall symptomatology measured by the SRS* and AA total scores, patients treated with DRUG ALONE and PSYCHOTHERAPY PLUS DRUG did significantly better than patients treated with PSYCHOTHERAPY ALONE or MILIEU, with ECT somewhere in between. The effect of *drug* in reducing symptoms was extremely significant, while the effect of *psychotherapy* was non-significant. There was no particular difference between the two sexes in their response to the five treatments, and no evidence of significant interaction between the effects of *psychotherapy* and *drug*.

By CMS Friendly, Clear-Thinking, Energetic and Depressed, the grouping was much the same, with best results from DRUG ALONE and PSYCHOTHERAPY PLUS DRUG; ECT in the middle; MILIEU and

---

* A list of conventional terms, abbreviations and notations will be found at the end of Chapter 3.

PSYCHOTHERAPY ALONE the least effective. *Drug* had an extremely or highly significant beneficial effect. *Psychotherapy* did not affect outcome materially except for Clear-Thinking, where its effect was significantly positive (but less than *drug* or *ECT*) and Energetic, where its effect approached significance. Here also there was no evidence of sex differences or of significant interaction between the effects of *psychotherapy* and *drug*.

The differences for CMS Aggressive were small but suggestive. Female patients were described by their therapists as on the average significantly more Aggressive at the end of treatment than males; this applied whatever the form of treatment, but particularly so for ECT (approaching significance); less so for DRUG ALONE and MILIEU. *Psychotherapy* had an effect that approached significance in the direction of making patients more Aggressive (and further away from the normal), and there was some indication of interaction between *psychotherapy* and *drug*. *Drug alone* increased the final level of Aggressive very slightly, but when *drug* was given in combination with *psychotherapy*, the aggression-increasing effect of *psychotherapy* was neutralized.

By CMS Jittery there was no significant difference between the outcome of the five treatments and no evidence of significant interaction or sex differences.

INTRODUCTION

How did the physicians who were directly responsible for the patients' treatment view the outcome of the five treatment methods? To answer this question, we will consider their ratings on two scales that reflect overall symptomatology—the Symptom Rating Scale (SRS) and the Ann Arbor Psychotic Confusion Scale (AA); and on the six aspects of emotional and behavioral functioning included in the Clyde Mood Scale (CMS).

SYMPTOM RATING SHEET (SRS)

Table 8.1 summarizes the analysis of variance for the SRS (Total Score) and Figure 8.1 shows the means for the five treatments in rank order with a Duncan Multiple Range test (lower scores indicate less pathology). There was an extremely significant difference between the five treatments: After separating out the effect of sex, the F-ratio for overall treatment differences was 7.16 (.0001, W_0: < .0005, Co-V). DRUG ALONE with a mean score of 23.4 and PSYCHOTHERAPY PLUS DRUG (23.0) were close together at the low end, indicating less severe symptomatology; they were not significantly different from each other (D > .05). MILIEU (27.7) and PSYCHOTHERAPY ALONE (29.3) were at the worse end, highly significantly different (D < .01) than the first two groups, but not significantly different from each other (D > .05). ECT (25.6) was in the middle, distinguishable from PSYCHOTHERAPY ALONE (D < .05) but not from anything else. There was no significant difference between the two sexes in their response to the five treatments.

Table 8.1.   SRS (TOTAL): ANALYSIS OF VARIANCE

Significance levels for the various effects at three successive stages of Winsorization, computed to four decimal places. The most representative, W_0, also shows the appropriate F-values in parentheses and a directional sign, (+) indicating better final values (or more change) for a particular treatment or for the female sex.

	W_0 Change		W_0 Final	W_1 Final	W_2 Final
Five treatments in general		.0001		.0001 (7.16)	.0001	.0001
Ataraxic drug	+	.0000	+	.0000 (26.67)	.0000	.0000
Psychotherapy	+	.1948	−	.5539 (0.35)	.4502	.3815
Sex (ECT included)	+	.2157	−	.3765 (0.80)	.3366	.2938
Sex (ECT excluded)	+	.2902	−	.7953 (0.07)	.8069	.7988
Interaction						
Sex × psychotherapy	−	.3873	−	.9259 (0.01)	.8836	.8626
Sex × drug	−	.9103	+	.8040 (0.06)	.7558	.7574
Psychotherapy × drug	−	.4061	−	.3297 (0.95)	.2477	.2565

Omitting the ECT group from consideration, a three-way analysis of variance shows that the main factor in reducing symptomatology was an extremely significant *drug* effect (F 26.67/.0000, W_0). For *psychotherapy* effect there is a disparity between the results obtained for *change* (+1948, W_0) and *final status* (−5539, W_0). If co-variance is used to resolve this, adjusting for differences in respect of sex and initial level, *psychotherapy* is determined to have increased symptomatology but to a clearly nonsignificant extent (> .80, Co-V). There was no evidence of significant interaction between *psychotherapy* and *drug* in either *change* scores (.4061) or *final* scores (.3297).

Figure 8-1   THERAPISTS' SRS (TOTAL): FINAL SCORES IN RANK ORDER FOR THE 5 TREATMENTS

Scores are non-Winsorized (W_o), expressed to one place of decimals, unadjusted and adjusted by co-variance for sex and initial level. Higher scores indicate more severe overall symptomatology.

The lines depict Ducan Multiple Range Tests at the 95% and 99% protection levels, non-Winsorized data (W_o). Groups not connected by these lines are significantly different from one another at that level.

████ = a lack of statistical significance at the 95% level

▪▪▪▪ = a lack of statistical significance at the 99% level

	(P+D)	(D)	(E)	(M)	(P)
MEAN					
co-varied	22.7	23.6	25.7	27.9	29.1
unadjusted	23.0	23.4	25.6	27.7	29.3
S.D.	4.5	5.9	6.7	8.1	7.8
N	44	47	47	43	46
MAX.	36	42	41	48	46
MIN.	16	16	16	16	16

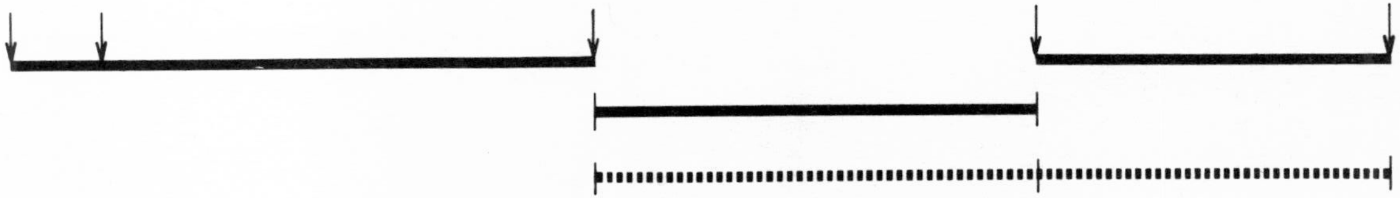

95% LEVEL

99% LEVEL

ANN ARBOR (AA)

Table 8.2 summarizes the analysis of variance for the AA (Total Score) and Figure 8.2 depicts the five treatment means in rank order (a high score indicates more severe overall symptomatology). The F-value for general intertreatment differences is extremely significant (F 8.91/.0001, W_1: $<$ .0005, Co-V). There is the now-familiar appearance of a higher (sicker) cluster, composed of PSYCHOTHERAPY ALONE (11.9) and MILIEU (12.5), highly significantly different (D $<$ .01) from a lower (healthier) cluster of DRUG ALONE (10.5) and PSYCHOTHERAPY PLUS DRUG (10.5); with ECT (11.3) in the middle. There is no evidence of significant difference between the sexes.

Table 8.2.   AA (TOTAL): ANALYSIS OF VARIANCE

Significance levels for the various effects at three successive stages of Winsorization, computed to four decimal places. The most representative, W_1, also shows the appropriate F-values in parentheses and a directional sign, (+) indicating better final values (or more change) for a particular treatment or for the female sex.

	W_0 Final	W_1 Change	W_1 Final	W_2 Final
Five treatments in general	.0001	.0001	.0001 (8.91)	.0001
Ataraxic drug	.0000	+ .0001	+ .0000 (33.27)	.0000
Psychotherapy	.3323	+ .0335	+ .3674 (0.81)	.3380
Sex (ECT included)	.7952	+ .4984	− .8077 (0.06)	.7578
Sex (ECT excluded)	.6533	+ .2737	+ .5056 (0.44)	.5029
Interaction				
Sex × psychotherapy	.4789	− .6566	− .4737 (0.51)	.5735
Sex × drug	.5878	− .3600	+ .7112 (0.14)	.6856
Psychotherapy × drug	.4138	+ .9648	+ .3289 (0.95)	.2437

The three-way analysis of variance for the AA yields results similar to the SRS. The effect of *drug* in reducing symptomatology was extremely significant (F 33.27/.0000, W_1), with no evidence of interaction between *psychotherapy* and *drug*. For *psychotherapy* effect, the figures for *change* (+.0335, W_1) and *final status* (+.3674, W_1) are somewhat discrepant. *Co-varied* scores would declare the effect of *psychotherapy* to be beneficial but not significantly so (.20–.30, Co-V). However, considering that the SRS showed a nonsignificant effect in the opposite direction, it would seem wise to conclude that according to their therapists, *psychotherapy* seems to have had little effect on patients' general symptomatology.

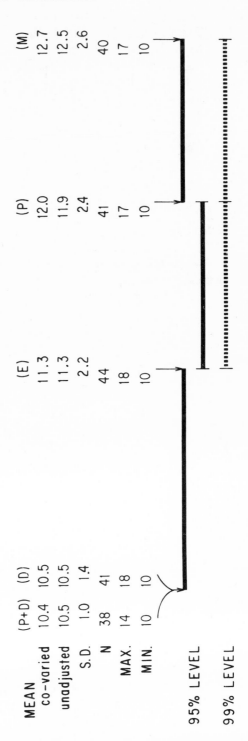

Figure 8-2 THERAPISTS' AA (TOTAL): FINAL SCORES IN RANK ORDER FOR THE 5 TREATMENTS

Scores are non-Winsorized (W_o), expressed to one place of decimals, unadjusted and adjusted by co-variance for sex and initial level. Higher scores indicate more severe overall symptomatology.

The lines depict Ducan Multiple Range Tests at the 95% and 99% protection levels, non-Winsorized data (W_o). Groups not connected by these lines are significantly different from one another at that level.

▬▬▬ = a lack of statistical significance at the 95% level

▪▪▪▪▪▪ = a lack of statistical significance at the 99% level

MEAN	(P+D)	(D)	(E)	(P)	(M)
co-varied	10.4	10.5	11.3	12.0	12.7
unadjusted	10.5	10.5	11.3	11.9	12.5
S.D.	1.0	1.4	2.2	2.4	2.6
N	38	41	44	41	40
MAX.	14	18	18	17	17
MIN.	10	10	10	10	10

95% LEVEL

99% LEVEL

In general the differences between the results from the SRS and the AA are minor and insignificant. First, the rank order of MILIEU and PSYCHOTHERAPY ALONE is reversed in the AA—but the scores remain indistinguishable (D > .05). The net result is that for the AA, ECT was distinguishable from MILIEU (D < .05) and not from PSYCHO-THERAPY ALONE (D > .05)—the other way around from the SRS. Second, for the AA it was necessary to use one stage of Winsorizing to obtain suitable representative statistics, as there was one patient in each of the female DRUG ALONE and male ECT groups with an unusually high (sick) score.

CMS (FRIENDLY AND CLEAR-THINKING)

In the CMS a higher numerical score for a particular subscale means that the patient is described as showing that factor to a greater extent. The scores are standardized so that the normal score will be somewhere around 50.

Table 8.3. CMS (FRIENDLY AND CLEAR-THINKING): ANALYSIS OF VARIANCE

Significance levels for the various effects at three successive stages of Winsorization, computed to four decimal places. The most representative, W_0, also shows the appropriate F-values in parentheses and a directional sign, (+) indicating better final values (or more change) for a particular treatment or for the female sex.

8.3A. FRIENDLY	W_0 Change		W_0 Final	W_1 Final	W_2 Final
Five treatments in general		.0031	.0001 (6.93)	.0001	.0001
Ataraxic drug	+	.0001	+ .0000 (28.14)	.0000	.0000
Psychotherapy	+	.5547	− .8820 (0.02)	.8237	.8011
Sex (ECT included)	+	.7855	− .9929 (0.00)	.9693	.9999
Sex (ECT excluded)	+	.5383	+ .5115 (0.43)	.4553	.4702
Interaction					
Sex × psychotherapy	−	.1709	+ .8953 (0.02)	.8077	.9144
Sex × drug	−	.7403	− .6010 (0.27)	.5464	.4714
Psychotherapy × drug	+	.8732	+ .4576 (0.55)	.3909	.4024

8.3B. CLEAR-THINKING	W_0 Change		W_0 Final	W_1 Final	W_2 Final
Five treatments in general		.0010	.0001 (5.95)	.0001	.0001
Ataraxic drug	+	.0007	+ .0000 (19.62)	.0000	.0000
Psychotherapy	+	.0071	+ .1284 (2.31)	.1026	.1050
Sex (ECT included)	+	.7530	+ .8101 (0.06)	.9760	.9299
Sex (ECT excluded)	+	.7060	+ .4541 (0.56)	.5168	.4814
Interaction					
Sex × psychotherapy	−	.9882	− .7471 (0.10)	.8138	.7793
Sex × drug	−	.9559	− .4383 (0.60)	.5054	.4962
Psychotherapy × drug	+	.9700	+ .1027 (2.67)	.0947	.1041

Tables 8.3 (A and B) contains the analyses of variance for Friendly and Clear-Thinking; the treatment means are given in rank order in Figure 8.3.

In the case of Friendly, the means for DRUG ALONE (47.3) and PSYCHOTHERAPY PLUS DRUG (46.2) are grouped at the more healthy end, significantly (D < .01) different from MILIEU (39.4) and PSYCHOTHERAPY ALONE (40.0) at the other end. ECT (42.5) is in the middle, distinguishable from DRUG ALONE (D < .05) but not from anything else. *Drug* had an extremely significant beneficial effect (F 28.14/.0000, W_0), but the effect of *psychotherapy* was nonsignificant (.8820, W_0). As with the AA and SRS, there is no significant difference between the sexes in their response to the various treatments and no evidence of significant interaction between *drug* and *psychotherapy*.

In the case of Clear-Thinking, although the final order of the groups was the same as Friendly and the differences among the five groups were extremely significant (F 5.95/.0001, W_0:< .0005, Co-V), one can only be confident (D < .05) that MILIEU was worse than the other four

Figure 8-3   THERAPISTS' CMS: FINAL SCORES AND RANK ORDER FOR THE 5 TREATMENTS

Scores are non-Winsorized (W_0), expressed to one place of decimals, unadjusted and adjusted by co-variance for sex and initial level. Normal score is about 50: lower scores indicate less friendly or clearthinking.

The lines depict Ducan Multiple Range Tests at the 95% and 99% protection levels, non-Winsorized data (W_0). Groups not connected by these lines are significantly different from one another at that level.

━━━ = a lack of statistical significance at the 95% level

▪▪▪▪▪▪▪▪ = a lack of statistical significance at the 99% level

(FRIENDLY)

MEAN	(M)	(P)	(E)	(P+D)	(D)
co-varied	39.3	40.1	42.4	46.3	47.1
unadjusted	39.4	40.0	42.5	46.2	47.3
S.D.	10.3	10.3	9.9	7.1	6.6
N	43	46	46	44	46
MAX.	60	58	58	62	60
MIN.	20	19	23	31	33

95% LEVEL

99% LEVEL

(CLEARTHINKING)

MEAN	(M)	(P)	(E)	(P+D)	(D)
co-varied	38.2	42.3	43.1	46.6	45.2
unadjusted	38.1	42.1	43.2	45.9	46.0
S.D.	9.8	9.8	9.6	7.6	7.7
N	43	46	46	44	46
MAX.	57	62	65	65	62
MIN.	22	24	24	27	32

95% LEVEL

99% LEVEL

groups. By three-way analysis of variance, *drug* had an extremely significant beneficial effect (F 19.62/.0000, W_0). The figures for *psychotherapy* effect are a little confusing (final status + .1284, W_0; change + .0071, W_0). However, when co-variance adjustment is made for sex and initial level, it is demonstrated that *psychotherapy* had, on the average, a significant positive effect (.05–.025, Co-V) although not as much as *drug* or *ECT*. There is no significant interaction between *psychotherapy* and *drug* (change .9700, W_0; final .1027, W_0; .30, Co-V). ECT is in the middle again, and there is no significant difference between the sexes for any of the treatments.

CMS (DEPRESSED AND ENERGETIC)

Table 8.4 (A and B) contains the relevant analyses of variance for the Depressed and Energetic subscales; the treatment means are given in rank order in Figure 8.4.

Table 8.4. CMS (DEPRESSED AND ENERGETIC):
ANALYSIS OF VARIANCE

Significance levels for the various effects at three successive stages of Winsorization, computed to four decimal places. The most representative, W_0, also show the appropriate F-values in parentheses and a directional sign, (+) indicating better final values (or more change) for a particular treatment or for the female sex.

8.4A. DEPRESSED	W_0 Change		W_0 Final	W_1 Final	W_2 Final
Five treatments in general		.0626	.0219 (2.94)	.0163	.0128
Ataraxic drug	+	.0046	+ .0012 (10.45)	.0009	.0009
Psychotherapy	+	.7431	− .5914 (0.29)	.5084	.4011
Sex (ECT included)	+	.8148	− .0432 (4.18)	.0313	.0251
Sex (ECT excluded)	+	.8181	− .1575 (2.00)	.1275	.1383
Interaction					
Sex × psychotherapy	−	.4170	− .7173 (0.13)	.6495	.6074
Sex × drug	+	.7163	− .5101 (0.43)	.4932	.4396
Psychotherapy × drug	−	.5238	− .8446 (0.04)	.8814	.8923

8.4B. ENERGETIC	W_0 Change		W_0 Final	W_1 Final	W_2 Final
Five treatments in general	+	.0101	+ .0357 (2.64)	.0181	.0138
Ataraxic drug	+	.0057	+ .0056 (7.68)	.0036	.0028
Psychotherapy	+	.0507	+ .1773 (1.82)	.1236	.1168
Sex (ECT included)	+	.5413	+ .4652 (0.54)	.4562	.3734
Sex (ECT excluded)	+	.6557	+ .3852 (0.84)	.3560	.3083
Interaction					
Sex × psychotherapy	+	.7195	+ .5447 (0.37)	.4319	.4354
Sex × drug	+	.3650	− .9754 (0.00)	.9447	.9124
Psychotherapy × drug	+	.4583	+ .2776 (0.18)	.2621	.2386

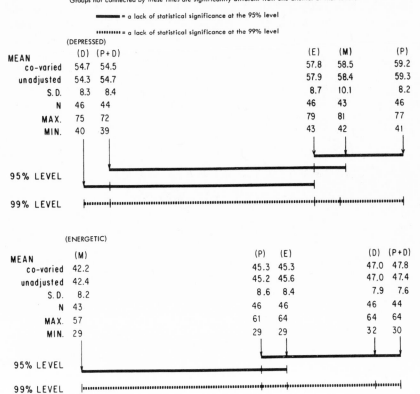

Figure 8-4   THERAPISTS' CMS : FINAL SCORES IN RANK ORDER FOR THE 5 TREATMENTS

Scores are non-Winsorized (W$_0$), expressed to one place of decimals, unadjusted and adjusted by co-variance for sex and initial level. Normal score is about 50: lower scores indicate less depression or more energetic.

The lines depict Ducal Multiple Range Tests at the 95% and 99% protection levels, non-Winsorized data (W$_0$). Groups not connected by these lines are significantly different from one another at that level.

━━━ = a lack of statistical significance at the 95% level

••••••• = a lack of statistical significance at the 99% level

(DEPRESSED)

	(D)	(P+D)		(E)	(M)	(P)
MEAN co-varied	54.7	54.5		57.8	58.5	59.2
unadjusted	54.3	54.7		57.9	58.4	59.3
S.D.	8.3	8.4		8.7	10.1	8.2
N	46	44		46	43	46
MAX.	75	72		79	81	77
MIN.	40	39		43	42	41

95% LEVEL

99% LEVEL

(ENERGETIC)

	(M)		(P)	(E)		(D)	(P+D)
MEAN co-varied	42.2		45.3	45.3		47.0	47.8
unadjusted	42.4		45.2	45.6		47.0	47.4
S.D.	8.2		8.6	8.4		7.9	7.6
N	43		46	46		46	44
MAX.	57		61	64		64	64
MIN.	29		29	29		32	30

95% LEVEL

99% LEVEL

There are significant differences among the five treatments for Energetic (.0357, W$_0$:.025–.01, Co-V) and Depressed (.0219, W$_0$:.05–.025, Co-V). By both of these criteria, DRUG ALONE and PSYCHOTHERAPY PLUS DRUG give the best result (i.e., closer to normal), significantly (D < .05) better than the least effective treatment. When co-variance adjustment is made for sex and initial level, PSYCHOTHERAPY PLUS DRUG did have an (insignificantly) better score than DRUG ALONE by both criteria. However, the mean scores are very close either way. ECT was in the middle again by both criteria, not distinguishable with confidence (D > .05) from either the best or the least effective treatments.

The effect of *drug* was highly significant in increasing Energetic (*F* 7.68/.0056, W$_0$) and in reducing Depressed (*F* 10.45/.0012, W$_0$).

Psychotherapy seemed to have no significant effect on Depressed (.5914, W_0). As for its possible effect on Energetic, there is an apparent disparity between the significance figures obtained from *final status* (+.1773, W_0) and from *change* (+.0507, W_0). If this is resolved by co-variance, *psychotherapy* is demonstrated to have increased Energetic to an extent that approached significance (.10–.05, Co-V). There was no indication of significant interaction between the effects of *psychotherapy* and *drug* for either Energetic or Depressed.

The sex of the patient seemed to make no difference to the response to any of the treatments for Energetic (.4652, W_0), but for Depressed there was a general tendency for females to be worse at the end of treatment (.0432, W_0): this was not significant for any one of the treatments separately, but was most apparent for ECT and MILIEU.

CMS (JITTERY AND AGGRESSIVE)

Table 8.5 (A and B) gives the relevant analyses of variance for the Jittery and Aggressive subscales; the treatment means in rank order are shown in Figure 8.5. In the case of *Jittery,* DRUG ALONE (50.7) was the most effective treatment by co-varied mean scores, and ECT (52.9) was the least effective, PSYCHOTHERAPY PLUS DRUG (51.8), MILIEU (51.7) and PSYCHOTHERAPY ALONE (52.2) were very close together in the middle. However, the differences between the groups are all very small (nonsignificant), and a three-way analysis of variance shows that there was no significant effect from either *drug* or *psychotherapy.* There was no indication that the patient's sex made any difference or that there was interaction between the effects of *psychotherapy* and *drug.*

The findings for Aggressive are also food for thought. As in the case of Jittery, none of the differences among the individual treatments were significant, and the average amount of change was small. However, the F-ratio for overall differences among the treatments approached significance (.0588, W_1:.25–.10, Co-V) and some of the other statistics are suggestive, despite a disparity between the figures for *final status* and *change.* Co-variance adjustment is inappropriate in this case because outcome appears to depend on initial level differently from one treatment to another* and it seems to be wiser to take *final status* as the best indicator. (One stage of Winsorizing is necessary to provide the most representative statistics, lessening the impact of one male patient in the MILIEU group who had an unusually high score.)

The conclusion from *final* scores is that *psychotherapy* had on the

---

* The regressions are determined to be insufficiently homogeneous by the rule given in Chapter 3.

average the effect of making patients more Aggressive (further away from normal) to an extent that approached significance (.1472, W_1)— about the same as *ECT*. The interaction between *drug* and *psychotherapy* approached significance, both for *final* scores (.0821, W_1) and for *change* scores (.0941, W_1). *Drug alone* increased the final level of Aggressive very slightly, but when *drug* was given in combination with *psychotherapy*, the aggression-increasing effect of *psychotherapy* was neutralized.

Table 8.5. CMS (JITTERY AND AGGRESSIVE):
ANALYSIS OF VARIANCE

Significance levels for the various effects at three successive stages of Winsorization, computed to four decimal places. The most representative, W_0 (8.5A) and W_1 (8.5B), also shows the appropriate F-values in parentheses and a directional sign, (+) indicating better final values (or more change) for a particular treatment or for the female sex.

8.5A. JITTERY	W_0 Change	W_0 Final	W_1 Final	W_2 Final
Five treatments in general	.6597	.6617 (0.60)	.6886	.7322
Ataraxic drug	+ .9292	+ .4613 (0.54)	.4354	.4730
Psychotherapy	− .2837	− .5804 (0.31)	.5530	.5951
Sex (ECT included)	+ .5421	− .3051 (1.07)	.2149	.2587
Sex (ECT excluded)	+ .4865	− .7333 (0.12)	.7118	.7931
Interaction				
Sex × psychotherapy	− .5434	− .7467 (0.10)	.6798	.6405
Sex × drug	− .5491	− .9723 (0.00)	.9609	.9210
Psychotherapy × drug	− .3822	+ .4897 (0.48)	.4784	.4687

8.5B. AGGRESSIVE	W_0 Final	W_1 Change	W_1 Final	W_2 Final
Five treatments in general	.1298	.4644	.0588 (2.32)	.0458
Ataraxic drug	.2549	− .7688	+ .2829 (1.15)	.2567
Psychotherapy	.2459	− .4234	− .1472 (2.10)	.1359
Sex (ECT included)	.0051	− .1032	− .0021 (10.18)	.0010
Sex (ECT excluded)	.0314	− .2549	− .0131 (6.15)	.0070
Interaction				
Sex × psychotherapy	.4046	− .0543	− .3362 (0.92)	.2930
Sex × drug	.9215	+ .7980	+ .9864 (0.00)	.9668
Psychotherapy × drug	.1453	− .0941	− .0821 (3.02)	.0766

As a final "teaser," whatever the form of treatment, female patients on the average were rated by their therapist at the end of treatment as more Aggressive than males (.0021, W_1)—and perhaps with less *change* in this respect (.1032, W_1). This was most marked for ECT (approaching significance), less for DRUG ALONE and MILIEU, and least for PSYCHOTHERAPY ALONE and PSYCHOTHERAPY PLUS DRUG.

Interpretation of mean values for Aggressive is not a simple matter, since deviation from the norm in either direction might legitimately be

Figure 8-5   THERAPISTS' CMS : FINAL SCORES IN RANK ORDER FOR THE 5 TREATMENTS

Scores are non-Winsorized (W_o), expressed to one decimal place, unadjusted and adjusted by co-variance for sex and initial level. Normal score is about 50. Higher scores mean more jittery or aggressive.

The lines depict Ducan Multiple Range Tests at the 95% and 99% protection levels, non-Winsorized data (W_o). Groups not connected by these lines are significantly different from one another at that level.

━━━ = a lack of statistical significance at the 95% level

••••••••• = a lack of statistical significance at the 99% level

(JITTERY)

	(D)		(P+D)	(P)	(M)		(E)
MEAN							
co-varied	50.7		51.8	52.2	51.7		52.9
unadjusted	50.5		51.9	52.0	52.1		52.9
S.D.	6.7		6.9	8.2	7.8		8.0
N	46		44	46	43		46
MAX.	66		66	71	68		75
MIN.	38		38	38	40		40

95% LEVEL ⎫
99% LEVEL ⎬

(AGGRESIVE)

	(P+D)	(M)	(D)		(E)	(P)
co-varied	51.2	50.9	52.0		54.3	54.7
unadjusted	51.0	51.1	51.5		54.6	54.8
S.D.	8.7	10.1	9.6		10.4	10.8
N	44	43	46		46	46
MAX.	71	80	74		76	74
MIN.	37	37	39		37	39

95% LEVEL ⎫
99% LEVEL ⎬

regarded as a manifestation of psychological difficulty. It is also necessary to consider the effect of the raters themselves. I suspect that when they made their ratings they may have made some private allowance for sex-role differences, manifestations of Aggression being seen by our society as more appropriate to men than to women. But when a therapist rates a patient whom he is treating with *individual psychotherapy* as more Aggressive at the end of treatment than a patient who is not getting *individual psychotherapy,* does this mean that the patient is truly more Aggressive—or is it perhaps that the therapist has had more opportunity to see or to provoke his Aggression?

More sophisticated analyses may perhaps clarify these problems. For the moment it seems wiser to stay with the facts and to say only that, whatever the reason, the patients' therapists described the women patients in general—and in particular those treated with *psychotherapy alone, ECT* and *milieu*—as being more Aggressive and further away from the normal at the end of treatment.

CHAPTER IX

Psychoanalysts' Assessment of Treatment Outcome

PHILIP R. A. MAY, M.D.

AS THE PSYCHOANALYSTS saw it, the overall differences among the five treatments were very highly or extremely significant for MHS*, CDAS (Total) and CDAS (Anxiety). By these three measures, patients treated with PSYCHOTHERAPY PLUS DRUG did best, although not distinguishably better than with DRUG ALONE ($D > .05$). Patients treated with PSYCHOTHERAPY ALONE or MILIEU did significantly worse ($D < .05$), fourth and fifth in rank order of effectiveness. ECT was in the middle, significantly worse ($D < .05$) than DRUG ALONE and PSYCHOTHERAPY PLUS DRUG, but not distinguishably different ($D > .05$) from PSYCHOTHERAPY ALONE or MILIEU.

By these same three measures, *drug* had an extremely significant positive effect, while the effect of *psychotherapy* was nonsignificant, with no evidence of interaction between the effects of *psychotherapy* and *drug*. There was some suggestion that males did

* A list of conventional terms, abbreviations and notations will be found at the end of Chapter 3.

better than females on ECT, and vice versa for MILIEU and PSYCHO-THERAPY ALONE; however, these sex differences were not statistically significant.

In terms of Insight, the results were somewhat different. First, the patients did not change as much, and the overall differences among the treatment groups were less apparent, although statistically significant (.05–.025, Co-V). Second, the effects of treatment were, as determined by analysis of variance, less obvious. On the average, *drug* had a significant positive effect on Insight (.05–.02, Co-V)—more so than *psychotherapy* (.40, Co-V)—and there was some evidence of interaction between these two that tended toward significance. *Psychotherapy* alone had no effect on Insight, but when given with *drug,* the combined effect of the two treatments was greater than from *drug* alone. Third, ECT was the last in rank order, being in this particular respect the least effective of the five treatments—a definite contrast to its position in the middle of the rank order by the other criteria. There was no particular evidence of differences between the sexes in Insight for any of the treatments, except ECT, where males did better than females although not significantly so.

INTRODUCTION

We will now consider outcome as seen by the psychoanalysts' rating teams in terms of two global measures, the Menninger Health-Sickness Scale (MHS) and the Camarillo Dynamic Assessment Scale (CDAS) Total; and in terms of two major sectors of psychological functioning, CDAS Insight and Anxiety.

MHS

The relevant analysis of variance is shown in Table 9.1 and the treatment means in rank order in Figure 9.1. (Higher scores indicate health, lower scores sickness.)

The overall differences among the treatment groups are extremely significant (.0001, $W_0: < .0005$, Co-V). A Multiple Range test shows that the mean ratings for PSYCHOTHERAPY PLUS DRUG (33.6) and DRUG ALONE (33.1) are not distinguishable from each other (D > .05), but they are highly significantly (D < .01) better than PSYCHOTHERAPY ALONE (28.0) and MILIEU (26.5). PSYCHOTHERAPY ALONE and MILIEU are not distinguishable from each other with confidence (D > .05), while ECT (29.9) is in the middle, not significantly (D > .05) different from any other treatment.

Table 9.1.   MHS: ANALYSIS OF VARIANCE

Significance levels for the various effects at three successive stages of Winsorization, computed to four decimal places. The most representative, W_0, also shows the appropriate F-values in parentheses and a directional sign, (+) indicating better final values (or more change) for a particular treatment or for the female sex.

	W_0 Change		W_0 Final	W_1 Final	W_2 Final
Five treatments in general		.0001	.0001 (6.09)	.0001	.0001
Ataraxic drug	+	.0000	+ .0000 (21.30)	.0000	.0000
Psychotherapy	+	.4754	+ .4656 (0.53)	.4669	.4811
Sex (ECT included)	−	.9760	+ .8038 (0.06)	.6121	.6734
Sex (ECT excluded)	+	.4905	+ .3294 (0.95)	.2014	.2225
Interaction					
Sex × psychotherapy	−	.9917	+ .8120 (0.06)	.7926	.8578
Sex × drug	−	.8790	+ .2670 (1.23)	.1703	.1323
Psychotherapy × drug	−	.6084	+ .7132 (0.14)	.6467	.6751

Omitting the ECT group from consideration, a three-way analysis of variance shows that the main factor in improving MHS was an extremely significant *drug* effect (*F* 21.30/.0000, W_0). *Psychotherapy* had no significant effect (.4656, W_0), nor was there any evidence of interplay between *psychotherapy* and *drug* (.7132, W_0). There was no significant difference between the two sexes in their response to the various types of treatment.

CDAS (TOTAL)

The relevant analysis of variance and treatment means are shown in Table 9.2 and Figure 9.2. (Higher scores indicate health, lower scores sickness.) The overall differences among the five treatment groups are highly significant for *final status* (.0011, W_0); very highly significant for *co-varied* (.0010–.0005, Co-V) and extremely significant for *change* (.0001, W_0). Here again we find the best mean ratings for PSYCHO-THERAPY PLUS DRUG (38.7) and DRUG ALONE (37.6), not significantly different (D > .05) from each other. There was an extremely significant positive effect from *drug* (*F* 16.41/.0001, W_0), no significant effect

Figure 9-1   ANALYSTS' MHS: FINAL SCORES IN RANK ORDER FOR THE 5 TREATMENTS

Scores are non-Winsorized (W_o), expressed to one place of decimals, unadjusted and adjusted by co-variance for sex and initial level. Higher scores indicate health, lower scores sickness.

The lines depict Ducan Multiple Range Tests at the 95% and 99% protection levels, non-Winsorized data (W_o). Groups not connected by these lines are significantly different from one another at that level.

▬▬▬ = a lack of statistical significance at the 95% level

▪▪▪▪▪▪▪▪ = a lack of statistical significance at the 99% level

	(M)	(P)	(E)	(D)	(P+D)
MEAN					
co-varied	26.7	27.8	30.0	32.9	33.8
unadjusted	26.5	28.0	29.9	33.1	33.6
S.D.	12.4	10.4	7.0	5.7	5.5
N	43	46	47	48	44
MAX.	50	50	45	46	45
MIN.	5	7	15	19	23

95% LEVEL
99% LEVEL

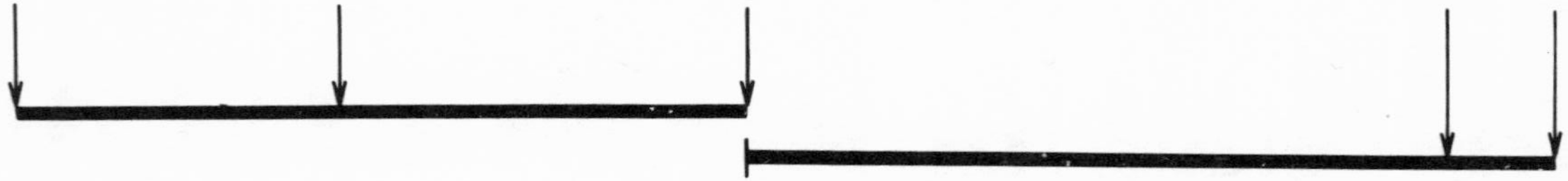

from *psychotherapy* (.7246, W_0) and no significant interaction between the effects of *drug* and *psychotherapy* (.7199, W_0).

Table 9.2.   CDAS (TOTAL): ANALYSIS OF VARIANCE

Significance levels for the various effects at three successive stages of Winsorization, computed to four decimal places. The most representative, W_0, also shows the appropriate F-values in parentheses and a directional sign, (+) indicating better final values (or more change) for a particular treatment or for the female sex.

	W_0 Change	W_0 Final	W_1 Final	W_2 Final
Five treatments in general	.0001	.0011 (5.01)	.0001	.0001
Ataraxic drug	+ .0001	+ .0001 (16.41)	.0000	.0000
Psychotherapy	+ .2804	+ .7246 (0.12)	.7572	.7161
Sex (ECT included)	+ .5913	+ .8699 (0.03)	.8332	.8359
Sex (ECT excluded)	+ .3859	+ .3937 (0.73)	.3660	.3297
Interaction				
Sex × psychotherapy	+ .5396	+ .4740 (0.51)	.4909	.4848
Sex × drug	+ .5854	+ .1453 (2.12)	.1083	.0868
Psychotherapy × drug	− .8530	− .7199 (0.13)	.6334	.6868

In general, the main difference between the results from MHS and CDAS (Total) is that, to judge by the latter, there was very little difference* at the lower end between MILIEU (31.8), ECT (32.3) and PSYCHOTHERAPY ALONE (31.7), all three being significantly worse than DRUG ALONE (D < .05) and highly significantly worse than PSYCHOTHERAPY PLUS DRUG (D < .01). There was also some evidence (not very strong) that treatment response differs according to sex. In terms of both *final status* and *change,* females did better than males on MILIEU, almost significantly so (D > .05), but they did worse than males on ECT.

CDAS (ANXIETY)

Table 9.3 and Figure 9.3 show the analysis of variance and treatment means for CDAS (Anxiety). (Higher scores indicate less anxiety.) The differences among the five treatment groups are extremely significant (.0001, W_0; .0005, Co-V). By the mean ratings on this measure also,

---

* Not only are the scores close, but the rank order varies according to the precise criterion chosen. PSYCHOTHERAPY ALONE is fifth in rank order of final scores, fourth by co-varied scores and third by change scores, ECT and MILIEU retaining their same relative positions. (Co-variance adjustment is indicated to be the most suitable indicator by the rule given in Chapter 3.)

Figure 9-2   ANALYSTS' CDAS (TOTAL): FINAL SCORES IN RANK ORDER FOR THE 5 TREATMENTS

Scores are non-Winsorized (W_O), expressed to one place of decimals, unadjusted and adjusted by co-variance for sex and initial level. Higher scores indicate health, lower scores sickness.

The lines depict Ducan Multiple Range Tests at the 95% and 99% protection levels, non-Winsorized data (W_O). Groups not connected by these lines are significantly different from one another at that level.

━━━ = a lack of statistical significance at the 95% level

▪▪▪▪▪▪▪ = a lack of statistical significance at the 99% level

MEAN	(P)	(M)	(E)	(D)	(P+D)
co-varied	31.8	31.6	32.2	37.5	38.9
unadjusted	31.7	31.8	32.3	37.6	38.7
S. D.	11.8	14.0	9.3	8.2	8.6
N	46	43	47	48	44
MAX.	57	55	54	52	54
MIN.	12	8	20	23	22

95% LEVEL

99% LEVEL

PSYCHOTHERAPY PLUS DRUG (5.5) and DRUG ALONE (5.4) were the best forms of treatment, not significantly different from each other (D > .05), but distinguishable with a high degree of confidence (D < .01) from PSYCHOTHERAPY ALONE (4.5) and MILIEU (4.3), and with a lesser degree of confidence (D < .05) from ECT (4.8). ECT, in the middle, was not significantly better than either PSYCHOTHERAPY ALONE or MILIEU, nor were these two latter groups readily separable (D > .05).

Table 9.3.   CDAS (ANXIETY): ANALYSIS OF VARIANCE

Significance levels for the various effects at three successive stages of Winsorization, computed to four decimal places. The most representative, W_0, also shows the appropriate F-values in parentheses and a directional sign, (+) indicating better final values (or more change) for a particular treatment or for the female sex.

	W_0 Change		W_0 Final	W_1 Final	W_2 Final
Five treatments in general		.0001	.0001 (6.51)	.0001	.0001
Ataraxic drug	+	.0000	+ .0000 (22.92)	.0000	.0000
Psychotherapy	−	.9918	+ .5345 (0.39)	.5776	.5982
Sex (ECT included)	+	.4929	+ .8724 (0.03)	.9456	.9472
Sex (ECT excluded)	+	.1885	+ .2321 (1.43)	.1978	.2056
Interaction					
Sex × psychotherapy	−	.8905	+ .7649 (0.09)	.9213	.7905
Sex × drug	+	.4896	+ .2733 (1.20)	.1940	.2403
Psychotherapy × drug	+	.9301	+ .7495 (0.10)	.9121	.8649

Drug had an extremely significant effect in reducing the final level of Anxiety (F 22.92/.0000, W_0). The effect of *psychotherapy* was nonsignificant (.5345, W_0), and there was no evidence of interaction between the effects of *psychotherapy* and *drug* (.7495, W_0).

The sex of the patient seemed to make a significant difference (D < .05) only for ECT, where males (5.2) did better than females (4.3). In the two DRUG groups there was very little difference between the sexes, while for MILIEU and PSYCHOTHERAPY ALONE females did slightly better (nonsignificantly) than males.

CDAS (INSIGHT)

The relevant statistics for CDAS (Insight) are given in Table 9.4 and Figure 9.4. (Higher scores indicate more Insight.)

By this measure there was a significant difference among the five treatments, but only at a fairly low level (change .0213, W_0; final .0523, W_0; .05–.025, Co-V), and the amount of change was relatively small,

Figure 9-3 ANALYSTS' CDAS (ANXIETY): FINAL SCORES IN RANK ORDER FOR THE 5 TREATMENTS

Scores are non-Winsorized (W_0), expressed to one place of decimals, unadjusted and adjusted by co-variance for sex and initial level. Higher scores indicate less anxiety.

The lines depict Ducan Multiple Range Tests at the 95% and 99% protection levels, non-Winsorized data (W_0). Groups not connected by these lines are significantly different from one another at that level.

▬▬ = a lack of statistical significance at the 95% level

▪▪▪▪▪▪▪ = a lack of statistical significance at the 99% level

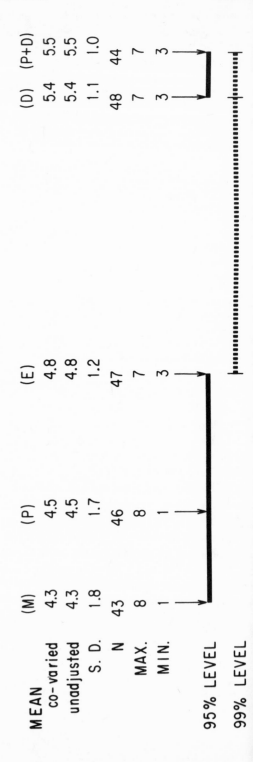

MEAN	(M)	(P)	(E)	(D)	(P+D)
co-varied	4.3	4.5	4.8	5.4	5.5
unadjusted	4.3	4.5	4.8	5.4	5.5
S. D.	1.8	1.7	1.2	1.1	1.0
N	43	46	47	48	44
MAX.	8	8	7	7	7
MIN.	1	1	3	3	3

95% LEVEL

99% LEVEL

contrasting sharply with the statistics for MHS, CDAS (Total) and CDAS (Anxiety).

Table 9.4. CDAS (INSIGHT): ANALYSIS OF VARIANCE

Significance levels for the various effects at three successive stages of Winsorization, computed to four decimal places. The most representative, W_0, also shows the appropriate F-values in parentheses and a directional sign, (+) indicating better final values (or more change) for a particular treatment or for the female sex.

	W_0 Change	W_0 Final	W_1 Final	W_2 Final
Five treatments in general	.0213	.0532 (2.39)	.0194	.0107
Ataraxic drug	+ .0255	+ .1049 (2.63)	.0676	.0476
Psychotherapy	+ .1273	+ .9762 (0.00)	.9727	.9696
Sex (ECT included)	+ .8818	− .9806 (0.00)	.9787	.9979
Sex (ECT excluded)	+ .4954	+ .5229 (0.41)	.5123	.4901
Interaction				
Sex × psychotherapy	+ .3672	+ .1371 (2.21)	.1270	.1135
Sex × drug	− .5488	+ .3450 (0.89)	.3290	.2722
Psychotherapy × drug	− .6221	− .1277 (2.32)	.0842	.0632

There is some disparity between the statistics for *final status* and *change.* In this case it is wise to give special attention to the figures for change and co-variance, which take initial level into consideration, since a supplemental analysis indicated that outcome depended on sex and initial level to about the same extent for all five treatments. Accordingly, unless specified otherwise, the following discussion will focus on statistics that apply to scores adjusted by co-variance.

By either *change* or *final status,* ECT had the least effect on Insight, although one cannot distinguish with an acceptable degree of certainty (D > .05) among the average *co-varied* scores for ECT (3.0), PSYCHOTHERAPY ALONE (3.3), MILIEU* (3.4) and DRUG ALONE (3.7). PSYCHOTHERAPY PLUS DRUG had the best result in terms of Insight, significantly more than ECT, MILIEU and PSYCHOTHERAPY ALONE (< .05, Co-V) and nearly significantly more than DRUG ALONE (.20–.10, Co-V).

On the average, lumping together PSYCHOTHERAPY and PSYCHOTHERAPY PLUS DRUG, *psychotherapy* had the effect of increasing co-varied Insight scores to an extent that does not reach significance (.40, Co-V). By contrast, *drug* had a significant positive effect (.05–.02, Co-V). However, there was perhaps some indication of interaction between the

---

* MILIEU is second in rank order of final scores, third by co-varied scores and fourth by change scores; the DRUG ALONE and PSYCHOTHERAPY ALONE groups retain their same relative positions. (As already indicated, co-varied scores would be selected as the most appropriate indicator.)

Figure 9-4   ANALYSTS' CDAS (INSIGHT): FINAL SCORES IN RANK ORDER FOR THE 5 TREATMENTS

Scores are non-Winsorized (W_o), expressed to one place of decimals, unadjusted and adjusted by co-variance for sex and initial level. Higher scores indicate more insight.

The lines depict Ducan Multiple Range Tests at the 95% and 99% protection levels, non-Winsorized data (W_o). Groups not connected by these lines are significantly different from one another at that level.

▬▬▬ = a lack of statistical significance at the 95% level

▪▪▪▪▪▪▪▪ = a lack of statistical significance at the 99% level

MEAN	(E)	(P)	(D)	(M)	(P+D)
co-varied	3.0	3.3	3.7	3.4	4.1
unadjusted	3.0	3.2	3.6	3.7	4.1
S.D.	1.6	2.1	1.6	2.1	1.6
N	47	46	48	43	44
MAX.	7	8	7	7	7
MIN.	1	1	1	1	1

95% LEVEL

99% LEVEL

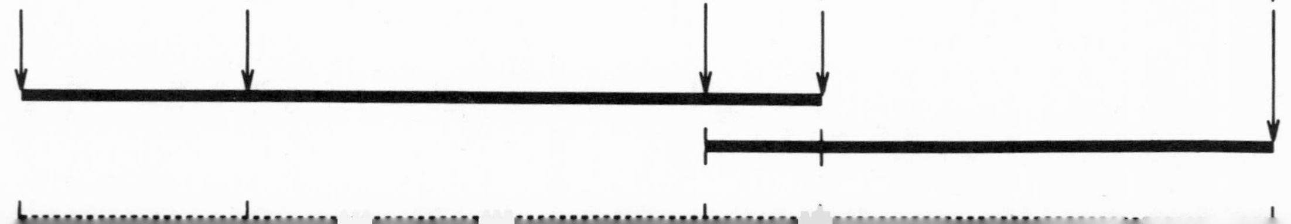

effects of *drug and psychotherapy* (change .6221, W_0; final .1277, W_0; .20–.30, Co-V). *Psychotherapy alone* had no effect on Insight (actually the mean co-varied score for PSYCHOTHERAPY ALONE was fractionally less than MILIEU), but when *psychotherapy* was given together with *drug,* the combined effect was greater than the (beneficial) effect of *drug* alone. In fact, the difference between DRUG ALONE and PSYCHO-THERAPY PLUS DRUG approached significance (.20–.10, Co-V).

Winsorization has very little effect on the group means for Insight, indicating that the differences among the treatment groups are likely to be representative for most of the patients, rather than confined to a few unusual or extreme cases. However, it is of interest that the two highest Insight ratings (8.0) were given to two patients in the PSYCHO-THERAPY ALONE group (one male and one female). If taken as a true nonchance finding, this might be interpreted as an indication that a small proportion of unusual patients who are given INDIVIDUAL PSYCHO-THERAPY ALONE may do very well in terms of Insight. If so, this would be counterbalanced by an equivalent number who do worse, since the average end result for PSYCHOTHERAPY ALONE was no better than for MILIEU. It must also be remembered that this particular finding is very likely to be a matter of chance; after all, it is only two cases and only one scale point higher than the highest scores in the four other treatment groups.

There was little difference in outcome between the two sexes except for ECT, where females did worse than males, although not significantly so.

CHAPTER X

The Use of Psychological Tests to Measure Treatment Outcome in Schizophrenic Patients

PHILIP R. A. MAY, M.D. AND
LUTHER S. DISTLER, PH.D.

SCHIZOPHRENIC PATIENTS POSE definite problems in psychological testing because the very nature of the illness makes it difficult or even impossible for the more seriously ill patients to cooperate. This diminishes the extent to which the data obtained may be taken as representative of the true state of affairs for the patient group as a whole. In addition, the absence of data for nontestable patients creates a major risk that a bias has been introduced *against* any treatment that is effective in increasing cooperation.

The results of psychological testing in this study show that *testability* can be used effectively as an outcome criterion for schizophrenic patients, with the results correlating well with clinical and administrative criteria. In terms of improving testability, DRUG ALONE* and PSYCHOTHERAPY PLUS DRUG were shown to be highly significantly more effective than MILIEU or PSYCHOTHERAPY ALONE, with ECT occupying an intermediate position.

The significant effects of treatment on testability made it necessary to take into consideration the degree of bias introduced by differential changes in testability as a result of treatment. When this was done, the psychological test scores could be used to provide useful additional information, in general consistent with the clinical and administrative criteria, although not as clear-cut.

On the MMPI, *psychotherapy* had a beneficial effect on *D* (Depression) that was nearly significant; *drug* had a beneficial effect that approached significance or better on *?* (Cannot say), *F* (Validity), *Mf* (Masculinity-Femininity), *Pa* (Paranoia), *Sc* (Schizophrenia), *Pa + Pt + Sc* (Psychotic Triad) and *Cn* (Control). *Drug* may also have had a beneficial effect on scales *Pd* (Psychopathic deviate), *Hs* (Hypochondriasis) and *Es* (Ego Strength), but the evidence is dubious. *Psychotherapy* had an adverse effect that was significant or approaching significance for *?* (Cannot say), *Mf* (Masculinity-Femininity) and *Cn* (Control). *Drug* had an adverse effect approaching significance on *Si* (Introversion).

By the Similarities-Proverbs, Shipley Verbal I.Q. and Shipley Abstract I.Q., there was no evidence of significant effect from either *psychotherapy* or *drug*.

There was no important difference between PSYCHOTHERAPY ALONE and MILIEU, and no significant interaction between the effects of *psychotherapy* and *drug,* except perhaps for the MMPI *F* (Validity) and *D* (Depression) scales and for the Shipley Abstract I.Q. For the *F* scale and Shipley Abstract I.Q., there was some indication that the combination of *psychotherapy* and *drug* was superior to either treatment given separately, the evidence being stronger but still not entirely satisfactory for the Shipley Abstract I.Q. In the case of the *D* scale, there was some unimpressive evidence that the two forms of treatment interfered with each other. This was the only measure in the entire *administrative, clinical* and

---

* A list of conventional terms, abbreviations and notations will be found at the end of Chapter 3.

psychometric spectrum for which there was any evidence of significant negative interaction.

ECT occupied in general a middle position among the five treatments: it might perhaps be declared to have had a significant beneficial effect by MMPI scales *Si* (Introversion) and *At* (Anxiety), but not by any of the other *psychometric* criteria.

Considerable differences were found between the mean scores for males and females for many of the MMPI scales, but the precise interpretation of this phenomenon must await further analysis and research. It may be that the differences are explicable on the basis of differential cooperation in testing, as females were generally less cooperative than males. However, other factors must also be considered such as test-standardization problems, differential response to treatment and true differences in the severity of illness at the time of admission.

THE PROBLEM OF NONTESTABILITY:
REPRESENTATIVENESS AND SELECTIVE BIAS

Testing before and after treatment would seem to be a forthright and relatively uncomplicated approach to the assessment of treatment effects. In practice with hospitalized schizophrenic patients, however, it turns out not to be quite so straightforward.

A considerable number of our study patients were so disturbed or uncooperative that acceptable* tests could not be obtained even though considerable time and effort were expended to obtain their cooperation. Table 10.1 shows that only 69 percent of the total patient sample were testable before treatment was started, and 87 percent at the end of treatment. Since a patient may be testable on admission but not at termination and vice versa, only 63 percent of the patients were testable both before and after treatment.†

There are some who might maintain that there are no untestable patients, only failures on the part of the examiner. We would be the first to agree that a greater number of acceptable tests might have

---

* The term "acceptable" is used deliberately in this context to enable a rigorous distinction to be made between *patient* problems of cooperation and testability and *instrument* problems of validity and reliability.

† These figures are for the MMPI, which seemed to be the most troublesome test for our patients. The proportions for the other tests are reasonably comparable.

been obtained by persons more talented and highly skilled, or by those with more time available than our research staff had.* Thus, when we say that a patient was nontestable this means only that, even exerting considerably more effort than is usual in routine psychological testing, we were not able to get him to cooperate sufficiently well to complete the test in a satisfactory and acceptable manner.

Table 10.1.   NON-TESTABILITY (MMPI) BY TREATMENT GROUP*

		Testable % Pre-treatment	Testable % Post-treatment	Testable % Pre and Post
MALES				
M		65	90	65
E		74	96	70
D		83	96	83
P		77	77	64
P+D		67	100	67
FEMALES				
M		79	70	61
E		54	79	46
D		64	100	64
P		67	75	50
P+D		65	96	65
BOTH SEXES				
M		72	80	63
E		64	87	58
D		73	98	73
P		72	76	57
P+D		66	98	66
	TOTAL	69	88	63

* Percentage testable in each group to nearest whole number

The presence of a sizeable number of untestable patients brings up the problems already referred to in the discussion of sample attrition (Chapter 2). Analyses that are based only on testable patients may seriously misrepresent the state of affairs for the total group: The tests provide no information on the untestables, and the entire question of the effect of treatment on these particular patients is ignored. It is of course possible to guess at what a particular patient's score might have been if he were tested by a magician, or even to compute a hypothetical value from other available information by regression or other missing-value techniques. However, in a situation where the nontestable patients

* We are inclined to believe, however, that even the most expert would have found it difficult to obtain satisfactory tests from patients such as #217, #239, #93, #145 (see Chapter 4) and #80 (see Appendix II).

are clearly different (in behavior at least) from the rest of the group, and particularly when a sizeable number of cases is involved, the optimum solution to this missing-value problem is far from certain. It is doubtful whether any of the commonly used replacement techniques would inspire any more confidence in the clinician than the current practice of sweeping the problem under the rug.

An important conclusion from Table 10.1 is that *final* scores are the most representative of the treatment group as a whole (87 percent of the total sample). The pre-post *change* and *co-varied* scores represent only 63 percent of the sample, a degree of attrition that in our judgment is too severe to justify their use as major criteria.*

There are further indications in Table 10.1 that caution is necessary in attempting to interpret the psychological test data. Although the five treatment groups included equivalent numbers of untestable cases at the time of admission, there were considerable differences among the five treatments in the proportion of untestable cases at termination. For example, the percentage of patients for whom post-treatment tests could be obtained ranges from 74 percent for PSYCHOTHERAPY ALONE to 98 percent for DRUG ALONE and PSYCHOTHERAPY PLUS DRUG. The proportion testable both before and after treatment ranges from 57 percent (ECT and PSYCHOTHERAPY ALONE) to 73 percent (DRUG ALONE).

This suggests that the five treatments had different effects on *testability*. It is therefore important to consider whether the absence of data for the untestables may have introduced any selective bias into the analyses. To put it another way, what would be the effect on the results if these untestable cases were somehow testable by a magician?

We would imagine that most clinicians with hospital experience would agree without further ado to the proposition that with schizophrenic patients the untestable cases would be, by and large, at the "higher pathology" end of the spectrum. (It is agreed, of course, that some seriously ill schizophrenics may be reasonably cooperative with testing.) For those who require evidence to support an assumption that non-cooperation (in testing and in other situations) is related to schizophrenic pathology, the case histories of patients #80 (see Appendix II), #93, #145, #217, and #239 (see Chapter 4) are offered as graphic illustrations.

There is also statistical evidence to support this hypothesis. First, discriminant analysis shows that nurses' ratings of Cooperation (MACC)

---

* The reader would be well advised to examine closely results reported in the literature for schizophrenic patients to determine to what extent the psychological test data for a particular study are genuinely representative of the patient sample, and to what extent the patient sample truly represents the ordinary run of schizophrenic hospital patients. It would seem that rigorous criteria and genuine representativeness are the exception rather than the rule.

discriminate powerfully among the treatment groups. By this scale the *F*-ratios for *drug* effect and for differences in *final status* among the five treatment groups are 45.8 and 12.2 respectively, both extremely significant (.0000, W_0). MACC (Cooperation) is very close indeed in discriminating power to MACC (Total), which was the best single discriminator among all the clinical, psychometric and administrative outcome criteria.

Second, Cooperation (MACC) *final* scores correlated highly with other independent criteria of outcome such as Release Rate ($r = .65$); analysts' MHS ratings ($r = .73$); therapists' SRS ratings ($r = .63$); and Admission Stay (L.R. 432) ($r = .65$).

Third, testability correlated strongly with Cooperation (MACC) ($r = .61$).

Fourth, testability correlated substantially with independent outcome measures such as Release Rate ($r = .61$); analysts' MHS ratings ($r = .59$); therapists' SRS ratings ($r = .57$); and Admission Stay (L.R. 432) ($r = .56$).

Assuming that the nontestable patients had a higher level of schizophrenic pathology, the absence of data for the untestable patients in a group would result in mean *final* scores that underestimate the average level of pathology (or overstate the degree of health). As a consequence, if a particular treatment group had a relatively larger proportion of untestable cases at the end of treatment, the *final* scores would be biased in favor of that treatment.

There would be a similar biasing effect on *change* and *co-varied* scores. These would overstate the worth of a poor treatment because data would not be included for a number of poor responders (those who were either untestable to start with and did not change, or those who were testable at the beginning and became worse). *Change* and *co-varied* scores would also underestimate a treatment that was truly effective, because in this case test scores would not be available for a number of positive responders who improved during treatment from nontestable to testable.

THE POSSIBLE BIASING EFFECTS OF UNTESTABLE CASES

If we follow the line of reasoning that has been detailed above, the figures in Table 10.1 can be used to provide some indication of the probable direction and degree of any biases that may have been introduced by testability problems. The *initial* (pretreatment) tests are all affected severely but more or less equally, i.e., there is not likely to be selective bias for or against any particular treatment group. The *final* scores would be assumed to be strongly biased (in absolute terms) in favor of PSYCHOTHERAPY ALONE (only 74 percent testable) and MILIEU (79 percent). There is somewhat less chance of bias in favor of ECT (87 percent), and in the case of DRUG ALONE and PSYCHOTHERAPY PLUS DRUG (98 percent) it would be negligible. The *change* and *co-varied* scores would be the most seriously affected (in absolute terms) as only 63 percent of the total patient group were testable both before and after treatment. There would be a risk of selective bias in favor of PSYCHOTHERAPY ALONE and ECT (only 57 percent testable) by comparison with DRUG ALONE (73 percent) and PSYCHOTHERAPY PLUS DRUG (66 percent). MILIEU (63 percent) stands somewhere in the middle.

The reader will now observe that we are faced with a dilemma. Although *final* scores are, on the average, more representative of the patient group as a whole and of the DRUG ALONE and PSYCHOTHERAPY PLUS DRUG groups in particular, we would be justified in assuming that they are also heavily biased against these two groups. On the other hand, the *change* and *co-varied* scores, although far less representative, may be assumed to show somewhat less selective bias against DRUG ALONE and PSYCHOTHERAPY PLUS DRUG.

A further point worth noting is that comparisons between treatments that have similar proportions of untestable cases may be accepted with a fair degree of confidence as a measure of their relative (but not absolute) effectiveness.* Thus, in the case of *final* scores the comparison between MILIEU and PSYCHOTHERAPY ALONE, which have nearly the same proportion of testable patients (79 percent and 74 percent respectively), might be reasonably acceptable, although perhaps a little biased in favor of PSYCHOTHERAPY ALONE. The comparison between DRUG ALONE and PSYCHOTHERAPY PLUS DRUG might also be reasonably acceptable as both were 98 percent testable. However, the comparisons between the two former and the two latter groups may well be seriously biased in favor of MILIEU and PSYCHOTHERAPY ALONE. For *change* and *co-varied* scores the comparisons between PSYCHOTHERAPY ALONE and ECT might be accepted as each group has 57 percent testable; also the comparison between DRUG ALONE and PSYCHOTHERAPY PLUS DRUG (73 percent and 66 percent respectively)—but it would be assumed that the comparisons with MILIEU (63 percent) are biased in favor of PSYCHOTHERAPY ALONE and ECT and against DRUG ALONE and PSYCHO-THERAPY PLUS DRUG.

---

* The snag is, of course, that the patients who are not included in the analysis because no test data are available, although equal in numbers among the groups, might react to the different treatments in an entirely different way than those who are testable.

The incidence of nontestability will also affect the results of the two-way and three-way analyses of variance for sex and treatment effects. Table 10.2 shows that fewer females were testable than males. This involves *initial*, *final* and *change* or *co-varied* scores to about the same degree and whether or not the ECT group is included. Thus one would assume that there would be a bias in favor of females in the direction of overestimating the beneficial effect of treatment for them. This would give rise to a spurious "sex effect."

Table 10.2. NON-TESTABILITY (MMPI) BY SEX*

	Testable % Pre-treatment	Testable % Post-treatment	Testable % Pre and Post
INCLUDING ECT GROUP			
Males	73	92	70
Females	66	83	50
EXCLUDING ECT GROUP			
Males	78	91	70
Females	56	84	60

* Percentage testable to nearest whole number.

Table 10.3 shows that for *final* scores, the proportion of testable patients in the combined *psychotherapy* groups* is about the same as for the combined *nonpsychotherapy* groups (86 percent and 89 percent respectively). However, in the case of *change* scores, there were slightly more untestables in the combined *psychotherapy* groups (61 percent testable versus 68 percent).

Table 10.3. NON-TESTABILITY (MMPI) BY
TREATMENT EFFECT CATEGORY*

	Testable % Pre-treatment	Testable % Post-treatment	Testable % Pre and Post
Psychotherapy	69	86	61
No Psychotherapy	73	89	68
Ataraxic Drug	70	98	70
No Drug	72	76	60

* Percentage testable to nearest whole number

Thus we might accept the analysis of *final* scores for *psychotherapy* effect with some confidence, although we would consider that the correspond-

* In the three-way analysis of variance the combined PSYCHOTHERAPY ALONE and PSYCHOTHERAPY PLUS DRUG groups are contrasted with the combined DRUG ALONE and MILIEU groups to determine *psychotherapy* effect. Similarly, to determine *drug* effect, the combined DRUG ALONE and PSYCHOTHERAPY PLUS DRUG groups are contrasted with the combined MILIEU and PSYCHOTHERAPY ALONE groups.

ing estimate from *change* scores might be biased somewhat in favor of *psychotherapy*.

There would seem to be a strong risk of bias against *drug* in the analysis for *drug* effect, particularly for *final* scores where 98 percent of the combined *drug* groups were testable, but only 76 percent of the combined *no-drug* groups. The same bias against *drug* would be present in the change scores, but to a lesser degree—70 percent testable pre and post in the combined *drug* groups, but only 60 percent in the combined *no-drug* groups.

TESTABILITY AS A GUIDE TO INTERPRETATION OF RESULTS

It is obvious from these considerations that the interpretation of the psychological test results in this study calls for some degree of finesse. The basic guidelines that were inferred by the authors from the testability data can be summarized as follows:

> (1) *Final* scores are the most representative for the patient group as a whole, although in general they are likely to overstate (in absolute terms) the effect of all the treatments, including the MILIEU group. In addition, however, where one is comparing MILIEU with the other four groups, it could reasonably be assumed that the *final* scores are a little biased in favor of PSYCHOTHERAPY ALONE, somewhat biased against ECT, and strongly biased against DRUG ALONE and PSYCHO-THERAPY PLUS DRUG. The relative position comparisons between MILIEU and PSYCHOTHERAPY ALONE and between DRUG ALONE and PSYCHOTHERAPY PLUS DRUG may be acceptable, but the distance between these two clusters would likely be greater if all the untestable cases could be somehow included. The three-way analysis of variance of *final* scores for *psychotherapy* effect is acceptable. It is assumed, however, that any beneficial effect from *drug* is likely to be understated considerably, while any adverse *drug* effect is likely to be correspondingly overstated.
>
> (2) The *change* and *co-varied* scores are not sufficiently representative to be acceptable to the clinician as major criteria. Nevertheless, they provide useful information that can be used to supplement the analysis of *final* scores. In comparing MILIEU with the four other treatment groups, it is assumed that the *change* and *co-varied* scores are biased relatively in favor of PSYCHOTHERAPY ALONE and ECT; against DRUG ALONE and against PSYCHOTHERAPY PLUS DRUG. The comparison between PSYCHOTHERAPY ALONE and ECT and the comparison between DRUG ALONE and PSYCHOTHERAPY PLUS DRUG may be acceptable, but the distance between these two clusters may be greater than the results suggest. In three-way analysis of variance of *change* and *co-varied* scores, any beneficial *psychotherapy* effect may be somewhat exaggerated (or adverse effects minimized); any beneficial effect of *drug* may be underestimated (or its adverse effects overstated).

(3) There is reason to presuppose that the *final, change* and *co-varied* scores are biased in favor of females, and that analysis for sex effect would result in a spurious indication that females do better than males. This would be most marked in the analysis of *change* scores including the ECT group, and least marked in the analysis of *final* scores not including the ECT group.

PROPOSED METHOD OF ADJUSTING FOR NONTESTABILITY

The results of the analyses comprise a formidable and complex body of information. In interpreting the information, it is necessary to keep constantly in mind the limitations and caveats imposed by the testability problems discussed in the preceding three sections. Accordingly, the authors have felt it desirable to assist the reader by providing as we go along some simple indication as to where bias may be operating and how we think the results should be interpreted. If this is taken by the critical as a departure from the scientific convention of strict separation between facts and interpretation, we ask for indulgence: It is in a good cause—communication with the clinician.

To this end, the following notations have been used throughout the remainder of this chapter to indicate the degree and direction of the correction for bias that the authors think may be necessary:

(Adjust significance +): Biased *somewhat against* this treatment (or sex); the true value might be somewhat more significant.

(Adjust significance ++): Biased *considerably against* this treatment (or sex); the true value might be appreciably more significant.

(Adjust significance −): Biased *somewhat in favor* of this treatment (or sex); the true value might be somewhat less significant.

(Adjust significance − −): Biased *considerably in favor* of this treatment (or sex); the true value might be considerably less significant.

To lighten the presentation further, only a minimum of pertinent figures have been given. Unless specified otherwise, the rank order and other data for a treatment are given in terms of mean *final* scores at the appropriate level of Winsorization (determined by the rules given in Chapter 3). Where mean *change* scores appear they are also at the appropriate level of Winsorization. *Co-varied* scores are always non-Winsorized; they are given only if relevant and if it was determined that co-variance was legitimately applicable (using the rule given in Chapter 3).

TESTABILITY AS AN INDEX OF OUTCOME

Testability can be used as an outcome criterion for it is an objective measure of the patient's performance, understanding and cooperation in a standardized test situation. Of course, increased testability at the end of a patient's hospital stay is not entirely a matter of improvement: The testors may be more willing to make demands on a subject than they were at the time of admission since the patient is more of a known quantity. The patient himself is more accustomed to hospital procedures and to research testing, particularly if this is repeated at intervals during his stay. Nevertheless, despite these practice effects, testability provides a simple objective basis for comparison between groups.

The use of testability as an objective measure of outcome gains support from the fact that it correlated quite strongly with the independent clinical measures of outcome provided by nurses, therapists and psychoanalysts and also with the administrative criteria (see second section of this chapter).

Analysis of post-treatment testability (MMPI) shows that the F-ratio for overall differences among the five treatment groups is very highly significant (F 5.03/.0007, W_0). There is a significant difference between the sexes, females being less testable than males (.0423, W_0). A Multiple Range test shows two clusters, as in the case of many of the clinical and administrative measures. DRUG ALONE and PSYCHOTHERAPY PLUS DRUG have the highest proportion of testable patients (98 percent in each group), highly significantly more ($D < .01$) than MILIEU (79 percent) and PSYCHOTHERAPY ALONE (74 percent). These two latter groups are not distinguishable from each other ($D > .05$). ECT is in the middle, significantly different ($D < .05$) from both clusters.

RELEVANCE AND SENSITIVITY OF THE MMPI AS AN INDEX OF PATIENT CHANGE

Are the MMPI scales reasonable criteria for the examination of change in schizophrenic patients? A number of previous reports would indicate that they are.[1] However, there has been no satisfactory reported comparison of their discriminating ability with other outcome criteria in an adequately controlled study of the treatment of schizophrenic patients.

[1] See references 3, 6, 8.

Further, there is good reason to question whether the scales are sufficiently sensitive to measure relevant dimensions of change in this kind of patient.

For instance, many of the items in the MMPI are cast in historical terms.* It would seem that the responses to this kind of item are not likely to change very much over a relatively brief period of time, even though the patient's psychiatric condition might change considerably.

There is particular reason to doubt the discriminating ability of certain MMPI scales that might be presumed to have relevance for the schizophrenic patient. For instance, the present form of the Pa (Paranoia) scale was considered to be only preliminary,[2] while the Sc (Schizophrenia) scale has never been satisfactory in terms of its ability to identify schizophrenic patients[3] although this may be improved somewhat by the now standard K-correction.[4]

However, the F scale has been widely recognized and used as an index of psychosis[5] and so has $Pa + Pt + Sc$ (Psychotic Triad).[6] It would therefore seem reasonable to include the F, Pa, Sc and $Pa + Pt + Sc$ scales as outcome criteria despite their obvious limitations and handicaps.

A simple way of determining whether the MMPI basic scales might be useful indices of change for our particular patient sample is to examine whether they reflect the fact that, in general, the patients were much better at the time they left the hospital than when they first came in. Figure 10.1 shows a profile of the mean standard scores for the entire patient group before and after treatment. There is a consistent pattern of reduction in scores between the pre-treatment and post-treatment tests for all of the scales except ? (Cannot say), L (Lie) and K (Correction). As expected, the most marked changes were in F (Validity), Pa (Paranoia), Pt (Psychasthenia) and Sc (Schizophrenia).

Figures 10.2 and 10.3 show the profiles for males and females separately. Both sexes show the same pattern of elevated F, Pa, Pt and Sc scores with reduction at the end of treatment. The main differences seem to be that males have generally higher scores both before and after treatment (except on Pd and Hy) and that women show more change on Pd and Hy but none on Mf.

It may be concluded that the MMPI scores for our patient sample

---

* "I have never been in trouble with the law; One or more members of my family is very nervous; I have never seen things doubled; I used to like 'drop the handkerchief.' "

[2] See reference 2.
[3] See references 1, 5, 7.
[4] See references 1, 7.
[5] See reference 1.
[6] See reference 10.

did change in a clinically meaningful direction during the course of treatment and that therefore they may be relevant for evaluation of treatment effectiveness—as long as the limitations and caveats imposed by testability bias are kept in mind.

THE MMPI: RESULTS

The analyses for this section included the standard scores for the basic clinical scales (*Hs* + *.5K**, *D*, *Hy*, *Pd* + *.4K**, *Mf*, *Pa*, *Pt* + *.1K**, *Sc* + *.1K**, *Ma* + *.2K**) and the validity scales (*?*, *L*, *F*, *K*); the Social Introversion scale (*Si*); the Psychotic Triad (the sum of *Pa*, *Pt* + *1K** and *Sc* + *1K**); Caudra's Control scale (*Cn*); Barron's Ego Strength scale (*Es*); and Taylor's Anxiety scale (*At*). (Pattern analysis of profiles was not included.)

MMPI: COMPARISON BETWEEN THE EFFECTS OF PSYCHO-THERAPY AND DRUG. In general the results of the three-way analy-

---

* For simplicity the *K*-correction has been omitted from the abbreviations used in the rest of this chapter and elsewhere.

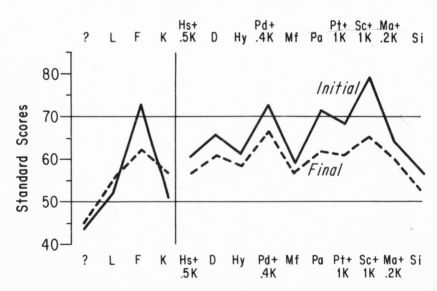

FIGURE 10-1 MMPI STANDARD SCORES
(ALL PATIENTS)

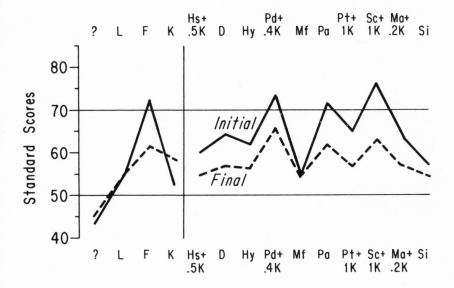

FIGURE 10-2   MMPI STANDARD SCORES (FEMALES)

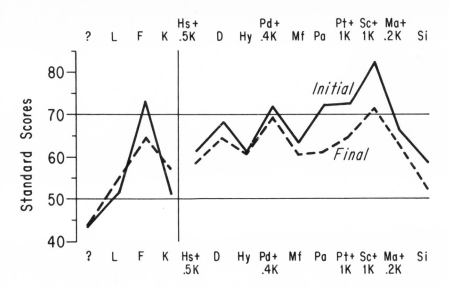

FIGURE 10-3   MMPI STANDARD SCORES (MALES)

sis of variance for the eighteen MMPI scales were consistently in the same direction as the clinical, administrative and testability criteria, i.e., little or no effect from *psychotherapy,* but a beneficial effect from *drug.* However, the findings were not nearly as impressive or as significant as was the case with these other criteria; in fact, the effects were clear-cut by only two scales—*F* and *Cn.*

(1) On scale *F* (Validity) *drug* had what might be taken to be a highly significant beneficial effect, producing lower *final* scores (.0217, W_0; adjust significance ++) and more *change* (.0025, W_0; adjust significance +).

(2) On scale *Cn* (Control) *psychotherapy* had at least a significant or nearly significant adverse effect by both *final* (.0700, W_0) and *change* scores (.0046, W_0; adjust significance +). On this same scale (*Cn*) there was a beneficial *drug* effect at least approaching significance evident in higher *final scores* (.0882, W_0; adjust significance ++) and more *change* (.1869, W_0; adjust significance +).

On seven more of the scales there was indication of a difference approaching significance between the effects of *psychotherapy* and *drug.* These were *?, D, Mf, Pa, Sc, Si* and *Pa + Pt + Sc.*

(1) On scale *D* (Depression) *psychotherapy* appeared to have a beneficial effect approaching significance, evidenced by lower *final* scores (.1316, W_0), and more change (.0480, W_1; adjust significance −).

(2) On the *Si* (Social Introversion) scale there was some rather weak evidence that *drug* had an adverse effect approaching significance, with higher *final* scores (.0130, W_0; adjust significance − −), less *change* (.4679, W_0; adjust significance −) and higher *co-varied* scores (.20–.10, Co-V; adjust significance −).

(3) On the *?* (Cannot say) scale *psychotherapy* made patients worse to an extent that was significant or nearly so, apparent in higher *final* scores (.1343, W_2) and less *change* (.0020, W_1; adjust significance +). On this same scale (*?*) *drug* appeared to have a beneficial effect that was significant or nearly so by *final* scores (.2518, W_2; adjust significance ++) and *change* (.0187, W_1; adjust significance +).

(4) There was reason to believe that *psychotherapy* had an adverse effect on the *Mf* (Masculinity-Femininity) scale that approached significance in terms of *final* scores (.1338, W_0) and *change* (.4367, W_1; adjust significance +). On this same scale (*Mf*) *drug* seemed to have had a beneficial effect approaching significance by *final* scores (.1619, W_0; adjust significance ++) and *change* (.2956, W_1; adjust significance +).

(5) By scale *Sc* (Schizophrenia) *drug* had a beneficial effect approaching significance, apparent in *final* scores (.1087, W_0; adjust significance ++), *change* (.0828, W_0; adjust significance +) and *co-varied* scores (.10–.05, Co-V; adjust significance +).

(6) By scale *Pa* (Paranoia) there was evidence that the effect of *drug* was beneficial to an extent approaching significance with lower *final* scores (.2444, W_1; adjust significance ++), more *change* (.0529,

W_1; adjust significance +) and lower *co-varied* scores (.10–.05, Co-V; adjust significance +.)

(7) On *Pa + Pt + Sc* (Psychotic Triad) it seemed that *drug* had a beneficial effect approaching significance by *final* scores (.2139, W_0; adjust significance ++), *change* (.0649, W_1; adjust significance +) and *co-varied* scores (.10–.05, Co-V; adjust significance +).

On three other scales there was weak and somewhat dubious evidence that *drug* might have had a beneficial effect approaching significance— *Es, Pd* and *Hs*.

(1) On *Es* (Ego Strength) the *drug* effect was evidenced by higher final scores (.3570, W_0; adjust significance ++), more *change* (.1712, W_1; adjust significance +) and higher *co-varied* scores (.40–.30, Co-V; adjust significance +).

(2) On the *Pd* (Psychopathic deviate) scale the *drug* effect was evidenced by lower *final* scores (.8344, W_0; adjust significance ++), more *change* (.0658, W_1; adjust significance +) and lower *co-varied* scores (.30–.20, Co-V; adjust significance +).

(3) On scale *Hs* (Hypochondriasis) *drug* had a beneficial effect in terms of *final* scores (.4078, W_1; adjust significance ++), *change* (.0863, W_1; adjust significance +) and *co-varied* scores (.30, Co-V; adjust significance +).

By the other six scales—*L, K, Hy, Pt, Ma* and *At*—the effects of *psychotherapy* and *drug* were small and clearly not significant.

MMPI: COMPARISON BETWEEN PSYCHOTHERAPY ALONE AND MILIEU. The PSYCHOTHERAPY ALONE group did better than the MILIEU group by both *final* and *change* scores on six scales—*D* (Depression), *Pd* (Psychopathic deviate), *Pt* (Psychasthenia), *Sc* (Schizophrenia), *Ma* (Mania) and *At* (Anxiety). The reverse situation applied to the *final* and *change* scores for five scales—? (Cannot say), *L* (Lie), *K* (Correction), *Mf* (Masculinity-Femininity) and *Cn* (Control). On the other seven scales, one of the two groups had better *final* scores but the other had better *change* scores.

The differences between MILIEU and PSYCHOTHERAPY ALONE were neither impressive nor statistically significant for any of the eighteen scales except *D* (Depression). In this case the *F*-ratio for differences among the five treatments approached significance (final .0727, W_0; *change* .0613, W_1). The PSYCHOTHERAPY group (55 8) was significantly better than MILIEU (64.7) in terms of *final* scores (D < .05) and *co-varied* scores (.025, Co-V; adjust significance −). However, the difference in *change* scores was not significant.*

* By strict interpretation the results of the Duncan Multiple Range test for the *final* scores are not fully acceptable because the *F*-test does not reach a significant level.

This one exception is no more than would be expected by chance, and it seems reasonable to conclude that there is no evidence from the MMPI that either of these two methods of treatment is superior to the other.

MMPI: PSYCHOTHERAPY-DRUG INTERACTION. The interpretation of interaction effects in the psychological tests for this study is necessarily uncertain because of the bias introduced by the untestable patients. However, the proportion of patients missing from each side of the necessary computation for interaction effect is very close, and it would therefore seem reasonable to take the observed results as a fair indication of the true state of affairs.

If this assumption is accepted, the results are in general consistent with the clinical, testability and administrative criteria. There was no significant interaction between *drug* and *psychotherapy* on *final* or *change* scores for any of the MMPI scales except the *change* scores for *F* (Validity) (.0207, W_1), and the *final* scores for *D* (Depression) (.0206, W_0). By the *F* scale, DRUG ALONE had higher *change* scores than PSYCHOTHERAPY ALONE but not significantly so (D > .05); adjust significance +). However, PSYCHOTHERAPY PLUS DRUG was highly significantly better than either DRUG ALONE (D < .01) or PSYCHOTHERAPY ALONE (D < .01; adjust significance +).

Even so, the balance of evidence for interaction on the *F* scale is not impressive. By *final* scores for this variable the interaction was in the opposite direction (not significant; .3785, W_0): in fact DRUG ALONE was actually (trivially) superior to PSYCHOTHERAPY PLUS DRUG, the mean scores being 60.1 and 60.2 respectively. (Co-variance is not applicable.)

The evidence for interaction on the *D* scale is also inconsistent and unimpressive (final .0205, W_0; change .5778, W_1; co-variance not applicable). The *final* mean score for PSYCHOTHERAPY ALONE was not significantly better than the mean score for DRUG ALONE (D > .05), but it was significantly better than the mean score for either MILIEU (D < .01) or PSYCHOTHERAPY PLUS DRUG (D < .05). However, by *change* scores, PSYCHOTHERAPY PLUS DRUG was slightly (not significantly) better than either PSYCHOTHERAPY ALONE or DRUG ALONE. It should be noted that the *D* scale was the only measure from the entire spectrum of clinical, administrative and psychometric criteria for which there was any evidence of significant interference between the effects of *psychotherapy* and *drug*.

Interaction was not significant on the 16 other MMPI scales and the mean *final* score for PSYCHOTHERAPY PLUS DRUG was superior to DRUG ALONE only for *Pd* (Psychopathic deviate)—trivially so. DRUG ALONE was superior to PSYCOTHERAPY PLUS DRUG on the remaining 15 scales, but not to a significant extent (D > .05) except in the case of *Cn* (Control) where the mean *final* scores for the DRUG ALONE and PSY-CHOTHERAPY PLUS DRUG groups were 25.4 and 22.9 respectively.

MMPI: OUTCOME OF ECT. The results for *ECT* were also consistent with the clinical, administrative and testability criteria, placing *ECT* somewhere in the middle of the general rank order.

ECT was first of the five treatments in rank order of effectiveness by *final* scores on five of the eighteen scales (*Hs, Pt, Es, Si, At*). However, for three of these five the *F*-ratio for overall treatment differences did not even approach significance—*Hs* (Hypochondriasis) (.2610, W_1), *Pt* (Psychasthenia) (.4507, W_1), and *Es* (Ego Strength) (.3462, W_0).

On *Si* (Social Introversion) the *F*-ratio for overall differences among the five treatments approached significance (.0750, W_0), and ECT was significantly* better than DRUG ALONE or PSYCHOTHERAPY PLUS DRUG (D < .05; adjust significance −).

On *At* (Anxiety) the *F*-ratio for differences between the treatments approached significance (.0907, W_0) and ECT was significantly* better (D < .05; adjust significance −) than PSYCHOTHERAPY PLUS DRUG (but not better than the other four groups).

On *Cn* (Control), *Sc* (Schizophrenia) and *Pa* + *Pt* + *Sc* (Psychotic Triad), ECT was second in rank order of effectiveness, but not significantly better than any of the other treatments.

ECT was third in rank order on two scales—*F* (Validity) and *D* (Depression); fourth in rank order on six scales—*?* (Cannot say), *L* (Lie), *Hy* (Hysteria), *Pd* (Psychopathic deviate), *Mf* (Masculinity-Femininity) and *Pa* (Paranoia); and fifth (last) in rank order on two scales—*K* (Correction) and *Ma* (Mania).

MMPI: SEX DIFFERENCES. Table 10.4 shows that there were significant differences between the two sexes in *initial* or *final* scores on all of the scales except *F, K, Pa, Si* and *At*.

On four scales—*Mf* (Masculinity-Femininity), *Pt* (Psychasthenia), *Sc* (Schizophrenia) and *Pa* + *Pt* + *Sc* (Psychotic Triad)—females scored substantially better than males at the time of both *initial* and *final* testing, with little change in the significance level of the difference. Thus these scores cannot be taken as a reflection of differential response to treatment between the sexes.

On five scales, the *initial* scores for males and females were not

---

* By strict interpretation the results of the Duncan Multiple Range test are not fully acceptable because the *F*-test does not reach a significant level.

significantly different, but there were substantial differences in favor of women for *final* scores—*Hs* (Hypochondriasis), *D* (Depression), *Hy* (Hysteria), *Pd* (Psychopathic deviate) and *Ma* (Mania).

Table 10.4.   MMPI SEX DIFFERENCES

Significance levels for sex effect from analyses of variance for Initial and Final scores (at the appropriate level of Winsorization). (+) sign indicates that females have healthier scores.

Scale	Initial	Final
?	—.6921	—.0376
L	—.0041	—.2289
F	+.5988	+.1758
K	—.2704	—.7804
Hs	+.4866	+.0050
D	+.1813	+.0001
Hy	—.8674	+.0060
Pd	—.3890	+.0661
Mf	+.0001	+.0001
Pa	+.8351	—.8296
Pt	+.0088	+.0001
Sc	+.0712	+.0021
Ma	+.3339	+.0001
Si	+.6953	—.1634
Es	—.1212	—.0272
Cn	—.2180	—.0357
At	—.5004	—.8277
Triad	+.0852	+.0188

On three scales, males scored significantly better than females in terms of *final* scores (but not *initial* scores)—? (Cannot say), *Cn* (Control) and *Es* (Ego Strength).

On scale *L* (Lie), males scored significantly better than females at *initial* testing, but not at *final* testing.

It must be remembered that considerable bias in favor of females may have been introduced as a result of their relatively high incidence of nontestability, females being significantly less testable after treatment than males ($.0423$, W_0). The precise interpretation of these findings must therefore be in some doubt, but it would seem possible that on some of the scales at least (particularly those for which the *final* scores for males were better than for females) there may be a sex difference even after allowing for the biasing effect of untestable patients.

Several possible explanations for such a difference might be suggested, apart from the possibility that the sex differences are an artifact due to chance or to the biasing effect of untestable patients. It may be that the standardization of some of these scales is inappropriate for schizophrenic patients. Or alternatively, it is possible that the sexes respond differently to treatment in certain ways. Or perhaps the male patients were truly sicker in some particular respects at the beginning than the females and this was reflected both in their initial testing and in their response to treatment. We hesitate, however, to use the current analyses as a basis for reaching any final conclusion on this matter, and would prefer to designate this as a subject for future research.

INTELLECTUAL FUNCTIONING

The Similarities-Proverbs and Shipley Verbal I.Q. show no significant differences among the five treatments; no indication of significant interaction between *psychotherapy* and *drug;* and no significant difference between the two sexes in response to treatment.

By the Shipley Abstract I.Q. there was no significant effect from *drug, psychotherapy* or *ECT*. There is, however, some indication of interaction between the effects of *psychotherapy* and *drug* (final .3907, W_0; change .0076, W_0; .01–.005, Co-V). DRUG ALONE is worse than PSYCHOTHERAPY ALONE, although not significantly so (.40– 30, Co-V). However, when *psychotherapy* and *drug* are given together, the combination is better than PSYCHOTHERAPY ALONE (.20–.10, Co-V) or DRUG ALONE (.02–.01, Co-V).

REFERENCES

(1) Dahlstrom, W. G. & Welsh, G. S.: Appraisal of symptomatic status. In *An MMPI Handbook*. University of Minnesota Press, Minneapolis, 1960: 276–299.
(2) Dahlstrom, W. G. & Welsh, G. S.: The basic scales. In *An MMPI Handbook*. University of Minnesota Press, Minneapolis, 1960: 43–85.
(3) Feldman, M. J.: The use of the MMPI profile for prognosis and evaluation of shock therapy. In *Basic Readings on the MMPI in Psychology and Medicine*. Welsh, G. S. & Dahlstrom, W. G., eds. University of Minnesota Press, Minneapolis, 1960: 553–559.
(4) Gough, H. G.: Diagnostic patterns on the MMPI. *J. Clinical Psychology*, 2:23–37, 1946. (Reprinted as pp. 340–350 in *Basic Readings on the MMPI in Psychology and Medicine*. Welsh, G. S. and Dahlstrom, W. G., eds. University of Minnesota Press, Minneapolis, 1960.)
(5) Hathaway, S. R.: Foreword. In Dahlstrom, W. G. & Welsh, G. S.: *An MMPI Handbook*. University of Minnesota Press, Minneapolis, 1960: vii–xi.
(6) Kaufmann, P.: Changes in the MMPI as a function of psychiatric therapy. In *Basic Readings on the MMPI in Psychology and Medicine*. Welsh, G. S. and Dahlstrom, W. G., eds. University of Minnesota Press, Minneapolis, 1960: 525–533.

(7) McKinley, J. C., Hathaway, S. R. & Meehl, P. E.: The *K* scale. In *Basic Readings on the MMPI in Psychology and Medicine*. Welsh, G. S. and Dahlstrom, W. G., eds. University of Minnesota Press, Minneapolis, 1960: 112–123.

(8) Schofield, W.: Changes following certain therapies as reflected in the MMPI. In *Basic Readings on the MMPI in Psychology and Medicine*. Welsh, G. S. & Dahlstrom, W. G., eds. University of Minnesota Press, Minneapolis, 1960: 534–547.

CHAPTER XI

Comparative Cost of Treatments for the Schizophrenic Patient

PHILIP R. A. MAY, M.D.

~~~~~~

BY ALL THE cost indices considered in this chapter, *individual psychotherapy** was the most expensive form of treatment and *ataraxic drug* was the cheapest. The cost-reducing effect of *drug* was major and substantial by all cost indices, while the cost-increasing effect of *psychotherapy* was major and substantial for all the indices except Cost (L.R. 432). This particular index gives no credit for the speed with which a decision as to failure can be reached (by contrast with Cost, Admission to Termination), as all failures are assigned 432 days stay, no matter how quickly or slowly the decision could be reached. In this case the cost-increasing effect of *psychotherapy* is less apparent, so that it only approaches significance.

It may be concluded that *individual psychotherapy* increases cost not only by adding to the expense of whatever the physician

* A list of conventional terms, abbreviations and notations will be found at the end of Chapter 3.

himself does (or orders), but also by increasing the length of time that a patient will be kept in the hospital until treatment is declared to be either a success or a failure. If (as in Cost, L.R. 432) it is assumed that there was no effective alternative that could be tried in the event of failure, then the longer length of stay for the *psychotherapy* failures would be discounted as the patients would presumably remain in the hospital anyway, whether or not they continued to receive *psychotherapy*.

There was evidence of significant interaction between the effects of *drug* and *psychotherapy* in the case of Cost of Physician-Ordered Treatment, where giving *drug* reduced cost more if the patients were also receiving *psychotherapy* than if they were not receiving *psychotherapy*. There was a tendency in the same direction for Cost (Admission to Release) and Cost (Admission to Termination).

MILIEU was the second most expensive treatment by the three indices that consider the entire cost of the hospital stay; if nursing care and meals are excluded, then it was third.

ECT and PSYCHOTHERAPY PLUS DRUG occupy varying and intermediate places in the cost hierarchy, depending upon the particular index under consideration. If one considers only cost to whenever a decision is made as to success or failure, then ECT is cheaper than PSYCHOTHERAPY PLUS DRUG, but not to a significant extent. On the other hand, if the lower release rate with ECT is taken into consideration, giving more weight to the failures, then PSYCHOTHERAPY PLUS DRUG is cheaper than ECT, but again, the difference between the two is not significant.

The cost of treating patients in the ECT group was greater for females than for males, whatever the cost index used, success or failure; the same applied for MILIEU, except in the case of Cost of Physician-Ordered Treatment. In general, whatever the treatment, females were given a longer and more expensive trial of treatment before being declared a failure than males.

INTRODUCTION

Undoubtedly some will think it unusual, if not actually incongruous, eccentric or improper, to include cost as a major criterion in a controlled scientific study of the outcome of psychiatric treatment. Psychiatric research investigators, it is said, should be consecrated to the pure-hearted contemplation of subjects of theoretical and scientific interest, not to mundane practical matters. Without wishing to detract from the undoubted virtues of pure science, it would seem that the time has come to lay aside this elegant—and perhaps self-serving—Edwardian image. Someone has to make practical decisions, and it is possible that accountants, politicians and administrators of medical care, as well as the physician and his patient, might welcome a little practical assistance as an alternative to being forced to rely entirely on phantasy and speculation or on the misleading ratios and indices devised by persons with no practical experience in hospital treatment. With the computational facilities now available, research investigators have the capacity necessary to develop the data; it is now necessary to devise explicit guidelines and limitations for their interpretation.

This chapter should be taken as a tentative exploration in this direction. I hope that it will stimulate further discussion and more exact examination of the subject, and that others will be encouraged to include this area in their investigations. It is assumed that the serious reader will have some wish to understand the problems involved, and that he will read with care the introductory section on assessment of cost (Chapter 2) and related Appendix VI.

THE COST OF SUCCESSFUL TREATMENT

It is important that the reader understand the different implications and limits of interpretation for each of the various cost indices. Cost (Admission to Release) considers the total cost of hospital care for the successes only—defined for our purposes as those who could be successfully released after a thorough treatment trial with a maximum limit of one year. This index may be interpreted as a response to the question, "Assuming that it were possible for each treatment to select out ahead of time, and with 100 percent efficiency, only those patients who were going to respond successfully within one year, how much would their treatment cost?" Thus, length of hospital stay is taken into consideration, but not the number of releases.

Table 11.1 summarizes the relevant analysis of variance. There was an extremely significant difference between the cost of the five treatments. After separating out the effect of sex differences, the F-ratio for overall differences among the five treatments was 5.88 (.0001, W_1). The significance level remains substantially the same (.005–.001, Co-V) if co-variance adjustments are made to estimate the Cost (Admission To Release) that would theoretically occur if the groups had been equated on sex and initial level on the Menninger Health-Sickness scale. It increases successively through two stages of Winsorization, as we pay less attention to the more extreme cases—apparently the differences observed were spread throughout each treatment group and were not the result of a few atypical cases.

Table 11.1. COST (ADMISSION TO RELEASE):
ANALYSIS OF VARIANCE

Significance levels for the various effects at three successive stages of Winsorization, computed to four decimal places. The most representative, W_1, also shows the appropriate F-values in parentheses and a directional sign, (+) indicating better values for a particular treatment or for the female sex.

	W_0		W_1	W_2
Five treatments in general	.0010		.0001 (5.88)	.0001
Ataraxic drug	.0110	+	.0074 (7.17)	.0080
Psychotherapy	.0090	−	.0021 (9.43)	.0013
Sex (ECT included)	.1845	−	.1813 (1.81)	.1805
Sex (ECT excluded)	.3394	−	.3601 (0.84)	.3718
Interaction				
Sex × psychotherapy	.1015	−	.0959 (2.77)	.0645
Sex × drug	.0668	−	.0420 (4.13)	.0376
Psychotherapy × drug	.4057	−	.2853 (1.14)	.2848

Figure 11.1 shows the mean Cost (Admission to Release) for the five treatments in rank order with a Multiple Range test. On the average, DRUG ALONE and ECT cost the least ($2680 and $2810 respectively). Next, and distinguishable from DRUG ALONE and ECT to an extent approaching significance (D > .05), were PSYCHOTHERAPY PLUS DRUG ($3290) and MILIEU ($3390). PSYCHOTHERAPY ALONE ($4470) was the most expensive form of treatment, significantly different (D < .05) from PSYCHOTHERAPY PLUS DRUG and MILIEU and highly significantly different (D < .01) from DRUG ALONE and ECT.

The mean for MILIEU is somewhat influenced by the inclusion of one female patient whose treatment cost $2750 more than any other patient in this group: one stage of Winsorization reduces the mean to $3270, the same as the mean (W_1) for PSYCHOTHERAPY PLUS DRUG. It would then be wise to judge that the Cost (Admission to Release) of these two forms of treatment is generally close to the same, except for unusual cases.

Setting aside the ECT group from consideration, a three-way analysis of variance shows that *drug* had a highly significant effect (F 7.17, .0074, W_1) in reducing Cost (Admission to Release), and that *psy-*

Figure 11-1   COST (ADMISSION TO RELEASE) FOR THE 5 TREATMENTS

S figures, non-Winsorized (W_o) and rounded off to nearest $10, for the cost of treating only those patients who could be planned for successful release within the first year. Failures are not included. Unadjusted and adjusted by co-variance for sex and initial level of health-sickness.

The lines depict Ducan Multiple Range Tests at the 95% and 99% protection levels, non-Winsorized data (W_o). Groups not connected by these lines are significantly different from one another at that level.

━━━ = a lack of statistical significance at the 95% level

▪▪▪▪▪▪ = a lack of statistical significance at the 99% level

	(D)	(E)	(P+D)	(M)	(P)
MEAN					
co-varied	2700	2820	3260	3380	4480
unadjusted	2680	2810	3290	3390	4470
S. D.	1740	1170	1820	2520	2250
N	46	37	42	25	30
MAX.	7190	5130	7980	10980	9770
MIN.	510	840	690	970	1240
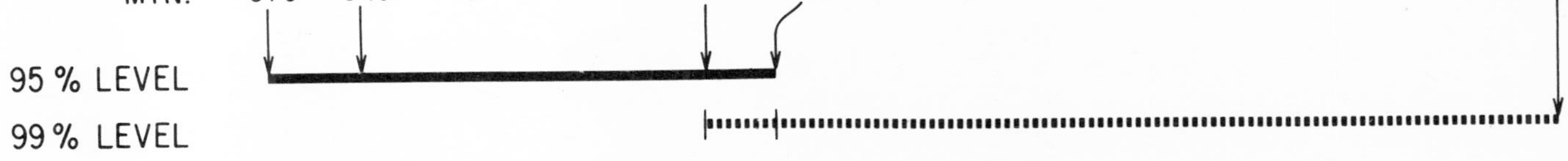 95 % LEVEL					
99 % LEVEL					

Figure 11-2   COST (ADMISSION TO RELEASE) FOR EACH TREATMENT AND SEX SEPARATELY

S figures, non-Winsorized (W_O) and rounded off to nearest $10, for the cost of treating only those patients who could be planned for successful release within the first year. Failures are not included.

The lines depict Ducan Multiple Range Tests at the 95% and 99% protection levels, non-Winsorized data (W_O). Groups not connected by these lines are significantly different from one another at that level.

■ = a lack of statistical significance at the 95% level

▪▪▪▪▪▪ = a lack of statistical significance at the 99% level

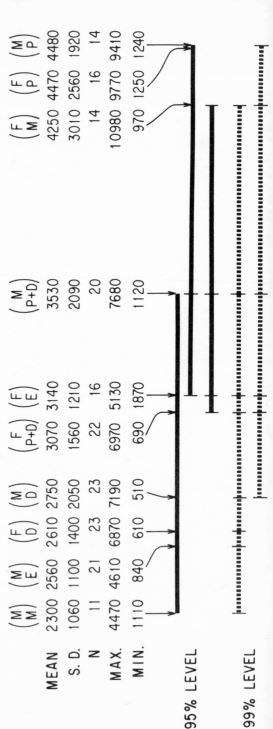

	$\binom{M}{M}$	$\binom{M}{E}$	$\binom{F}{D}$	$\binom{M}{D}$	$\binom{F}{P+D}$	$\binom{F}{E}$	$\binom{M}{P+D}$	$\binom{F}{M}$	$\binom{F}{P}$	$\binom{M}{P}$
MEAN	2300	2560	2610	2750	3070	3140	3530	4250	4470	4480
S.D.	1060	1100	1400	2050	1560	1210	2090	3010	2560	1920
N	11	21	23	23	22	16	20	14	16	14
MAX.	4470	4610	6870	7190	6970	5130	7680	10980	9770	9410
MIN.	1110	840	610	510	690	1870	1120	970	1250	1240

95% LEVEL

99% LEVEL

chotherapy had a highly significant effect in increasing it (F 9.43, .0021, W_1). There is some (nonsignificant) indication of interaction (.2853, W_1). Giving *drug* reduced Cost (Admission to Release) more if the patients were also receiving *psychotherapy* than if they were not receiving *psychotherapy*.

Figure 11.2 shows the figures for the five treatments and two sexes separately. The influence of the patient's sex on cost that is indicated by the statistics for sex effect is seen to be largely due to a marked difference in the cost of MILIEU for males ($2300) and females ($4250). Winsorizing reduces the average for females by about $180 (largely because of one extreme case), but the difference remains significant (D < .05).

For ECT the average Cost (Admission to Release) was greater for women ($3140) than for men ($2560), but not significantly so (D > .05). For PSYCHOTHERAPY ALONE the costs for the two sexes are very close together, the non-Winsorized means being $4480 (males) and $4470 (females). (In the male PSYCHOTHERAPY ALONE group there was one patient whose treatment cost $2360 more than anyone else in that group; one stage of Winsorizing lessens the impact of this aberrant case so that the mean for males is lowered to $4440, while for females it remains $4470.)

The figures for Cost (Admission to Release) include a per diem charge for the initial period of evaluation before treatment was actually started. They also assume that there is no charge when the patient is away from the hospital for a weekend or similar short periods of leave. It may therefore be of interest that these two items make very little difference to the statistical discrimination between the various treatment groups. Subtracting the cost of initial evaluation leaves the rank order unchanged, but increases the F-ratio for treatment differences by a small amount (.13, W_0). Adding a charge for leave also makes no difference to the rank order, but increases the F-ratio fractionally (by .058, W_0).

COST FOR ALL PATIENTS TREATED TO MAXIMUM OF ONE YEAR

Table 11.2 summarizes the relevant analysis of variance for Cost (L.R. 432).

In contrast to the preceding section, this index presupposes that there is no effective way of predicting ahead of time which patients will respond to which particular type of treatment. All patients are included whether success or failure, taking into consideration their length of stay in the hospital and responding to the question, "How much does it cost to treat comparable average groups of schizophrenic patients with each of the five treatments until they are well enough to be released or else have been given treatment for a year?" From the viewpoint of the administrator, Cost (L.R. 432) assumes that patients who are not successfully released are dropped from the budget of the treatment unit at the end of approximately one year, either by discharge or by transfer to another treatment or custodial unit. Further, it must be understood that there is no attempt to take into account the cost of any treatment that might be given after a patient has been released from the hospital.

Table 11.2. COST (L.R. 432): ANALYSIS OF VARIANCE

Significance levels for the various effects at three successive stages of Winsorization, computed to four decimal places. The most representative, W_0, also shows the appropriate F-values in parentheses and a directional sign, (+) indicating better values for a particular treatment or for the female sex.

	W_0	W_1	W_2
Five treatments in general	.0001 (12.65)	.0000	.0000
Ataraxic drug	+ .0000 (45.48)	.0000	.0000
Psychotherapy	− .1076 (2.89)	.1297	.1115
Sex (ECT included)	− .0632 (3.50)	.0557	.0458
Sex (ECT excluded)	− .4714 (0.52)	.4702	.4880
Interaction			
Sex × psychotherapy	− .2262 (1.46)	.1985	.2047
Sex × drug	− .4260 (0.63)	.4160	.3539
Psychotherapy × drug	− .8406 (0.04)	.6893	.7069

For Cost (L.R. 432) there was an extremely significant difference among the five treatments. After removing the effect of sex variation, the F-ratio for overall treatment differences was 12.65 (.0001, W_0). Co-variance adjustments for sex and initial level on the Menninger Health-Sickness scale make very little difference ($<$ .0005, Co-V), and the F-ratio is increased by Winsorization, indicating that the significant differences should not be attributed to a few extreme cases.

Figure 11.3 shows the average Cost (L.R. 432) of the five treatments in rank order with a Multiple Range test. DRUG ALONE (with a mean of $2960) and PSYCHOTHERAPY PLUS DRUG ($3640) are the least expensive forms of treatment by this index, not confidently distinguishable from each other (D $>$ .05), but highly significantly less expensive (D $<$ .01) than MILIEU ($6230) and PSYCHOTHERAPY ALONE ($7080). These two latter are not significantly different from each other (D $>$ .05). ECT ($4440) is in the middle, set apart on the one side as sig-

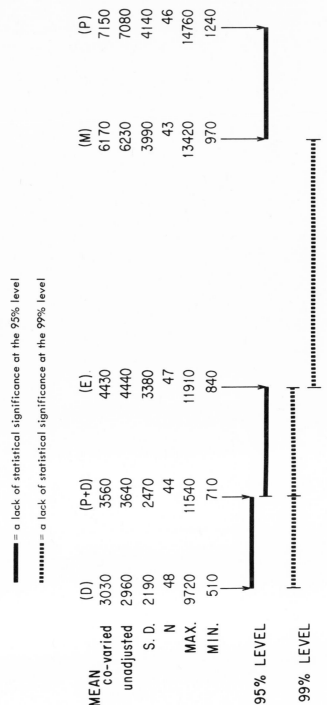

Figure 11-3   COST (LR 432) OF THE 5 TREATMENTS

$ figures, non-Winsorized (W_o) and rounded off to nearest $10, for cost of treating all patients up to maximum of one year on their original treatment. Unadjusted and adjusted by co-variance for sex and initial level of health-sickness.

The lines depict Ducan Multiple Range Tests at the 95% and 99% protection levels, non-Winsorized data (W_o). Groups not connected by these lines are significantly different from one another at that level.

▬▬▬ = a lack of statistical significance at the 95% level

▪▪▪▪▪▪▪▪ = a lack of statistical significance at the 99% level

MEAN	(D)	(P+D)	(E)	(M)	(P)
co-varied	3030	3560	4430	6170	7150
unadjusted	2960	3640	4440	6230	7080
S. D.	2190	2470	3380	3990	4140
N	48	44	47	43	46
MAX.	9720	11540	11910	13420	14760
MIN.	510	710	840	970	1240

95% LEVEL

99% LEVEL

nificantly less expensive than MILIEU (D < .05) and highly significantly less expensive than PSYCHOTHERAPY ALONE (D < .01); and on the other side as significantly more expensive than DRUG ALONE (D < .05), but not clearly more expensive than PSYCHOTHERAPY PLUS DRUG (D > .05).

If we omit the ECT group, a three-way analysis of variance demonstrates that *drug* had an extremely significant effect (F 45.48/.0000, W_0) in reducing Cost (L.R. 432), while *psychotherapy* had a cost-increasing effect that approached significance (F 2.89/.1076, W_0). There was no significant interaction between the effects of *drug* and *psychotherapy* (.8406, W_0).

Figure 11.4 shows the means for the five treatments and two sexes separately; their rank order and absolute values are not materially affected by Winsorization.

The patients' sex seems to make very little difference to the Cost (L.R. 432) of treatment with *ataraxic drug* or *individual psychotherapy,* alone or in combination. Thus for PSYCHOTHERAPY ALONE, Cost (L.R. 432) was virtually the same for men and women. For DRUG ALONE the average Cost (L.R. 432) for males was $400 less than for females, while for PSYCHOTHERAPY PLUS DRUG it was $480 more for males than females. However, it cost significantly more to treat female ECT patients than males—by an average of $2650 (D < .05). MILIEU was also a more expensive treatment for women than men, although here the difference ($1500) only approached significance (D > .05).

COST FOR ALL PATIENTS, ADMISSION TO TERMINATION

This index is similar to Cost (L.R. 432), but instead of providing for the treatment of all nonresponders to a defined maximum of one year, it affords the possibility that treatment might be given up as a failure before then under certain circumstances—had there been a full and reasonable trial and had it seemed reasonably clear that the patient would not be getting out within one year. The administrator should interpret Cost (Admission to Termination) as assuming that there is a well-supervised consultation system to ensure that treatment will be abandoned if, at any point after six months, there seems to be less than one chance in ten that the patient will be discharged by the end of the one-year period. It is also assumed that once treatment has been declared a failure the patient is dropped from the budget of the treatment unit by discharge or transfer to some other unit, and that there is no need to take into account the cost of any treatment that might be given to either the failures or the successes subsequent to discharge from the unit.

Figure 11-4 COST (LR 432) FOR EACH SEX AND TREATMENT SEPARATELY

$ figures, non Winsorized (W_o) and rounded off to nearest $10, for cost of treating all patients up to maximum of one year on their original treatment.

The lines depict Ducan Multiple Range Tests at the 95% and 99% protection levels, non-Winsorized data (W_o). Groups not connected by these lines are significantly different from one another at that level.

━━━ = a lack of statistical significance at the 95% level

┄┄┄ = a lack of statistical significance at the 99% level

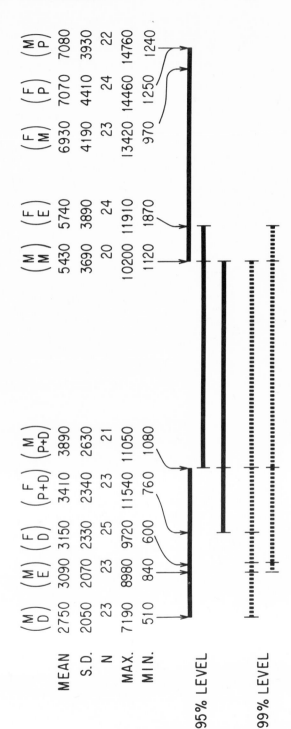

	(M/D)	(M/E)	(F/D)	(F/P+D)	(M/P+D)	(M/M)	(F/E)	(F/M)	(F/P)	(M/P)
MEAN	2750	3090	3150	3410	3890	5430	5740	6930	7070	7080
S.D.	2050	2070	2330	2340	2630	3690	3890	4190	4410	3930
N	23	23	25	23	21	20	24	23	24	22
MAX.	7190	8980	9720	11540	11050	10200	11910	13420	14460	14760
MIN.	510	840	600	760	1080	1120	1870	970	1250	1240

95% LEVEL

99% LEVEL

The relevant analysis of variance (Table 11.3) reveals that, by this particular cost index, there was an extremely significant difference among the five treatments. After allowing for differences between the two sexes, the F-ratio for overall treatment differences was 12.85 (.0000, W_0). It increases through two successive stages of Winsorization, indicating that the differences are not likely to be confined to a few unusual or extreme cases. The significance level is sustained if co-variance adjustments are made for sex and initial level on the Menninger Health-Sickness scale ($< .0005$, Co-V).

Table 11.3. COST (ADMISSION TO TERMINATION):
ANALYSIS OF VARIANCE

Significance levels for the various effects at three successive stages of Winsorization, computed to four decimal places. The most representative, W_0, also shows the appropriate F-values in parentheses and a directional sign, (+) indicating better values for a particular treatment or for the female sex.

	W_0	W_1	W_2
Five treatments in general	.0000 (12.85)	.0000	.0000
Ataraxic drug	+ .0000 (26.71)	.0000	.0000
Psychotherapy	− .0004 (12.39)	.0001	.0001
Sex (ECT included)	− .0578 (3.66)	.0582	.0482
Sex (ECT excluded)	− .2119 (1.56)	.2344	.2110
Interaction			
Sex × psychotherapy	− .6657 (0.19)	.5862	.5729
Sex × drug	− .0730 (3.21)	.0530	.0338
Psychotherapy × drug	− .3851 (0.75)	.1824	.1755

Figure 11.5 shows the average values for Cost (Admission to Termination) for the five treatments with a Multiple Range test. DRUG ALONE ($2780) is the least expensive, highly significantly (D $< .01$) cheaper than both MILIEU ($4260) and PSYCHOTHERAPY ALONE ($5720). ECT ($3310) ranks as the second cheapest; it is also significantly less expensive than MILIEU (D $< .05$) and highly significantly less expensive than PSYCHOTHERAPY ALONE (D $< .01$). PSYCHOTHER-APY PLUS DRUG ($3660) ranks third, highly significantly less expensive than PSYCHOTHERAPY ALONE (D $< .01$), but not significantly different from any of the other groups (D $> .05$). PSYCHOTHERAPY ALONE is the most expensive, highly significantly more than any of the other four methods (D $< .01$).

A three-way analysis of variance, leaving out the ECT group, demonstrates that *drug* had an extremely significant effect in reducing Cost (Admission To Termination) (F 26.71/.0000, W_0), and that *psychotherapy* had a very highly significant effect in increasing it (F 12.39/

Figure 11-5   COST (ADMISSION TO TERMINATION) OF THE 5 TREATMENTS

$ figures, non-Winsorized (W$_0$) and rounded off to nearest $10, for cost to termination of a reasonably adequate trial of treatment for all cases. Unadjusted and adjusted by co-variance for sex and initial level of health-sickness.

The lines depict Ducan Multiple Range Tests at the 95% and 99% protection levels, non-Winsorized data (W$_0$). Groups not connected by these lines are significantly different from one another at that level.

▬▬▬ = a lack of statistical significance at the 95% level

▪▪▪▪▪▪▪ = a lack of statistical significance at the 99% level

	(D)	(E)	(P+D)	(M)	(P)
MEAN					
co-varied	2820	3300	3620	4230	5760
unadjusted	2780	3310	3660	4260	5720
S. D.	1720	1450	2280	2260	2690
N	48	47	44	43	46
MAX.	7170	7080	10680	10820	11630
MIN.	510	840	670	970	1240
95% LEVEL					
99% LEVEL					

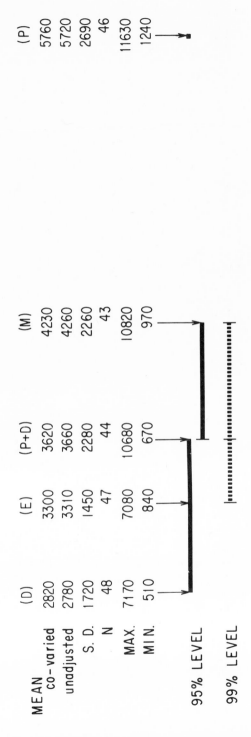

Figure 11-6   COST (ADMISSION TO TERMINATION) FOR EACH SEX AND TREATMENT SEPARATELY

$ figures, non-Winsorized (W_o) and rounded off to nearest $10, for cost to termination of a reasonably adequate trial of treatment for all cases.

The lines depict Ducan Multiple Range Tests at the 95% and 99% protection levels, non-Winsorized data (W_o). Groups not connected by these lines are significantly different from one another at that level.

▬▬▬▬ = a lack of statistical significance at the 95% level

▪▪▪▪▪▪▪▪ = a lack of statistical significance at the 99% level

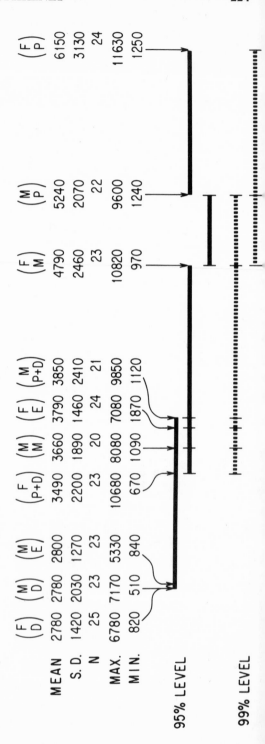

	$\binom{F}{D}$	$\binom{M}{D}$	$\binom{M}{E}$	$\binom{F}{P+D}$	$\binom{M}{P+D}$	$\binom{M}{M}$	$\binom{F}{E}$	$\binom{M}{P+D}$	$\binom{F}{M}$	$\binom{M}{P}$	$\binom{F}{P}$
MEAN	2780	2780	2800	3490	3660	3790	1460	3850	4790	5240	6150
S. D.	1420	2030	1270	2200	1890	1890	1460	2410	2460	2070	3130
N	25	23	23	23	20	24	24	21	23	22	24
MAX.	6780	7170	5330	10680	8080	7080	1870	9850	10820	9600	11630
MIN.	820	510	840	670	1090	1090	1870	1120	970	1240	1250

95% LEVEL

99% LEVEL

.0004, W_0). *Drug* reduced Cost (Admission to Termination) more if the patient were also receiving *psychotherapy* than if the patient were not receiving *psychotherapy*, but the *F*-ratio for interaction was not significant (.3851, W_0).

Figure 11.6 shows the means for the treatments and sexes separately. Winsorization has no effect on the rank order and little effect on the means themselves. For ECT females cost more than males, but to an extent that only approached significance (D > .05). Apart from ECT, there are differences between the costs for the two sexes in MILIEU, where the average Cost (Admission to Termination) for males ($3660) was less than for females ($4790), approaching significance (D > .05); and in PSYCHOTHERAPY ALONE, where the cost for males ($5240) was also less than for females ($6150). For DRUG ALONE, the Cost (Admission to Termination) for male and female patients was the same ($2780).

COST OF PHYSICIAN-ORDERED TREATMENT ONLY

Treatment is sometimes seen as only whatever the physician orders or does himself. It is therefore necessary to give a figure for the total cost of all those items that, during the entire course of treatment up to eventual success or failure, are given personally by the physician or that are (usually) ordered by him on the Physician's Order Sheet. This includes sedatives, hydrotherapy and seclusion, as well as *electro-*

Table 11.4. COST (PHYSICIAN-ORDERED TREATMENT ONLY): ANALYSIS OF VARIANCE

Significance levels for the various effects at three successive stages of Winsorization, computed to four decimal places. The most representative, W_1, also shows the appropriate F-values in parentheses and a directional sign, (+) indicating better values for a particular treatment or for the female sex.

	W_0	W_1	W_2
Five treatments in general	.0000	.0000 (57.56)	.0000
Ataraxic drug	.0002	+ .0000 (17.94)	.0000
Psychotherapy	.0000	− .0000(149.66)	.0000
Sex (ECT included)	.3992	− .6687 (0.19)	.6507
Sex (ECT excluded)	.9901	− .6295 (0.23)	.6330
Interaction			
Sex × psychotherapy	.3596	− .2555 (1.29)	.2649
Sex × drug	.3246	− .2567 (1.29)	.2355
Psychotherapy × drug	.0266	− .0113 (6.42)	.0098

Figure 11-7   COST OF PHYSICIAN-ORDERED TREATMENT ONLY, FOR THE 5 TREATMENTS

$ figures, non-Winsorized (W_o) and rounded off to nearest $10, for cost of all such treatment, to termination of a reasonably adequate treatment trial.

The lines depict Ducan Multiple Range Tests at the 95% and 99% protection levels, non-Winsorized data (W_o).
Groups not connected by these lines are significantly different from one another at that level.

▬▬▬ = a lack of statistical significance at the 95% level

▪▪▪▪▪▪▪▪ = a lack of statistical significance at the 99% level

	(D)	(E)	(M)	(P+D)	(P)
MEAN	240	340	350	820	1230
S.D.	200	270	370	500	640
N	48	47	43	44	46
MAX.	1250	1330	1720	2040	3170
MIN.	40	70	20	230	250

95% LEVEL

99% LEVEL

convulsive therapy, ataraxic drugs and *individual psychotherapy*. Meals and nursing care are specifically excluded.

Table 11.4 shows the relevant analysis of variance and Figure 11.7 shows the group means in rank order.

The differences among the five treatments were extremely significant, the F-ratio after allowing for sex effect being 57.56/.0000, W_1. PSYCHO-THERAPY ALONE, with an average cost of $1230, and PSYCHOTHERAPY PLUS DRUG ($820) were highly significantly more expensive (D < .01) than the other groups and highly significantly different from each other (D < .01). DRUG ALONE ($240) was actually the cheapest, but it is not confidently distinguishable (D > .05) from ECT ($340) or MILIEU ($350). ECT and MILIEU are very close together and, indeed, their positions are reversed by paying less attention to extreme cases (Winsorization).

A three-way analysis of variance indicates that *drug* had an extremely significant effect in *reducing* Cost (Physician-Ordered Treatment Only) (F 17.94/.0000, W_1), while *psychotherapy* had an extremely significant effect in *increasing* it (F 149.66/.0000, W_1).

There is a significant interaction between the effects of *psychotherapy* and *drug* (.0113, W_1). Giving *drug* to patients who are also receiving *psychotherapy* reduced Cost (Physician-Ordered Treatment Only) more than giving *drug* to patients who were not receiving *psychotherapy*.

Figure 11.8 shows the means separately by sex and treatment group. ECT for the average male patient cost $240 less than for the average female ($460), approaching a significant difference between the sexes (D > .05). For the other treatments, the sex of the patient made little difference to Cost (Physician-Ordered Treatment Only).

COST—A POSTSCRIPT

Some months after the cost computations had been completed and after the main text of this chapter had been written, the author heard, for the first time and admittedly with mixed feelings, of *Operation Red Ball*.[1]

In January 1965 the State of California Director of Mental Hygiene commissioned his Bureau of Management Analysis ". . . to identify and pin a price tag on every element of cost, direct or indirect, connected with early treatment, defined as the first thirty days of hospitalization." The accounting included (1) a time-measurement study with direct time charging by all personnel having personal or paperwork contact

[1] See reference 1.

Figure 11-8   COST OF PHYSICIAN-ORDERED TREATMENT ONLY, FOR EACH SEX AND TREATMENT

$ figure, non-Winsorized (W_o), rounded off to nearest $10 for cost of all such treatment to termination of a reasonably adequate treatment trial.

The lines depict Ducan Multiple Range Tests at the 95% and 99% protection levels, non-Winsorized data (W_o). Groups not connected by these lines are significantly different from one another at that level.

━━━ = a lack of statistical significance at the 95% level

▪▪▪▪▪▪▪▪ = a lack of statistical significance at the 99% level

	$\binom{M}{E}$	$\binom{M}{D}$	$\binom{F}{D}$	$\binom{M}{M}$	$\binom{F}{M}$	$\binom{F}{E}$	$\binom{F}{P+D}$	$\binom{M}{P+D}$	$\binom{M}{P}$	$\binom{F}{P}$
MEAN	220	230	250	290	400	460	750	900	1220	1250
S.D.	90	160	240	260	450	330	430	580	550	720
N	23	23	25	20	23	24	23	21	22	24
MAX.	430	550	1250	920	1720	1330	2040	2040	2350	3170
MIN.	70	40	60	20	30	110	230	230	250	290

95% LEVEL

99% LEVEL

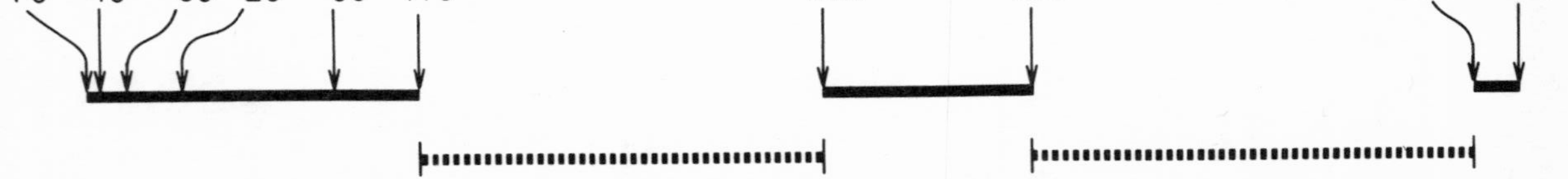

with the patients, and (2) prorating expenses that, for practical purposes, were considered to be constant and applicable to all patients in the hospital.

Their study, titled *Operation Red Ball,* was carried out at three hospitals within the California State Department of Mental Hygiene (unfortunately not including Camarillo, the hospital at which the *S.R.P.* was conducted). It included 337 patients admitted over the last fourteen days of October 1965. Of these, 124 left the hospital in less than thirty days. Their closest comparable figures are for a subgroup of 51 first admissions (mentally ill other than geriatric and alcoholic) who stayed for the full thirty days. These can be compared with the computations of per diem cost already made for the 228 patients in our study.

The findings of *Red Ball* provide striking confirmation that the cost estimates obtained in our research study are likely to be respectably close to the figures that might be derived by professional accounting personnel and management analysts. Both studies found a definite difference between the sexes, and the two estimates of average per diem costs are remarkably close. The *S.R.P.* per diem average for males was $23.93; *Red Ball* found variation from one hospital to another with a range of $18.24–$23.95, average $20.95. For females, the *S.R.P.* per diem figure was $27.14; *Red Ball* found a range from hospital to hospital of $22.52–$28.37, average $24.10.

The higher *S.R.P.* figures are readily accounted for by the fact that the *S.R.P.* level of care was deliberately set at the highest level that would seem reasonably attainable in a public hospital in the forseeable future. By contrast, *Red Ball* considered only the current average level of care in the first thirty days, which, in the judgment of the principal investigator, is appreciably less than that of the *S.R.P.*

The *S.R.P.* figures provide an interesting and important dimension of per diem cost that does not appear in *Red Ball*—the effect of differences in treatment method. In *Red Ball* costs were averaged for all patients regardless of the type of treatment. The *S.R.P.* figures show that the per diem cost varied according to the type of treatment being given from $21.95 to $26.67 for males and from $25.21 to $30.08 for females. Moreover, the *S.R.P.* data provide estimates of the *total* cost of treatment for the patient's entire hospital stay, as well as per diem cost.

As a matter of technical accounting detail, there is happily a reasonable correspondence between the allowances for *indirect* costs in the two studies. *Red Ball* figures show that their estimate of indirect costs (excluding food and food services which were included as direct costs in the *S.R.P.*) amounted to 21–22 percent* of the direct costs, compared with the *S.R.P.* assumption of 20 percent.

REFERENCES

(1) *Operation Red Ball:* A survey of costs of early treatment in California's hospitals for the mentally ill. State of California Department of Mental Hygiene Division of Administration, Management Analysis Assignment #115. Feb. 1966.

* *Red Ball* report shows indirect costs as 23.7 percent and direct costs as 76.3 percent, i.e., their indirect costs were (approximately) 32 percent of direct costs. However, food and food service costs ($1.29–$1.54 per day varying from hospital to hospital) comprise 32–35 percent of *Red Ball's* indirect costs. If these are removed, the indirect cost for *Red Ball* becomes 21–22 percent of the direct costs. The indirect cost figures from *S.R.P.* and *Red Ball* are still not entirely comparable because of the different approaches to various associated and treatment and diagnostic services, but it is clear that they correspond substantially.

CHAPTER XII

The Results of Treatment of Schizophrenia —An Overview

PHILIP R. A. MAY, M.D.

~~~~~~~~~~~~~~~~~~~~~~~~~~~~~~~~~~~~~

THIS CHAPTER SUMMARIZES the main findings to give reasonable overall perspective to the detailed material given in Chapters 5–11, reviewing the outcome of the five treatments in terms of four general criterion categories—*clinical, psychometric, movement* and *cost*.

DRUG ALONE* and PSYCHOTHERAPY PLUS DRUG were the most effective treatments and also the least costly in time and money. By the *clinical* criteria, the advantage between these two was generally with PSYCHOTHERAPY PLUS DRUG, but the differences between them were mainly small and insubstantial and never impressive. The largest difference was in the case of Insight, where PSYCHOTHERAPY

* A list of conventional terms, abbreviations and notations will be found at the end of Chapter 3.

PLUS DRUG was superior to DRUG ALONE to an extent that approached significance. For the *psychometric* criteria, the situation was reversed, DRUG ALONE being superior to PSYCHOTHERAPY PLUS DRUG by almost all the test measures. However, the differences between the two were small and not statistically significant except in one instance where DRUG ALONE was more effective. By all the *movement* and *cost* criteria, DRUG ALONE was superior to PSYCHOTHERAPY PLUS DRUG. However, these two treatment groups were distinguishable with an acceptable degree of statistical significance only in terms of Cost (Physician-Ordered Treatment Only), where PSYCHOTHERAPY PLUS DRUG was highly significantly more expensive.

PSYCHOTHERAPY ALONE and MILIEU were clearly the least effective and the most expensive forms of treatment with little to choose between them. ECT occupied an intermediate position.

Analysis of the different components of treatment effect indicates that by almost all the clinical, movement and cost criteria, *drug* had a powerful beneficial effect, while the effect of *psychotherapy* was nonsignificant. There was no evidence of antagonism between *drug* and *psychotherapy*. On the contrary, such little interaction as did seem to occur was in the direction of potentiation of positive *drug* effect on certain variables where *psychotherapy alone* appeared to have little effect or even a slightly adverse one. The psychometric results confirm or are consistent with these findings.

As for differences in outcome between the sexes, female patients did significantly or nearly significantly worse than males on *ECT* by several of the clinical, movement and cost criteria. There was also some indication that *milieu therapy* tended to take more time and be more expensive for females, and that *psychotherapy* (with or without *ataraxic drugs*) was likely to be given a longer trial of treatment in females before being declared a failure.

There were considerable differences between the mean scores of males and females on many of the MMPI scales, but it is possible that this may be an artifact, the result of differences in cooperation with testing or of standardization problems.

INTRODUCTION

The preceding chapters have considered the results in terms of 53 different measures and 101 separate variables* which may be classified in four main categories as follows:

   (1) *Clinical:* The independent ratings of nurses, therapists and psycho-analysts
   (2) *Psychometric:* The MMPI, Similarities-Proverbs and Shipley scales
   (3) *Movement:* Release rate and measures of hospital stay.
   (4) *Cost:* The various cost of treatment indices

The differences among the five treatment methods were most apparent in the clinical, movement and cost criteria. The psychometric criteria follow in general the same pattern as the other data, but they are less conclusive and pose substantial problems in interpretation due to nontestable patients. For this reason they will be considered separately at the end of this resumé.

PSYCHOTHERAPY PLUS DRUG VERSUS DRUG ALONE

PSYCHOTHERAPY PLUS DRUG and DRUG ALONE were the two most effective forms of treatment by all the clinical measures except for the therapists' ratings of Aggressive and the analysts' ratings of Insight where DRUG ALONE was third in rank order. PSYCHOTHERAPY PLUS DRUG was slightly the better of the two by all eleven of the analysts' and nurses' measures;** by both of the therapists' global measures (AA and SRS) and by their ratings of Energetic, Clear-Thinking,† Depressed† and Aggressive. DRUG ALONE was rated slightly better by the therapists on the other two Clyde subscales, Jittery and Friendly.

One would hesitate, however, to assert with any substantial degree of confidence that combined treatment is superior by the clinical cri-

---

* For each clinical measure, *final status* and *change* are counted as separate variables, but not the *co-varied* scores. IDIORAT is counted as a variable that is transformed into a derived measure, TROUBLERAT. For the stay and cost criteria, adjustments for leave and initial evaluation are considered to be additional variables, but not separate measures.

** In the case of nurses' MHS, the *change* and *co-varied* scores were higher for PSYCHOTHERAPY PLUS DRUG, although the *final* scores were lower.

† For Clear-Thinking and Depressed, DRUG ALONE had better *final* scores, but the *change* and *co-varied* scores gave the advantage to PSYCHOTHERAPY PLUS DRUG.

teria, as the differences between PSYCHOTHERAPY PLUS DRUG and DRUG ALONE were often tiny or trivial and never impressive or statistically significant. For the average patient the six largest differences in *co-varied* scores were as follows:*

Analysts' measures:	MHS +0.9 points (1/8)
	CDAS (Total) +1.4 points (1/5)
Therapists' measures:	Clear-Thinking +1.4 points (1/5)
	Jittery −1.1 points (1/2)
Nurses' measures:	TROUBLERAT +8.5 points (1/5)
	MHS +0.9 points (1/8)

For the other thirteen clinical measures, the differences were even less substantial.

Furthermore, analysis of the different components of treatment effect indicates that by thirteen out of the nineteen clinical measures, the effect of *psychotherapy* was not significant, but *drug* was effective beyond all reasonable doubt.† Two other clinical measures followed a similar path but to a lesser degree—therapists' ratings of Clear-Thinking and Energetic. By the former, *psychotherapy* had a significant positive effect, but not as much as *drug,* whose effect was extremely significant. Similarly, the effect of *drug* in increasing Energetic was highly significant, while that of *psychotherapy* only approached significance.

For the remaining four clinical measures—analysts' ratings of Insight, therapists' ratings of Jittery and Aggressive, and nurses' ratings of Motility—the differences between the effects of *psychotherapy* and *drug* were smaller and less conclusive, although clearly in the same direction as the others. Neither treatment had much effect on Motility and Jittery. *Psychotherapy* increased Aggressive to an end result that was further away from the normal to an extent that approached significance, while *drug* had an insignificant effect in the same direction. The end effect of *drug* on Insight was significantly positive, while the effect of *psychotherapy* in this respect was positive but nonsignificant.

Where do DRUG ALONE and PSYCHOTHERAPY PLUS DRUG stand by nonclinical criteria? DRUG ALONE was the cheapest and most effective treatment by all of the movement and cost measures. This latter group had the highest release rate; it also had the shortest average length of

---

* (+) indicates PSYCHOTHERAPY PLUS DRUG to be superior. The figure in parentheses expresses the difference as a fraction of the spread between the means of the best and the worst of the five treatment groups.
† Extremely significantly—eleven measures
  Very highly significantly—one measure
  Highly significantly—one measure

hospital stay and the lowest average cost per patient, whatever method was used to measure stay or cost.*

| PSYCHOTHERAPY PLUS DRUG ranks second of the five treatments in terms of Release Rate and the stay and cost measures that take the number of failures into consideration by giving them all equal weight.† If only the successes are considered,‡ then PSYCHOTHERAPY PLUS DRUG ranks third, and it ranks fourth if one considers only Cost (Physician-Ordered Treatment Only). In general, PSYCHOTHERAPY PLUS DRUG was somewhat inferior but fairly close to DRUG ALONE by the movement and cost criteria. In fact, these two treatment groups were distinguishable with an acceptable degree of statistical significance only in terms of Cost (Physician-Ordered Treatment Only), where PSYCHOTHERAPY PLUS DRUG was highly significantly more expensive than DRUG ALONE. Their Release Rates were virtually identical, although the results for stay and cost are somewhat in favor of DRUG ALONE over PSYCHOTHERAPY PLUS DRUG.

Analysis of the different components of treatment effect for the movement and cost criteria indicates that drug had a powerful and extremely significant effect in increasing the number of successful releases and, even despite the increased number, a highly significant effect in reducing the average stay and cost for those released. By contrast, *psychotherapy* had no appreciable effect on Release Rate, and it did seem to increase the length of time that a patient will be kept in treatment in the hospital until treatment is declared to be either a failure (to an extent that was extremely significant) or (to an extent that approached significance) a success. In fact, if the patients had remained in the hospital as long as their physicians wanted them to, the treatment-prolonging effect for the successes would have been highly significant.

It was also demonstrated that by all the cost indices *psychotherapy* had similar but somewhat more pronounced effects in increasing the average cost of treatment.

ECT

It is also necessary to consider the positions of DRUG ALONE and PSYCHOTHERAPY PLUS DRUG in relation to their closest competitor, ECT,

* For the purposes of discussion in this chapter, Ideal Stay and Admission Stay to Failure are not included under the rubric of movement criteria, as it is not easy to make a direct unqualified value judgment as to the relative virtue of high or low figures for these two variables. If lower figures are accepted as "good," then DRUG ALONE was superior by these two criteria also.

† I.e., Stay and Cost (L.R. 432 or L.R. 407).

‡ I.e., Stay and Cost (Admission or Selection to Release).

which was third in rank order of treatment effectiveness by all the *clinical* criteria except therapists' ratings of Jittery, analysts' ratings of Insight and nurses' ratings of Motility where it was fifth (last); and by therapists' ratings of Aggressive and nurses' MHS where it was fourth.

The differences between ECT and the other four treatments were considerably greater than those between DRUG ALONE and PSYCHOTHERAPY PLUS DRUG. To illustrate this point, the differences observed between ECT and the most effective treatment were 2½–5 times as great as the differences for the six measures listed in the previous section between DRUG ALONE and PSYCHOTHERAPY PLUS DRUG. Moreover, ECT was often substantially less effective by measures where the differences between DRUG ALONE and PSYCHOTHERAPY PLUS DRUG were trivial.

By the eleven nurses' and analysts' measures, the differences were such that ECT could be distinguished with some confidence (D < .05) as being inferior to DRUG ALONE, except for analysts' MHS and Insight* ratings and nurses' Motility and TROUBLERAT, and as inferior to PSYCHOTHERAPY PLUS DRUG except for analysts' MHS and nurses' Motility ratings.

The therapists did not see as clear differences among ECT, DRUG ALONE and PSYCHOTHERAPY PLUS DRUG as did the nurses and analysts.† Although like the analysts and nurses, they rated ECT third, in the middle of the rank order (except for Jittery where it was fifth and Aggressive where it was fourth), none of their eight measures distinguished ECT with confidence from PSYCHOTHERAPY PLUS DRUG, and it could only be separated clearly (D < .05) from DRUG ALONE by one criterion—Friendly.

On the other side of the rank order, ECT patients did worst (i.e., fifth in rank order) in terms of three clinical measures—analysts' ratings of Insight, therapists' ratings of Jittery and nurses' ratings of Motility. Of the other sixteen clinical measures, ECT was distinguishably better (D < .05) than the least effective treatment in terms of three global measures (therapists' AA Total and SRS Total; nurses' MACC Total) and two subscales (therapists' Clear-Thinking and nurses' Communication).

By the *movement* criteria also, ECT generally occupied an intermediate position, somewhere in between the most and the least effective treatments. If one considers only patients successfully released, the average number of days Stay (Admission to Release) was almost the same for ECT (135), DRUG ALONE (130) and PSYCHOTHERAPY PLUS DRUG (138). However, the release rate for ECT (78.7 percent) was substantially and significantly lower than for DRUG ALONE (95.8 per-

---

* The difference approached significance for Insight.
† Or else the rating scales used were not sufficiently precise to reflect their perceptions.

cent) and PSYCHOTHERAPY PLUS DRUG (95.5 percent). If the number of failures is taken into consideration by giving them all equal weight, as in Admission Stay (L.R. 432), the length of stay for ECT is significantly longer than for DRUG ALONE and nearly so for PSYCHOTHERAPY PLUS DRUG.

Much the same situation applies for *cost* where ECT ranked second cheapest by all the criteria except Cost (L.R. 432). By this criterion in which due weight is given to the number of failures, ECT was on the average $1480 (significantly) more expensive than DRUG ALONE, and $800 (not significantly) move expensive than PSYCHOTHERAPY PLUS DRUG.

On the other side of the *cost* and *movement* rank order, ECT had a significantly higher release rate than MILIEU (but not than PSYCHOTHER-APY ALONE). ECT patients who were successfully released had a significantly shorter stay than patients treated with PSYCHOTHERAPY ALONE (but not MILIEU). When due weight is given to the proportion of failures, as in Admission Stay (L.R. 432), the length of stay for ECT patients is substantially and highly significantly shorter than for PSYCHO-THERAPY ALONE or MILIEU. The same applies to Cost (L.R. 432) where, allowing due weight for the number of failures,* ECT was $2640 cheaper per patient than PSYCHOTHERAPY ALONE and $1790 cheaper per patient than MILIEU.

There was no support for the notion that ECT increases the incidence of discharge against medical advice, although their therapists would have liked ECT patients to stay a (nonsignificantly) little longer in the hospital than they did. On the contrary, the data suggest that it is patients who are treated with *milieu* and not given some kind of "specific" treatment such as *electroconvulsive therapy, ataraxic drugs* or *individual psychotherapy,* who are likely to remove themselves from the hospital prematurely and against medical advice. However, ECT was the only treatment where physical complications or therapist resistance forced premature termination of treatment before the patient was well enough to leave the hospital.

MILIEU VERSUS PSYCHOTHERAPY ALONE

MILIEU and PSYCHOTHERAPY ALONE were the least effective forms of treatment by fourteen of the nineteen *clinical* measures, i.e., all except the five instances where ECT displaced them upward one rank by being last or next to last in the rank order (analysts' Insight; therapists' Jittery

---

* Cost (Admission to Termination), by which ECT was second in rank, does not give due weight to the number of failures. On the contrary, it gives credit to ECT for the speed with which therapists can come to a rapid decision as to success or failure. Cost (L.R. 432) weights the failures as if they had all remained on their original treatment (whatever that might be) for a full year's trial.

and Aggressive; nurses' MHS and Motility). One would hesitate to designate either MILIEU or PSYCHOTHERAPY ALONE as clinically more or less (in)effective than the other. By the criterion of number of measures, there was no particular advantage, MILIEU being higher ranking than PSYCHOTHERAPY ALONE by ten of the nineteen. By the criterion of the size of the differences, there was also no clear advantage to either treatment. The difference betwen MILIEU and PSYCHOTHERAPY ALONE by sixteen of the nineteen measures was clearly insubstantial. Of the other three, *psychotherapy* could be declared to have a significant beneficial effect on therapists' ratings of Clear-Thinking and a beneficial effect approaching significance on therapists' ratings of Energetic. However, the adverse effect of *psychotherapy* on therapists' ratings of Aggressive approached significance.

By the *movement* and *cost* criteria also, MILIEU and PSYCHOTHERAPY ALONE were close together at the bottom of the ladder, generally the least effective and most costly forms of treatment, with little to choose between them. The release rate for PSYCHOTHERAPY ALONE (65 percent) was slightly higher than for MILIEU (58 percent), but the difference between the two is not significant. There was nothing to support the notion that *psychotherapy* diminishes the incidence of discharge against medical advice.

In general *psychotherapy* (with or without *drug*) seems to increase the length of time that a patient will be kept in the hospital until treatment is declared to be either a success or a failure. Compared with DRUG ALONE, patients who were released successfully stayed in the hospital 33 days longer on MILIEU and 55 days longer on PSYCHOTHERAPY ALONE. This increasing effect applies even more so to the cost of treatment. In fact, the average cost of treating patients with PSYCHOTHERAPY ALONE was materially and significantly (or highly significantly) greater than MILIEU, both for the successes and the failures; except that the difference between the two groups was less apparent (only $850) and the cost-increasing effect only approaches significance if no credit is given for the speed with which a decision can be made that treatment is likely to be a failure—as in Cost (L.R. 432).*

It should be noted that *milieu* is the second most expensive form of treatment by the three indices that consider the total cost of hospitalization, and the third most expensive if one is considering only the cost of treatment specifically ordered by or given by the physician.†

---

* In other words, if it is assumed that there is no effective alternative to *psychotherapy* that could be tried in the event of failure, then the longer Stay to Failure for the *psychotherapy* failures would be discounted, as they would presumably have remained in the hospital anyway whether or not they continued to receive *psychotherapy*.

† I.e., in general, all treatment apart from nursing care and meals.

PSYCHOTHERAPY-DRUG INTERACTION

On the whole there was little *clinical* evidence that *drug* interfered with or potentiated *psychotherapy* or vice versa, the interactions being clearly non-significant for sixteen of the nineteen clinical measures. For the other three clinical measures, the evidence was somewhere in the region of unimpressive to suggestive and certainly not in any way conclusive. However, it all tended to be in the same direction. *Psychotherapy* alone would have little effect (or even a nonsignificant adverse effect) compared with *milieu*. *Drug* alone would have a definite beneficial effect; but when *drug* and *psychotherapy* were combined, the beneficial effect would be greater than the effect of *drug* alone. However, even by the three criteria that indicated some interaction effect, the difference between DRUG ALONE and PSYCHOTHERAPY PLUS DRUG was not very great—at the most just approaching significance.

This applied to nurses' MHS, by which measure *drug* had an extremely powerful therapeutic effect; to analysts' Insight, where *drug* effect is less evident but nevertheless significant; and to therapists' Aggressive. In this last instance, *psychotherapy* increased Aggressive to an extent that borders on the significant; *drug* alone increased it by an insignificant amount; but the combination of *psychotherapy plus drug* resulted in a level that was slightly lower (more normal) than that of *drug* alone.

Thus the *clinical* measures show beyond reasonable doubt that *drug* and *psychotherapy* did not interfere with each other in the treatment of our average hospitalized schizophrenic patient. On the contrary, such little interaction as may have occurred seems to have been in the direction of potentiation for the better in a few specific sectors of the patients' functioning.

Much the same state of affairs was found with the *movement* and *cost* criteria. For Cost (Physician-Ordered Treatment), there was a significant interaction between the effects of *drug* and *psychotherapy;* giving *drug* reduced cost more if the patients were also receiving *psychotherapy* than if they were not receiving *psychotherapy*. There was a tendency in the same direction for Cost (Admission to Termination) and Cost (Admission to Release).

This potentiation in the direction of reduced cost applies only to the successes; the opposite seems to apply to the failures. If a patient is given both *psychotherapy* and *drug* and fails to respond, there is likely to be a considerable increase in the length of the treatment trial and in cost before treatment is abandoned as a failure.

SEX-TREATMENT INTERACTION

There was some evidence of difference in response between the two sexes by all three categories of criteria, *clinical, movement* and *cost*. The evidence is somewhat stronger than for interaction effects between *psychotherapy* and *drug;* perhaps it might be regarded as strongly suggestive. The differences were apparent mainly for *ECT,* which was less effective for females than males; highly significantly so for nurses' ratings of Affect, significantly so for Release Rate, Cost (L.R. 432) and analysts' ratings of Anxiety, and to an extent approaching significance for therapists' ratings of Aggressive, Cost (Admission to Termination), Cost (Physician-Ordered Treatment Only) and Stay (L.R. 432). Analysts' MHS, CDAS (Total) and CDAS (Insight); therapists' Depressed; nurses' ISR, MACC Total, Cooperation and Communication; and Cost (Admission to Release) suggestively followed the same trend, although for these measures the differences between the two sexes were not significant.

Apart from ECT, the differences in outcome between the two sexes by the *clinical* criteria were relatively insignificant and scarcely enough to make much of a fuss about. There was a general tendency (nonsignificant) for therapists to rate females as being more Aggressive and Depressed, especially in the MILIEU group. On the other hand, females were rated by the analysts as doing better (not significantly) than males in terms of MHS, CDAS (Total) and Anxiety, especially in the MILIEU and PSYCHOTHERAPY ALONE groups.

By the *movement* and *cost* criteria, the sex differences apart from ECT were a little more tangible for MILIEU and PSYCHOTHERAPY ALONE. MILIEU tended to take more time and greater expense for females than males, significantly so for Admission Stay and Cost (Admission to Release) and to an extent approaching significance for Cost (L.R. 432) and Cost (Admission to Termination). In the case of PSYCHOTHERAPY ALONE, females were given a highly significantly longer and more expensive trial on treatment before being declared a failure than males.

PSYCHOLOGICAL TEST CRITERIA

The results of psychological testing in this study show that, for schizophrenic patients, *testability* can be used effectively as an outcome criterion, and that the *testability* results correlate well with the *clinical, movement* and *cost* criteria. In terms of improving testability, DRUG ALONE and PSYCHOTHERAPY PLUS DRUG were shown to be highly significantly more effective than MILIEU or PSYCHOTHERAPY ALONE. ECT occupied an intermediate position, significantly better than MILIEU or PSYCHOTHERAPY ALONE and significantly worse than DRUG ALONE and PSYCHOTHERAPY PLUS DRUG.

If one takes into consideration the degree of bias introduced by differential change in testability as a result of treatment, the psychological test scores provide useful additional information, generally consistent with the findings for clinical, movement and cost criteria although not as clear-cut.

By the test scores, PSYCHOTHERAPY PLUS DRUG and DRUG ALONE are the two most effective forms of treatment with little to choose between them. By final scores, which should be taken as the most representative of the sample as a whole, DRUG ALONE was superior to PSYCHOTHERAPY PLUS DRUG on seventeen of the MMPI scales, the Similarities-Proverbs and Shipley Verbal I.Q. However, the differences between DRUG ALONE and PSYCHOTHERAPY PLUS DRUG were small and not statistically significant except in the case of Cn (Control) where DRUG ALONE was more effective. PSYCHOTHERAPY PLUS DRUG was superior to DRUG ALONE, nonsignificantly on the Pd (Psychopathic deviate) scale and significantly on the Shipley Abstract I.Q.

Analysis of the separate components of treatment effect showed that *drug* had a beneficial effect as judged by certain MMPI scales: highly significantly so in the case of F (Validity); to an extent that was significant or nearly so for $?$ (Cannot say); and to an extent that approached significance for Mf (Masculinity-Femininity); Pa (Paranoia); Sc (Schizophrenia); $Pa + Pt + Sc$ (Psychotic Triad); Es (Ego Strength) and Cn (Control). On three other MMPI scales there was weak and somewhat dubious evidence that *drug* might have a beneficial effect approaching significance: These were Es (Ego Strength); Pd (Psychopathic deviate) and Hs (Hypochondriasis). It had an adverse effect on Si (Introversion) that approached significance.

Psychotherapy had a beneficial effect that approached significance on MMPI scale D (Depression); an adverse effect that approached significance on Mf (Masculinity-Femininity); and an adverse effect on $?$ (Cannot say) and Cn (Control) that was significant or nearly so.

There was no significant interaction between the effects of *psychotherapy* and *drug,* except perhaps for the MMPI F (Validity) and D (Depression) scales and for the Shipley Abstract I.Q. For the F scale and Shipley Abstract I.Q. there was some indication that the combination of *psychotherapy* and *drug* was superior to either treatment given alone; the evidence being stronger, but still not entirely satisfactory, for the Shipley Abstract I.Q. In the case of the D scale, there was some unimpressive evidence that the two forms of treatment interfered with each other. This was the only measure in the entire administrative, clinical and psychometric spectrum for which there was any evidence of significant negative interaction.

MILIEU and PSYCHOTHERAPY ALONE were generally the two least effective forms of treatment by the psychological test scores. The *final* and *change* scores for PSYCHOTHERAPY ALONE were better than for MILIEU in the case of six MMPI scales, the Similarities-Proverbs and the Shipley Verbal I.Q. The reverse applied for five MMPI scales and the Shipley Abstract I.Q. By the other seven MMPI scales, one of these two treatment groups had better *final* scores, but the other had better *change* scores. None of the differences between PSYCHOTHERAPY ALONE and MILIEU were significant for any of the measures except for *D* (Depression). In this case, PSYCHOTHERAPY ALONE was significantly better than MILIEU in terms of *final* and *co-varied* scores, but the difference for *change* scores was not significant.

If we take into consideration the fact that the results may be biased in favor of *psychotherapy* by the nontestable patients, it is clear that there is no convincing evidence in the psychological test data to support the notion that either PSYCHOTHERAPY ALONE or MILIEU are superior to each other.

ECT occupied in general a middle position among the five treatments by the test scores, with perhaps some shaky evidence that it had a significant beneficial effect on MMPI scales *Si* (Introversion) and *At* (Anxiety).

Considerable differences were discovered between the mean scores of males and females on many of the MMPI scales, but it is possible that this may be an artifact attributable to differences in cooperation with testing or to standardization problems.

Chapter XIII

Conclusions: The Hospital Treatment of the Schizophrenic Patient

PHILIP R. A. MAY, M.D.

OUR CONCLUSIONS, CONTAINED in two chapters, are in the form of a presentation by the principal investigator followed by a formal discussion. In this present chapter the principal investigator has felt free to abandon the rigid limits of bare-facts presentation, to stick his neck out, and to comment without equivocation. To preserve a spirit of spontaneity, his conclusions were not discussed with anyone before the chapter was written, and the text was not materially changed after the draft had been given to the other investigators. The other investigators were asked to comment particularly on points of agreement and disagreement and to expand on areas of their individual interest. Thus their discussion in the next chapter appears as a free-style elaboration and development. This approach was chosen deliberately in preference to attempting to come to some well-meaning and tidy—but colorless—committee-style report.

The findings of the Schizophrenia Research Project are discussed in terms of their application to other patient groups; to other therapists of different levels of training and experience; to alternative techniques of administration and supervision of the five particular treatments; and to different treatment settings.

It is concluded that the results may be applied to the immediate outcome for the general run of schizophrenic patients in all good hospitals (and probably in most hospitals) when treated with suitable, realistic dosage by the usual therapist, perhaps even by the gifted (p) specialist. (The meaning of each phrase in this definition is discussed in the text.)

The role of the five different treatment methods and the design and operation of an optimum treatment program are discussed, followed by the teaching and research implications of the study.

INTRODUCTION

I will start with some comments on the application of the findings of this study to other patient groups; to other therapists of different levels of training and experience; to alternative techniques of administration and supervision of the five treatments; and to different treatment settings. There are also a few special problems of interpretation. I will then discuss the role of the different treatment methods, the formulation of an optimum treatment program when resources are not unlimited, and finally the teaching and research implications.

APPLICATION TO OTHER PATIENT GROUPS

The extent to which one can generalize from our particular group of schizophrenics to other patients is a crucial issue. Certainly our findings relate only to hospital patients whose diagnosis falls into the category of "schizophrenia"; they have nothing to do with the treatment of other disorders. They relate particularly to *the general run of schizophrenic patients,* a phrase that I have chosen to refer to the fairly wide range of types of schizophrenic patients to whom I think the results apply, and to indicate my belief that the findings are likely to be representative of schizophrenics in general aside from outlying, unusual or extreme cases.

For instance, I would have real hesitation in applying our results directly to outpatients or to those under the age of 16 or over 45. I would also think it entirely possible that different treatment tactics and results may apply on the one hand to those who improve rapidly within the first week or two without any particular treatment, and on the other hand to those who have already had substantial prior treatment or hospital care.

Another question is whether the results may be applied to patients from other social levels or in other communities, states or countries. Leaving aside the problems of comparability of therapist and treatment milieu (which I will discuss later) and concentrating strictly on the issue of the patient and his illness, there is little evidence to suggest that mental illnesses differ from culture to culture in any way other than in their superficial content.[1] Certainly I had the impression that our schizophrenic patients were fundamentally and closely comparable to those that I have seen elsewhere in private, university and public hospitals in California, in other states and in Great Britain.

THE EFFECT OF THERAPISTS' TRAINING AND EXPERIENCE

The general level of skill, ability and enthusiasm of our therapists was quite comparable with that of the residents and post-residents that I have encountered in other private, university and public hospitals: some very good and some not so good. It would seem safe to assume that our findings can be generalized to other therapists of the same level of training and experience, i.e., in general to those in residency training and beyond that to "post-residents" up to the level of board certification.*

The important question is whether the results, particularly for *individual psychotherapy,* might have been different with more experienced therapists. There is a common underground belief that inexperienced therapists, being relatively simple and enthusiastic, may get better results with schizophrenic patients than those who have been disillusioned by experience. However, the relatively few scientific studies of this matter point to the conclusion that private psychiatrists (who have completed their residency training) and residents (in any of the three to four years of training) all obtain somewhat similar results with schizophrenic patients. For example, Cole found that under comparable conditions psychiatrists in private practice obtained somewhat worse results than residents with both *ataraxic drug* and *placebo* in neurotic outpatients.[2]

---

* Three to four years' training and two to three years' subsequent experience.
[1] See reference 19.
[2] See reference 11.

However, with hospitalized patients, Goldberg found that *placebo-ata-raxic drug* differences were similar in private, university and public hospitals.[3] This would indicate that the same differences between treatments are likely to be found whatever the setting, even if there are general outcome differences that depend on the therapist's level of experience, patient selection or hospital setting.

As for the kind of results obtained by residents, Lichtenberg studied 27 residents in the four years of residency training at Sheppard and Enoch Pratt Hospital.[4] He found no significant differences whatever the length of their experience. Moreover, for schizophrenic patients there was no significant relationship between outcome and supervisor's rating of the resident's skill. At the Henry Phipps Psychiatric Clinic, Betz and Whitehorn reported that their residents' improvement rates for schizophrenic patients also did not change during the three years of residency training.[5]

The point must be made that these results do not necessarily mean that training and experience make no difference—obviously an inexperienced and unsupervised therapist could sabotage any form of treatment. The most likely interpretation would be that the kind of reasonable supervision provided in residency training is sufficient to compensate in actual practice for any differences in results that might otherwise be found.

THE EFFECT OF THERAPISTS' PERSONALITY AND CLINICAL STYLE

The suggestion has been made by Betz,[6] Betz and Whitehorn,[7] and Whitehorn and Betz[8] that the effectiveness of individual residents in *individual psychotherapy* may not vary with experience but according to the type of patient and the resident's personality style. They reported that success with schizophrenic patients does not correlate highly with success with other patients. In particular, certain residents—designated as Type (A)—showed nearly three times as high an improvement rate for schizophrenic patients (in comparison with Type (B) residents of the same level of training and experience). This was associated with differences in the residents' tactical approach to the understanding and treatment of their patients. Type (A) residents were characterized by

[3] See reference 14.
[4] See reference 20.
[5] See reference 7.
[6] See references 1, 2, 3, 4, 5, 6.
[7] See reference 7.
[8] See references 28, 29, 30, 31.

active personal participation, whereas Type (B) residents were either passive and permissive or tended to rely on pedagogic interpretations.

Later, working with the same patient sample, they reported that the vocational interests of the therapist (determined by the Strong Vocational Interest Blank) may be related to the outcome of treatment. Improvement was more frequent in schizophrenic patients treated by therapists whose interest patterns resembled those of lawyers and accountants (Type A) than in patients treated by therapists whose interest patterns resembled those of printers and mathematics-physical science teachers (Type B).

In general, attempts to validate the A-B concept for the treatment of schizophrenic patients have been far from convincing.* Betz reported from a study of 336 schizophrenic patients treated by 22 residents at the Sheppard and Enoch Pratt Hospital that the improvement rate of patients treated by Type (A) residents (60 percent improvement rate) was significantly ($<$ .05) greater than that of patients treated by Type (B) residents (49 percent).[9] This is not nearly as impressive as the first report of a 75 percent–25 percent difference.[10] Moreover, Stephens and Astrup found no correlation between patients' clinical status at discharge or follow-up and their therapists' A-B type, even though 98 of their 334 patients were included in the original Betz and Whitehorn criterion group that defined the (A) and (B) types.[11] Nor were they able to confirm the report that the differences in success rates between (A) and (B) therapists were more striking with (difficult) "process" patients than with (easier) "non-process" patients.[12] They concluded that both short- and long-term outcome in schizophrenic illness was far more dependent on the total clinical status of the patient when he came for treatment than on the (A) or (B) type of the therapist who treated him.

The (A)-(B) hypothesis is still very much alive, however. The most recent development is an "Extended (A)-(B) doctor" scale of eighty items from the Strong Vocational Interest Blank developed by Campbell, Stephens, Uhlenhuth and Johansson.[13] This new scale was effective in separating Type (A) residents (whose patients had an improvement rate of 68 percent or more) from the Type (B) residents (whose improvement rate was lower than 68 percent). These investigators also applied

---

* Studies that attempt to relate B-type characteristics to success in the treatment of neurosis and depression have been omitted as not sufficiently germane to this brief review of A–B differences and the schizophrenic patient.
[9] See reference 1.
[10] See reference 29.
[11] See reference 25.
[12] See reference 2.
[13] See reference 10.

the "Extended (A)-(B) doctor" scale to a sample of men in other occupational groups who were reasonably satisfied and successful in their jobs. This showed that those in verbally-oriented occupations (author, journalist, lawyer and librarian) scored high at the (A) end of the scale—as did artists, advertising men and ministers. At the other (B) end of the scale were the practical, straightforward, nonintellectual doers, the carpenters, pilots, mathematics-science and business education teachers. Even so, there was major and substantial overlap between their patient sample and those of Whitehorn and Betz. It remains to be seen whether the new scale will stand up to cross-validation study. As the authors comment, the essential question is "Does this scale give reasonable results when applied to other samples?"[14]

It should also be remembered that a survey of how things turn out at hospital X is open to many hidden biases in patient selection, retention, treatment and evaluation. At best, it cannot be regarded as anything more than suggestive. To take an (imaginary) example suggested by the results of our study: If a therapist's personality determines whether or not he favors the use of *ataraxic drugs,* and *if* the therapists have the usual freedom in prescribing (or not prescribing) *ataraxic drugs, then* it would be unwise to assume that the therapist's personality alone is the immediate causal explanation of a high (or low) success rate.

In this connection, Rickels has demonstrated that superior results may be erroneously attributed to some special quality of the therapist, when in fact they may be due to a difference in the type of patient that he selects to treat. He found that a certain group of "introvert, intuitive, nonauthoritarian" private psychiatrists obtained better results with the combination of *placebo plus individual psychotherapy* than the "extrovert, authoritarian, action-oriented" therapists. Further investigation revealed that the former had selected for treatment a group of patients with characteristics often regarded as indicative of a better prognosis for *individual psychotherapy*—higher I.Q., more acute illness, expressing a greater wish for *individual psychotherapy,* and more active in reporting happenings in their personal lives.

The "A-B" literature is in some respects confusing. At least seven different methods have been used to label therapists as (A) or (B) with apparently little recognition that the A's and B's of one method may not be the same as the A's and B's of another. In a study of four of these methods, Stephens and Astrup found that only 27 of 63 physicians were classified in the same way by all four scales.[15]

[14] See reference 10.
[15] See reference 25.

The reporting of overlapping samples can also lead to circular reasoning. If a method of distinguishing (A) from (B) has been developed from analysis of a particular patient sample, then one cannot legitimately use further analysis of the same sample (or of one that has substantial overlap) to cross-validate hypotheses relating to (A) and (B). Thus Stephens and Astrup point out that the Betz studies[16] that showed a strongly positive correlation between patients' clinical condition at the time of discharge from the hospital and their therapists' A-B rating were not meant to confirm earlier correlations that had been reported, since the patients used were predominantly the same as those originally used to devise the methods for determining A-B status.

The serious reader who may wish to refer to the various original articles is advised to note carefully, for each article, the precise method(s) used to distinguish between (A) and (B) therapists; the composition of the patient group from which the method was derived; and the composition of the patient and physician groups to which it is now being applied.

THERAPISTS' ATTITUDE AND OTHER FACTORS

Inconclusive or conflicting results have also been obtained in other work that suggested that response to *ataraxic drug therapy* might vary according to therapist attitude and style of approach. Fisher, Cole, Rickels and Uhlenhuth first reported in a carefully controlled study of psychoneurotic anxious outpatients that the drop-out rate for *ataraxic drug* (but not for *placebo*) was increased when the therapist assumed an attitude of experimenting skepticism and reduced when his attitude was one of therapeutic enthusiasm.[17] However, a later report of the results for those patients who stayed in treatment for six weeks suggests that the therapist's attitude had only a temporary and transient effect at the beginning of treatment.[18] Moreover, the effect varied from one setting to another. At one clinic, patients taking *ataraxic drug* improved more for enthusiastic doctors than patients taking *placebo;* the opposite applied for the skeptical doctors. At the other two clinics the results were reversed, with *ataraxic drug* tending to be superior for skeptical doctors.

To complicate matters further, these findings were associated with (but not necessarily due to) differences between the clinics. At the

---

[16] See references 1, 2.
[17] See reference 13.
[18] See reference 27.

clinic where enthusiasm was associated with improved results from *ataraxic drug,* the patients were from a lower social class. Their doctors came from lower social-class backgrounds and had a greater preference for an enthusiastic rather than a skeptical role. This is of interest because of the suggestion of McNair, Callahan and Lorr that the A-B differences reported by Betz and Whitehorn might be due to the Type (A) therapists' either being from a life background similar to their patients' *or* having more interests in common with them.[19]

Finally, and more directly related to the subject of this study, Tuma and May reported that, for a major subsample (210) of our patients in the Schizophrenia Research Project, there was very little relationship between the therapists' attitudes toward a treatment modality* and the eventual outcome of treatment.[20]

THE USUAL THERAPIST AND THE GIFTED (P) SPECIALIST

At this point I suggest that we come up to the surface for air and start off again with two basic assumptions. First, an incompetent and unsupervised therapist could contrive to render any treatment ineffective by giving it in homeopathic doses or not at all, or at the wrong time or in the wrong way. Second, there is no scientific evidence that experienced therapists get any better results in the hospital treatment of schizophrenia than inexperienced therapists working under reasonable supervision, and that the burden of proof is on the person who wishes to assert otherwise.

Beyond this is more or less speculation. My own particular notion is that the kind of psychiatrist, psychotherapist or psychoanalyst who has little contact with hospital patients and spends only a small part of his time working with psychotics will not do any better with schizophrenic patients than did our therapists, no matter how old or experienced he is in the treatment of other types of patient. On the other hand, I can readily believe that the therapist who specializes in the treatment of the schizophrenic patient with persistent vigor, enthusiasm and style, is likely to become increasingly more effective.

Our findings might therefore apply only to *the usual therapist,* i.e., to all therapists except those (relatively few) who are both gifted and experienced in the treatment of the psychotic (i.e., schizophrenic) patient; and those (also relatively few) who are both incompetent and unsupervised.

A difficulty is that there is no experimental evidence to indicate

[19] See reference 21.
[20] See reference 26.
* As determined by the three scales and preference list described in Chapter 2.

whether the benefits of being treated by a gifted (p) specialist* (as I will now call him) accrue equally to each of the five methods of treatment used in our study. If they do, then our conclusions as to the relative efficacy of the five methods may reasonably be applied whatever the caliber of the therapist. However, if the treatments do not all benefit to the same extent, then our conclusions should be applied only to *the usual therapist*.

It is my impression that *the gifted (p) specialist* will get better results with any of the five methods used in our study, not just with *individual psychotherapy*. This is supported by the preliminary report of Grinspoon, Ewalt and Shader that when chronic schizophrenic patients are being treated with *individual psychotherapy* by experienced therapists, the addition of *ataraxic drug* results in improvement in symptomatology and in communication.[21]

After all, *individual psychotherapy* is not the only method of treatment that can combine art with science. Elegance in *ataraxic drug therapy,* for instance, calls for the (relatively rare) combination of expertise in drug effect, continuous understanding of the patient and of the process of his illness and sensitivity to the nuances of the patient-therapist relationship.

It may be that I am wrong and that *a gifted (p) specialist* makes more difference to the outcome of *individual psychotherapy* than to the outcome of the other forms of treatment. We have at the moment no certainty either way, so it will do no great harm if the reader accepts the possibility that this hypothesis might be true—as long as it is recognized that such an assumption has absolutely no bearing on the results for *the usual therapist;* and that the combination of *individual psychotherapy plus ataraxic drug* is likely to be potentiated by *the gifted (p) specialist* to a greater extent than *individual psychotherapy alone*.

SPECIAL THERAPIST-RELATED PROBLEMS IN THE ECT AND PSYCHOTHERAPY GROUPS

It is necessary to refer briefly to two other therapist-related matters. First, the fact that therapists with less than six months' experience were

---

* The "(p)" in this neologism stands for *psychosis:* it may be silent or not, depending on whether or not one wishes to make explicit the distinction from those who might be gifted and experienced in the treatment of some other kind of patient.

    The gifted (p) specialist is flexible: he is able to prescribe and administer (or willing to arrange for someone else to administer) whatever treatment or treatment combination is likely to help his patient most and to adjust his approach continuously according to the process of the illness. He should be distinguished from the *gifted (p) specialized technician* who is only able to carry out (or accept) one approach.

21 See reference 16.

permitted to treat patients with DRUG ALONE, MILIEU and ECT, but not with PSYCHOTHERAPY ALONE or PSYCHOTHERAPY PLUS DRUG. The review of the literature on the effect of therapists' experience would indicate that this had no material effect on the results, but it must be admitted that if six months of additional residency training means that a physician is going to get significantly better results with *individual psychotherapy,* then there was a slight bias in favor of PSYCHOTHERAPY ALONE and PSYCHOTHERAPY PLUS DRUG and in favor of estimates of *psychotherapy* effect.

Although some might question the wisdom of our providing a somewhat more favorable comparison for *individual psychotherapy,* it should be recognized that the study was deliberately designed this way in an attempt to ensure that *individual psychotherapy* would be given under conditions that would be considered a fair trial by its proponents. It could, with good reason, be maintained that physical methods of treatment and *ataraxic drug therapy* are so well taught in medical school and during internship that the physician entering psychiatric residency is already well-equipped to handle this particular type of therapeutic relationship. On the other hand, he has usually had little or no experience with *individual psychotherapy,* so it was considered reasonable to require this small amount of additional experience with this particular treatment.

Second, there is the matter of the three cases dropped from the ECT group (see Chapter 2). Fortunately the number is small and is composed of one probable failure (#19) and two possible successes (#17 and #18). This is very close to the ratio of success to failure for the remainder of the ECT group, so the actual effect on the end result would be likely to be small. In our judgment, the inclusion in the final analysis of the data from these three cases would introduce problems of comparability and confidence in interpretation that would far outweigh the possible bias from their exclusion.

It follows, however, that our ECT findings can apply strictly only to cases where treatment did not have to be stopped because of complications or because of therapist resistance—in practice, a very small limitation as these conditions are the realities of hospital treatment.

TREATMENT TECHNIQUE AND ITS SUPERVISION

It is common usage to lump many substances together under the rubric "ataraxic drugs," although they vary considerably, not only in chemical composition and toxicity, but also in the nature and extent of their therapeutic effect. In this chapter, except where discussing the work of other investigators, the terms *"ataraxic drug therapy"* and *"ataraxic drugs"* have been used to refer to the particular type of drug treatment given to our patients, i.e., adequate dosage of trifluoperazine (Stelazine), combined (if necessary) with supplemental dosage of chlorpromazine (Thorazine).

Comparison of one drug with another was not our purpose and was beyond the scope of this study. We simply used the two drugs that were considered at the time to be generally the most effective in the treatment of schizophrenic patients. The reader is therefore cautioned to apply our results to other drugs only to the extent that he knows (or believes) that they are generally as effective with schizophrenic patients as the specific drugs used in this study. He should also bear in mind that although the dosage schedule and choice of *ataraxic drugs* was completely at the discretion of the therapist and his supervisor, it is possible that a more flexible use of a wider spectrum of different drugs might produce even better results than the one-or-two-drug-across-the-board approach that was actually used in our study. This is suggested by recent experimental evidence that the effectiveness of *ataraxic drug therapy* in schizophrenia might be increased by using specific drugs for specific subsyndromes.[22]

In the case of *individual psychotherapy,* however, we did use a flexible rather than an across-the-board approach, to ensure that the technique used was the best possible for the given conditions of therapist and patient. A wide variety of maneuvers and approaches are labeled as *individual psychotherapy,* and our supervisors concentrated on helping the therapist to use them flexibly to obtain the best result, taking into consideration both the patient's particular difficulties and the therapist's characteristic personality. Under these circumstances, the safest assumption would be that the maximum use was made of the individual therapist's psychotherapeutic potential. There may be some who will feel that things would have gone differently if only we had used their particular "brand" of individual or group psychotherapy or family therapy. Perhaps. But the burden of proof is on them—and a few case anecdotes will not be sufficient. Scientific standards require objective research study of methods and results, as in the case of Rosen.[23]

To turn to the matter of supervision. From what I have seen elsewhere, I think the reader may safely assume that the supervision provision provided for all five treatment groups in this study was of high quality. It should be inferred that the results for any of the five treatments might be less favorable than those obtained in this study if they

[22] E.g., see references 15, 18, 22.
[23] See references 8, 9, 12, 17, 24.

are given "wild" (with no supervision at all) or under inept or inadequate supervision. Great care was taken to ensure that each treatment was given properly and in adequate dosage; the reader (and particularly the administrator) should not kid himself that treatment at a level less adequate than that described will produce the same results.

|TREATMENT DOSAGE

The "failures" of each treatment method were, in general, given a substantial trial of treatment under good battlefield conditions, supervised by an experienced clinician. It would, I think, be unreasonable to quibble about the *length* of the treatment trial, but it must be admitted that we did not push the *dosage intensity* for *ataraxic drug, ECT* or *individual psychotherapy* as high for a few of the failures as some might wish. The facts given in Chapter 2 indicate that it is most unlikely that better results would have been obtained by heroic dosage of *ataraxic drugs* or *ECT,* but I think it a legitimate point to question whether *individual psychotherapy* was sufficiently intensive.*

Therapists have only a certain limited amount of time available, and it is therefore easier, timewise, to increase the dose of *ataraxic drug* or the frequency of *ECT* than to see a patient more often in *individual psychotherapy.* It should be made clear, therefore, that we have not studied the effectiveness of psychoanalysis—as a matter of fact, our group considers orthodox psychoanalysis to be inappropriate for the hospitalized schizophrenic patient. Nor do we claim to have investigated the outcome of the kind of superintensive psychotherapy in which the patient is seen for seven hours or more a week.† The cost of these two particular methods is so great that they are likely to be used justifiably only in research or for the relatively wealthy hospital patient.

We were determined to be practical in our study. For example, *individual psychotherapy* was given within the realistic limits of the therapists' available time under what we judged to be the best conditions that might be available for the general run of schizophrenic hospital patients in the forseeable future; and it was given at an intensity that would certainly apply to a very great number of the patients being treated in private and university hospitals throughout the United States at the present time.

Accordingly, the phrase *suitable realistic dosage* will be used in this

* I.e., frequent enough interviews.
† Research evaluation of one such technique (Direct Analysis) does not support the claim that it results in a high degree of recovery. Another separate study also showed that the results with this method were not significantly better than a random control group or a designated control group. (See references 8, 17.)

chapter to denote my belief that the findings of this study apply to a reasonably practical treatment optimum for any of the five treatments under good, but not lavish, conditions and with sound supervision of dosage and other treatment details.

APPLICATION TO OTHER TREATMENT SETTINGS

Psychiatric hospitals vary a good deal in their staffing patterns and in style and amenities. It was assumed in planning our study that this variation in treatment milieu may influence the outcome of treatment.

Accordingly, a deliberate attempt was made to set up *milieu therapy* at a level that would seem to be the maximum reasonably attainable in a public hospital in the forseeable future, and that was at least equivalent to that found in a considerable number of private and university hospitals.* Undoubtedly a higher level is provided at certain private hospitals, but my impression is that the level of *milieu therapy* for our patients was, in general, of a relatively high order, although the physical amenities were less attractive than in some of the more elegant establishments.

It was thought that setting a high standard for *milieu therapy* would obtain close to the best possible results for the *milieu* (control) group and so allow the findings of our study to be applied to *all* good hospitals, i.e., to those with a good or superior level of *milieu care*. It was also thought that the results of our study would not apply directly to inferior hospitals where *milieu therapy* would be expected to be less successful and so the effects of the specific treatments would be more evident.

There is, however, recent evidence that would suggest that our findings are likely to apply to *most* hospitals and not just to the good ones. The NIMH Psychopharmacology Service Center Collaborative Group studied the effectiveness of *ataraxic drug therapy* for acute schizophrenia in a variety of settings—two psychiatric units in general municipal hospitals, four state hospitals, one private hospital, one university hospital and one small state-supported psychiatric unit in a general hospital closely affiliated with a university. Somewhat to their surprise, they were unable to confirm their hypothesis that the effect of *ataraxic drugs* would be less apparent in the university and private hospitals with higher levels of basic and physician care and a different class and type of patient. On

---

* The staffing patterns of teaching hospitals cannot be taken at their face value when one is considering patient care. In institutions of this type the total staff time available is not translated directly into patient care, as a substantial proportion of personnel effort is taken up in conferences and other teaching and research functions.

the contrary, they found that although there were enormous differences in general level of outcome among the nine hospitals, the size of the *placebo-ataraxic drug* differences did not differ significantly, whatever the setting.[24]

It would seem, therefore, that although it is possible that the effects of a specific form of treatment (such as *ataraxic drug* or *individual psychotherapy*) might be less apparent at some exceptional hospitals because of their unusually high level of *milieu care,* it would be necessary to justify any such claim with scientific study before it could be accepted.

However, at the other end of the scale, things may be different—the NIMH Collaborative Study did not include any hospitals with poor and inferior staffing. It would perhaps be wise to assume that hospitals with grossly deficient staffing would get poor results with *milieu therapy*— and that therefore the effects of specific treatments might be more evident at such institutions.

The use of the phrase *in most hospitals* indicates my belief that our findings may be applied to all hospitals except those where *milieu therapy* is grossly deficient.

LIMITATIONS OF COST DATA

The limitations of the cost estimates have been discussed at some length in Chapter 2 and Appendix VI, with further comment in Chapter 11. Thus the professional administrator should be able to determine their applicability to his specific situation on the basis of the information provided.

For the purpose of this chapter it should be sufficient to make two general comments. First, the cost figures were computed in terms of price and salary levels at the end of the treatment phase of the study (1963–1964); suitable adjustments must be made if the reader wishes an expression in terms of current levels. Second, the various components of the cost of hospital treatment vary considerably from one hospital system to another. The mental hospitals operated by the State of California Department of Mental Hygiene are probably sufficiently similar to permit reasonably direct use of the figures as they stand. For other hospital systems, I would advise that the figures be taken as indicators of relative rather than absolute costs.

DOUBT IN GENERAL

In deciding how far afield to apply our results, it is important to consider the degree of certainty or uncertainty with which a particular

[24] See reference 14.

conclusion has been demonstrated for our specific patient group. It is of course true that anything could happen by chance, and one has to consider seriously the possibility that some of the findings are the result of sheer happenstance error in the selection or evaluation of the patient sample.

Many of the findings are obviously at a level of probability that puts them *beyond all reasonable doubt*. But those that are at a low or marginal level of probability are a different matter. Life cannot be divided rigorously into black and white, and in the end it is up to the reader to determine for himself the level of certainty at which he feels comfortable. However, as a rough sort of guide, I have used in this chapter phrases such as "if this means anything at all" or "it might perhaps be that" to indicate a certain degree of reluctance in proposing a particular conclusion, even for our patient group—a state of troubled doubt that would be indicated by the old Scottish verdict of "Not Proven."

Another kind of uncertainty occurs where there is a negative (i.e., not statistically significant) result. In this case it might be that the particular measure that was used was in some way not sensitive enough; or insufficiently valid; or merely just too inaccurate and unreliable to demonstrate what we were seeking. These are legitimate possibilities for every such negative result, but it may be that these are the facts and there is no sense in denying them. In any case, the measures that we used seemed to be the best we could get for these particular items, and until someone comes up with better ones, the negative results must be taken as the most likely answer. Accordingly, except in a few instances when special reference has been made to this problem (in this chapter or in Chapter 2) I have assumed that our measures were (for practical purposes) sufficiently valid and reliable, and that nonsignificant results can be accepted as such. The appearance of the phrase "as far as we can tell" will indicate where I feel that there may be a special problem of this kind.

SHORT-TERM OUTCOME

Finally, it should be remembered that the findings reported in this volume relate only to short-term immediate outcome, up to the end of the first year of treatment. It cannot seriously be denied that short-term improvement is important, both for the patient and for his physician, but it is not the same as long-term results.

Some are quick to suggest that their favored method (whatever that might be) has better long-term results. They may be right—but it would be wise to wait for the results of our follow-up study to test the validity of such an assumption.

APPLICATION: SUMMARY POSITION

It should now be reasonably clear to the reader what is meant when I take the position that the results of this study may be applied *to the immediate outcome for the general run of schizophrenic patients in most hospitals when treated with suitable realistic dosage by the usual therapist, perhaps even by the gifted (p) specialist.* He should also understand what lies behind such hedging remarks as *if this means anything at all, perhaps* and *as far as we can tell.*

The remainder of this discussion, which will be directed toward the actual use of the various treatment methods and to the implications for training and research, is intended to refer only to this kind of patient and treatment situation, unless specified otherwise.

THE ROLE OF DRUG THERAPY

The results of our research demonstrate beyond reasonable doubt that *ataraxic drug therapy* is the most effective single* form of "specific" treatment for *the general run of schizophrenic hospital patients,* and also the cheapest.

It is particularly impressive to find that this superiority applies to all the criterion sources explored in this report—to the *clinical* judgments of the nurse, therapist and psychoanalyst as well as to the *psychometric, movement* and *cost* measures. There can be no doubt that *ataraxic drug therapy* relieves the symptoms of schizophrenia—it would be a poor treatment that did not. But from the theoretical standpoint, such sweeping generalized effects may be taken as an indication that there is more to it than mere symptom relief. Surely it must be that *ataraxic drugs* exert their effect in a manner that is closely related to some basic mechanism in the schizophrenic process?† A reappraisal of some of the different concepts of drug action in the process of restitution in schizophrenia may be in order.

A prevalent view of the restitution process is based on a supposed fundamental role of affect and impulse in drug response. According to this concept the primary effect of *ataraxic drugs* is to reduce the schizophrenic patient's overwhelming anxiety and aggressive impulses. This

---

* I.e., not including combinations of more than one treatment given simultaneously.
† In this context there is little to be gained by discussing at its face value the fashionable dictum that *ataraxic drugs* provide merely "symptomatic relief." This subject will be taken up later.

would mean that they either do not improve ego functioning at all, or else that any improvement is entirely secondary, the result of the reduction in affect and impulse. Restated in neuro-psycho-pharmacological terms, the hypothesis is that schizophrenia is a disturbance of some affect-related chemical substance or activity center that is counteracted by *ataraxic drugs*.

An opposing and less popular view (but more congruent with Bleuler's proposition that the primary disorder of the schizophrenic is associational) is that drug-induced restitution in schizophrenia is primarily a matter of improved ego functioning. By this concept any change in affective behavior would be purely secondary.

How do these two theoretical hypotheses stand up to the observations that have been made for our real-life sample of 228 patients? By and large, the findings are compatible with either theory, in that improvement in general clinical condition and in ego functioning is roughly parallel with improvement in affect. For example, the effect of *ataraxic drug* seems to be equally apparent in all the ratings of general overall clinical condition, in the nurses' evaluations of cooperation, communication and paranoid affect, and in the psychoanalysts' assessments of anxiety. However, there are some interesting and perhaps important exceptions and inconsistencies.

First, there was no significant effect from *drug* on therapists' ratings of Jittery (CMS), although there was a powerful effect on psychoanalysts' ratings of Anxiety (CDAS). This should not be lightly brushed aside with the glib assumption that one of the two scales is less sensitive or less reliable, since in point of fact the two scales actually measure quite different things. It seems to me that Jittery (CMS) appraises essentially the externally observable manifestations of free-floating unattached anxiety.* The psychoanalysts' ratings on the other hand go much wider and deeper, including inferred subjective experiences that may not be apparent in the patient's overt behavior, anxiety attached to specific situations or ideas, and symptoms that are interpreted by the rater as manifestations of an underlying anxiety. In other words, the psychoanalysts measured not only free-floating, unattached anxiety, but also a substantial segment of anxiety that had been bound by the defense mechanisms of the ego (i.e., virtually all psychopathology except shame, guilt and the symptoms and manifestations of the mechanism of denial). Thus, as far as we can tell, *drug* appeared to have little or no effect on free-floating anxiety, but a powerful effect on that portion of the patient's

---

* Jittery is scored positively for the following items: excited, excitable, nervous, jittery and shaky; negatively for calm and relaxed. It is not likely that the raters would have confused these items with the restless muscular movements (akathisia) that may appear as a side effect of trifluoperazine (Stelazine).

anxiety that had been handled by the defense mechanisms of the ego.

A second point of interest is that *drug* had no significant effect on the therapists' ratings of Aggressive (CMS), a scale which measures some of the external manifestations of aggression.* However, there was a definite (positive) *drug* effect on Depressed (CMS)† It can be theorized that depression is a manifestation of the ego's defenses against aggression, the defense mechanism being the turning inward of the aggressive impulses. If so, this finding can be interpreted as another instance where, as far as we can tell, *drug* appeared to have little or no effect on the straightforward appearance of an impulse, but a definite effect when that impulse had been transformed by the defense mechanisms of the ego.

There is a third group of instances that could also be interpreted as an indication that *ataraxic drugs* have more effect on ego functioning than on affective behavior. *Drug* had no significant effect on the nurses' ratings of boisterous or agitated overactivity (MACC Motility), but there was a definite positive effect on the psychoanalysts' ratings of Insight (CDAS) and the therapists' ratings of Clear-Thinking, Friendly and Energetic** (CMS).

To summarize these three points, it would seem that as far as we can tell *ataraxic drugs* have little observable effect on some of the external behavioral manifestations of aggression and free-floating anxiety—precisely the kind of affective behavior that the "Affect is primary" hypothesis would suggest as their prime target of action. On the contrary, there was much more positive change in areas where this hypothesis would suggest that the effect of *ataraxic drugs* would be less apparent or nonexistent.

The evidence is somewhat flimsy and by no means conclusive, but it is all in the direction of suggesting that drug-induced restitution is primarily a matter of improving ego function, and that affective change is secondary or of secondary importance. Powerful drugs such as chlorpromazine (Thorazine) do indeed have obvious short-term sedative effects, but we should not be misled into thinking that these sedative

---

* Aggressive is scored positively for the following items: critical, reckless, daring, boastful, bossy, demanding, forceful, sarcastic, bold, unpredictable, sexy.

† Depressed is scored on 59 separate items, too many to list here. The four principal items are depressed, troubled, unhappy and downhearted.

** Friendly is not scored as the opposite of Aggressive. It is scored positively for the following items: easy-going, light-hearted, ambitious, friendly, agreeable, obedient, earnest, talkative, considerate, kind, sociable, satisfied, happy, polite, cooperative, cheerful, good-natured, genial, affectionate, pleasant, warm-hearted.

Clear-Thinking is scored positively for: clear-thinking, able to concentrate, efficient, alert, dependable, independent.

Energetic is scored positively for: vigorous, confident, active, able to work hard, energetic, wide-awake, refreshed, lively.

effects are responsible for the long-term improvements in the manifestations of psychosis. Admittedly, it is possible that *ataraxic drugs* may exert their effect in both ways, by improving ego function and by directly reducing anxiety and aggression. Nevertheless, as far as we can tell, there is reason to consider that they are truly anti-psychotic rather than merely tranquilizers. Perhaps they are in some way effective in dealing with the nonspecific state of being overwhelmed, whether this results from internal sources or from sources external to the ego.

Before leaving the subject of restitution, the effect of *ataraxic drugs* on Insight is also of considerable theoretical interest. It will be remembered that *drug* was rated by the psychoanalysts as having in the end a significantly greater effect on Insight (CDAS) than *psychotherapy*. Few —except perhaps the proselytes of so-called consciousness-expanding drugs—would seriously suggest that pills can give magical insight into one's illness and personal problems. It would seem more plausible that in some way *ataraxic drugs* restore ego function to a level that enables the patient to see himself, his illness and his actions in a different light.

To return to more practical matters, it should be clear beyond reasonable doubt to both therapist and administrator that *ataraxic drugs* are likely to give better results at less cost than *milieu therapy alone, individual psychotherapy alone* or *electroconvulsive therapy,* being superior to these three by every criterion that we have studied so far.

However, this does not mean that all hospitalized schizophrenic patients should be given *ataraxic drugs* indiscriminately. Obviously, patients who are already on the way to restitution during the initial evaluation period should not receive any specific treatment, unless it can be established that there is a good probability that this will either improve their final condition or lessen their financial burden. Curiously, medical research tends to ignore the problem of deciding who *not* to treat, and as a consequence there is little scientific evidence to guide the clinician in this kind of decision. There is a real need to develop scientific guidelines for the selection of these patients for whom no specific treatment is indicated while they are in the hospital.

Just as obviously, at the other extreme, *ataraxic drugs* should not be given to these chronic cases who have failed to respond to previous *drug therapy* in adequate doses.

There is also the problem that in the present state of our knowledge we do not know enough to be able to say, one way or the other, whether there might be exceptional or unusual cases that would respond differently than *the general run of schizophrenic patients,* and for whom *milieu therapy, individual psychotherapy alone* or *electroconvulsive therapy* might give better results than *ataraxic drugs*. The results of Winsorization show that there are not likely to be many such patients, but the possibility does exist. Hopefully, further analyses from our study may throw some light on this matter. For *the general run of schizophrenic patients,* however, *ataraxic drug therapy is* undoubtedly the single treatment of choice at the present time—the only question is whether there is anything to be gained by giving *individual psychotherapy* as well.

THE ROLE OF PSYCHOTHERAPY

Judging by our results, the value of *individual psychotherapy alone* for the hospitalized schizophrenic patient has been greatly exaggerated in some circles. At this stage of the illness, *individual psychotherapy alone* without *ataraxic drugs* is an expensive and ineffective form of treatment that apparently adds little or nothing to conservative *milieu therapy.* Admittedly it may be that, compared with *milieu therapy,* there is some additional improvement in certain ego functions such as Clear-Thinking and Energetic. On the other hand, with *individual psychotherapy alone,* hospital stay will surely be prolonged; there is not likely to be any improvement in Insight, and it may even be that there will be some worsening in terms of Aggressive.*

Evidently a thoughtful reappraisal of our whole thinking about the *psychotherapy* of the schizophrenic patient is in order. Perhaps we need to give up some of our artificial concepts as to what is beneficial for the psychotic patient—but we must be careful not to throw the baby out with the bathwater. *Individual psychotherapy* may be of no great help in achieving restitution in the earlier stages of the schizophrenic illness, but this does not mean that it should never be used at all.

Obviously, *individual psychotherapy* should not be used alone as the only form of treatment. The question is whether there is any advantage to be gained by adding *psychotherapy* to *ataraxic drug therapy.* From the evidence in this project we can dismiss as a fairy tale the story that *ataraxic drugs* should be avoided because they interfere with the *psychotherapy* of the hospitalized schizophrenic patient. Not only was there no evidence of significant interference, but, on the contrary, such little interaction as occurred was almost entirely in the direction of potentiation in a few specific sectors such as Abstract I.Q., Insight and Aggressive. These findings are consistent with the preliminary report of Grinspoon, Ewalt and Shader that although *psychotherapy alone* (with experienced psychotherapists) did little or nothing for chronic schizophrenic patients in two years' time, the combination of *psychotherapy plus drug* seemed to work quite well in reducing florid symptomatology and perhaps in

---

* I am not able to accept the sophistical proposition that increased aggression is a good thing—not when the direction is away from normal.

making the patient more reachable and more receptive to communication with the therapist.[25]

All in all, the addition of *psychotherapy* to *ataraxic drug therapy* in this stage of the illness does not seem to be much of an advantage. By comparison with *ataraxic drug alone,* the patient's stay in the hospital is likely to be prolonged, and the cost of treatment will be increased. There may (perhaps) be some slight additional improvement over *ataraxic drug alone* in items such as Clear-Thinking and Energetic and some minor gains in Insight and Aggressive, but the differences between *drug alone* and *psychotherapy plus drug* were never impressive or statistically significant.

In certain situations where cost and stay are of no concern, it may be justifiable to recommend the addition of *psychotherapy* to *ataraxic drug therapy* for the hospitalized schizophrenic patient with so little chance of additional benefit—as long as both the patient and the therapist understand clearly that this is either a research enterprise or, if presented as treatment, that it is, statistically speaking, more or less a gamble. As far as one can tell, the odds are generally less than even that there will be any particular benefit at all from the addition of *psychotherapy* to *ataraxic drug therapy,* and in any case, the gains are likely to be relatively small and confined to a few areas of functioning. For a few patients such a gamble is well worth taking. For the general run of hospitalized schizophrenics, however, I would advise against the use of *psychotherapy plus drug.* The money and time available should be spent on something that might have a greater chance of helping. There may be far more to be gained, for instance, from working with some other nonhospitalized member of the family; or by conserving resources to provide adequate *psychotherapeutic management, psychotherapy, ataraxic drug therapy, social service casework* or *rehabilitation* in the community after the patient leaves the hospital.

I have the impression that the additional stay associated with *individual psychotherapy* is often the result of the therapist's reluctance to give up the case. If this is true, it would follow that if *psychotherapy* is to be given, the extra hospital stay and cost might be reduced if it can be given by the same therapist who will be responsible for the case after the patient leaves the hospital.

These remarks should not be interpreted as meaning that we should pay no attention to the schizophrenic patient's psychological needs while he is in the hospital. In fact, it is in precisely this area of treatment that our techniques may need the most reappraisal. A distinction needs to be made between *psychotherapy* and *what is therapeutic for the psyche.*

[25] See reference 16.

Instead of formal *psychotherapy,* particularly the kind of orthodox *psychotherapy* that is commonly used with psychoneurotic outpatients and which is seemingly not very helpful in the process of restitution, we should concentrate on improving what I shall call *psychotherapeutic management.*

By this I mean the application of understanding of psychopathology and psychodynamics to the remedial management of the individual patient. *Psychotherapeutic management* should include not only helping the patient to identify and learn how to deal with his current life problems, but also work with other family members and in the community; appropriately sensitive techniques of nursing care and social casework; thoughtfully nondoctrinaire *milieu therapy;* goal-directed occupational therapy and rehabilitation; even perhaps a perceptive intervention along the lines of behavioral conditioning.

Here again, let us watch out for the baby. *Individual psychotherapy,* conducted by *gifted (p) specialists* and not by *the usual therapist,* may be indicated as a research technique for the understanding and treatment of the chronic, poor prognosis, failure patient who has not responded to adequate *ataraxic drug therapy* combined with proper *psychotherapeutic management.* Radical as this proposal may seem, in the light of our findings it makes much more financial and clinical sense than the prevalent custom of applying *individual psychotherapy* indiscriminately to all cases or reserving it for patients with a good prognosis.

As another basis for the recommendation that *individual psychotherapy* should be employed particularly for the chronic inpatient, it is my position that this kind of person needs all the help he can get. Moreover, there is the possibility that in these cases the extra cost of *psychotherapy* might be eventually offset by the saving that would result if the patient responds and can be discharged. This is not such a wild hope as it might seem. If there are indeed unusual patients who respond better to *psychotherapy alone* or to *psychotherapy plus drug* than to *ataraxic drug alone,* they are likely to be concentrated in the group of patients that has failed to respond to *ataraxic drug alone.*

I should add that I cannot agree with the seductive suggestion that *individual psychotherapy* should be given selectively to hospital patients with good or average prognosis who want it and who are thought *by the usual therapist* to be capable of benefiting. It is not acceptable medical practice to give an expensive treatment to a patient merely because he asks for it or because the therapist is eager to give it. The usual therapist should remember that our research has shown that there is generally likely to be little or no benefit from formal *psychotherapy* given by him at this stage of the illness. He should reflect that the money and time available might be used more effectively in some other way, such as to provide adequate treatment after the patient leaves the hospital (including *psychotherapy*) or to provide a better level of *psychotherapeutic management* while he is still in the hospital.

It is true that our findings indicate that there might be a small number of patients who can benefit in a few limited ways from the addition of *individual psychotherapy* to *ataraxic drug*. Further analysis of our data will enable us to tell whether they can be identified by the criteria such as age, education and motivation that have been ritually employed by the *usual therapist*. In the meantime, although there may be *gifted (p) specialists* who can accomplish this critical selection, it would be wise to submit their criteria for doing so to scientific validation before assuming that the *usual therapist* can do likewise.

For the schizophrenic outpatient, continuing *psychotherapeutic management* is indicated, whatever else is done. In addition, formal *individual psychotherapy*—or even *psychoanalysis*—may be an appropriate therapeutic (or research) technic for certain schizophrenic outpatients, particularly those who have reached a reasonably high level of ego functioning. Since our study did not extend to out-patients, I will leave to my colleagues the major role in discussing the position of *psychotherapy, psychoanalysis* and *psychotherapeutic management* in outpatient treatment.

Finally, there is the matter of the relationship between *psychotherapy* and Insight. As far as we can tell for the schizophrenic patient, *psychotherapy alone* did not on the average lead to any greater level of Insight than *milieu therapy*. The best that can be said is that it may have done so in a few unusual cases, but this was counterbalanced by some who did worse. *Ataraxic drug alone,* however, had a significant beneficial effect on Insight and it might be that there was some further additional improvement from the combination of *psychotherapy plus drug*.

At this point it is crucial to define what we mean by the term "Insight." As used for our patients, Insight does not mean the kind of deep understanding that may be encountered in the psychoanalysis or psychotherapy of the neurotic outpatient. The general run of schizophrenic patient is nowhere near this when he leaves the hospital. The usual state of affairs is recognition of the reality that he has been ill, perhaps with identification of some precipitating circumstance. At best, there may be a degree of understanding that there have been disturbed personal relationships in the past and that this is still existent.

To illustrate this point, the mean post-treatment Insight score for our 228 patients was 3.5. Scale point 3.0 is defined as:

> The patient recognizes that he acts peculiarly or suffers symptoms, but rationalizes these peculiarities or symptoms as inevitable or "normal"

reactions to the environment which in his conviction has fostered or forced his disorder.

Scale point 4.0 is defined as intermediate between points 3.0 and 5.0. Scale point 5.0 is defined as:

The patient realizes that he is ill, that his behavior is peculiar and unnatural and that something is wrong, but has no or only slight awareness of the connection between the symptoms, his inner conflicts and/or the precipitating circumstances.

Only two of the 228 patients reached Scale point 8, intermediate between Scale points 7.0 and 9.0. Scale point 7.0 is defined as:

The patient has some affective and appropriate awareness that he is ill, that his environment is also related to particular precipitants in the environment and that the illness is also related to a sensitivity on his part to similar precipitants in the past.

Scale point 9.0 is defined as:

The patient is aware with appropriate affect that his illness is related to particular precipitants in the environment and also to a special sensitivity on his part to similar precipitants in the past, having to do with significant family relationships which have generated major inner conflicts.

In other words, the Insight of the restituted schizophrenic patient is essentially a matter of reality testing. The findings of this study are therefore in accord with the view that, at this stage of the illness, Insight is a secondary development in the process of recovery. Restitution leads to Insight and not vice versa. As ego functioning is restored, so reality testing improves and the patient develops the capacity to see himself and his illness in a more realistic way. Deeper psychological understanding comes later, if at all, after restitution has been achieved and consolidated.

It is now possible to see that in the treatment of the hospitalized schizophrenic patient *ataraxic drug therapy alone,* which is more effective in restoring ego functioning, will lead, on the average, to a greater degree of Insight than *psychotherapy alone.* Indeed, if lack of Insight is actually a symptom of a fundamental disorganization of the ego, it would be premature to attempt to induce Insight by *psychotherapy* at this stage of the patient's illness. It might even be alleged—I think with partial, but not complete, truth—that the application of so-called *insight psychotherapy* at this stage of the schizophrenic illness would be merely symptomatic therapy (defined as the attempt to remove or reduce directly a symptom that is actually a manifestation of some deeper underlying disorder).

THE ROLE OF ECT

It is reasonably clear that *electroconvulsive therapy* cannot be considered to be desirable as an alternative or serious rival to *ataraxic drug alone* or to *psychotherapy plus drug*. However, this does not mean that *electroconvulsive therapy* should be abandoned altogether. *ECT* gave generally better results than *psychotherapy alone* or *milieu*, and it may be that *ECT* has a place in the treatment of occasional cases such as those who develop toxic side effects or who fail to respond to *ataraxic drug alone* or to *psychotherapy plus drug*. It is also possible that there may be a few exceptional patients who respond specifically to *electroconvulsive therapy* and not to the other treatment methods. Further analysis of our data may throw more light on this matter.

I doubt that anyone will be surprised at the finding that patients treated with *ECT* had the lowest post-treatment level of Insight. Actually however, the differences between *ECT, milieu* and *psychotherapy alone* were not statistically significant, and they could easily be the result of chance. If they mean anything at all, then *electroconvulsive therapy* may have a specific effect in reducing the patient's awareness of his illness and personality problems. Two possible explanations for this phenomenon occur to me. It is well known that *electroconvulsive therapy* commonly produces both retrograde and anterograde amnesia and confusion; these could certainly interfere with the patient's perception of the circumstances and manifestations of his illness. It might also be that the unpleasant dramatic nature of the patient's phantasies* about *electroconvulsive therapy* foster the use of denial as a psychological defense against the possibility of a repeat performance.

It is of interest that female patients on *ECT* did significantly worse in many respects than male patients, and this might be kept in mind when considering whether or not to use this form of treatment for the exceptional case. There were no important differences between the sexes in response to the other treatments, so that if this finding means anything at all, *ECT* stands out as an exception in this respect. Further research study of this matter would seem to be indicated, but I would be interested to see if my colleagues have any comments to make on this matter from their own experience.

---

* The word *phantasies* is used deliberately here. When *ECT* is properly given under intravenous anesthesia, as in this study, the actual experience is in itself relatively innocuous.

\ THE ROLE OF MILIEU THERAPY

Our statistics demonstrate beyond reasonable doubt that for the general run of schizophrenic patients, *milieu therapy alone* is both expensive and relatively ineffective. However, as I have suggested above, there may be some patients with an extremely good prognosis for whom no specific treatment is indicated—at least while they are hospitalized. For these, *milieu therapy* combined with proper *psychotherapeutic management* may be the treatment of choice.

In general, however, although a hospital must of necessity conform to acceptable standards of *milieu care,* it is evident that it is generally fiscally unsound, penny-wise and pound foolish to propose a budget that relies on *milieu care alone* without adequate provision for specific methods of treatment. For the benefit of those who make decisions on treatment programs and budgeting, this point needs to be driven home by a concrete illustration of the importance of taking cost comparisons into account.

For the fiscal year 1966, 3,253 schizophrenic patients between the ages of 16 and 44 were admitted for the first time to psychiatric hospitals operated by the California State Department of Mental Hygiene. If we make the assumption that by and large it is reasonable to apply our figures directly to this group, then the cost of treating these patients up to release (or up to the end of the first year, whichever is earlier*) with a good level of *milieu care alone* (at an average per patient cost of $6,230) would be $20,270,000.†

By contrast, the cost of treating these same patients with the addition of *ataraxic drug alone,* the cheapest and most effective *single* form of specific treatment (at an average per patient cost of $2,960) is only $9,630,000. In other words, it would cost $10,640,000 *less*—and get better results—to treat these first admission patients adequately with *ataraxic drug* plus a good level of *milieu therapy* than it would cost to treat them with *milieu therapy alone.*

Even if we go to the limit of our available specific treatment methods and assume that there may be some additional benefit from using *individual psychotherapy* as well as *ataraxic drug* (at an average per patient cost of $3,640), the cost of treating these first admission patients is only $11,840,000. This is still $8,430,000 less than the cost of treatment with *milieu therapy alone.*

* Cost (L.R. 432)
† This does not take into account changes in prices and salary levels since 1963–1964, nor does it consider the treatment of additional patients who were readmissions or who were already chronic hospitalized cases.

Thus, by comparison with the cost of providing a good level of conservative *milieu therapy,* the net effect of using the most effective *single* treatment is a saving *per year* of $10,640,000, and the net effect of using the most effective *combination* is a saving of $8,430,000 per year.*

As a taxpayer I find a difference of the order of $10,000,000 per year most interesting, particularly when I consider the possible size of comparable figures that would include private, military and veteran patients and that would apply to the whole of the United States, not just to California.

In my capacity as a Clinical Director, and to put the whole thing in proportion, I note that $10,000,000 is roughly the same as the annual budget of two neuropsychiatric institutes such as the one in which I work.

Finally, as a research investigator I cannot help comparing $10,-000,000 per year with the cost of our research project, which so far has totalled rather more than $1,000,000 over the past ten years.† The comparison ought to be sufficient to convince even the most hardened skeptic that vigorous support for research may well prove to be the best form of economy. I also hope that the figure that I have just given as the cost of our research project will demonstrate to those involved in the various stages of planning and budgeting of research programs that thorough, careful clinical research costs a great deal of money and takes a lot of time.

AN OPTIMUM TREATMENT PROGRAM

In the light of what I have said already, certain recommendations can be made that might be helpful to those responsible for the design and

---

* No doubt someone will be tempted to misinterpret or misquote this illustration of the size of the sums involved to suggest that I think the State of California could save $8,000,000 to $11,000,000 per year by immediately putting into practice the results of this research. To set the record straight on this issue, the reader must recognize that at the present time a certain proportion of California first admissions are being treated with varying dosages of each of the five treatment methods that we have studied (and also with other additional treatments and combinations). It would be necessary to estimate these proportions and the efficacy of the other treatments and combinations to arrive at any figure for potential current savings. Even so, there would still be the practical problem of providing the same level of care as that provided for our patient group. The correct interpretation of this example is that the results indicate that in California it would cost (about) $10,000,000 a year *less* to provide the most effective available treatment for first admissions to state hospitals than it would cost to provide merely a good level of *milieu therapy* without special additional treatment.

† About half of this was in direct research grants. The remainder represents the cost of personnel provided through other sources.

operation of institutional treatment programs for first admission schizophrenic patients when financial resources are not unlimited. I will summarize a program starting from the time of first admission (the problem
of readmissions and those already chronically institutionalized is beyond
the scope of this book and is specifically excluded from consideration).

(1) Provision should be made for the early identification of those
patients for whom no "specific" treatment is indicated. (In the present
state of our knowledge, this might be taken as those who have already
restituted or who show clear signs of restitution within the first two
or three weeks.) These "good prognosis" patients should be treated
with *psychotherapeutic management* and *milieu therapy*. They should
not be given formal *psychotherapy* or *ataraxic drugs* while they are in
the hospital, although it would be well to encourage them in some
way to consider seriously the possibility of *psychotherapy after* they
leave the hospital. They should be discharged at the earliest reasonable
moment to be followed in an after-care unit that can continue adequate *psychotherapeutic management* and also arrange for outpatient
ataraxic drug therapy or *psychotherapy* if indicated.
(2) Provision should be made for the early identification of those
patients who, although this is their first hospital admission, have already had a fully adequate trial of *ataraxic drugs** or who have in the
past developed some special drug sensitivity or toxic reaction. These
patients should be transferred at once to a special treatment research
unit [see (4) below].
(3) The remainder of the patients should be treated on an ordinary
treatment unit with *ataraxic drugs* and *psychotherapeutic management*.
Ataraxic drug therapy should be fully adequate in terms of dosage
and properly supervised by experienced consultants. This group of
patients should not receive formal *psychotherapy* while they are in the
hospital—although an attempt should be made to provide a climate
that will detect and encourage those who might profit from *psychotherapy after* they have been released from the hospital. The general
goal of hospital treatment for these patients should be discharge at
the earliest reasonable moment to the after-care unit described in (1)
above.
(4) Those patients who develop toxic reactions to the administration
of *ataraxic drugs or* who do not show any improvement after an
adequate trial of *ataraxic drugs* (say six months at effective dosage)
or who are not well on the way to discharge at the end of one year
should be transferred to a special multidisciplinary treatment research
unit.
This treatment research unit should have better staffing and facilities than the remainder of the hospital. It should be able to provide
(as necessary and desirable) any form of treatment, including, for
example, *behavioral therapy, individual psychotherapy,* specialized
drugs or *electroconvulsive therapy* as well as the most recent research
developments.
(5) It may be that some patients who fail to respond to the maximum

---

* In my opinion, a most unusual circumstance.

efforts of the treatment research unit and who cannot be discharged into the community should eventually be transferred to some type of chronic care unit—a true asylum (in the best sense of the word) for those who need it, and one of the legitimate functions of a state hospital. Even so, this is not a valid excuse for denying any patient the potential benefits of a trial of treatment in a treatment research unit. (6) Before dismissing recommendations (2), (4) and (5) as utterly impractical, the reader would do well to reflect on the conspicuously dismal consequences of the current practice of transferring the failures of an initial period of "intensive treatment" to less well-staffed custodial "continued care" units—an accumulating group of expensive chronically institutionalized dependents. The taxpayer, if no one else, may have an interest in seeing the results of a controlled comparison of the two alternate approaches.

(7) Patients discharged to the community from a treatment research unit should be followed in a special after-care research unit.

(8) *Gifted (p) specialists* are likely to be in short supply.* They will probably do the most good in an after-care research unit or a treatment research unit, although they would have a valuable function as consultants and teachers in the ordinary units.

(9) *Gifted (p) specialized technicians* who are not flexible enough to be able to administer other forms of therapy outside their own narrow field of specialization or to work in cooperation with other forms of therapy pose a special problem. They also will probably do the most good in an after-care research unit or in a treatment research unit, but some may do better in an ordinary treatment setting. In any case, it would be wise to arrange for the overall management and direction of the patient's treatment to be in the hands of someone with more general flexibility—otherwise both the patient and the unit will surely suffer from his therapeutic rigor.

(10) *The usual therapist* can probably be used anywhere, but is likely to be most useful and effective in an ordinary treatment or after-care unit.

TEACHING IMPLICATIONS

The findings of this study have definite implications for teaching the treatment of the schizophrenic patient.

PSYCHIATRIC RESIDENTS AND CLINICAL PSYCHOLOGISTS.

First, in relation to training programs for psychiatric residents and clinical psychologists, it is demonstrably not in anyone's best interest to expect beginning residents to treat hospitalized schizophrenic patients successfully with *individual psychotherapy alone;* to lead them into the

---

* The administrator should note that he is not likely to have any *gifted (p) specialists* at all unless he has a salary structure that allows them to function as therapists and research investigators without becoming burdened with administration.

belief that this is the treatment of choice; and to devote several hours a week of so-called supervision to the scrutiny of what goes on under these circumstances. It can be expected that the residents and their patients will do much better if the emphasis is on *psychotherapeutic management* rather than on formal *psychotherapy;* and if this is combined with full and adequate teaching of the realistic use of *ataraxic drug therapy.*

By this latter, I do not mean laissez faire reliance on drug-house giveaways and the latest uncontrolled reports in the literature with a few additional lectures on the mythology of neuropsychopharmacology. Nor do I mean the scarcely helpful routine designation of medication by mouth as oral gratification or of injection as some form of assault. I mean that a substantial block of time and supervision should be assigned to serious study of matters such as nondrug factors in response to medication; dose-response curves; timing; prediction of response; target symptoms; drug specificity; estimation of change; bias in evaluation of results; and how to evaluate advertisements and research reports.

It is also important for the clinical instructor to realize that psychoanalytic terminology may be used by the resident as an intellectualizing defense against deeper understanding of the dynamics of drug response. For example, it is a common cliché that *ataraxic drugs* represent to the patient a fantasied incorporation of the good or bad therapist. If you inquire further of the resident precisely what he means and what bearing it has on his patients anyway, it may become apparent that this lofty phraseology is a real barrier to understanding. Simple English would make a better introduction to the richness and complexity of the interaction between *ataraxic drug* effect and patients' attitudes and expectations—"It may make quite a difference whether the patient sees the therapist as a good guy or a bad guy."

Instruction in formal *psychotherapy* (as opposed to *psychotherapeutic management*) of the schizophrenic patient should be given as an elective at a later stage of training, and only for those residents who intend to specialize to some degree in the therapy of psychosis. The preferred location for this kind of teaching would be in an outpatient department or an after-care unit or in an inpatient treatment research unit such as that previously described. The ordinary inpatient treatment unit is not a suitable place for this kind of teaching as it is bound to clash with the treatment unit's goal of speedy discharge to adequate after-care.

EDUCATING THE INSTRUCTORS. A second and important consideration is in connection with the education of those who do the teaching. It would seem to me that those who teach (or intend to teach) the treatment of the schizophrenic patient should be encouraged to become serious students of *ataraxic drug therapy* and of the problems of integrating it with *psychotherapy* and *psychotherapeutic management*. In this day and age this must necessarily involve knowing more about *ataraxic drug therapy* than the average psychiatric resident and thereby poses a practical problem. Many of the psychiatric residents' and clinical psychologists' instructors received their training before *ataraxic drugs* were even heard of. Who will accept the responsibility for educating these instructors? Or will they accept the responsibility for educating themselves in *ataraxic drug therapy* and the psychodynamics of drug response?

RESEARCH IMPLICATIONS

FUTURE AIMS OF THE SCHIZOPHRENIA RESEARCH PROJ-ECT. In future research we hope to go beyond the analyses reported in this volume. For instance, it is necessary to analyze the follow-up information and the results of further treatment of the failure cases. We will also attempt to determine whether it is possible to predict which patients will respond or not respond to a particular treatment method. In the final analysis, it is the treatment of the individual patient that counts, and not just the mass average. What is the right treatment for most or even almost everyone is not necessarily right for all. This is a much more difficult problem to solve, and it will be some time before we are in a position to publish any findings in this respect.

When we started this project I was convinced that we would probably find substantial numbers of patients who would respond more or less specifically to each of the five treatment methods. However, the findings from Winsorized data seem to indicate that *ataraxic drug* had a substantial effect on the majority of patients. Accordingly, if I were forced to speculate from the facts available at the moment, I would say that there are likely to be few, if any, patients who respond *specifically* to *electroconvulsive therapy* or to *individual psychotherapy*. There is perhaps more to be gained by attempting to identify the occasional patient who may do better with *psychotherapy plus drug* than with *drug alone,* but even in this case I have some reservations about our chances of success. I hope I am wrong, as I find it very hard to give up the idea of "the right treatment for the right patient."

Along the same line, we also intend to analyze the data to investigate whether there are certain types of patient who might get just as well just as quickly with *milieu therapy alone* as with *drug alone.*

POSSIBLE AREAS FOR RESEARCH BY OTHERS. I would hope that our study will stimulate further research on schizophrenia in areas beyond our reach. For example, in the area of treatment choice it would seem most important to determine whether specific treatments such as *ataraxic drug* or *individual psychotherapy* have any merit at all for the kind of good prognosis patients who restitute rapidly in the first few weeks. Or are the results just as good without pushing the patient with unnecessary intrusive interventions? Drug specificity is also an important matter: Are there perhaps certain types of patient who respond better to other drugs than trifluoperazine (Stelazine)?

Study of the influence of therapist experience on treatment outcome is another obvious focus for future research. The crucial information that is needed could be obtained in a fairly simple experiment—a comparison of the results of *ataraxic drug alone* with the results of *individual psychotherapy plus drug* when the patients are treated by *gifted (p) specialists* and by *the usual therapist*. A deluxe version of this experiment would include an additional comparison group of patients treated by *gifted (p) specialists* with *individual psychotherapy alone*.

In another area for research, there are certain problems relating to drug effect that deserve special and serious study by the psychoanalyst research investigator. Can teachable techniques be devised that will utilize psychodynamic understanding to maximize drug effect and to integrate *ataraxic drug therapy* with *individual psychotherapy* or *psychotherapeutic management*? What are the best ways of lessening the potential psychological hazards of *ataraxic drugs,* such as passivity, dependence and resistance to psychological self-examination? Is drug-induced restitution the result or the cause of anxiety reduction? There is also a need to improve techniques of *psychotherapy* and of *psychotherapeutic management* for the schizophrenic patient, and to establish the optimum role for *psychotherapy* in the treatment of both the outpatient and the chronic failure.

ISSUES IN PSYCHIATRIC RESEARCH METHODOLOGY. Finally, there are three issues that have to do with psychiatric research methodology. First, our study has demonstrated beyond reasonable doubt that testability poses a serious problem in the use of psychological test measures to evaluate status and change in hospitalized schizophrenic patients. Whenever the patient's cooperation is required for a particular test, it is imperative to have adequate information on the incidence of noncooperation in order to assess not only the extent to which the data are truly representative of the patient sample as a whole, but also whether there has been selective bias as a result of the confounding effect of treatment on testability. A research report should not be taken seriously unless this information is provided.

If the original patient sample in a study of hospitalized schizophrenic patients is such that it includes only patients who are testable before treatment is started, it cannot be considered to be truly representative of the general run of schizophrenia, which can be expected to include a substantial proportion of uncooperative patients. Accordingly, the reports from such studies should be treated with considerable reserve until they have been cross-validated with nonpsychometric criteria on a sample that includes sicker, untestable patients. On the other hand, if a substantial proportion of the original patient sample is nontestable, the psychometric measures should be treated as confirming rather than major criteria.

It is important that the research investigator should understand that for treatment research with hospitalized schizophrenic patients, even relatively unreliable measures that do not depend on the patient's cooperation (such as clinicians' and nurses' judgments of behavior and other characteristics) may give better and more consistent discrimination between treatment groups than psychometric measures that depend on the patient's cooperation.

Obviously, there is a need for further research in the application of psychological tests to the assessment of schizophrenia and to develop measures that are less dependent on the patient's cooperation. The work on the influence of nontestability reported in this volume is a step in this direction, but more sophisticated study of the problem should be undertaken.

The second issue relates specifically to the MMPI, which is widely used for research and other purposes. The findings of this study show that the F (Validity) scale may be more useful than the Pa (Paranoia) and Sc (Schizophrenia) scales for the assessment of outcome in schizophrenic patients. In fact, if one did not have to consider the resistance to change imposed by a generation of usage, it would seem appropriate to consider changing the name of the F scale from "Validity" to some other title that would be more indicative of its relationship to psychotic, autistic or idiosyncratic thinking.

It would also seem that in terms of discrimination between treatment groups, the MMPI is a relatively insensitive instrument, at least when the scale scores are used directly for the assessment of final status and change in schizophrenic patients. It might be made more useful if further effort could be directed toward improving the Pa (Paranoia) and Sc (Schizophrenia) scales, which were apparently regarded as provisional and have never been entirely satisfactory. Another possible approach would be the application of Winsorizing as a research technique in conjunction with a more sophisticated study of noncooperation and testability. An analysis along these lines is planned as a part of our own future work. (It may be that pattern analysis of the MMPI profiles might give better results than the straightforward use of individual scale scores. A comparison of the discrimination and sensitivity of the two methods is currently in process.)

Third, and perhaps most important, it should now be apparent that multivariate studies of treatment outcome are both feasible and highly desirable from the clinician's point of view. Research investigations that are restricted to observation of one or two variables will undoubtedly continue to take a valuable place as training exercises; or when resources are limited; or in certain other situations such as some types of rapid screening and the determination of narrow theoretical issues. However, the computing capacities that are now available have made it possible to explore the potential of multivariate studies, and it seems likely that in the future these will play an increasingly prominent role in professional clinical research studies. I hope that our steps in this direction will be an encouragement to others.

REFERENCES

(1) Betz, B. J.: Bases of therapeutic leadership in psychotherapy with the schizophrenic patient. *American J. of Psychotherapy*, 17:196–212, 1963.
(2) Betz, B. J.: Differential success rates of psychotherapists with process and with non-process schizophrenic patients. *American J. of Psychiatry*, 119:1090–1091, 1963.
(3) Betz, B. J.: How do personal attitudes and interests influence psychotherapeutic effectiveness? *Proceedings 6th Annual Psychiatric Institute*, Princeton, N. J., 14:14–28, 1958.
(4) Betz, B. J.: Strategic conditions in the psychotherapy of persons with schizophrenia. *American J. of Psychiatry*, 107:203–215, 1950.
(5) Betz, B. J.: The problem solving approach and therapeutic effectiveness. *American J. of Psychotherapy*, 20:45–56, 1966.
(6) Betz, B. J.: Validation of the differential treatment success of "A" and "B" therapists with schizophrenic patients. *American J. of Psychiatry*, 119:883–884, 1963.
(7) Betz, B. J. & Whitehorn, J. C.: The relationship of the therapist to the outcome of therapy in schizophrenia. *Psychiatric Research Reports*, 5:89–117, 1956.
(8) Bookhammer, R. S., Meyers, R. W., Schober, C. C. & Piotrowski, Z. A.: A 5-year clinical follow-up study of schizophrenics treated by Rosen's "Direct Analysis" compared with controls. *American J. of Psychiatry*, 123:602–604, 1966.
(9) Brody, M. W.: *Observations on Direct Analysis.* Vantage Press, New York, 1959.
(10) Campbell, D. P., Stephens, J. H., Uhlenhuth, E. H. & Johansson, C. B.: The therapist's vocational interests versus success with schizophrenic patients. An extension of the Whitehorn-Betz A-B scale. (To be published.)
(11) Cole, J. O. Personal communication.
(12) English, O. S., Hampe, W. W., Bacon, C. L. & Settlage, C. F.: *Direct Analysis and Schizophrenia.* Grune & Stratton, New York, 1961.
(13) Fisher, S., Cole, J. O., Rickels, K. & Uhlenhuth, E. H.: Drug-set interaction: the effects of expectations on drug response in outpatients. In *Neuropsychopharmacology*, Volume III. Bradley, P. B., Flugel, F. and Hoch, P., eds. Elsevier Publishing Co., Amsterdam, 1964: 149–156.

(14) Goldberg, S. C.: Personal communication.
(15) Goldberg, S. C., Cole, J. O. & Klerman, G. L.: Differential prediction of improvement under three phenothiazines. In *Prediction of Response to Pharmacotherapy.* Wittenborn, J. R. and May, P. R. A., eds. Charles C Thomas, Springfield, Ill., 1966: 69–84.
(16) Grinspoon, L., Ewalt, J. R. & Shader, R.: A preliminary report on long term treatment of chronic schizophrenia. *International J. of Psychiatry,* 4:116–128, August 1967.
(17) Horwitz, W. A., Polatin, P., Kolb, L. C. & Hoch, P. H.: A study of cases of schizophrenia treated by direct analysis. *American J. of Psychiatry,* 114:780–783, 1958.
(18) Katz, M. M.: A typological approach to the problem of predicting response to treatment. In *Prediction of Response to Pharmacotherapy.* Wittenborn, J. R. and May, P. R. A., eds. Charles C Thomas, Springfield, Ill., 1966: 85–101.
(19) Kiev, A.: The study of folk psychiatry. In *Magic, Faith and Healing.* Free Press of Glencoe. (Reprinted in *International J. of Psychiatry,* 1:524–552, 1965).
(20) Lichtenberg, J. D.: A statistical analysis of patient care at the Sheppard & Enoch Pratt Hospital. *Psychiatric Quarterly,* 32:13–40, 1958.
(21) McNair, D. M., Callahan, D. M. & Lorr, M.: Therapist type and patient response to psychotherapy. *J. of Consulting Psychology,* 26:425–429, 1962.
(22) Overall, J. E., Hollister, L. E., Honigfeld, G., Kimball, I. H., Meyer, F., Bennett, J. L. & Caffey, E. M.: Comparison of acetophenazine with perphenazine in schizophrenics: determination of differential effects based on computer-derived diagnostic models. *Clinical Therapeutics,* 4:200–208, 1963.
(23) Rickels, K.: Personal communication.
(24) Scheflen, A. E.: *A Psychotherapy of Schizophrenia: Direct Analysis.* Charles C. Thomas, Springfield, Ill., 1961.
(25) Stephens, J. H. & Astrup, C.: Treatment outcome in 'process' and 'non-process' schizophrenics treated by 'A' and 'B' types of therapists. *J. of Nervous and Mental Disease,* 140:449–456, 1965.
(26) Tuma, A. H. & May, P. R. A. The effect of therapist attitude on outcome of drug treatment and other therapies in schizophrenia. In *Psychotropic Drug Response—Advances in Prediction.* May, P. R. A. and Wittenborn, J. R., eds. Charles C Thomas, Springfield, Ill. (In Press.)
(27) Uhlenhuth, E. H., Rickels, K., Fisher, S., Park, L. C., Lipman, R. S. and Mock, J.: Drug, doctors' verbal attitude and clinic setting in the symptomatic response to pharmacotherapy. *Psychopharmacologia,* 9:392–418, 1966.
(28) Whitehorn, J. C. and Betz, B. J.: A comparison of psychotherapeutic relationships between physicians and schizophrenic patients when insulin is combined with psychotherapy and when psychotherapy is used alone. *American J. of Psychiatry,* 113:901–910, 1957.
(29) Whitehorn, J. C. and Betz, B. J.: A study of psychotherapeutic relationships between physicians and schizophrenic patients. *American J. of Psychiatry,* 111:321–331, 1954.
(30) Whitehorn, J. C. and Betz, B. J.: Further studies of the doctor as a crucial variable in the outcome of treatment with schizophrenic patients. *American J. of Psychiatry,* 117:215–223, 1960.
(31) Whitehorn, J. C. and Betz, B. J.: Studies of the doctor as a crucial factor for the prognosis of schizophrenic patients. *International J. of Social Psychiatry,* 6:71–77, 1960.

CHAPTER XIV

Open Forum

~~~~~~

THIS CHAPTER PRESENTS the viewpoints of a number of the other investigators who were associated with the Schizophrenia Research Project—Drs. Gerald J. Aronson, Luther S. Distler, Edward G. Feldman, Sidney Fine, Maimon Leavitt, Genevieve S. May, A. Hussain Tuma and Milton Wexler.

They were given a draft of the preceding chapters and invited to discuss the principal investigator's conclusions and to add any other comments that they might care to make. As in a discussion, the contributions appear without material editing in the order that they were received, with comments by the principal investigator.

The chapter concludes with a section by Dr. Jonathan O. Cole, formerly Chief of the Psychopharmacology Research Branch, National Institute of Mental Health, and now Superintendent, Boston State Hospital. Dr. Cole provides an additional viewpoint from outside the project.

ONE PATH TO RECOVERY LIES IN THE DEVELOPMENT OF STABLE OBJECT RELATIONSHIPS WITH SOMEONE IN THE OUTSIDE WORLD
MILTON WEXLER, PH.D.

I think Dr. May has been enormously careful to point out in detail what it is that is being researched. I have no optimism that his caution will meet with equal caution in the minds of many readers. In fact, if I am candid, I suspect that there are moments when even Dr. May sweeps over the limited boundaries of his research and generalizes beyond his data. Since his work has such a significant potential for hospital administration, it would be a sad result if his findings are misused by either a too general and enthusiastic endorsement or by a total and critical rejection. Kept within realistic bounds, the results of this study can be of enormous importance to the treatment of hospitalized schizophrenic patients.

The key problem lies in constantly keeping in mind the issue that Dr. May himself has reiterated many times. This research constitutes an investigation into certain well-defined, limited and practical treatment modalities in a public hospital. When the word *psychotherapy* is used, or *drug,* or *milieu,* it refers only to the highly specific, closely defined prescriptions for psychotherapy, drug administration, or milieu therapy given in this study. It does not, cannot, must not be taken to refer to any and all forms of psychotherapy, any and all forms of drug administration, any and all forms of milieu. Dr. May says this over and over again. And yet I am afraid that there are times when he slips from the throne of objectivity and forgets his own clear cautionary statements. Not often, but just enough to raise a little dust that may get in the eye of the observer.

Let's take a few instances. They are not major, but may serve both as guides for reading this report as well as questions for future research. It seems best to quote Dr. May:

> First, in relation to training programs for psychiatric residents and clinical psychologists, it is demonstrably not in anyone's best interest to expect beginning residents to treat hospitalized schizophrenic patients successfully with *individual psychotherapy alone;* to lead them into the belief that this is the treatment of choice; and to devote several hours a week of so-called supervision to the scrutiny of what goes on under these circumstances. It can be expected that the residents and their patients will do much better if the emphasis is on *psychotherapeutic management* rather than on formal *psychotherapy;* and if this is combined with full and adequate teaching of the realistic use of *ataraxic drug therapy.*

And further:

> A second and important consideration is in connection with the education of those who do the teaching. It would seem to me that those who teach (or intend to teach) the treatment of the schizophrenic patient should be encouraged to become serious students of *ataraxic drug therapy* and of the problems of integrating it with *psychotherapy* and *psychotherapeutic management.* In this day and age this must necessarily involve knowing more about *ataraxic drug therapy* than the average psychiatric resident and thereby poses a

practical problem. Many of the psychiatric residents' and clinical psychologists' instructors received their training before *ataraxic drugs* were
even heard of. Who will accept the responsibility for educating these
instructors? Or will they accept the responsibility for educating themselves in *ataraxic drug therapy* and the psychodynamics of drug response?

There is nothing terribly objectionable in these statements by Dr.
May except that they reveal a subtle, encroaching bias that tends to
equate the psychotherapy used in this study with all psychotherapy,
that tends to inject in the mind of the reader as an established fact that
an adequate program of drug therapy under any and all circumstances
is better than psychotherapy in general. While he does not quite say
so, I am inclined to think that Dr. May occasionally falls from grace
by believing that the five modalities of treatment explored in this study
are the *only* methods practically available to state hospitals for the
treatment of schizophrenic patients, and that the psychotherapy employed in this study is a fairly representative sample of psychotherapy
in general.

I would not give up on the teaching of psychotherapy to residents, nor
would I be inclined to give any special stress to the teaching of drug
therapy to psychoanalytic candidates even though there is certainly
some usefulness in their knowing about drugs in the management of
schizophrenic patients. Where I might agree with Dr. May is in rejecting training either residents or candidates in the techniques of psychotherapy as employed in this study. But I would have expressed that
notion from the very beginning of the study. And I am sure many of
my colleagues would have done the same. The type of psychotherapy
employed in this study is standard for institutional practice at a certain
level, is the only level that is deemed even remotely practical in terms
of utilizing residents and supervisors, and is the only psychotherapeutic
technique investigated at Camarillo. This does not mean that other
forms of psychotherapy could not be imagined; even practical forms
that proceed on a very different basis. And until all forms of suggested
psychotherapeutic practice have been investigated, I think it might be
wise to withhold suggestions concerning training, or to advance them
rather tentatively.

To understand this fully we need to go off on a tangent. Some therapists of schizophrenia with a theoretical bent suggest that a developing
insight in the patient stemming from correct interpretation leads to ego
integration and subsequent recovery from the illness. Others tend to
emphasize object relatedness, identification, internalization processes as
the condition precedent to developing insight and restitution. It makes
a vast difference in psychotherapeutic technique, even in psychothera-

peutic management or milieu arrangements, when one opts for the first or the second theoretical prejudice. Let me give a single instance.

If one believes in the basic merit of the interpretive approach, then the procedures employed in this study do represent a fair and practical compromise approach to the problem of psychotherapy in a public hospital. The doctor sees the patient as often as is practical in private sessions held two or three times per week and attempts to understand the patient and communicate his understanding. More frequent sessions are too costly, and even this type of arrangement might not be very practical for large populations not under research scrutiny. While it is true that even here and quite apart from interpretation, there is an opportunity for contact, object relatedness, identification, etc., this is necessarily minimized by time limitations and may even be interfered with by interpretive interventions.

On the other hand, if one puts theoretical emphasis on contact and internalization elements in the therapeutic process, the types of approaches employed could be altogether different. I can recall some time back going to see a patient in consultation in a hospital back East. The patient was extremely withdrawn and skittish and would not engage in any conversation for a major part of the day. So I sat during most of the day on the ward, watched, read, talked with anyone who cared to talk, including patients, doctors, nurses, maids. I saw the residents coming in busily, giving their shots, taking patients out for brief private sessions, reading charts. I had marvelous interchanges with at least a dozen patients on that ward, a major number of whom (most quite schizophrenic) begged me to take them on as private patients. I came away absolutely convinced that the psychotherapeutic interchanges on that single day were more significant than if I had spent twelve separate hours with twelve separate patients in intensive interviews with a therapeutic intention.

Now Dr. May will say that in the first place this is merely anecdotal and requires research validation. I will endorse his statement completely. I will even go further and say that there are many such formats for psychotherapeutic interventions that move very far from the method employed in his study, that may be quite cheap and practical, that can utilize the services of nurses and aides as well as residents, that fall within the framework of a definition of *psychotherapy,* and that have not been tested by his research.

I do indeed believe that seeing a patient daily is terribly important in the psychotherapy of schizophrenia, even if such contact has no formal office structure by way of personal interview. And my belief is based on a theoretical formulation that loss of object representation is crucial to the development of a schizophrenia, and that one path to recovery lies in the development of stable object relationships with someone in the outside world. Seeing a patient two or three times per week in office consultation is inadequate for the task at hand. And Dr. May's reference to the research on Direct Analysis where the patient is supposedly seen seven times per week does not convince me otherwise. After all, even Dr. May will admit that there were a few other variables in the Direct Analytic method than mere frequency of seeing the patient. In my view, even if the patient is seen seven times per week in Direct Analysis, a fact which is in some doubt, one must be aware that this frequently is accompanied by a mode of interpretation that many consider both assaultive and destructive of relationships rather than constructive in the sense of building stable object constancy.

As Dr. May correctly anticipates, those of us with investments in the psychotherapeutic process will incline to hold him tight to the line in the kinds of conclusions he draws from his study. I, at least, feel quite strongly that there is some real danger in that his method of writing up his conclusions, despite extreme caution, may lead to great generalizations about the ineffectiveness of psychotherapy in general without a limiting qualification that we are only talking about this *specific* procedure for *psychotherapy*. And I believe that Dr. May, himself, would be the first to push for precision in this area.

Apart from this issue there are many fascinating things to be learned from the study, a great many challenging findings, and a wealth of suggestions for hospital administrators. I would like to comment on a miscellany of items that I find stimulating, provocative and valuable.

In an era which tends to assume the value of expertise in the treatment of schizophrenia, it awakens the senses to read Dr. May's blunt statement that there is no scientific evidence to show that experienced therapists get any better results with their patients than inexperienced therapists working under reasonable supervision, "and the burden of proof" lies with the one who wishes to assert otherwise. I agree about where the burden of proof should lie. I only hope it is understood that Dr. May is stating an assumption, not that his research or any other research really proves this proposition in the broad terms in which it is stated. And particularly, I hope that nothing is implied about any single definition for psychotherapy or any proof that any old psychotherapeutic approach is as good as another. What is needed is a really sound research effort which would compare therapists as well as techniques. Perhaps Dr. May will get around to this some day. I am sure he will do a superb job.

It is fascinating to me to read Dr. May's discussion of the effects of ataraxic drugs. He suggests that the drug-induced restitution in schizophrenia has more to do with improved ego function directly produced by drug action than to reduction in overwhelming anxiety and aggressive impulses, followed by some reconstitution of ego functioning. His research is not designed to answer this question definitively, but he has surely used his limited data quite effectively to tease out such an implication.

One element in his analysis of data in this area interested me in particular. If we accept Dr. May's conclusions, it would seem that a patient's insight into his illness follows on the restoration of ego function by way of the administration of drugs. To quote: "It would seem more plausible that in some way they [drugs] restore ego function to a level that enables the patient to see himself, his illness and his actions in a different light." One can easily see that such a conclusion fits more neatly into the theoretical bias of those therapists who hold that the process of recovery follows a pattern of internalization, restored ego function, insight than those who hold to a pattern of interpretation, insight, internalization, restored ego function. To quote Dr. May, "Restitution leads to Insight and not vice versa." Quite frankly, even though this conclusion suits my own biases rather generally, I would certainly wish to be quite as tentative as Dr. May and merely suggest that this whole area deserves far more investigation.

When Dr. May says that the "value of *psychotherapy alone* for the hospitalized schizophrenic patient has been greatly exaggerated in some circles," I am again tempted to wish that he had developed some neologism to represent the kind of psychotherapy given in this study. Not that this kind is so unusual; in fact it is quite general for hospitals. But sentences of the above type seem to arise from the kind of generalizing tendency which may mislead readers into thinking that all psychotherapy is being challenged rather than a specific mode of administration exposed to study here. If Dr. May really does not want us to throw the baby out with the bathwater, I would urge him to give clear definition to that baby so that we can keep a tight grip on it.

I must confess to an evil delight in the following sentence written by Dr. May: "It is not acceptable medical practice to give an expensive treatment to a patient merely because he asks for it or because the therapist is eager to give it." Here we have, in a nutshell, the problem presented by defining psychological disturbance in medical terms, as illness. Medical shibboleths become the criteria for behavior whether it makes sense or not. Who cares about "acceptable medical practices" in this situation? If asking and offering is what does people good, if that defines the type of person who could benefit and that defines the type of person who can help, the eager seeker and the eager giver, then "acceptable medical practice" should go out the window. For once I find myself in favor of some learning theory for psychological disturbance. At least teachers and students would find it most acceptable practice to join forces when there existed a climate of urgent asking and urgent giving. I would recommend the use here of a most "accepted pedagogical practice" and throw the medical model out as part of the bathwater.

The Cost figures in this study are intriguing to say the least. If the general findings are valid—and since they fit my preconceptions I am inclined to think they are—Dr. May has made a most significant contribution that could save millions of dollars and more than justify the cost of the research. In fact, I think he makes a great case for on-going research which elaborates the present endeavor. I would hold that, among other things, his own personal development as a researcher along with that of several of his collaborators is a value that must not be lost. But it can only be readily utilized if responsible sources will support him in some continuing efforts at exploration.

In one small instance, however, I would have some skepticism. He has shown that for the age group 16–44 in terms of California first admission, the cost of *drug alone* therapy would be $9,630,000. For *drug* and *psychotherapy* the cost increases to $11,840,000. As a hunch, as a statement of prejudice, I am inclined to suggest that if the type of psychotherapy given were altered, naturally according to my own predilections, the combination would pay off in the long run despite the $2,000,000 differential. This does not alter Dr. May's conclusion, however, and under the defined conditions I also would feel that he has put his finger on the best and cheapest approach for the average schizophrenic patient in the given milieu. For that one finding alone I think we can be very grateful to the authors, and can hope that hospital administrators will heed his recommendations. But even more, we can hope that further and even more intensive studies will be possible for the basic team that, under Dr. May's guidance, has produced such a careful and controlled investigation.

PHILIP R. A. MAY, M.D.

Happily, the kind of dust in the eyes that Dr. Wexler attributes to me has nothing to do with the technical aspects of research design. He refers to the sort of human frailty that afflicts us all—a tendency to see (or to interpret) the facts a little differently. When discussing this subject, I am very fond of illustrating the dilemma of the search for objectivity by referring to the stories by Ryunosuke Akutagawa that were composed into the classic film *Rashomon,** depicting the killing of a Samurai in a mountain grove through the conflicting testimony of

---

* R. Akutagawa (translated by Takashi Kojima). *Rashomon and Other Stories.* Liveright Publishing Corporation, New York, 1952.

a woodcutter, a traveling Buddhist priest, a policeman and an old woman; the separate confessions of the bandit and the Samurai's wife; and the spirit of the dead Samurai speaking through a medium. The series of contradictory statements portray the precarious balance between illusion and reality, and undermine our customary confidence in distinguishing between subjective and objective, between truth and fiction. There are beams or motes in the eyes of all of us, including even those who seem to be the most objective.

In the case of this study, the reader can see the facts for himself in the preceding chapters. I hope he will now review all of our conclusions and comments, deciding where in each of us—and in himself—the truth and the biases lie.

Actually, the first page or two of Dr. Wexler's comments make it appear that he and I disagree about *psychotherapy* more than I think we really do. As he explains his position more fully, he makes qualifications that bring us closer together. Apparently he would agree with my statements that a thoughtful reappraisal of our whole thinking about the *psychotherapy* of the schizophrenic patient is in order; that it is necessary to discard some of the notions derived from the kind of orthodox *psychotherapy* that is commonly used with psychoneurotic outpatients; and that we need to improve our techniques for the application of understanding of psychopathology and psychodynamics to the remedial management of the psychotic patient. As far as I can see, then, a great part of the difference between our positions may be purely semantic, having to do with the fact that he uses the term *psychotherapy* to cover more than I do, including a great deal of what I had included under the neologism *psychotherapeutic management*. To resolve this, I suggest we distinguish between two babies and the one lot of bathwater by the terms *"object relations therapy," "psychotherapeutic management"* and *"interpretation-insight psychotherapy."*

If I understand correctly, Dr. Wexler and I agree that the kind of *interpretation-insight psychotherapy* that is generally used as standard practice in most hospitals and that is usually taught to psychiatric residents and psychology interns is unsuitable for the general run of schizophrenic patient. This is the kind of *psychotherapy* that I had in mind in the first of the two paragraphs that he quotes, and I have no hesitation in substituting therein the neologism *interpretation-insight psychotherapy*.

The style of approach that Dr. Wexler advocates, which I will call *object relations therapy* until he invents a more adept neologism, is an entirely different kind of baby. He is talking about something that is radically different from the kind of *psychotherapy* that is usually taught, for it concentrates not on insight or interpretation but on object relations, identification and internalization. It also includes a great deal that in my own mind I was including under the rubric *psychotherapeutic management,* such as the type of "psychotherapeutic interchange" that Dr. Wexler describes in his vignette, and also that he refers to as ". . . psychotherapeutic interventions that move very far from the method employed in [this] study, that may be quite cheap and practical, that can utilize the services of nurses and aides . . . ."

I think it advisable to make a clear distinction between this style of approach and orthodox *interpretation-insight psychotherapy.* Otherwise, if both are included under the same *psychotherapy* label, some therapists will be tempted to confuse the two and to use Dr. Wexler's comments as an excuse for continuing to do the same old thing in the same old way. Let us, therefore, distinguish *interpretation-insight psychotherapy* from *object relations therapy,* and both of these from *psychotherapeutic management.*

To this end, *object relations therapy* might be defined pragmatically for the moment as something that the therapist himself does directly with the patient along the lines that Dr. Wexler advocates, and including the therapist-patient part of what I described in my discussion of *psychotherapeutic management* (see Chapter 13). The term *psychotherapeutic management* could then be limited to whatever the therapist does on behalf of the patient with other family members and anything else that is done by others under the therapist's direction to help the patient's psyche.

I can now restate a little more clearly my position in the first paragraph that Dr. Wexler quotes:

> First, in relation to training programs for residents and clinical psychologists, it is demonstrably not in anyone's best interest to expect beginning residents to treat hospitalized schizophrenic patients successfully with *interpretation-insight psychotherapy alone;* to lead them into the belief that this is the treatment of choice; and to devote several hours a week of so-called supervision to the scrutiny of what goes on under these circumstances. It can be expected that the residents and their patients will do much better if the emphasis is on *psychotherapeutic management* and *object relations therapy* rather than on orthodox *interpretation-insight psychotherapy;* and if this is combined with full and adequate teaching of the realistic use of *ataraxic drug therapy.*

In making this statement it must in all fairness be admitted that our study does not provide (and was not designed to provide) any evidence as to the efficacy of the combination of *object relations therapy* and *psychotherapeutic management* (except perhaps to the extent that our therapists and supervisors may have used *object relations* rather than *interpretation-insight* techniques for patients asigned to treatment with *psychotherapy* or *psychotherapy plus drug*). But I think it does provide a good basis for directing further research toward the development and integration of these two approaches to the treatment of the schizophrenic patient.

Knowing that Dr. Wexler is an expert fisherman, I will nibble only gently on "acceptable medical practice" by altering very slightly the last passage that he quotes to read as follows:

> It is not acceptable *to me* to give an expensive treatment to a patient *merely* because he asks for it or because the therapist is eager to give it.

I was really not trying to be contentious on behalf of the medical profession; all I meant to convey was that I think there should be some objective evidence that a treatment is likely to be helpful before it is recommended to a patient, and it should also be reasonably clear that his financial resources could not be better expended in some other way. I was trying to make the point that there may be more prudent ways of spending money for the schizophrenic patient than on giving formal orthodox psychotherapy *during the phase of restitution, while he is in the hospital.* For instance, there might be more to be gained by working with other members of the family; or by saving the money to be spent later to provide a better level of after-care *after he has left the hospital* —and both *psychotherapeutic management* and *psychotherapy* would be important components of after-care. It is my prejudice that *object relations psychotherapy* may be more appropriate for outpatient schizophrenics where adjustment is borderline than *interpretation-insight psychotherapy,* and that *interpretation-insight psychotherapy* may be more appropriate for those who have reached a higher level of restitution, but of course our study cannot throw any light on this particular matter.

As Dr. Wexler says, "Kept within realistic bounds, the results of this study can be of enormous importance to the treatment of hospitalized schizophrenic patients." We do need to improve our techniques, and I am pleased that he has used the results to point to some possible paths for future development and research in the field of psychotherapy of psychosis in which he himself is so expert.

THE IMPORTANCE OF GOOD PSYCHOTHERAPEUTIC MANAGEMENT
EDWARD G. FELDMAN, M.D.

I agree with Dr. May's conclusions that *drug therapy* plus proper *psychotherapeutic management* is the treatment of choice for the average acute schizophrenic psychosis. Dr. May is careful in his emphasis on proper *psychotherapeutic management.* The acutely psychotic patient who is suffering from ego disorganization and disintegration and who sees other people as persecutors can certainly benefit much more from proper 24-hour intensive *psychotherapeutic management* than from two hourly *psychotherapy* sessions a week. Repeated brief contacts with the psychiatrist and ancillary personnel are much more beneficial with the acutely psychotic patient at this stage than any attempt to establish a psychotherapeutic relationship.

Ataraxic drug (Stelazine) does appear to exert an anti-psychotic effect, and this effect seems to be mainly in facilitating ego integration and synthesis. This then results in improved impulse and emotional control. I would add that good *psychotherapeutic management* also aids in improved ego integration and secondarily improves impulse control.

In the study, the term *milieu therapy* is used synonymously with *psychotherapeutic management*. It might be better to substitute the term *psychotherapeutic management* for *milieu therapy* in order to emphasize its importance, as there may be a tendency on the part of some people to believe that *drug therapy* and custodial care constitute adequate treatment. I do not wish to raise semantic problems, but to emphasize that proper *psychotherapeutic management* does not mean custodial care plus the administration of *ataraxic drugs*. Adequate treatment includes not only *drug therapy* where indicated but also nursing care and milieu therapy.

I was somewhat surprised to find that male patients responded better than female patients to *ECT*. In my experience, depression has been a prominent symptom in female schizophrenic patients and depression usually responds well to *ECT*. On the other hand, paranoid symptoms are more common in male patients and these symptoms are more resistant to *ECT*. Perhaps further analysis of the results will shed further light on this question.

Although insulin shock therapy has been largely supplanted by the newer somatic treatments, there may still be a select group of patients who may benefit from it, if the other treatment modalities fail.

PHILIP R. A. MAY, M.D.

I am glad that Dr. Feldman has emphasized both the importance of *psychotherapeutic management,* and the fact that proper *psychotherapeutic management* does not mean custodial care. It would be most unfortunate if anyone were to draw the conclusion that *custodial care plus ataraxic drugs* constitute an adequate treatment program.

Dr. Feldman's clinical impression that depression tends to be more prominent in female schizophrenic patients is certainly supported by the therapists, who rated females as more depressed (CMS) than males, highly significantly so before treatment and significantly so after treatment. As he says, it is somewhat surprising to find that depression in schizophrenic patients does not respond particularly to *ECT*. We shall therefore certainly follow up his suggestion to investigate further the prognostic value of paranoid and depressive symptoms and their relationship to sex differences.

PSYCHIATRIC FIRST AID AND RESTITUTION VERSUS STABILIZATION OF THE PERSONALITY
GENEVIEVE S. MAY, M.D.

My association with this research project has been an impressive experience in serious disciplined scientific work requiring the integration of quite divergent skills and personalities. It was particularly impressive because many of the personalities were known individualists, not otherwise famed for group endeavors—including me. The impact of this quality of person on the residents, nurses and other personnel was quickly evident, both in the time spent working together and in subsequent careers. In fact, a separate paper could be written entitled "Secondary Gains." With the effort to develop an observant, experimental therapeutic attitude throughout the patients' daily life, the hospital staff learned something of the philosophy of approach of this group of psychoanalysts to the treatment of schizophrenia. In addition, everyone (including the psychoanalysts) experienced directly the disciplined attitude and the rewards of serious research, and learned more of the natural course of an important illness.

The primary gains of the study will, I hope, affect even more people, in that schizophrenic patients seem to be with us to stay, by the millions. Some of the ideas which came to my mind as I read the fresh and startling conclusions of the study have to do with the use of the hospital for psychiatric first aid and as a place to restore patients to an "ambulatory" (i.e., emotionally compensated) status by the use of thoughtfully designed *milieu* and *drug therapy*. Psychiatric first aid requires a staff that can develop an environment which is a therapeutic experience for the patient. It should include not only *drug therapy* but also introduce the patient to an actively introspective attitude in which management and personal problems can be discussed, i.e., an enculturation of the idea that breakdowns have meaning and that behavior can be understood. A general approach of preparation for psychological thinking is an important part of *psychotherapeutic management* during the weeks or months in the hospital.

If it can be anticipated that going to a hospital will help a patient to compensate so that he returns to his former life as soon as possible with the addition of *psychotherapy* and *psychotropic drug* support as indicated, a whole new concept of the function of the mental hospital and of the treatment of mental illness can develop in the public mind. With the use of *psychotropic drugs* and a therapeutic environmental experience, many patients can move rapidly to being well enough for *psychotherapy* and after-care planning. Movement in or out of the hospital can depend simply on the severity of symptoms as in other medical disabilities.

However, it has been demonstrated that patients who begin *psychotherapy* in the hospital are more likely to continue after returning home, especially if the same therapist is available to them, or if they return to the one who sent them in. If symptoms are relieved by *ataraxic drugs* and patients are then sent for *psychotherapy* to a stranger, the drop-out rate is enormous. This type of fragmentation in planning reinforces the internal fragmentation typical of the schizophrenic process.

Thus, in using the results of this study, one needs to adopt a long-term therapeutic attitude; to redefine the function of the hospital period of the illness and to lay greater emphasis on the related functions of after-care. Therapeutic after-care requires specific, imaginative, individual planning for rehabilitation on many levels, with high respect for the natural sources of support in each community. Many patients will not continue *psychotherapy* after leaving the hospital (for various reasons), but deeper insights and stabilization of personality should not be sought at the price of the detrimental effects and cost of prolonged hospitalization which deprives the patient of the sustaining, ego organizing, and satisfying effects of work, family and friends.

One of the remarkable and unexpected findings in this study is that insight seems to develop with *drugs alone* to a degree almost equal to *psychotherapy plus drug* and greater by far than with *psychotherapy alone* while the patient is in the hospital. This reminds me of an old saying: "Sleep on a problem and it will be solved in the morning." Sleep, it seems, has a profound effect on reautomatization. In psychoanalytic terms we might say "Regression in the service of the ego can result in reorganization." If the *psychotropic drugs* do indeed interrupt deep anxiety and afford the overwhelmed ego some respite and an opportunity for reautomatization and reorganization, then we can accept them as a true aid in the therapeutic process. In this study, 100 percent of the patients on *drug* left the hospital within one year* with no increase in readmission rate.†

---

* See Chapter 5, Figure 5.1.
† P. R. A. May and A. Hussain Tuma: Treatment of schizophrenia. *The British J. of Psychiatry*, 3:508, 1965.

Stabilization of the personality is another matter. The optimum result is obtained by the combination of *drug* and *psychotherapy* for the out-patient. In my concept and experience it rests on object relationships and the internalization of good objects, as well as upon increased insight into the specific precipitating circumstances and vulnerabilities of the individual patient. Unfortunately, the notion that psychoanalytic con-cepts and techniques for the treatment of neurotic patients can be di-rectly applied as a model for the treatment of psychosis is apparently often conveyed to residents, with disillusioning results to all concerned.

It should not be assumed that all patients will benefit from *psycho-therapy* after restitution in the hospital. If this experience has served to revitalize their internal objects and if their return to their former lives means reunion with a stabilizing natural habitat of work and meaningful relationships, the therapeutic restoration or initiation of such internal objects will often not be necessary. A therapeutic attachment is no adequate substitute for viable natural-life objects.

It has been said that the use of *psychotropic drugs* will invalidate *psychotherapy*. The findings of the study do not support this notion; indeed, there appeared to be a slight gain in insight and reality testing in patients treated with the combination of *psychotherapy* and *psycho-tropic drugs*. In my own work I have come to expect some support from *psychotropic drugs* not only in hospital patients, but also in the long, slow task of helping office patients to compensate and (hopefully even-tually) to stabilize their personality by learning with me to identify and deal with the alienized pathological part of themselves.

The therapeutic task with schizophrenic patients is an almost super-human undertaking. Schizophrenia is a very serious and widespread illness in which restitution and stabilization are both sought. Ameliora-tion of symptoms is not enough. The slow piecing together of a frag-mented personality that was often attempted by skilled therapists in the days before *psychotropic drugs* were introduced could be applied to no more than a handful of patients. This study supports the thesis that a sensitive combination of *drug* and dynamically oriented *psycho-therapy* holds promise as a true therapeutic for people suffering from a schizophrenic psychosis.

Dr. Philip May's research may well serve as a strong stimulant to the further development of this special field of the hospital phase of treatment of the schizophrenic illness.

PHILIP R. A. MAY, M.D.

I am in complete accord with Dr. Genevieve May's formulation that the hospital treatment of the schizophrenic patient should concentrate on psychiatric first aid and restitution, and that stabilization of the personality is the ultimate goal of the outpatient phase. Our findings indicate that it is in the stabilization phase (and not in the hospital phase) that *psychotherapy* is likely to be of most help.

Our treatment strategy should therefore center around the careful integration of hospital and outpatient care. There should be a vigorous effort to provide continuity of follow-up and after-care, and to integrate *drug therapy, psychotherapeutic management* and *psychotherapy* into a constructive and efficient treatment approach, rather than thinking of them in terms of some rigid organic-functional dialectic, as mutually exclusive competitors. In this context, what she refers to as ". . . [introducing] the patient to an actively introspective attitude . . . . [a] general approach of preparation for psychological thinking . . ." becomes an essential part of *psychotherapeutic management* that prepares the patients who can use it for *individual psychotherapy* in the stabilization phase *after* they leave the hospital.

We must learn to integrate the psychodynamic and somatic approaches with discretion and finesse, and to develop a science of timing that uses them both appropriately and in harmony. It would therefore be helpful if teaching and research could make a deliberate attempt (amongst other things) to focus on the problems of integration of *ataraxic drugs, psychotherapeutic management* and *individual psychotherapy*.

It seems to me that at least a part of the difference of opinion over the relative roles of *psychotherapy* and *ataraxic drugs* has come about because people frequently confuse what applies to the *psychotherapy* of the *psychotic* patient with what applies to the *psychoanalysis* of the *neurotic*. I can well believe that *ataraxic drugs* would do nothing for the kind of patient who is suitable for *psychoanalysis,* and that they would interfere with the analytic process. But the *psychotherapy* of the psychotic patient and of the restitution phase in particular (contrasted with what Dr. Genevieve May calls the stabilization phase) is an entirely different matter, and we should be very careful to avoid sweeping generalizations from the one to the other.

I see little sense in quibbling about whether or not the patient should actually start formal *psychotherapy* while he is still in the hospital. We would do better to start from two basic premises. First, if a schizophrenic patient is well enough to profit from formal *psychotherapy,* he is generally well enough to be seriously considered as ready (or almost ready) to leave the hospital. Second, as Dr. Genevieve May points out, the drop-out rate is likely to be enormous if ex-patients are sent to a stranger for psychotherapy (in fact, I would guess that this applies to any kind of therapy).

If the treatment program is properly planned so that continuity of inpatient and outpatient care is provided by the same treatment team, the transition from inhospital *psychotherapeutic management* to outpatient *psychotherapeutic management plus individual psychotherapy* will be easier and more effective.

If, on the other hand, the treatment program is fragmented so that a different therapist treats the patient after he leaves the hospital, it will be much more difficult to provide adequate care. Matters will be improved somewhat if the patient can be returned to a therapist who treated him before admission to the hospital. Otherwise, a possible approach would be to arrange for the new outpatient psychotherapist to see the patient in the hospital a few times to initiate a psychotherapeutic relationship.

PSYCHOTHERAPEUTIC HELP THROUGH THE TERRIBLE ORDEAL OF ILLNESS
SIDNEY FINE, M.D.

I am in substantial agreement with the conclusions. I am not generally in favor of *psychoanalysis* or *formal psychotherapy* in the treatment of acute schizophrenia. The supervision that I administered to the psychiatric residents was what I too would call *psychotherapeutic management.*

There is one main disagreement I have with Dr. May's statements. I think the acutely disturbed patient in his internal isolation and loneliness does much better if he has someone with psychotherapeutic knowledge to help him through the terrible ordeal of his illness. There is no doubt in my mind that *ataraxic drugs* reduce the overwhelming anxiety in these patients and help them perceive their environment more realistically. But all these crises, the "psychotic illness" itself as well as the disturbing changes which follow their becoming "sane" again, are somewhat ameliorated by the assistance and counseling of interested and trained persons. The psychotherapist, in my opinion, is the best qualified to do this in the psychiatric hospital today.

There are, of course, some apparent drawbacks to this besides the expense involved. The patient, because of his attachment to the therapist, is not eager to leave the hospital. But in my experience, that "attachment" is *the* necessary relationship with a person, in many instances, which triggers the remission.

The ideal situation is the one in which the hospital therapist follows the patient on discharge into the outpatient clinic and continues the treatment and the relationship. This occurs in private practice, but is very difficult if not impossible in a public hospital. For this reason it is necessary to avoid those techniques which would encourage or facilitate marked regression and dependence on either the psychotherapist or the hospital.

I also believe as Dr. May does that the patient should be discharged from the hospital as soon as it is realistically feasible, and that treatment should be continued in his home environment.

PHILIP R. A. MAY, M.D.

Dr. Fine depicts what I also would see as one of the main tasks for *psychotherapeutic management*—helping the patient through a period of isolation, loneliness and feeling overwhelmed. I really do not think we disagree about the major role of the psychotherapist in this, because both of us feel strongly that under optimum conditions the same therapist should follow the patient and continue the therapeutic relationship after discharge.

In fact, I would guess that all the S.R.P. investigators feel this way. And for this reason it is about time we got to work on those resistances to change that obstruct the attainment of optimum conditions outside private practice. From my experience as an administrator (Clinical Director) I believe that there is no valid excuse for the prevalent public and university hospital practice of making an artificial separation between inpatient and outpatient therapists. To call a spade a spade, it seems to me that the main difficulties are the sheer inertia of established custom and the attractive administrative convenience of the separation. I admit that these are formidable resistances—but they are not impossible.

A HUMAN THERAPIST MUST DECIDE WHEN A CHEMICAL MUST REPLACE HIM, SUPPLEMENT HIM OR BE DISCARDED BY HIM
GERALD J. ARONSON, M.D.

The conclusions are sound, sobering and practical; and I was fascinated by the considerations of cost. I can disagree with none of the conclusions, but will cavil and chip away, perhaps also add something in the following items:

(1) *The issue of psychotherapeutic management:* Although a definition of *psychotherapeutic management* and some of its essentials were given, I feel that if this therapeutic mode is important, more should be said about it. How does one know when management is therapeutic? How

does one instruct others to do it? Are there varieties of *psychothera-peutic management?* Examples would be helpful to delineate between *psychotherapeutic management* and *nonpsychotherapeutic management.* My own feeling is in agreement with the conclusions. No treatment can have any beneficial effect unless it is embedded in *psychotherapeutic management*—otherwise it is brainwashing, coercion, threat or indifference. If *psychotherapeutic management* is so important, how can we insure its presence and proliferation, extend its influence, persuade colleagues in the ancillary arts of its usefulness, and teach it to ourselves and to others? *Psychotherapeutic management* may well be the bath-water in which all the babies float (*drugs, psychotherapy,* etc.), but only *drugs* (and perhaps *psychotherapy*) enable the patient to be aware of, to be receptive to *psychotherapeutic management.* I can well imagine *drug treatment* a complete fiasco at hospitals other than Camarillo where no *psychotherapeutic management* is available.

An alarming idea occurs to me! Might it not be possible that in a *nonpsychotherapeutic management* environment, *drug treatment* might make the patient worse since he then becomes more aware (through the *drug treatment*) of the indifference or cruelty of the environment?

(2) *Insight:* I suppose we are all to snap to attention at this word. Do not *insight* and *psychotherapy* have some special connection which is threatened by the finding that insight more promiscuously aligns itself with *drug therapy* than with *psychotherapy?* Dr. May rescues us from this scandal by pointing out that the kind of insight discussed has to do more with reality testing than with a real understanding of internal dynamics.

An analogy: A man standing before a garden, frightened, with eyes closed, does not see the garden. If his fear is decreased by some means or another, he is able to open his eyes and see the garden (i.e., to realize his geographic situation). His awareness of the garden did not enable him to open his eyes, but vice versa. A decrease in fear or derangement will inevitably lead to two consequences: (a) an increased awareness of some elements of his psychological situation which were not properly apprehended in the confused state, (b) an increased ability to deny and/or repress other elements of his psychological situation, e.g., his ambivalence, his confusion, etc.

Thus new seeds of illness are planted by the process of recovery itself. We can add to our therapeutic obligations by trying to temper, minimize and lead off these recovery-generated abilities of denial, repression, isolation and sequestration. This obligation places us squarely on both sharpened horns of a dilemma. It comforts us not at all to realize that the patient has been in this painful situation for many more years than we have and has finally "broken down"—i.e., fled the dilemma entirely. What is this dilemma that he and his therapist are faced with? Simply this: To realize and deal with the hate (and all its variations) within and around him, or to blot it out, and with it eclipse important segments of reality and mental functioning. Perhaps this is the reason *psychotherapy* works over the long haul and why *drugs* work well in the acute illness. Perhaps *drugs* aid by permitting the patient selectively to diminish his hatred, or his reaction to the hatred of others, without having to pay the price (which would be demanded without *drugs*) of lessening his awareness of reality. *Psychotherapy* should, in theory, make him more aware (rather than disguise his awareness) of his hatred and enable him to become more skilled at dealing with it. Unfortunately, this greater awareness may be precisely what the patient is defending against.

To repeat then: The insight gained by *drugs* is the increased awareness of some of those aspects of reality which had been blotted out when the blotting out was a blanket operation. *Drugs* enable the blotting out to be selective rather than total, thus leading to some return to awareness of elements of the psychological situation. This "insight," however, can only be maintained if the selective blotting out is buttressed by *drugs,* alteration in the family situation, supportive relationship with the therapist, etc.

You will be grateful to learn that this brings me to my last point. (3) *Continued treatment as an outpatient:* There are two strategies of treatment: (a) to aid selective suppression so that total denial (i.e., psychosis) will not become necessary, or (b) quietly and persistently to assist in the growing awareness of internal conflicts and deficits in such a manner that ego restrictions are not called for by the surge of unwelcome impulses and affects. Both strategies call for human judgment and human intervention. It may even be that from time to time alterations, combinations, or oscillations between these two strategies are necessary. In any case, then, a treatment course cannot be set on auto-pilot. A human therapist must decide when a chemical must replace him, supplement him, or be discarded by him. And these decisions must constantly be reviewed as patient and therapist pause, fall back and move forward in the lurching process that is therapy.

PHILIP R. A. MAY, M.D.

Dr. Aronson depicts in his sensitive and inimitable way the dilemma of the patient and the therapist—and of *psychotherapeutic management.* In so doing, he provides us with a theoretical framework that should help us toward its resolution.

THE MAGNITUDE OF EFFECTS MAY BE DEPENDENT ON THE HIGH QUALITY OF MILIEU TREATMENT

LUTHER S. DISTLER, PH.D.

I would like to reinforce Dr. May's concern that some may interpret our results as supporting a bandwagon rush to phenothiazines as the *specific* and *sufficient* treatment for hospitalized schizophrenics, with a resultant decrease in concern for the schizophrenic patient's psychological needs while in the hospital (e.g., *drugs* work and *milieu* and *psychotherapy* do not).

Clearly trifluoperazine in adequate treatment levels is an impressively effective treatment agent in caring for the hospitalized schizophrenic. Its addition to a rich and intensive treatment program (*milieu* or *milieu plus psychotherapy*) produced demonstrably better treatment results. But while our results are probably relevant to other good hospitals (private and university), it must be remembered that our *milieu* program was designed to be the *maximum* reasonably attainable in a public hospital in the foreseeable future. The quality and number of nursing services available to all our research patients far exceeded that of the great majority of present treatment facilities caring for schizophrenics. The addition of somatic therapies and particularly phenothiazines such as trifluoperazine in adequate treatment levels may well produce similarly effective results in treatment settings which provide the patient fewer opportunities for "psychotherapeutic" experiences in his dealings with those in his immediate life environment.

By contrast to the clear gains afforded by the addition of *drugs* to an intensive *milieu* program (even if the magnitude of effects may be dependent on the high quality of *milieu* treatment), the addition of *psychotherapy* to such an intensive *milieu* treatment program appears to add little or nothing of value in the treatment of the general run of hospitalized schizophrenics. This may be due not so much to *psychotherapy* not working as to the amount of 'psychotherapeutic' contact already available from the nursing staff. *Milieu* in the present study may not constitute an adequate control group for assessing whether *psychotherapy* works for hospitalized schizophrenics. One would not expect to fairly demonstrate the effects of a new drug in patients already receiving a moderately effective treatment with another drug with highly similar properties.

In distinguishing between *psychotherapy* and *psychotherapeutic man-*

agement, Dr. May made the point that beneficial psychotherapeutic interventions occur outside formally defined psychotherapy relationships. However, his comments are focused on the psychiatrist or psychiatric resident as the major or only psychotherapeutic agent in the patient's environment. The mental health field has only recently acknowledged the possibility that housewives and other lay persons may make equally effective "psychotherapists." In many outpatient community treatment centers, nurses, psychiatric technicians and occupational and rehabilitation workers are carrying the same formal assignments of psychotherapy as the more traditional disciplines of psychiatry, social work and psychology.

The kind of intensive milieu therapy program characteristic of our research wards provided considerable individual and small group "psychotherapeutic" relationships with exceptionally sensitive, dedicated and experienced ward treatment staff. The psychiatric resident may in fact on occasion have been the least experienced and least available "therapist" with whom the patient had meaningfully intense contact. This is particularly problematic because the nursing staff tended to concentrate their therapeutic attention on those patients whom they felt were not otherwise getting adequate treatment, particularly those assigned to *milieu* only. *Psychotherapy alone* may not have done better than *milieu* because the real load of psychotherapy for our "untreated" patients and their families was being carried by our ward treatment staff.

By far the most interesting and intriguing aspect of our results to date deals with the speculations about the mode of action of the impressive *drug* effects noted in our research. Dr. May has concisely drawn two major conceptualizations of the drug induced restitutive process. Is the restitution due to the effect of the drug in reducing overwhelming anxiety and aggressive impulses, or does it effect changes in the core psychotic process of defective ego functioning? Dr. May presents some data which lend support to the hypothesis that the *drug* effects in our study are not simply tranquilizing, but are truly anti-psychotic. This was particularly interesting to me as I had reached a similar impression from working on the MMPI results prior to reading Dr. May's comments.

Despite the limitations of the MMPI data due to untestable cases, it does provide some additional support for the hypothesis that drug-induced restitution in schizophrenia is primarily a matter of improved ego functioning. The major MMPI changes with *drug* were in those scales reflecting the core schizophrenic processes of bizarre psychotic symptoms, social, emotional and self-alienation, lack of ego mastery over cognitive and conative functions, paranoid sensitivity, and psychotic suspiciousness (*F* or Validity, *?* or Cannot say, *Sc* or Schizophrenia, *Pa* or Paranoia and the Psychotic Triad). The favorable effects of *drug* on *Cn* (Control), *Es* (Ego Strength) and *Pd* (Psychopathic deviate) clearly suggest improved ego controls over the expression and disruptive experiencing of excessive fears, anxieties, unacceptable sexual, aggressive and anti-social impulses. These changes also suggest improved interpersonal relations and an increased capacity for effective adjustive reactions to life stresses, and a less primitive, egocentric reaction to their psycho-social environment. The reduction in *Hs* (Hypochondriasis) suggests an increased insight into the emotional basis underlying their previous primitive expression of conflicts in terms of abnormal concerns about their bodily functions.

On the other hand, those MMPI scales which should have been most sensitive to the effects of *drug*-induced reductions of affect, anxiety, agitation, and distress did not show changes (*At* or Manifest Anxiety, *Ma* or Hypomania, *Pt* or Psychasthenia and *D* or Depression).

Many of the findings interpreted above were not clear-cut, significant differences, and are by no means conclusive. But they do re-echo Dr. May's comment that they are ". . . all in the direction of suggesting that drug-induced restitution is primarily a matter of improving ego function and that affective change is secondary or of secondary importance." Further study of this issue is clearly indicated.

One last comment in defense of the MMPI and the use of self-report measures in studies such as the present one. The limitation due to attrition of data because of the patient's inability or refusal to cooperate does reduce the usefulness of the data as an outcome measure with acutely disturbed schizophrenics. However, in those cases where data can be obtained, a valuable additional body of information is provided. In such a study as the present one, there are a number of other questions that one will wish to address after the initial question of which treatment works best. The self-report measures such as the MMPI add essential and different data to such questions as whether one can develop screening procedures for selecting a treatment of choice for the individual patient. Even as an outcome measure, the above discussion of *drug* effects clearly demonstrates that the MMPI is not totally without value.

PHILIP R. A. MAY, M.D.

Dr. Distler's interpretation of the MMPI findings is very interesting, and naturally I am pleased that it goes in the direction of my own thinking as to the mode of action of *ataraxic drugs*. One has to agree with his comment that despite the limitations due to nontestability, in those cases where data can be obtained, valuable additional information is provided and ". . . as an outcome measure . . . the MMPI is not entirely without value."

He very properly emphasizes that our *milieu care* was of a high order and that *ataraxic drugs* might not produce similarly effective results in less therapeutic treatment settings. I would join with him in emphasizing the therapeutic value of contact with nurses, psychiatric technicians, occupational and rehabilitation therapists and other professionals besides the three disciplines traditionally associated with *psychotherapy*. However, please let us not call everything *psychotherapy*—and let us not get distracted into arguments about who is qualified to do it. Although individual contacts of many kinds, by many different people, may be therapeutic (in the sense of "beneficial"), accidentally or by design, they are not all *psychotherapy*. There is a real practical value to distinguishing between *psychotherapy* and *what is therapeutic for the psyche,* and between *psychotherapy* and *psychotherapeutic management*. The section on individual psychotherapy (page 74), to which I would ask the reader to refer, defines not only what we meant by *psychotherapy* in the S.R.P., but also the conditions under which it was given.

If we keep to these distinctions, we can stay on the right track when it comes to the subject of controls. The point is that the choice of a control group must always depend on the question one wishes to answer—as illustrated by the apocryphal story of the research investigator who replied to the inquiry "And how is your wife?" with a cautious "Compared to what?"

In the S.R.P. we asked (amongst other things) the practical clinical question whether *individual psychotherapy alone* (as specifically defined) adds anything to the results of a good general level of ward *milieu care* (as specifically defined). For this question, our choice of a high level of *milieu care* as a control was clearly appropriate and enabled us to meet our treatment obligations to the patient in an ethically acceptable manner.

Now, if one wishes to ask an entirely different question, whether either *psychotherapy* or *therapeutic human contact other than formal psychotherapy* add anything to *no care at all,* then a theoretical case can be made for using as a control a group of patients who receive a lower level of care or even some sort of custody without significant therapeutic contact. I suppose this comparison could be done, but I would not care to be the person who does it with schizophrenic patients.

Independent evidence does not support the speculation that the comparison between *milieu* and *psychotherapy alone* might have been somewhat prejudiced in favor of *milieu* because the nursing staff may have tended to concentrate their efforts on the MILIEU group. As the supervisor of the MILIEU group, I had no such impression, so I checked this out with two psychiatrists and two nurses who were in close contact with the wards. Their observation (and mine) was that nursing personnel did not give extra attention to any particular treatment group per se, but rather to those patients who were more troublesome or disturbed, or who failed to get better, or who were in some other way demanding of attention. Since the statistics show that the MILIEU and PSYCHO-THERAPY ALONE groups were not significantly different in general level of health-sickness either before or after treatment, it would seem reasonable to assume on this basis that the amount of attention was roughly the same in these two groups.

This view is supported by the findings for the research nurses' ratings of the amount of special nursing attention given to the patients (obtained as described in Chapter 2). By this criterion there was no significant difference between the MILIEU and PSYCHOTHERAPY ALONE groups. Although the male patients treated with MILIEU received more attention than those treated with PSYCHOTHERAPY ALONE, the difference was not significant. Moreover, for females the reverse applied: PSYCHOTHERAPY ALONE received more attention than MILIEU, but only to a small extent and again not statistically significant.

IT IS IN THE DEGREE OF DIFFERENCES, PERHAPS, WHERE THE SURPRISES LIE
MAIMON LEAVITT, M.D.

In general I find what Dr. May has written to be comprehensive and lucid. Considering the complexity of the statistical material (certainly for me), it is put in a very comprehensible way, easy to follow and to make comparisons between relevant factors, allowing the reader to arrive at conclusions rather than having them forced upon him, and at the same time leaving it sufficiently open-ended so that it is stimulating to parallel thoughts and extensions, provoking other lines of thought. For the type of reader who is not well-informed statistically, the statistical section is excellently done, clear and sufficient to make the data, tables and conclusions meaningful without obfuscation.

I think there might well have been a bit more indication of the magnitude of the task that was undertaken. It is of course implicit in the text, from the wealth of data, tests, etc., but I wonder if it would not be appropriate to toot the horn, setting this study in the proper framework and indicating both the need for a comprehensive, statistically sound study such as this, and the need for more such thorough work.

The results lead to conclusions of varying degrees of certainty; some support prior impressions and prejudices and some negate others. It is important to keep in mind the specific limitations of the study as well as what generalizations may be reasonably drawn.

Among the significant points specified in the design section, which define the limitations, are these: The population is of schizophrenic patients whose disorder has been sufficiently gross and manifest as to require a substantial period of hospitalization. The hospital care, as a baseline, was somewhat above that of the average public hospital situation. The psychotherapists, while in general more interested and probably better qualified than the usual ward psychiatrist in a public hospital, were nevertheless mainly quite limited in prior training and experience in psychotherapy. The results are based upon criteria such as length of stay, discharge rates, scale ratings, etc., up to the time of discharge only (or to one year) in this part of the study. All these, and other factors, may limit extrapolation to other situations.

The findings are quite significant, but perhaps not so surprising as far as general trends are concerned. It is in the degree of differences, perhaps, where the surprises lie. Since the advent of *ataraxic drugs,* we have all been pleasantly aware of the tremendous effect these have had on stay and discharge rates for hospitalized schizophrenic patients. The results reported here are specific evidence of this efficacy for psychic restitution which permits of discharge.

I am disappointed, but not surprised, that *psychotherapy* had so relatively little benefit for these patients. Since Freud himself there has been much doubt as to the efficacy of *psychotherapy* in patients such as these, so far as restitution is concerned. This has been particularly so for (relatively) short-term treatment, and one might imagine this to be even more the case for relatively untrained, rarely gifted therapists. (So few therapists are gifted in the treatment of schizophrenic persons, well-trained or not.)

It has always been my impression that *psychotherapy* with such severely ill schizophrenic patients is of restricted value, the principal indication being for research interest, and the principal beneficiaries being that limited number of patients treated by a small group of unusual therapists. The present results unfortunately only confirm my impression. *Psychotherapy* does not seem to interfere with *drug treatment* and may indeed be of additional help in the long run (e.g., in after-care). If economic considerations were not involved, it would still be of value to utilize *psychotherapy* with such patients, so long as it is in addition to, not instead of, *ataraxic drugs.* We must remember that this study was designed partly to evaluate from a hard-headed, pragmatic, economic, administrative point of view. From this view the conclusions stated above are valid and must be given most serious consideration in any treatment program where economics is a principal factor. But, in general, where *psychotherapy* has been utilized with such patients, economics has not been a principal determinant in the treatment program. Economics aside, these results do of course indicate that for such a patient's own restitution, *ataraxic drugs* should be utilized regardless of which of the other three treatment modalities may also be given.

The results of *ECT* were somewhat better than I should have expected. Here I would be particularly interested in the follow-up study.

This brings us to a vital consideration in interpreting this study. The results here deal mainly with the evidences of restitution over the short term. What will the follow-up over the long term show? The question of the degree and level of stabilization of the restituted state is most significant. While I would anticipate that the stabilization of the discharged patients would not differ significantly between groups (if the after-care is similar), nevertheless this would be even more significant than the data on hospital stay. If my supposition were correct, it would certainly further support the use of *ataraxic drugs* during hospitalization as a practical measure. A similar modality study should be undertaken for the after-care period.

In this connection, the statements in the conclusion about *psychotherapeutic management* and after-care *psychotherapy* appear to be presumptions with little in this study to support them, although I personally fully agree with them. While I heartily agree, I wonder on what basis the use of *psychotherapeutic management* for the outpatient is predicated. I do not see where this study lends itself to any conclusions in this regard.

Certain cautions must be underscored. The evidence in this study of the questionable value of *psychotherapy* contact with these patients cannot be extended to suggest that increased contact with caring personnel in general is not significant. There is no evidence here to support such a view, and a great deal of evidence from many other sources to confirm the opposite view.

There is nothing in this study directly applicable to questions of the relative effectiveness of these modalities in other patient populations and other types of settings. It is tempting to do so, but unwarranted. And the findings do not interdict the teaching and practice of *psychotherapy* with schizophrenic hospitalized patients, so long as the purposes and limitations are understood. Indeed, there is considerable research potential in combined *psychotherapy* and *drug therapy* to elucidate hypotheses such as that of the mode of action discussed above.

In the PSYCHOTHERAPY ALONE and PSYCHOTHERAPY PLUS DRUG groups, was there any indication of an ideal time to terminate treatment, i.e., a time after which there were few responders despite the additional length of treatment? It would be helpful to know if there is an established period of adequate trial. The length of stay of *psychotherapy* patients may have been excessively long because of the investment of the therapist, although this is probably negated by the shorter stay of the patients on *psychotherapy plus drugs* and the lower scale ratings of *psychotherapy* patients in general.

Despite comment to the contrary in the design section and conclusions, it would be worthwhile to compare results with similar modalities, where cases were chosen as "most suitable" for each. If the results did not correspond with those here, it might throw further light on the matter of efficacy. While I am by no means certain we have good criteria for such selection of modality, it is nevertheless possible that we do. There is the possible criticism that the present study may involve treating a variety of different disease entities by randomly selected treatments, and this would raise doubts as to what we are measuring.

In the discussion of "insight," the argument seems based upon some unspoken assumption on the part of others that insight leads to restitution and improvement. Since insight and reality testing are manifestations of ego functions, it is not a matter of consequence but rather of identity of functions.

The suggestions and recommendations in the last part of the conclusions are all provocative and well worth pursuing.

PHILIP R. A. MAY, M.D.

Dr. Leavitt's appreciation of the magnitude of the task and the need for thorough and careful work is most welcome. I feel strongly that if we are to get anywhere in systematic clinical psychiatric research we should discourage what the research fraternity refers to as "quick and dirty" studies. In fact, I am inclined to recommend as a rough general guideline that in outcome research one should allow at least as long to plan a study as to collect the data, and at least twice as long again to process and analyze it.

I must admit that his cautionary comments about presumptions as to the value of *psychotherapeutic management* and outpatient *psychotherapy* put a finger right on the border line between the factual results of our study and assumptions from experience and from other evidence. He is quite right in his implication that there is a need for more systematic study in this area.

However, even so, I think our position is justifiable. The S.R.P. results were obtained in the setting of a high standard of *milieu care,* and as Dr. Leavitt says, there is a great deal of evidence from other sources to support the view that increased contact with caring personnel in general does contribute materially to better results.

On the subject of controls, he anticipates the objection of proponents who may say that the results are all well and good for a heedless random treatment, but if you would only prescribe their particular therapy for whom it is truly suited, then you would see the difference. This subject, which I will refer to as the "Chosen Treatment" design, has already been dealt with to some extent in Chapter 2, to which I would ask the reader to refer. I have a few additional comments.

First, the "Chosen Treatment" argument could be advanced with equal reason for any of the five treatment methods.

Second, the part of the S.R.P. reported in this volume had the aim of comparing the general results of the five treatment methods assuming (as we believed to be true) that no one really knew the answers as to which treatment was best for what particular kind of schizophrenic patient. The "Chosen Treatment" design cannot make this comparison unless the patients so chosen are then assigned equally (as by a random method) to the other treatment modalities to enable a fair comparison to be made.

Third, there is little in the literature to support a claim to have identified practical criteria for the selective use of any specific method of treatment for schizophrenic patients—apart from merely the criteria for a good or bad prognosis in general. In fact, the S.R.P. findings so far indicate that some of the criteria that might be proposed (such as the amount of insight as a favorable indicator for *psychotherapy;* or overt signs of anxiety, hyperactivity and aggression for *drug therapy;* or depression for *ECT*) did not respond to the various forms of treatment in quite the way that we expected. An important part of this study will be further analyses to determine whether there is any objective evidence that it may be possible to select ahead of time those patients who will respond favorably to a particular treatment. If we are indeed able to derive suitable prediction criteria, then a good case could be made for doing what Dr. Leavitt suggests—a further (validation) study in which assignments to the various treatments would be made on the basis of these specific criteria. The results of this second validation study could then be compared with the results of the present study to see if any progress has been made toward the ultimate goal of maximizing the improvement rate.

The suggestion is most intriguing that we study response over time to see if an optimum period of treatment trial can be established. We have the data and will certainly attempt to do so.

DEGREE AND KIND OF INITIAL RESPONSE TO TREATMENT MAY PROVE TO BE ONE OF THE BEST PREDICTORS OF LONG-RANGE PROGNOSIS AND EVENTUAL OUTCOME
A. HUSSAIN TUMA, PH.D.

I have one comment regarding the findings of this study in general and a series of brief observations regarding specific points made in various parts of the present report. The general purpose of these comments is to supplement or clarify the author's statements rather than be critical of the views or interpretations reported in this volume.

In general I believe that due to certain important design features of this study, such as provision of control and comparison groups, "random" method of assignment of patients to treatment, attempt at selecting a generally more homogeneous sample of patients, multiplicity of outcome measures depicting a wide range of behaviors and sources of observations, etc., truly comparative observations about the efficacy of the five experimental treatments used in this study have become possible. It is my sincere hope and expectation that these findings will have meaning both to the clinician and the researcher and have the proper impact on the prevailing attitudes toward the treatment of schizophrenia.

The data presented in this report use treatment groups as the unit of analysis, utilizing their respective averages and measures of variability. This approach is quite essential and proper for the provision of overall comparative statements regarding their efficacy. The next step of data analysis must, however, focus on what is in my estimate a very crucial question, clinically and theoretically. It would be extremely important to identify, within each treatment group, those characteristics which distinguish patients who respond differentially to the given treatment and those who do not respond at all or get worse. The results of such analysis would hopefully provide the clinician with the needed information for more accurate estimates of prognosis, and provide the research theoretician with useful leads and hints for the understanding and delineation of the pathological states which were labeled, albeit carefully, in this study as schizophrenia. Such data may also be most essential in the analysis of data already collected in a two-year post-hospital follow-up study of these same patients. Degree and kind of initial response to treatment may prove to be one of the best predictors of long-range prognosis and eventual outcome.

My next few comments are on specific statements which appear in several different parts of the report.

In discussing release rate, it is suggested that patients who are not given a specific treatment such as *ataraxic drugs, ECT* or *psychotherapy* are more likely to remove themselves prematurely from the hospital. I seriously doubt that schizophrenic patients, or their therapists for that matter, view *psychotherapy* as a specific treatment unique to schizophrenic disorders. I know that the author does not imply specificity in the sense of being the most indicated, appropriate or curative method. What is intended is a distinction between these methods and general *milieu care*. It is perhaps true that physical forms of treatment come closer to fulfilling patients' expectations of typical medical treatment with its concrete events and its defined procedures and schedules of administration. The regularity of the patient-doctor contacts at predetermined times and in the doctor's private office all tend to give *psychotherapy* some degree of definiteness. This is certainly lacking from the experiences of the MILIEU group. However, although regular psychotherapeutic interviews over several months did not reduce or ameliorate symptomatology as effectively as *drugs* and *ECT,* they apparently served to provide the patients and perhaps the staff with some assurance of expert psychiatric attention and thus the hope that if the patient stays in treatment longer he will eventually get better. There is reason to believe that MILIEU patients did not develop similar expectations and hope for relief. This may in part explain the greater premature departures from the hospital among the MILIEU (control) patients.

In the discussion of sex differences in relation to the therapist's persistence before giving up, the possibility is pointed out that if a female patient is given *psychotherapy,* the physician is likely to persist longer before giving up than if he is treating the patient with *ECT, ataraxic drugs alone,* or similar therapy, and that this is not so for the male patients.

It is important to point out that this does not justify a possible inference about the sex of the patient alone. Thirty-five of the therapists were male physicians and only six were women. Also, all but one of the senior treatment supervisors were men. Therefore, if the observed sex differences among the patients were true differences, they are so when there is a preponderance of male therapists and supervisors. This is in general a rather typical situation in present-day psychiatry in the United States.

Regarding the value of short-term improvement versus long-term results of treatment, I might add that they both constitute important criteria of outcome. My guess is, however, that long-range outcome is far more difficult to study and assess and much more difficult to interpret or attribute to a particular treatment. As the reader certainly realizes, this is so because of the wide range of uncontrolled and uncontrollable experiences in and out of treatment which may influence long-range outcome. Perhaps certain innovative methods for analyzing prospective data collected continuously for a number of years following hospital release can help overcome some of the problems in this area. It is hoped that post-hospital data collected as part of this study will throw some light on the relationship between short-term and long-term outcome.

On the interpretation of the positive effects of *anti-psychotic drug therapy,* it is essential to stress that firm conclusions about the primacy of improved cognitive ego functions and the relatively secondary role of better affect cannot be justifiably made on the basis of present data. In order to be able to do so, further systematic clinical and laboratory studies of the effect of the phenothiazines on various cognitive functions and a range of emotional states are needed. Without such data, inferences about the role of *drugs* in a treatment and their mechanisms of action are likely to reflect personal belief and suffer from circularity.

Finally, the statements regarding the advisability of *psychotherapy* after patients leave the hospital seem contrary to the evidence furnished in this report on the effectiveness of *psychotherapy* in the hospital. Two points are in order here: (a) that these statements seem to be more an expression of faith and hope than an inference based on presently available data; (b) for these statements to be consistent with present evidence, one must assume that the patient is no longer psychotic and hence *psychotherapy may* be useful to him.

Psychologically sound management in social, familial and occupational settings is by definition a good thing not only for schizophrenics whose reality testing is perhaps still impaired, but for all people—and most particularly the mentally healthy person—for it is the kind of management that makes possible other health-enhancing interactions and experiences in our everyday encounters.

PHILIP R. A. MAY, M.D.

Dr. Tuma's comments on prediction and long-term versus short-term outcome are most appropriate and timely. In particular, he makes the important point that the next stage in our data analysis—examination of the characteristics of those who do or do not respond to a particular treatment—has considerable theoretical interest, for it may help to distinguish different types of "schizophrenia" and so lead to a better understanding of this condition. As he comments in his introductory chapter on the background of this study, a particular treatment may be extremely valuable in helping us to understand "schizophrenia" even if it is not effective in a great number of patients. So even though I am now not as optimistic as I used to be about our chances of finding many patients (in the average prognostic range) who respond better to some treatment other than *ataraxic drug,* the effort will be worthwhile anyway. I am glad he brought this up, because, as I said earlier, I find it very hard to give up the idea of "the right treatment for the right patient."

He also comments that just because the female patients stayed longer with certain treatments, we must not leap to the conclusion that this is just a patient problem. Maybe, he says, it has something to do with the sex of the therapist. He is, of course, quite right, and this points up the need for further study of the subject.

His explanation of the higher incidence of AMA discharges in the MILIEU group is exactly what I had in mind, but had not made explicit. If the patient is given something that he can understand as a "treatment" intended to help his illness, then he is likely to remain willingly in the hospital—and *milieu therapy* is not so readily perceived as "treatment."

Dr. Tuma properly and cautiously recommends that we wait for further clinical and laboratory studies of the effect of *ataraxic drugs* on cognition and emotion before coming to a firm conclusion about the relationship between drug-induced restitution, ego functioning and affective change. Since I observed that the evidence in this respect is ". . . somewhat flimsy and by no means conclusive," and recommended further systematic study, we have no big disagreement here. But I would be very hesitant indeed in assuming that results from experiments with normal persons, or normal animals, or persons suffering from other psychiatric disorders can be applied directly to schizophrenia.

I cannot resist nudging him a bit about his final remarks to the effect that my expressed belief in the value of outpatient *psychotherapy* is based more on faith and hope than on the findings of this study. Apparently he himself has no hesitation in asserting that *psychotherapeutic management* ". . . is *by definition* a good thing not only for schizophrenics . . . but for all people . . ." (italics are mine). I am reminded of the cartoonist's question, "Are you an idealist upholding a principle or a cynic defending a prejudice?"

More seriously, I do think the research investigator has an obligation to go further than presenting his research findings in detached isolation; they should be set in the context of other evidence and of his own experience. So, whether it is faith, hope, prejudice, logical deduction or reasonable extrapolation, my opinion is that, with the schizophrenic patient, the main indication for formal *psychotherapy* (as distinct from *psychotherapeutic management*) is in the outpatient phase, after release from the hospital and after restitution has been substantially achieved. I doubt, however, that it is indicated in every case.

A UNIQUE STUDY WHICH MAY NEVER BE REPEATED

JONATHAN O. COLE, M.D.

This is a neat, competent, effective and unique study which may never be repeated. The weight of scientific and clinical evidence which has accumulated since this study was initiated would make it difficult to justify including in any study a group of acute schizophrenic patients who were to receive no specific therapy for many months.

The handful of controlled studies of specific nondrug treatments *(psychotherapy, intensive milieu therapy)* of which this is, I believe, the best, would make most clinical investigators reluctant to place acutely ill schizophrenics even on psychotherapy without drugs for any prolonged period. The clear, overwhelming results of this study serve, in fact, to make any replication attempt improbable.

In some ways this is a shame. One would like to know, and one suspects, that some schizophrenics should do better on *milieu therapy alone* or on *psychotherapy alone.* From the data presented here, the number of such patients would seem to be small. However, the total numbers of patients in each treatment group may be a little small for optimal application of multivariate techniques like multiple regression or discriminate function to the data in a search for characteristics of patients doing particularly well on any single therapy. However, I am currently spoiled by N's of 100 to 160 per treatment group and may be overestimating the power of numbers alone.

Purists will note the absence of placebo controls. I wish merely to note that I prefer the strategy employed here for this particular kind of study. I am unconvinced that there is any large response to the administration of inert pills on the part of schizophrenic patients, as distinct from the natural course of the illness or responses to the total treatment context.

I strongly applaud the collection and analysis of Cost data. This is unique to this study and badly needed in psychiatry in general.

In addition to rejoicing in the firm and reasonable findings of the study, I also applaud Dr. May's emphasis on the concept of *psychotherapeutic management,* an area which may well be of far greater importance in the treatment of most patients than is *psychotherapy* more narrowly defined.

I take particular pleasure in having received the opportunity to read the body of this volume before it went to press because my staff and I had a somewhat larger role in bringing the work to this point than is often the case. There came a time about two years ago when the faith of formal reviewing groups at NIMH had worn somewhat thin. Problems in the collection, cleansing, rechecking and processing of data had delayed all major analyses of the findings on the full patient sample, and the reviewing groups began to doubt the value of investing further in the research. At this point we shifted from the grant to the contract mechanism to support the final phases of the work and to insure that the lack of a few thousand dollars in 1966 did not render futile the granting of hundreds of thousands of dollars in earlier years.

In fairness, it must be noted that assistance from the UCLA Health Sciences Computing Facility was every bit as important as our contract support in getting the study done, and the doggedness and thoroughness of Dr. May and his staff was the most important of all. Nevertheless, I take particular pleasure in the publication of this part of the study and look forward eagerly to further reports, particularly on the follow-up of these patients.

APPENDIX I

Assignment of Patients to Treatment and to Therapists

PREPARATION OF ASSIGNMENT CARDS

A statistician prepared a master deck of a large number of sequentially numbered sealed opaque envelopes: each of these contained a card indicating assignment to one of the five treatments, the treatments being randomly distributed within each set of five cards. Each set of five cards in the master deck was randomly different from other sets.

ASSIGNMENT OF SUBDECKS TO THERAPIST·

From the master deck, subdecks were prepared for each therapist in units of five to maintain random distribution of treatment for each therapist. Each therapist had two decks—one for male patients, one for female patients.

ASSIGNMENT OF PATIENT TO DOCTOR

By a rotation system, the research patients were assigned to a physician's case load up to a maximum of seven (for residents, other nonresearch cases might raise his case load to not more than 12–15) or to a maximum case load of twenty for staff psychiatrists. When a resident had a vacancy on his case-load roster, he would get the next case selected in sequence. There was no special selection of a particular patient; in fact, the assignment method assured that the resident could not know ahead of time who his next patient might be.

ASSIGNMENT OF PATIENT TO TREATMENT METHOD

After the research work-up had been completed by the physician assigned to the case and by the research staff, the research psychiatrist (who did not treat the patient) was notified. He in turn requested the project psychologist to make a treatment assignment for the patient. To do this, the psychologist pulled the next envelope in sequence from that particular doctor's deck according to the sex of the patient; when opened, this would indicate the treatment to which the patient was to be assigned. The research psychiatrist and the patient's physician were notified of the treatment to which the patient had been assigned. The psychologist recorded on the card the date, patient's name, research number and therapist's name and filed the envelope in the patient's research folder.

RE-ASSIGNMENT BEFORE TREATMENT

In three or four cases in each of the treatment groups it was necessary for proper continuity of patient care to reassign the patient before treatment was started to a physician other than the one who had done the initial work-up. For example, if the original physician assigned to the case was soon to change from one service to another, or was about to go on extended vacation, the patient was reassigned to the next doctor in sequence. There was clearly no significant difference among the five treatment groups in respect to the number of patients reassigned in this manner, and no evidence of bias.

PROCEDURE IF A PHYSICIAN LEFT THE HOSPITAL OR THE TREATMENT SERVICE AFTER TREATMENT HAD BEEN STARTED

Normally, a patient remained under the care of his original therapist throughout his entire stay in the hospital. However, if the therapist left the hospital or if other circumstances prevented him from continuing the case to completion, the patient was then reassigned to another physician thought by the research staff to be comparable to the first in terms of sex, experience, etc. This meant that patients who remained longer in the hospital, presumably the cases who responded the least to treatment, were more likely to be reassigned to another physician than those who stayed in the hospital only a short while. A record was kept of the dates and circumstances of reassignment from one doctor to another.

CLOSURE PROCEDURE AT END OF STUDY

The first patient was selected for the study on June 18, 1959, and the last on December 19, 1962. It was originally intended to continue assignment until at least 25 patients of each sex had been included in each of the five treatment groups, but unfortunately our resources proved insufficient. Accordingly, in the last two months of the 42 months of patient selection, we adopted a procedure for closure that would aim at approximately equal number for each sex in each of the specific treatment groups.

Up to then, larger numbers of females than males had been selected (roughly five females to four males). For females, we set 25 as the target sample size for each treatment group.* For males, who were in relatively short supply, we decided to close the control group at 21 and to continue admission to the other groups, hoping to reach as close to 25 as possible within the limits imposed by our resources. When the specified number of patients was reached for a particular treatment and sex, assignment to that treatment for that sex was terminated. Thus, two months before the end of patient selection, patients of both sexes were still being assigned to the five treatments. Then one treatment after another was dropped until selection stopped with nearly equal numbers of patients in each group. During the closure period, the treatment envelopes were still pulled in the manner previously described. However, if a card was obtained that would add to a group for which selection had been stopped, it was destroyed and the next random card was pulled. The final numbers assigned to each treatment and included in the final analysis are shown in Table I.1, 20–25 in each treatment for the sexes separately and 43–48 for both sexes combined.

Table I.1. NUMBERS OF PATIENTS ASSIGNED TO TREATMENT GROUPS AND INCLUDED IN FINAL ANALYSIS

Treatment Group	Assigned			Final Analysis		
	Male	Female	Total	Male	Female	Total
M	22	25	47	20	23	43
E	25	26	51	23	24	47
D	24	27	51	23	25	48
P	24	25	49	22	24	46
P+D	21	28	49	21	23	44
TOTAL	116	131	247	109	119	228

Closure to equal group size introduces the possibility of bias vis-à-vis the first group to close if the last patients added are in any way different from those included before first closure. Accordingly, precautions were taken to minimize the possibility of influencing the selection teams. They and the research psychiatrist

* The target sizes were based on the numbers believed at that time to be eligible for the final analysis; some patients were subsequently excluded.

were deliberately kept under the impression that selection would continue as usual for much longer, while the actual decisions on closure were a close-kept secret by the principal investigator, project psychologist and statistician. For this reason and because only a few patients were assigned during the relatively short closure period, the possibility of closure bias in this study is small. Actually, for males, one patient was assigned to each of the other four groups over the 49-day period after closure of intake to MILIEU (3.7 percent of the number over 3.8 percent of the time). For females, after closure of the DRUG ALONE group, seven patients were assigned to the other four groups over a 68-day period (5.9 percent of the number over 5.3 percent of the time). PSYCHOTHERAPY PLUS DRUG was the first to close intake for both sexes—after this, seven patients were assigned to the other four groups over a period of 34 days (3 percent of the number over 2.4 percent of the time).

When random assignment and staggered intake are used, one of the groups has to be last, and small "runs" in assignment are to be expected. In our study, the workings of random assignment were such that the last group to close was ECT. Three patients (one male and two females) were assigned to this treatment over a 23-day period after intake to all other groups had ceased (1.3 percent of the patients over 2.0 percent of the time). Table I.2 shows that these last three patients did not differ from the remainder of the ECT group or from any of the other patients in age, I.Q., initial level and two-year prognosis on the Menninger Health-Sickness scale, education and duration of illness. It may reasonably be concluded that there is no evidence that the method of closure introduced any systematic bias into the experiment.

Table I.2. CHARACTERISTICS OF THE LAST THREE PATIENTS ASSIGNED TO THE ECT GROUP

Patient	Age	Verbal I.Q.	Menninger Scale Initial	Two-Year Prognosis	Educa- tion*	Duration of Psychosis (wks)
251	34	122	23	36	4	32
252	36	111	22	32	4	14
253	27	83	20	34	6	2
TOTAL PATIENT GROUP						
Mean	28.1	107.0	19.4	36.3	4.2	38.5
SD	6.2	18.3	3.9	4.9	1.2	66.1

* 4 = High School (completion of 12th grade).
  6 = Junior High School (completion of 7th, 8th or 9th grade).

ASSIGNMENT OF PATIENT NUMBERS

Each patient was assigned a research number at selection. At the end of the study the numbers for each treatment group were stratified by sex and divided into halves by a random method. This made it possible to compare the results for two randomly selected halves as well as for the first and second halves of the patient group.

*Amounts of Individual Psychotherapy
and Other Individual Contact, by Treatment Group*

INDIVIDUAL PSYCHOTHERAPY

None of the MILIEU, ECT or DRUG ALONE patients received anything designated as *psychotherapy*. For the two PSYCHOTHERAPY groups, the amount of therapy per week was in conformity with the instructions to therapists and supervisors—"An average of not less than two hours per week and a minimum of not less than one hour." As one would expect, the total amount varied considerably according to the length of hospitalization.

For patients assigned to PSYCHOTHERAPY and released successfully, the total amount ranged from 7–87 hours (12–106 interviews).* The sixteen patients not released successfully from this group (limited responders) were given a reasonable trial before it was decided to give up; the number of hours for the individual cases being 20, 32, 39, 40, 44, 53, 54, 56, 58, 62, 66, 82, and 91 respectively (38, 39, 49, 55, 68, 69, 70, 70, 72, 76, 85, 81, 110 interviews). Complete information was not obtained for patients #1, #11 and #50, but it seems safe to assume that the amount was substantial as they were in treatment for 252, 365 and 364 days respectively. The patient who received only 20 hours of therapy (38 interviews) before being designated a "limited responder" did so poorly that treatment had to be terminated 166 days after admission, 141 days after treatment was started. The case report below suggests that he might have been a problem for even the most experienced psychotherapist.

Patient # 80: This male patient, age 27, was assigned to PSYCHOTHERAPY. On admission he talked continuously, heard voices and was frightened, saw visions, said he was dead or being chased and spied on; attempted to escape; masturbated openly; and would often assume bizarre positions or lie naked on the floor. After one month of treatment (1½ months from admission) his hallucinations and agitation were more severe. He then became progressively mute and withdrawn, often refused to eat and remained in bed most of the time. After two months of treatment (2½ months from admission) his condition began to fluctuate. During mute periods he would sit on the toilet for hours at a time or remain in bed. At other times he would be hyperactive, occasionally strike patients or staff or try to escape. He attempted to smuggle knives from the table, started shadowboxing and riding on his bed, calling it a horse and telling it to go faster. Three months after admission he was worse: When excited he would attack patients and staff or pace around in circles, hitting his head and body against the wall. Five months after admission, despite all management efforts, he was almost continually hallucinated and frightened; his condition oscillated daily between mute withdrawal and severe excitement, and every day or two there would be an episode in which he would strike patients or staff. After 141 days of treatment (166 days from admission) it was finally decided by the therapist and treatment supervisor that treatment was not likely to succeed and that it would be unwise to attempt to

---

* One hour = 60 minutes (not 50!). These figures do not include time spent by the (future) therapist with the patient during initial work-up and evaluation: This probably amounted to some three to ten hours. Nor do they include individual contact between physician and patient of the kind that was not designated as *psychotherapy*. If this is included, the figure for "hours" and "interviews" are increased by about 10 percent and 60 percent respectively.

continue any longer. Accordingly, an exception was made and he was declared a "limited responder" before the end of the full six months.

For patients assigned to PSYCHOTHERAPY PLUS DRUG and released successfully, the total amount of *psychotherapy* ranged from 10–66 hours (10–80 interviews). As for the two patients not released, one received 200 hours before being designated a "limited responder"; complete information is not available for the other, but it is safe to assume that a fair trial was given—he was in treatment for 377 days.

ANY TYPE OF INDIVIDUAL PHYSICIAN-PATIENT CONTACT

Although the patients assigned to MILIEU, DRUG ALONE and ECT did not receive any formal *psychotherapy*, they did of course have some contact with the physician even if it was not characterized as *psychotherapy*. Accordingly, it is advisable to examine the figures for all individual contacts, whether designated as *psychotherapy* or not, to determine the extent to which the two PSYCHOTHERAPY groups differed from the others in this respect.

In terms of the *frequency* of individual contacts, there was little difference among the five groups, although the means for the PSYCHOTHERAPY ALONE, DRUG ALONE and PSYCHOTHERAPY PLUS DRUG groups tended to be somewhat higher than the others (two-way analysis of variance, F-ratio for differences among the five treatments = 1.47, $p = .21$).

However, there was a clear and substantial distinction between the two PSYCHOTHERAPY groups and the others in terms of the *total number of hours of individual contact*, as shown in Table II.1.

Table II.1.   MEAN NUMBER OF HOURS: INDIVIDUAL CONTACT ALL TYPES

	M	E	D	P	P+D
Male	9.9	9.6	7.9	48.5	39.9
Female	10.1	11.5	9.1	49.2	25.6

A two-way analysis of variance shows that the differences between the groups are extremely significant ($F = 49.6$, $p = .0000$).

There was also a clear and substantial difference between the groups in terms of the duration of each contact with the physician. The mean duration of contacts that were designated as *not psychotherapy* ranged from a low of eight minutes for male and female PSYCHOTHERAPY ALONE and female MILIEU, to a high of thirteen minutes for male MILIEU, female ECT and female DRUG ALONE. By contrast, *psychotherapy* sessions conformed pretty much to the fifty or sixty minute hour: Their mean length ranged from a low of 49 minutes for female PSYCHO-THERAPY PLUS DRUG to a high of 53 minutes for male PSYCHOTHERAPY PLUS DRUG.

INDIVIDUAL CONTACT OTHER THAN PSYCHOTHERAPY

Only ten of the *nonpsychotherapy* patients had individual contact with their physician at a rate of more than four hours a month sometime during their hospital careers. In all except two, the contact was increased above four hours per month only during one or two "crisis" months and was well below this limit for the remainder of the patient's hospital stay.

The two exceptions were patients #75 and #122 who were seen individually by their physicians for more than four hours a month during ⅔ of their hospital stay. However, the duration of each contact was only about fifteen minutes, and the average number of hours per month for both cases was 3.5, comfortably below the level defined as *psychotherapy*. It seems reasonable to conclude that there was no attempt to give systematic *psychotherapy* (as defined) to any of the MILIEU, ECT or DRUG ALONE patients.

Patient #75: (ECT) was seen 125 times (27 hours) over six months' hospital stay. In the first and second months she was seen 20 times (5 hours), and in the third and fourth months, 25 times (6 hours), in the fifth month, 20 times (3 hours) and in the sixth, 15 times (2¼ hours). Successful release.

Patient #122: (DRUG ALONE) was seen 110 times (27 hours) over six months' hospital stay, 20 times (5 hours) in the first, second, third and fifth months; 20 times (4 hours) in the fourth month and 10 times (3 hours) in the sixth month. Successful release.

APPENDIX III

Instructions for Rating Idiosyncratic Symptoms (ISR)

List on the form not more than four brief descriptive statements which you feel best characterize the patient's behavior, in the order which they concern you most (i.e., require the most nursing concern or attention—are most serious), the most important first. Rate the severity of these symptoms initially and bimonthly.

If later in the patient's hospital course it is necessary to add any new symptoms, you may add to a total of not more than six including those listed originally. Indicate the date of addition beneath the additional symptom described, and assign new ranks to indicate the order of importance (seriousness, concern) within the modified list, giving a rank value of 1 to the most serious symptom, a rank value of 2 to the next most serious, etc. (Enter these new ranks in the time-interval boxes corresponding to the date of the new list of symptoms.) When adding new symptoms, you should rate their severity all the way back to the initial period.

For ratings of severity, use the following scale: (4) severe or almost always; (3) moderate or fairly often; (2) mild or occasional; (1) not present.

Record your ratings for each idiosyncratic symptom by marking the appropriate level at each time interval. Connect these marks to form a line graph as in a temperature chart.

APPENDIX IV

Criteria for Movement Statistics

In studying treatment outcome, it is important to distinguish between patients who have had prior treatment experience and those who have not, since the response to a particular treatment may be partially determined or modified by prior experience. The multiple-readmission group in particular poses a serious problem in interpretation of results, being strongly contaminated by previous treatment and, as Smith and Wittson[1] point out, heavily loaded with patients who may respond equally well, albeit only temporarily, to different therapies.

As patients are seldom admitted to the hospital without having had something that someone might call prior treatment, even if only a few days' observation or a single outpatient visit, the following criteria were used for first significant admission:

Either (1) Admitted directly for the first time and not hospitalized elsewhere in any kind of hospital or sanitarium at any time for a psychiatric disorder,

Or (2) Admitted for the first time as a transfer from another hospital in which they had been for not more than 31 days; provided that the patient had not received any major somatic therapy (defined as electroshock, lobotomy or more than 21 days of continuous treatment in hospital with ataraxic drugs),

Or (3) Admitted for the first time with a history of hospitalization elsewhere for psychiatric disorder at some other time provided that: (a) The patient had not received any major somatic therapy as defined above *and* (b) The patient had not been in any one hospital for more than 31 days *and* (c) The total period of hospitalization for all hospitals had been not more than 45 days.

SIGNIFICANT RELEASE

A patient was said to have achieved a significant release on the day he (physically) left the hospital if he subsequently remained out for more than 21 days. If there were a series of leaves and returns, returning for less than two full days in between, the brief returns were disregarded in computing the time spent continuously in the community. (It is reasonably clear that in these cases the patient is actually being managed as an outpatient and that the return to the hospital and rapid turn-around was prearranged.) However, if the patient spent two full days or more in the hospital in between leaves, then he was not counted as released.

When a patient was transferred from Camarillo to another hospital, this was counted as a single continuous admission, the release date being when the patient left the other hospital. This particular point will no doubt seem logical, even superfluous, but the reader should note that at the time of the study it was common practice in official statistics in California and elsewhere to treat transfers as if they were regular new admissions for the purpose of calculating hospital stay, even though this results in marked distortion.

Freeman and Simmons used "30 days or more" as their criterion for release.[2] Twenty-one days seems to be more consistent with our clinical experience. In fact, a criterion of fifteen days would have been set for this study if it had not been necessary to allow for the two- to three-week leaves that are traditional at most psychiatric hospitals over Christmas and New Year's. By and large, if a

[1] See reference 2.
[2] See reference 1.

patient has not returned within 21 days it may be assumed that either he, his family or his physician felt that he was well enough to stay out. After 21 days, the distinction between AWOL and official leave seems to disappear. With the two exceptions described below, all the project patients who left the hospital AWOL and subsequently remained out for more than 21 days were eventually converted to an official leave status.

Two patients posed particular and exceptional situations that required special management—both clinically and in terms of analysis of results. They illustrate vividly the trials and tribulations that beset the research investigator and the type of error that may occur in studies that use official dates of leave and discharge without making a careful study of intervening events:

Patient #211: A married female assigned to PSYCHOTHERAPY ALONE. Five months after admission and having shown little or no change or progress, she failed to return from a visit with her husband and infant son and was placed on AWOL status. The telephone at home was not answered, the shades were drawn and no one answered the door, but eventually a persistent social worker did manage to see her. She seemed thin, worn and manifestly still psychotic: Apparently she had been staying at home all the time with the shades drawn, watching TV and looking after her baby in lackadaisical fashion. She said she was not getting on with her husband, that she knew she needed treatment, that she wished to return to the hospital and would have done so except her husband insisted she stay home and look after the baby. He had told her not to go out or to speak to anyone (she said); was out all day himself and returned late at night. The social work agency was not willing to place the child without the husband's permission—but he could not be contacted. Eventually, however, arrangements were made for the placement and the patient returned voluntarily to the hospital 87 days after she had left. Thirteen months after initial admission, six months after her return and having received a total of nine months of *individual psychotherapy,* she was declared a "limited responder." Her condition at that time was perhaps a trifle better in general, although worse in some ways and unchanged in many others.

From the point of view of data analysis, any way of handling this case is open to question. If the date she left the hospital AWOL was counted as the date of first release, one would be ignoring the strenuous efforts that were made to get her back. Moreover, the assigned experimental treatment (PSYCHOTHERAPY ALONE) would be credited with a successful release when, in fact, treatment at that point (and later) was a manifest failure. If the release was not counted, then the length of stay for this particular patient would be artificially inflated by 87 days and the AWOL statistics would be seriously distorted.

It was finally decided, on an arbitrary but carefully considered basis, that the fairest way that would produce the least distortion of results would be to count the patient as a "limited responder" (treated and never released) and to subtract 87 days from her hospital stay and AWOL figures; the "Six Months" psychometric tests, due while she was physically out of the hospital, were recorded as "Missed, not scheduled."

Patient #98: A single male assigned to MILIEU. Thirty-eight days after admission he was sent home for a seven-day leave, on the last day of which he was put in jail for beating up the man who was going to marry his ex-girlfriend. Every effort was made to get him back to the hospital, but he remained in jail for 29 days without specific treatment before being returned. According to the jail physician, he was, during this time, loud, abusive, irritable, hallucinating and obviously psychotic. He finally left the hospital in apparent remission 191 days after admission or 117 days after his return from jail.

This case was handled in a similar manner to Case #211. The first seven days that he was out were counted as leave; the period that he was in jail was not counted at all, and accordingly, 29 days were subtracted from his stay figures.

SIGNIFICANT READMISSION

A significant readmission was defined as a return to the hospital for 21 continuous days or more, this period being chosen to be consistent with the criteria for significant release. Readmissions for less than 21 days were not counted (although we did keep track of them). Readmissions for physical illness were not counted if it could be clearly verified that this was the only reason for readmission. If a patient was readmitted to one hospital and then transferred to another, it was counted as a single continuous readmission.

STAY

Several different measures of stay in hospital (Stay) were derived from the movement data. In keeping with the usual practice in hospital statistics, in all computations of Stay the first day is counted but not the last.

ADMISSION STAY. For patients released from the hospital after completion of the original experimental treatment—the number of days from admission to first significant release.

TREATMENT STAY. For patients released from the hospital after completion of the original experimental treatment—the number of days from assignment to treatment to first significant release.

STAY (ADMISSION TO TERMINATION). For all patients—the number of days from admission to termination of the original experimental treatment. For obvious reasons it is necessary to distinguish between responders and nonresponders in analyzing this variable. Admission to Termination Stay (Responders) may be seen as "success time," the time taken for successful release from hospital. Admission to Termination Stay (Nonresponders) may be seen as "failure time" or "despair time," the time taken for the treatment staff to give up with that particular treatment.

ADMISSION STAY TO FAILURE. The same as Stay (Admission to Termination), but computed for limited responders (failures) only.

STAY (TREATMENT TO TERMINATION). For all patients—the number of days from assignment to treatment to completion of the post-treatment evaluation, regardless of whether treatment was a success or failure.

TREATMENT STAY TO FAILURE. The same as Stay (Treatment to Termination), but computed for the limited responders (failures) only.

ADMISSION STAY (L.R. 432). Similar to Admission Stay, except that patients who were not released from the hospital after completion of experimental treatment (the limited responders) are arbitrarily assigned a length of Stay of 432 days. This measure was used because Admission Stay applies only to those patients who were successfully released after treatment, not including the limited responders where treatment was abandoned as a failure. It seemed important therefore, to create an assessment of Stay that would somehow take the failures into consideration and give some weight to them. After considering several possible methods, it was decided to assign the failure cases an arbitrary Stay value based on the manner in which failure was defined—a committee decision that if the course of treatment was continued, there was small chance that the patient would be successfully released by the end of the maximum treatment period. It would seem both reasonable and conservative to assume that if the failures had remained on their original treatment they would, on the average, have stayed in the hospital at least one day longer than the longest Admission Stay for a success. Accordingly, for this assessment the failures were assigned a Stay of 432 days, one day longer than the longest Admission Stay for any patient successfully released.

TREATMENT STAY (L.R. 407). Using the same reasoning as for Admission Stay (L.R. 432), a variable was formed in which patients who were not released from the hospital after completion of experimental treatment were arbitrarily assigned a length of Treatment Stay of 407 days, one day longer than the longest Treatment Stay for any patient successfully released.

IDEAL STAY. When the patient was released, his therapist was asked how long he felt the patient *should* have stayed in hospital.

OFFICIAL STAY TO RELEASE. The number of days from official date of admission to the official date of discharge or indefinite leave (trial visit), whichever was earlier.

OFFICIAL STAY TO DISCHARGE. The number of days from official date of admission to official date of discharge. As many readers know, it is customary in mental hospitals to keep patients on hospital records and registers after their actual release, the general intent being the extension of observation and care during convalescence. When the patient continues to do well outside the hospital or does not require further hospitalization, he is officially discharged from the records.

If a patient had not been officially discharged from the hospital records by July 1, 1965, the last date that it was practical for us to keep track, this was taken as the official date of discharge. This will shorten Official Stay to Discharge for a few cases.

Official Stay to Discharge is heavily determined by administrative policy and custom. For example, at Camarillo at the time of the study, patients who were released from the hospital by leave rather than direct discharge were usually kept on leave status for one year unless there was some specific reason for doing otherwise.

RECIPROCAL STAY. Any of the Stay measures may be converted to a reciprocal, giving a variable that is more a measure of speed of release. By weighting early release more heavily, this tends to lessen any error that might be inherent in the arbitrary assignment of a constant Stay period to the treatment failures.

LOG, STAY AND OTHER TRANSFORMATIONS. Various other transformations were tried in an attempt to fit the Stay data to a "normal" bell-shaped curve. (The closest fit was obtained with the reciprocal of the logarithm of Selection Stay Minus 19 Days.)

ADJUSTED STAY. Any of the Stay measures may be adjusted to exclude the number of days spent out of the hospital on authorized or unauthorized leave.

AUTHORIZED LEAVE

The number of days away from the hospital with the permission of the treating physician. For each separate leave, fractions of a day are counted as a whole day, including the first and last days. Although this may lead to some exaggeration of the actual numbers of days away, the reasoning is that the patient is seldom available for much treatment on the fractional days.

UNAUTHORIZED LEAVE

The number of days absent from the hospital without the permission of the treating physician. For each separate leave and for the same reasons outlined above for authorized leave, fractions of a day are counted as a whole day, including the first and last days.

REFERENCES

(1) Freeman, H. E. & Simmons, O. G.: *The Mental Patient Comes Home.* John Wiley & Sons, New York, 1963.
(2) Smith, J. A. & Wittson, C. L.: Evaluation of treatment procedures in psychiatry. *Diseases of the Nervous System,* 18:1–4, 1957.

\ APPENDIX V

Criteria for Onset and Duration of Illness

DURATION

Duration of illness according to the various different definitions was estimated in weeks for the present episode and for the sum of all episodes, a fraction being counted to the nearest highest number:

$$1\text{–}7 \text{ days} = 1 \text{ week}$$
$$8\text{–}14 \text{ days} = 2 \text{ weeks}$$
$$15\text{–}21 \text{ days} = 3 \text{ weeks, etc.}$$

AGE AT ONSET

The age at onset according to the various different definitions of illness was recorded as the patient's age at his last birthday.

PREVIOUS PSYCHOTIC EPISODE

It is necessary to recognize that a patient may have a transient circumscribed psychotic episode without being admitted to the hospital. A patient was considered to have suffered from a previous psychotic episode if he had had symptoms that were clearly psychotic on some previous occasion and had subsequently "recovered" to the extent of being apparently symptom-free and functioning reasonably well in society for at least a year. If the "recovery" lasted less than a year, it was not counted as an "episode," but as a continuous illness.

DURATION OF PSYCHOTIC SYMPTOMS

The number of weeks that the patient had suffered from symptoms that were clearly and definitely classifiable as psychotic. If the symptoms fluctuated, duration was estimated from the first appearance of definite psychotic symptoms, and all the intervening time up to admission was counted, as long as he had serious symptoms of any kind, even though these might not be definitely classifiable as psychotic. However, if at some time after the first appearance of psychotic symptoms and before admission to the hospital he became symptom-free, or had only mild nondisabling and clearly nonpsychotic symptoms for as long as a month, the nonpsychotic period was not included. In other words in estimating duration of psychosis the first task is to establish the point at which the symptoms can clearly be called psychotic; all subsequent symptoms are then considered to be manifestations of psychosis unless clearly definable otherwise.

DURATION OF PERSONALITY DISORDER

The number of weeks that there had been definite (but not necessarily severe) incapacity as the result of a behavioral or interpersonal problem. If the patient had neurotic or psychotic symptoms it was assumed that a personality disorder has been present from at least the time of the first appearance of symptoms.

The following are case examples that were taken to have definite incapacity:
a) Shy, no dates, no parties
b) Truant, lonely, never held job more than a year, always quiet and disinterested
c) Shy, left school at age 16, irregular work record
d) Belonged to teen-age gang, stayed out overnight against parents' wishes
e) Enuresis, irritable, sensitive and withdrawn with other children, defiant, runaway

f) Wild, runaway

g) Flighty, restless, would leave spouse unpredictably, became hysterical if did not have own way

h) Unable to hold a steady job

i) Frightened, always daydreaming, lonely, lost

j) Stuttered, stammered, always shy and fearful, difficulty in kindergarten

k) Enuresis, stammered

l) Hard to handle, always wanted own way, would scream and stamp and kick if thwarted

m) Promiscuous nightclub singer and stripteaser, lived with many men, always moving from place to place

n) Temper tantrums, fear of dark, constant strife in marriage

o) Homosexual, inferiority feelings

p) Slow at school, in special classes, timid, runaway, tense, awkward

In the absence of other evidence, the following case examples were not considered to have definite incapacity:

a) Shy, restless, fidgety, nervous

b) Shy and extremely good

c) Somewhat nervous

d) Demanding, bossy, tomboy

e) Enuresis alone

f) Illegitimate pregnancy

g) Overly good, meticulous, needs to impress others

h) Left school to join Navy

i) Negative and difficult in school but stayed with it and graduated from high school

j) Quit school at age 16: afterward attended school part-time and worked. Charged with battery once, but case dismissed

k) Nail biting and knuckle cracking

l) Living in common-law relationship

DURATION OF OCCUPATIONAL INCAPACITY

The number of weeks that the patient had been unable to carry out his occupation full-time because of psychiatric illness. He was not considered to be disabled if he was able to support himself, even if there were repeated job changes, but unemployment with financial dependence on others was counted as disability. For housewives, looking after the family and household was considered to be a full-time occupation.

DURATION OF SYMPTOMS

The number of weeks that the patient had had any identifiable subjective or objective indication of psychotic or neurotic disorder. Personality-related behavioral disturbances were not counted as symptoms unless they caused a considerable degree of distress or incapacity such as inability to earn a living; legal difficulty to the extent of having a juvenile court petition filed or being placed on probation; substantial subjective distress; having to give up school; or severe social isolation.

The following examples illustrate the kind of disturbances that were considered to be severe enough to be categorized as "symptoms":

a) Physical fights with neighbors

b) Gross denial of spouse's very obvious carcinomatous illness

c) Drunk arrests, theft, runaway several times

d) Barbiturate addiction

e) Would go as long as three weeks without saying a word to parents

f) Severe withdrawal and isolation after illegitimate pregnancy
g) Excessive gambling, running up debts and concealing them from spouse; threatened mortgage foreclosure, repossession of purchases
h) So suspicious and difficult that spouse divorced him
i) Runaway from home and school, psychiatric treatment recommended
j) Insomnia, alcoholism, itching in bed, temper tantrums

NUMBER OF PREVIOUS ADMISSIONS (SIGNIFICANT OR OTHERWISE)

In recording the number of times the patient had been in hospitals other than Camarillo, each time in each hospital was counted as a separate admission, no matter how briefly the patient had been hospitalized. The purpose was to record the number of hospitals in which the patient had been. Accordingly, this rule was applied even if the patient was transferred from one hospital to another so as to make hospitalization virtually continuous.

Cost of Treatment

GENERAL

Cost was expressed as the *total cost* of all treatment and services provided during the patient's entire stay in hospital. Per diem costs were also computed, but were not used as a criterion for comparison between treatments as they are considered to be inappropriate and misleading for this purpose (see Chapter 2).

The cost figures for the individual items and categories were computed separately and then summed in different ways to provide a number of indices of the cost of hospital care for each individual patient from admission to release or termination of treatment.

A percentage was added as "overhead" to make allowance for items such as furnishings, equipment, maintenance and business services, special medical services and allied medical services.

Our limited financial resources could not provide professional accounting, personnel and management analysts to keep cost accounting records and to conduct a specific professional cost analysis according to the standardized procedures developed by the American Hospital Association[1] and the California Hospital Association.[2] Nor were the hospital accounts kept in this manner. Accordingly, I trust that the professional accountant will accept the methods and procedures for what they are—the humble best that a clinician could do under the circumstances.

COMPONENT ITEMS

The following items were considered as components of cost:

BASIC NURSING CARE. It was obviously not possible for us to determine by direct observation exactly how much time the nursing staff spent with each patient each day. Accordingly, the assumption was made that on the average all patients receive an equal level of basic care over a period of time. The cost of basic nursing care, excluding items such as housekeeping supplies and equipment which were costed under overhead, was therefore obtained by multiplying the number of days in hospital by a sex-appropriate per diem factor. This was determined by the following formula:

$$\text{Per diem Nursing cost} = \frac{\text{Total daily salary all nursing staff on ward}}{\text{Number of beds on ward}}$$

For males, the per diem was \$15.81925; for females, \$18.06335.*

To obtain the total daily salary for the ward, the number of assigned staff (over a sample fifteen-month period when the patients were on twenty-bed units) was multiplied by the appropriate daily salary. (The research nurses, whose assignment was to carry out or to coordinate the obtaining of research data rather than to provide patient care, were not included; nor were the staff of the hydrotherapy section which was costed separately.) Tables VI.1 and VI.2

---

[1] See references 1, 2.

[2] See reference 3.

* Unit costs are expressed to several decimal places if this was the most likely estimate of the actual cost, rounding off being done as late as possible in computation. This has resulted in some apparent minor inconsistencies between different unit costs in the last place of decimals.

show, for female and male wards separately, the numbers of staff assigned and the appropriate salaries.

For senior nursing staff (State of California Civil Service position titles: Senior Psychiatric Nurse, Registered Nurse, Psychiatric Technician II, Psychiatric Technician I) the salary of the incumbents was usually at the top or middle of the salary range. For the rank-and-file psychiatric technician staff there was considerable variation, so their salary was taken as the middle step of the range. Ten percent was added for fringe benefits such as retirement and health insurance. Ten percent was also added as an allowance for nursing supervisory personnel (such as nursing education, nursing supervisors and assistant superintendents), while 10 percent was subtracted to allow for the separate costing (described in the next section) of specific nursing duties in connection with the administration of *ataraxic drugs, sedatives, ECT* and *seclusion.*

Table VI.1. FEMALE TWENTY-BED UNIT: STAFF AND SALARY

Category	Average # Assigned	Daily Salary*	Cost per Day
Senior Psychiatric Nurse	1.0	$31.42	$31.420
R.N.	1.13	28.51	32.216
Psychiatric Technician I	1.0	23.50	23.500
Psychiatric Technician	12.87	21.30	274.131
TOTAL	16.00	—	361.267

Per patient per diem = $361.267 ÷ 20 = $18.06335.
* Includes 10 percent fringe benefits—retirement, insurance, etc.

Table VI.2. MALE TWENTY-BED UNIT: STAFF AND SALARY

Category	Average # Assigned	Daily Salary*	Cost per Day
Senior R.N.	0.6	$31.42	$18.852
Psychiatric Technician II	0.4	28.51	11.404
Psychiatric Technician I	1.0	23.50	23.500
Psychiatric Technician	12.33	21.30	262.629
TOTAL	14.33	—	316.385

Per patient per diem = $316.385 ÷ 20 = $15.81925.
* Includes 10 percent fringe benefits—retirement, insurance, etc.

These two latter 10 percent figures are arbitrary estimates, arrived at after discussion with the superintendent of nurses and with nursing supervisory and ward staff. It would obviously have been more satisfactory to carry out an actual observational study to determine the true values, but our resources did not permit this. Since the per diem figures are based on the number of staff *assigned,* not on the number *on duty,* there is no need to adjust further for vacation, sick leave or days off.

SPECIFIC NURSING DUTIES. Nursing staff spend time directly in the administration of two of the "specific" types of treatment used in this study (*ECT* and *ataraxic drugs*), also in other "secondary" treatments that have been reported to be reduced according to the effectiveness of the "specific" treatment given. For example, they chart and administer *ataraxic drugs* and *sedatives,* assist in giving *ECT,* administer *hydrotherapy,* and give special care to patients whose condition requires *seclusion.* Accordingly, (as described above) the staff of the hydrotherapy unit were costed separately and the per diem for basic nursing care was reduced 10 percent to compensate for the separate costing of nursing time used in connection with *sedatives, ataraxic drugs, ECT* and *seclusion.* The cost estimates given below for each of these items therefore contain a factor for nursing time.

Hydrotherapy was staffed as a separate unit, and the cost of this accessory service was relatively accessible. For the other duties, staff estimates of the actual time spent for each task were obtained in discussion sessions with the research psychiatrist and the principal investigator. These estimates were then used to derive unit costs based on the salary levels shown in Tables VI.1 and VI.2. They should be looked upon as educated guesses by the professional staff of the average time consumed in a particular operation for the average patient. They are not based on time studies by management or industrial analysts, and there are obvious limitations and many potential sources of error. Nevertheless, they are the best we could do within the limits of our resources and they do seem, on the surface at least, to be reasonable approximations.

HYDROTHERAPY. The cost of the various forms of hydrotherapy was obtained by multiplying the number of hours spent in each type by a sex-appropriate unit factor:

Female:	Pack	$2.35423	per hour
	Tub	$2.55423	per hour
	Other	$2.35423	per hour
Male:	Pack	$1.68461	per hour
	Tub	$1.17533	per hour
	Other	$1.68461	per hour

This covers only staff time spent in administering the treatment, including preparation and cleanup time, with 20 cents per hour added for continuous tubs to allow for the cost of the warm water used (the latter based on engineer's rough estimate). No direct allowance was made for the use of sheets, towels, equipment, etc., this being included in the category of overhead.

On the female unit, where tubs, packs and other forms of treatment were given in approximately equal numbers, the staff were of the opinion that all forms of hydrotherapy took about the same amount of staff time per hour of treatment.

Accordingly, the staff cost per hour was obtained by dividing the total salary for the average number of staff assigned to the hydrotherapy unit (over a sample 32-month period) by the total number of hours of all treatments. (Salary levels shown in Tables VI.1 and VI.2.)

On the male hydrotherapy unit, the program was organized in a different way, reflected in a lower "male" cost factor for this type of treatment. Continuous tubs were used a great deal, wet packs somewhat less and other forms of treatment hardly at all. The staff time per hour of continuous tub was estimated to be lower than for packs and other forms of treatment.

SECLUSION. Seclusion,* the occasional enforced separation of a patient in his own separate room when his behavior is too disturbing or distressing to others or to himself, was used a good deal less frequently for males than for females.

---

* It is sometimes asserted that seclusion is never used at certain hospitals. For the purposes of cost comparison it may be assumed that a (perhaps) more polite, but at least equally costly procedure has been substituted.

However, if a male patient did require this kind of isolation, the incident absorbed much more personnel time than on the female side. This is reflected in the different unit cost estimates for males and females which are supported by the informal observations of the research staff.

The extra cost of seclusion (in comparison with the usual level of nursing care) may be thought of in terms of the time it takes to persuade the patient to go to his room and later to come out; plus the extra attention that has to be given at meal times and intermittently as long as the patient remains by himself.

It was estimated by the staff that the initial and terminal operation and charting for the usual case took eighty minutes of staff time on the male unit and only fourteen minutes on the female unit. For both male and female, the usual amount of continuing *extra* attention was judged to be ten extra minutes at each mealtime and two extra minutes per hour as long as the patient remained in seclusion. Since patients usually stayed in seclusion over only one mealtime, the cost was finally computed as a *cost per time* factor that included one meal and "in-out time" multiplied by the number of times the patient was secluded; plus a *cost per hour* factor multiplied by the number of hours.

Using the salaries shown in Tables VI.1 and VI.2, the *cost per time* factor was taken as $3.99 (90 minutes of staff time) for males; $1.064 (24 minutes of staff time) for females. The *cost per hour* factor of $0.08867 (2 minutes of staff time) was the same for both sexes.

ORAL ATARAXIC DRUGS. The cost of orally administered *ataraxic drugs* was expressed as the actual cost of the medication plus an allowance for "distribution time," i.e., the time it takes to get the medication from the pharmacy, do the necessary paper work and preparation and give it to the patient. No direct allocation was made for items such as pharmacy personnel, dispensing equipment, etc. which were costed under overhead.

The cost of the medication was obtained by multiplying the total dose given by the cost (at the hospital bulk purchase rate) of the tablet size normally used (i.e., trifluoperazine [Stelazine], 10 mgm.—$0.075; chlorpromazine [Thorazine], 100 mg.—$0.05). Since it was customary to give procyclidine (Kemadrin) in a dose of 5 mgm. ($0.02) per 10 mgm. of Stelazine or 100 mg. of Thorazine, the unit cost was increased accordingly.

Since it was not practical to count the number of doses actually given, distribution time was computed on the basis of a dose of 10 mgm. of Stelazine three times a day, close to the median dosage used. Distribution time is roughly the same regardless of the particular medication or the size of the dose—for these particular wards it was estimated that it usually took four minutes of staff time per patient per dose ($0.17732).

ORAL SEDATIVES AND HYPNOTICS. In this case, a record was made of the number of orders written by the physician. Hospital procedure required that these orders be rewritten every week, and they almost invariably provided that the medication might be given whenever necessary but not more often than every four hours. Accordingly, it was taken as an educated guess that seven doses (an average of one per day) of 0.2 gm. Sodium Amytal (the usual dose) were given for each order written. The limitations are obvious, but it does seem that it might be reasonably close to the actual average state of affairs—the possible range would be somewhere between 0–42 doses per order, with the extreme figures being most unlikely.

The cost of 0.2 gm. Sodium Amytal at the hospital bulk purchase rate was $0.0099. Distribution time was computed on the same basis as for *oral ataraxic drugs*. Thus the unit cost of each written order was established as follows:

Sodium Amytal	0.2 gm. × 7 =	$0.06930
Distribution	4 min. × 7 =	$1.24124
Total	=	$1.31054

INTRA-MUSCULAR ATARAXIC DRUGS. For orders that were not written "to be given as necessary," the number of days on intra-muscular medication was multiplied by a factor for staff time, based on three doses per day. It was estimated that it took fifteen minutes of staff time to procure, prepare and administer each injection—a unit cost for the three doses per day of $1.9950. To this was added the bulk purchase cost of the medication at the average intra-muscular dose given to that particular patient:

Trifluoperazine (Stelazine)—$0.1215 per mg.
Chlorpromazine (Thorazine)—$0.00616 per mg.

For orders that were written "to be given as necessary," the number of orders was multiplied by twice the unit cost factor, assuming that two doses were given for each written order. (Since these orders expired automatically after 48 hours and were written only for patients who required occasional injections, as an educated guess, this seemed likely to be a reasonable approximation to the true number of doses given.)

No direct allocation was made for items such as pharmacy personnel, syringes, etc., which were costed under overhead.

INTRA-MUSCULAR SEDATION. Orders for intra-muscular sedation were almost invariably "one-shot" affairs for 0.5 gm. Sodium Amytal. Accordingly, the number of orders was multiplied by the nursing cost factor for a single intra-muscular injection ($0.665) plus the cost of O.5 gm. Sodium Amytal at the hospital bulk purchase rate ($0.074).

PHYSICIAN CONTACT. For all patients, the number of hours spent with the physician in individual contact (other than *psychotherapy* and *electroshock*) after treatment was started was multiplied by an hourly salary factor of $6.3912. This factor is based on the "average" salary for the "average" kind of treating physician at California State Civil Service salary levels for the time of the project, with a 10 percent allowance for fringe benefits such as retirement and insurance (see Table VI.3). It was not practical to use the actual salary for each individual patient's doctor.

Table VI.3.   MEDICAL STAFF SALARIES

Category	Month*	Hour†
Psychiatric Resident (2nd Year)	$ 957	$5.52
Staff Psychiatrist (Middle Range)	1,415	8.16

* Includes 10 percent fringe benefits—retirement, insurance, etc.
† 40-hour week.

For *psychotherapy* and *ECT*, the unit cost estimates contain a separate factor for the time spent by the physician in giving these treatments, based on the same hourly rate.

By actual count, $\frac{2}{3}$ of the patients were treated by psychiatric residents, $\frac{1}{3}$ by staff psychiatrists. Accordingly, the salary factor was derived as follows:

Hourly Salary Factor = "average resident salary" × 67% + "average staff psychiatrist salary" × 33%
= (5.52 × 67%) + (8.16 × 33%) = $6.3912

The residents ranged from those just starting their first year of training to those who were just about to complete the third year, so the *average resident salary* was taken from the second year. The *average staff psychiatrist salary* was taken from the middle of the lower range for this position—this is appropriate for the staff psychiatrists who actually treated the patients.

ECT. The cost of *ECT* was taken as the number of treatments multiplied by a sex-appropriate cost factor (male—$4.6635; female—$7.6245).

On the male unit, three to four nursing staff were used to assist; it was estimated that each treatment took seventy minutes of nursing time ($3.1033) and ten minutes of physician's time ($1.0652). This includes preparation, set-up time, administration of treatment and supervision of the immediate recovery period. On the female unit, five nursing staff were used to assist and treatment took longer: The staff estimated that each treatment took 125 minutes of nursing time ($5.5317) and fifteen minutes of the physician's time ($1.5978). The sex differential in staff time corresponds to that observed informally by the research staff.

The cost of the medications used for each treatment (hospital bulk purchase rate for the time of the study) was as follows:

Atropine, grs. 1/100	$0.01
Succinyl-choline, 15 mgm.	0.075
Sodium pentothal, 0.5 mgm.	0.41

PSYCHOTHERAPY. The number of hours of *psychotherapy* was multiplied by a unit cost of $17.989. This includes the time of the physician at $6.3912 per hour of treatment plus an allowance to cover the estimated *extra* cost of individual supervision at the rate of half an hour's supervision for each hour of *psychotherapy*. (This extra cost is over and above the cost of supervision of other forms of treatment for which no separate allowance was made.)

Psychotherapy supervision is a time-consuming process. It was estimated that the resident spent about twice as much time in supervision for *psychotherapy* cases compared with supervision of other forms of treatment. Accordingly, 50 percent of the cost of the resident's time in *psychotherapy* supervision was added to the cost of *psychotherapy*.

It is also necessary to consider the cost of the *supervisor's* time. Since the other treatments were actually supervised in a small group setting, the *nonpsychotherapy* supervisor could handle (say) five times as many residents in a given time. Assuming that the actual cost of supervision is $25 per hour, the *extra* cost of the *psychotherapy* supervisor was therefore taken as $20 per hour of supervision (80 percent of $25). Thus the cost of one hour of *psychotherapy* with the *extra* cost of ½ hour of supervision is composed as follows:

Treating physician, one hour therapy	$ 6.3912
Treating physician, supervision time (50% of ½ hour)	1.5978
Supervisor, ½ hour	10.0000
Total, per hour of therapy	17.9890

MEALS. The cost of meals was obtained by multiplying the number of days in hospital by a per diem factor. The hospital yearly budget for food service staff in the last year of the study was $703,383, with a patient population of 5,800, giving a food service personnel salary factor per patient day of:

$$\frac{\$703,383}{5,800 \times 365} = 0.3323 \text{ per patient day}$$

The daily cost of the food itself was $0.755 per patient day, giving an estimated total per diem per patient food cost of $1.0873.

Patient labor was not taken into consideration in arriving at the figures: the author's private opinion is that the assignment of patients to work in the hospital food service did not alter the net cost of the operation. The reader should therefore consider that the true cost might be more or less than the stated figure, depending on whether it is believed that the assignment of patients to "industrial therapy" increases or decreases net costs.

DEPRECIATION, OVERHEAD AND SPECIAL SERVICES. Twenty percent was added to the Total Cost figures (not to any of the individual cost items) to make allowance for items such as the following:

a) Provision and depreciation of unit furnishings and medical equipment (not including depreciation of buildings for which a suitable guideline was not available).

b) Maintenance services, e.g., heat, light, fire prevention, building maintenance and repair, housekeeping and paperwork supplies, upkeep of grounds, post office, messenger service, laundry.

c) Business services, e.g., accounting, personnel services.

d) Special medical services, e.g., medical-surgical service, X-ray and laboratory, medical administrative staff, medical records, pharmacy, central supply.

e) Allied medical services, e.g., Occupational Therapy, Psychology, Social Service, Rehabilitation Services.

Exact determination of these costs is an involved affair, and we did not attempt to refine the estimates further into a "loading factor" for the expense of admission and discharge, plus a "per diem" cost. Instead, we merely applied the percentage figure used by the State of California for overhead in grant applications at the time of this study. The addition of a percentage for overhead is a standard practice; although the true percentage may in actuality be more or less than 20 percent and will certainly vary from one time and place to another, there is, fortunately for our research purposes, little to be gained by quibbling about the precise figure to be applied. Once it has been decided to allow for these items by the addition of a percentage to the total cost, then although the value chosen will affect the *absolute* cost figures, it makes no *relative* difference for the comparison we seek between individuals or treatment groups.*

TREATMENT OF PHYSICAL ILLNESS. No separate allowance was made for the cost of diagnosing or treating any concomitant or complicating physical illness, other than the overhead allowance described previously.

CHARGES FOR LEAVE. In some hospitals (as at Camarillo at the time of the study) patients are not charged for days out of the hospital on leave or AWOL. In other hospitals, patients may be charged for a full day if a bed is held for them. To allow for this variation in practice, each of the cost indices was computed in two ways: with and without allowance for days on leave or AWOL.

MISSING DATA. In one case the form containing figures for the number of times and hours of seclusion was lost. Also, the complete figures for hours of *psychotherapy* and *other individual contact* with the physician were not available in 25 and 68 cases respectively, because collection of detailed information did not start until we were approximately one-fourth through the study. All the other data necessary for the computation of cost for these cases was available, and it was felt that the comparative statistics would be more truly applicable for the entire patient group if the missing entries could be filled in with the most likely values. Accordingly, these particular missing values were estimated by the method described in Chapter 3.

* Unless the proportion of overhead varies from one treatment to another. The assignment of differential overhead charges to different treatments would require a major accounting and management analysis effort far beyond our limited capacities.

OVERALL COST INDICES

These were derived by summing the individual cost items in various ways to illustrate different aspects of the problem.

COST (ADMISSION TO RELEASE). Includes all component items. No allowance was made for cost of work-up period, except for basic nursing care, meals and overhead. Administrators should note that this particular index does not include the cost of treating patients who were not successfully released from the first experimental treatment.

COST (ADMISSION TO TERMINATION). Similar to Cost (Admission to Release), but based on the time from admission until *either* the patient was successfully released *or* until treatment had to be abandoned as a failure. Since Admission to Termination Stay is used as a basis for computation, administrators should interpret this index as assuming that patients who are not successfully released are dropped from the budget by transfer to some other unit either as soon as it is determined that their first treatment is very likely to be a failure or at the end of one year of treatment.

COST (L.R. 432). Similar to Cost (Admission to Release) but an arbitrary length of stay of 432 days has been assigned to the "limited responders" where treatment had to be abandoned as a failure before the end of the full one-year treatment period. The cost of the initial work-up period and of hospitalization after the first experimental treatment was officially terminated has been computed on the basis of the average per diem cost during the experimental treatment period. Since Admission Stay (L.R. 432) is used as a basis for computation, administrators should interpret this index as assuming that patients who are not successfully released are dropped from the budget at the end of approximately one year of treatment—either by discharge from the treatment unit or by transfer to another treatment (or custodial) unit.

UNADJUSTED COST (L.R. 432). Similar to Cost (L.R. 432) but not adjusted to allow for the cost of treatment during the initial work-up period and during hospital stay after the first experimental treatment has been terminated (except basic nursing care, meals, and overhead).

COST (ADMISSION TO FIRST RELEASE OF ANY KIND). Similar to Cost (L.R. 432) but instead of assigning an arbitrary length of stay (432 days) to "limited responders," their hospital stay has been taken as the actual time they stayed in the hospital until their first release, regardless of how many types of treatment they had been given. (It must be remembered that in this study all patients who failed to respond to the original experimental treatment were subsequently treated with the combination of *ataraxic drugs* and *group therapy*. Because of the confounding of this second treatment with the effects of the original experimental treatment, this particular cost index must therefore be interpreted with special caution.)

UNADJUSTED COST (ADMISSION TO FIRST RELEASE OF ANY KIND). Similar to Cost (Admission to First Release of Any Kind) but not adjusted to allow for the cost of treatment during the initial work-up period and during hospital stay after the first experimental treatment (except basic nursing care, meals and overhead).

COST (SELECTION TO RELEASE). Similar to Cost (Admission to Release) but with no allowance for the cost of the initial work-up period.

COST (SELECTION TO RELEASE—L.R. 407). Similar to Cost (L.R. 432) but with no allowance for the initial work-up period. An arbitrary length of stay of 407 days has been assigned to the "limited responders." [See also definition of Treatment Stay (L.R. 407), Appendix IV.]

COST OF PHYSICIAN-ORDERED TREATMENT. Includes only the cost of those treatments that are given personally by the physician or that are (usually) ordered by him on the Physician's Order Sheet. This includes items such as *sedatives, hydrotherapy, seclusion, ECT, ataraxic drugs* and *psychotherapy*. Meals and nursing care are specifically excluded.

REFERENCES

(1) *Cost finding for hospitals.* American Hospital Association, Chicago, 1961.
(2) *Uniform chart of accounts and definitions for hospitals.* American Hospital Association, Chicago, 1961.
(3) *Uniform Cost Analysis Manual.* California Hospital Association, San Francisco, 1964.

Pretreatment Patient Characteristics

KEY TO TABLES

The tables in this appendix present a statistical summary of a number of pretreatment characteristics that might be thought to have some bearing on the outcome of treatment and on the degree to which the five treatment groups were satisfactorily equated. The tables give for each variable the mean, range and standard deviation for the entire patient group with significance levels (p) from a two-way analysis of variance for differences among the five treatments (Rx) and between the two sexes (Sex). Data are non-Winsorized (W_o). For differences between the sexes, ($+$) indicates that females had higher scores and ($-$) that they had lower scores. Table VII.1 covers 22 demographic and clinical history items; Table VII.2 covers 24 items of initial clinical status; Table VII.3 covers 28 initial psychometric items.

Where relevant, the numerical coding for an item is explained in numbered footnotes which have been grouped together following the tables.

Table VII.1.   DEMOGRAPHIC AND HISTORY

	MEAN	SD	MAX	MIN	SEX (p)	Rx (p)
Age	28.1	6.2	45	16	+5515	0813
Education (1)	4.21	1.19	8	1	+7577	2610
Occupation (2)	5.24	1.49	7	1	−0526	6972
Religious Attendance (3)	1.95	.90	3	1	+4531	4258
Weight (pounds)	139	26	232	84	−0000	0544
Height (inches)	66	3.7	75	54	−0000	5960
Length Military Service (4)	1.5	1.9	13	0	−0000	0813
Physical disease on admission (5)	1.24	.5	4	1	+2977	4301
Language difficulty (6)	1.1	.3	3	1	−7640	7899
Ever married (7)	.6	.5	1	0	+0001	0288
Currently married (7)	.4	.5	1	0	+0001	6070
Protestant Religion (8)	.60	.49	1	0	−8696	8374
Catholic Religion (9)	.30	.46	1	0	−4898	8122
Voluntary Admission (10)	1.81	.39	2	1	+1384	9254
White (11)	1.32	.47	2	1	−6327	3235
Negro (12)	1.21	.41	2	1	+9331	2489
Mexican (13)	1.91	.29	2	1	+0813	8744
Age onset psychosis (yrs)	26.7	6.1	44	15	+4671	2415
Age onset personality disorder (yrs)	18.6	8.3	44	2	−8546	0720
Duration psychosis (yrs)	38.6	66	470	1	−0613	1766
Duration personality disorder (wks)	444.9	326	999+	1	+4757	1587
Precipitating Stress Intensity (14)	3.8	2.1	8	0	+0010	2470

NUMERICAL CODING: FOOTNOTES

(1) Education:
    (1) Graduate School training—Master's Degree
    (2) College or University graduation—Bachelor's Degree

      (3) Partial College or Business School
      (4) Completed 12th grade: High School graduate
      (5) Completed 10th or 11th grade: partial High School
      (6) Completed 7th, 8th, 9th grade: Junior High School
      (7) Completed 5th or 6th grade: Grammar School
      (8) Completion of less than five grades of school

(2) Occupation:
      (1) Higher executives, major professionals
      (2) Business managers, proprietors of medium-sized business and lesser professionals
      (3) Administrative personnel, small independent businessmen and minor professionals
      (4) Clerical—sales workers, technicians and owners of small businesses
      (5) Skilled manual employees
      (6) Machine operators and semiskilled workers
      (7) Unskilled employees
      (Not included) Student, housewife, or never worked

(3) Religious attendance:
      (1) None
      (2) Occasional
      (3) Regular

(4) Length Military Service:
      (1) None
      (2) Less than ½ year
      (3) ½–1 year
      (4) 1–1½ years
      (5) etc.

(5) Physical disease on admission:
      (1) None
      (2) Minor
      (3) Moderate
      (4) Major

(6) Language difficulty:
      (1) None
      (2) Some impairment or limited vocabulary
      (3) Considerable or severe problem

(7) Marital Status:
      (1) Married
      (2) Not married

(8) Religion:
      (1) Protestant
      (2) Not Protestant

(9) Religion:
      (1) Catholic
      (2) Not Catholic

(10) Type of Admission
      (1) Voluntary
      (2) Involuntary

(11) Race:
      (1) White
      (2) Non-White

(12) Race:
      (1) Non-Negro
      (2) Negro

(13) Race:
      (1) Mexican
      (2) Non-Mexican

(14) Precipitating Stress
    (0) None
    (1) Intermediate between (0) and (2)
    (2) Some
    (3) Intermediate between (2) and (4)
    (4) Moderate
    (5) Intermediate between (4) and (6)
    (6) Considerable
    (7) Intermediate between (6) and (8)
    (8) Extreme

Table VII.2.   INITIAL EVALUATION (CLINICAL)

	MEAN	SD	MAX	MIN	SEX (p)	Rx (p)
ANALYSTS						
MHS (present)	19.4	3.9	32	10	+5394	3485
MHS (2-year prognosis)	36.3	5.0	53	26	+4038	7515
CDAS Total	23.8	4.9	40	10	−3773	3891
Affective Contact	3.6	1.0	6	1	−5004	8905
Anxiety	3.1	.8	6	1	−2915	6990
Ego Strength	3.0	.7	5	1	−0595	6397
Insight	2.6	1.2	7	1	−8554	0790
Motivation	2.6	1.2	7	1	−3765	0376
Object Relations	3.0	.6	6	1	−9637	6539
Environment Suffers						
Personal Identity	3.0	.7	6	1	−9787	5911
NURSES						
MACC Scale						
Motility	6.9	2.6	15	3	+2860	3125
Affect	9.9	2.7	15	3	−0351	8874
Cooperation	13.5	3.9	20	4	+1633	9824
Communication	13.6	4.1	20	4	+1220	9532
(Total)	37.2	10.3	55	12	+5163	9792
THERAPISTS						
AA (Total)	13.7	2.3	18	10	+3539	2462
SRS (Total)	33.5	6.5	52	18	+0109	2016
CMS Friendly	36.7	8.7	61	19	−6539	9349
Energetic	40.9	8.8	71	29	−9518	6255
Clear-Thinking	37.3	8.2	62	21	−8796	2305
Aggressive	53.1	11.3	87	37	+3285	4082
Jittery	56.0	8.5	75	38	+0680	3399
Depressed	62.8	6.9	79	44	+0021	6968

Table VII.3.   INITIAL EVALUATION (PSYCHOMETRIC)

Shipley	MEAN	SD	MAX	MIN	SEX (p)	Rx (p)
VIQ	107	18	144	57	−4945	8801
AIQ	87	22	143	54	−7519	8710
I.Q.	95	21	139	54	−5843	9130
Similarities-Proverbs	14.3	5.6	28	0	−1095	8726
MMPI Scales						
?	43.2	5.3	72	41	+7671	2884
L	53.5	9.0	84	36	+0076	1141
F	72.9	19.2	119	44	−5988	2727
K	51.7	9.4	79	30	+2704	5553
Hs + .5K	60.8	14.0	99	33	−4866	5202
D	66.1	16.8	118	30	−1813	4150
Hy	61.6	11.6	91	39	+8674	9780
Pd + .4K	72.5	13.1	104	34	+3890	4110
Mf	59.3	11.4	90	31	−0001	4749
Pa	72.0	16.7	108	38	−8351	2996
Pt + 1K	68.7	17.3	112	36	−0088	5937
Sc + 1K	79.6	20.8	119	41	−0712	2461
Ma + .2K	65.0	14.0	103	26	−3339	1856
Si	58.3	11.4	86	28	−6953	4097
Es	36.6	9.1	55	13	−1212	5546
Cn	25.4	5.3	36	11	−2180	4773
At	22.1	10.6	49	1	+5004	2212
Pa + Pt + Sc	220	50	332	129	−0852	2993
CMS (Self-Sort)						
Friendly	49.9	11.4	75	18	+5773	5339
Energetic	51.5	10.6	71	29	−5273	9207
Clear-Thinking	49.5	11.4	70	22	−4820	8601
Aggressive	55.8	11.1	96	37	−7030	1399
Jittery	52.3	9.6	79	34	+2407	0576
Depressed	57.2	10.1	85	39	+3555	2196

APPENDIX VIII

Schizophrenia Research Project
Publications

Distler, L. S., May, P. R. A. and Tuma, A. H.: Anxiety and ego strength as predictors of response to treatment in schizophrenic patients. *J. of Consulting Psychology*, 28:170–177, April 1964.

A study of the predictive value of the respective MMPI scales for the first 50 male and 50 female patients in the study.

McKeever, W. F. and May, P. R. A.: The MACC scale as a predictor of length of hospitalization for schizophrenic patients—a cross validation. *J. of Consulting Psychology*, 28:474, October 1964.

An assessment of the usefulness of the MACC scale in predicting speed of release, using data obtained for the first 100 patients in the study.

McKeever, W. F., May, P. R. A. and Tuma, A. H.: Prognosis in schizophrenia: prediction of length of hospitalization from psychological test variables. *J. of Clinical Psychology*, 21:214–221, April 1965.

An examination of the relationship of 43 pre-treatment test variables to speed of release. Data from the first 100 patients in the study.

May, P. R. A.: Ataraxic drugs and electroshock therapy in schizophrenic patients—a preliminary report. *Neuropsychopharmacology*, 3:162–165. Bradley, P. G., Hoch, P. H. and Flugel, F., eds. Elsevier Publishing Company, Amsterdam, 1964.

A preliminary report comparing drug therapy, ECT and milieu care for the first 20 patients in each group, using as outcome criteria, release rate, length of hospital stay, final level on the Menninger Health-Sickness scale and the amount of supplemental treatment required.

May, P. R. A.: Prediction of psychiatric outcome: animal subjects and individual differences in response—a clinician's view. In *Prediction of Response to Pharmacotherapy*. Wittenborn, J. R. and May, P. R. A., eds. Charles C Thomas, Springfield, Ill., 1966: 147–155.

Discussion of the limitations of predicting the outcome of psychiatric treatment from animal experiments, with suggestions from clinical experience.

May, P. R. A. and Tuma, A. H.: Ataraxic drugs and psychotherapy: The effect of psychotherapy and Stelazine on length of hospital stay, release rate and supplemental treatment of schizophrenic patients. *J. of Nervous and Mental Disease*, 139:362–369, October 1964.

A preliminary report comparing psychotherapy alone, drug therapy alone, psychotherapy plus drug therapy, and milieu care, using as outcome criteria release rate, length of hospital stay, amount of supplemental treatment required and estimated change on the Menninger Health-Sickness scale. Data are presented for the first 20 patients in each group.

May, P. R. A. and Tuma, A. H.: Choice of criteria for the assessment of treatment outcome. *J. of Psychiatric Research*, 2:199–209, October 1964.

Illustration of the thesis that different disciplines and different measures perceive the patient differently and that inter-relationships are not so high that one can safely expect to reach a satisfactory verdict on outcome on the basis of assessment by a single measure. Analysis of the inter-correlations between a large number of outcome criteria from different sources for the first 100 patients in the study.

May, P. R. A. and Tuma, A. H.: Ataractic drugs and electroshock. *International J. of Neuropsychiatry*, 1, 1:84–89, January 1965.

A preliminary report comparing the results of ECT, drug therapy and milieu care for the first 20 patients in each group. Evaluation in terms of estimated change on the Menninger Health-Sickness scale, length of hospital stay, release rate, use of sedatives and hydrotherapy.

May, P. R. A. and Tuma, A. H.: Treatment of schizophrenia. *British J. of Psychiatry*, 3:503–510, June 1965.

A preliminary report for the first 100 patients in the study, comparing the outcome of the 5 treatments in terms of re-admission rate during the two years after first release from hospital; total time in hospital during a three year period from the date of first hospitalization; post-treatment Menninger Health-Sickness ratings; post-treatment MACC ratings.

May, P. R. A., Tuma, A. H. and Kraude, W.: Community follow-up of treatment of schizophrenia: issues and problems. *American J. of Orthopsychiatry*, 35:754–763, July 1965.

A discussion of the methodology and of the operational, procedural and practical problems associated with the execution of a follow-up study. Illustrated by experience in six years of data collection.

May, P. R. A., Tuma, A. H., Distler, L. S. and McKeever, W. F.: Selection of treatment for schizophrenic patients: Methodological problems in outcome and prognosis research. *Psychiatric Quarterly*, 40:236–247, April 1966.

A discussion of research in prediction that includes illustrations from correlational and other analyses for the first 100 patients in the study.

Tuma, A. H.: The prediction of response to pharmacotherapy among schizophrenics: an historical perspective. In *Prediction of Response to Pharmacotherapy*. Wittenborn, J. R. and May, P. R. A., eds. Charles C Thomas, Springfield, Ill., 1966: 43–68.

Highlights some of the salient issues and problems with illustrations from the literature.

Tuma, A. H. and May, P. R. A.: The effect of therapist attitude on outcome of drug treatment and other therapies in schizophrenia. In *Psychotropic Drug Response—Advances in Prediction*. May, P. R. A. and Wittenborn, J. R., eds. Charles C Thomas, Springfield, Ill. (In Press.)

Investigates the hierarchy of treatment preferences for a major subsample of the patients and therapists in the study and examines the relationship between attitude and outcome.

Index

Measurements, *see* Statistics; *specific tests*

Medication, *see* Treatments; *individual drugs*

Meehl, P. E., 49–50

Mendelsohn, G. A., 36–37, 93

Menninger Clinic
  Project supervisors from, 83
  psychotherapy research project of, 37, 88–89

Menninger Foundation Psychotherapy Research Project, 37, 88–89

Menninger Health-Sickness Rating Scale (MHS)
  average admission rating on, 127
  nurses' rating of patients on, 90, 156, 160–62, 214, 313
    MHS figure, 161
    MHS table, 160
  patient's highest pretreatment rating on, 133–34
  patient's highest two-year prognosis on, 135
  patient's lowest pretreatment rating on, 135
  patient's lowest two-year prognosis on, 134–35
  pretreatment ratings on, 128
  psychoanalysts' ratings of patients on, 179–81, 195, 234, 240
    MHS compared with CDAS, 183, 240
    MHS table, 81
  two-year prognosis on, 128
  use of, 88, 116, 120, 137, 143, 151

"Methods of Statistical Analysis" (Dixon and May), 106–125

MHS, *see* Menninger Health-Sickness Scale

Miami, University of, Biometric Laboratory of, 37

Middlebrook, R., 36

Milieu therapy
  optimum program of, 270
  in other hospitals, 255, 256
  role of, 268

Milieu therapy (as Project treatment method)
  amounts of individual contact in, 315–16
  application of, 255, 256
  comparative costs of, 212
    admission to release, 214–17
    admission to termination, 220–25
    all patients to maximum one year, 217–20
    physician-ordered treatment, 225–27
  data on, 97–98
  definition of 28–29
  high quality of, 297–101
  incidence of AMA discharges from, 139–141, 306, 307, 308–9
  length of stay with, 142, 144, 151
  nurses' rating of patients in, 155–65
    ISR, 162–65
    ISR figure, 164
    ISR table, 163
    MACC, 155–57
    MACC figure, 159
    MACC sex-differential, 160
    MACC table, 159
    MHS, 90, 156, 160–62
    MHS figure, 161
    MHS table, 160
  psychoanalysts' rating of patients in, 179–89
    CDAS (Total), 179–80, 81
    CDAS anxiety, 183–85
    CDAS figures, 182, 184, 186
    CDAS insight, 185–89
    CDAS sex-differential, 185–189
    CDAS tables, 183, 185, 187
    MHS, 179, 180, 181
    MHS table, 181
  psychotherapeutic management and, 289
  psychotherapy and, 300–301
  vs. psychotherapy, 237–38
  results of, 232–33
  sex differences in, 142, 147, 149
  sex-treatment interaction in, 240
  stay to failure with, 149
  testability of, 241–42